Christian Theological Seminary, Indianapolis

A History of Education for Ministry

Keith Watkins

Guild Press of Indiana, Inc.

Copyright 2001 by Keith Watkins

All rights reserved. No part of this book may be reproduced in any form without express permission from the publisher. For further information, contact

BV
4070
.C47
W38
2001

Guild Press of Indiana, Inc.
10665 Andrade Drive
Zionsville, Indiana 46077
317-733-4175 / fax 317-733-4176

All opinions, representations, and interpretations contained in this book are solely those of the author and in no way represent the opinions, representations, and interpretations of, and are not authorized or approved by, the Christian Theological Seminary, Indianapolis.

Library of Congress Cataloging-in-Publication Data
Watkins, Keith.
    Christian Theological Seminary, Indianapolis: A History of Education for Ministry / Keith Watkins.
      p. ; cm.
    Includes bibliographical references and index.
    ISBN 1-57860-092-8
    1. Christian Theological Seminary (Indianapolis, Ind.)—History. 2. Theological seminaries—Indiana—Indianapolis—History. 3. Indianapolis (Ind.)—Church history. 4. Theology—Study and teaching (Higher)—Indiana. 5. Christian Church (Disciples of Christ)—Education. I. Christian Theological Seminary (Indianapolis, Ind.) II. Title.
BV4070.C47 W38 2001
230.51771514
                                                      CIP 20-010862

Remembering
Clementine Miller Tangeman
1905–1996
Ronald E. Osborn
1917–1998

Contents

Preface vii

1 Stalemate in Indianapolis 1
   The Struggle to Create a Central Training School for the
   Disciples of Christ, 1855–1921

2 More Religion—Less Theology 24
   A Viable Plan for Ministerial Education at Butler
   University, 1917–1924

3 Training Men and Women "of All Faiths" for the
   Christian Ministry 47
   The Seminary's First Decade, 1924–1935

4 Catholicity and Conservatism 70
   The Bible, Unity, and Mission at the School of Religion,
   1935–1944

5 In the Best Possible Hands 94
   New Leaders and the Renewal of the Seminary's
   Commitments, 1943–1949

6 For the Sake of the Kingdom 116
   The Decision to Become Christian Theological Seminary,
   1950–1958

7 Recklessly Committed to Christ and the Gospel 142
   The New Seminary in a Decade of Cultural Crisis,
   1959–1970

8 The Liveliest Place in the Area 165
   The CTS Ethos Emerges, 1965–1974

9 Coping with Adversity 192
   Hard Times and the Deepening of Faith, 1974–1978

10 The Finest Institution of its Kind **214**
    A Center of Theological Education and Reflection,
    1979–1987

11 A Spirit Ever Restless **242**
    An Ecumenical Seminary of the Christian Church,
    1987–1997

12 Memory and Mission **267**
    The Seminary in its Seventy-fifth Year, 2000

    Appendix—Faculty of the Seminary, 1924–2000 .. **276**
    Endnotes **282**
    Index **313**

Preface

My associations with Christian Theological Seminary began in the 1940s when it was known among the churches as Butler—shorthand for the School of Religion of Butler University. My boyhood pastor in Portland, Oregon, and several of his friends were Butler graduates and frequently spoke of their years on campus with the professors whom they revered—Kershner, Holmes, Nakarai, and Walker. Later, as a student at Northwest Christian College, I met Ross J. Griffeth, who had come to that college presidency following more than a decade on the Butler faculty, and Ronald E. Osborn, who during my freshman year accepted a call to the Butler faculty. Following graduation from college, my wife, Billie, and I joined some forty Northwest graduates who were doing their theological studies at the School of Religion. In 1956, I graduated with the standard seminary degree in the university commencement which was held at the Hilton U. Brown Theatron, with President M. O. Ross presiding. We went to California for five years where I served as a pastor in the San Joaquin Valley and was a graduate student at Berkeley. In 1961, I returned, as assistant professor, to the red brick building on the Butler campus. During my absence the Seminary had become a separate corporation with a new name: Christian Theological Seminary. Thirty-four years later I retired.

In the early 1980s I wrote a twenty-five page retrospective essay outlining my personal understanding of the Seminary's history. Richard D. N. Dickinson, Jr., who was then the dean and later became the president, encouraged me to expand my work and develop a full history, using the Seminary's archives and other records. During brief periods of time in my final years on faculty and in longer periods of work since my retirement, I have continued my research and writing. Although the narrative is now much fuller than before, and the research much more substantial, this later version continues as it began. It is a personal account of the history of an institution with which I have been intimately connected for some fifty years.

The base for this history is the vast deposit of correspondence, memoranda, official minutes, academic records, published catalogs, and other matter—published and unpublished—at Christian Theological Seminary. Most of the unpublished material is in the Seminary's archives where it is classified in several categories, the most important of which are PRS (Presidents, School of Religion) and MC (Manuscript Collection). Papers of Frederick D. Kershner and Orman L. Shelton, who functioned as chief executive of the Seminary even though their title was dean, have been deposited in both categories. A considerable body of unclassified material has been deposited in the archives and gradually is being arranged and indexed, in some cases with other three-letter codes. The Seminary's library also contains major holdings in the history of the Christian Churches—Churches of Christ—Disciples of Christ movement with which Butler University and Christian Theological Seminary have been historically related.

Other unpublished correspondence and records used in this history are preserved in the papers of the Irwin-Sweeney-Miller family (in the care of the Irwin Management Company) at Columbus, Indiana, and have been used at the courtesy of members of the Miller family and the staff of the Irwin Management Company. A few papers that I have used are deposited with the Disciples of Christ Historical Society, Nashville, Tennessee, and the staff of that depository have made these materials available to me. I appreciate the assistance of the staff at the Disciples Seminary Foundation, Claremont, California, when I have used their Discipliana collection. George M. Waller's research on the history of Butler University has been taking place during the time that I have been preparing the history of the Seminary. His reseach in the official records of the University and my research in the papers of the Seminary's leaders provide the basis for contrasting narratives of Seminary-University relations. A copy of his manuscript, with the title "Butler and Its People: A History of Butler University, 1855–Present," is on deposit in the University's archives. The transcript of an interview that Virginia Geddes conducted with Thomas J. Liggett was made available by President Liggett. Copies of this transcript are on deposit in the libraries of the Graduate Theological Union at Berkeley, California, and Union Theological Seminary at New York.

The following books have been valuable sources of information and interpretation. Henry K. Shaw's *Hoosier Disciples: A Comprehensive History of the Christian Churches (Disciples of Christ) in Indiana* (St. Louis: The Bethany Press, 1966) provides extensive information about the history of Butler University and Christian Theological Seminary. Shaw drew upon archival material from the University and the Seminary. Lester G. McAllister's *Z. T. Sweeney: Preacher and Peacemaker* (St. Louis: Christian Board of Publication, 1968) provides an overview of a person who was important in the history of theological education in Indiana. An understanding of William G. Irwin's business career and J. Irwin Miller's career as a "values-driven" industrialist is presented in *The Engine That Could: 75 Years of Values-Driven Change at Cummins Engine Company*, by Jeffrey L. Cruikshank and David B. Sicilia (Boston: Harvard Business School Press, 1997). Hilton U. Brown's *A Book of Memories* (Indianapolis: Butler University, 1951) contains informal memoirs of the man who at the time the book was published had been a director of Butler University for sixty-eight years and for forty-nine of them its president. This book suggests the character of the University through the first century of its life. The Seminary's scholarly journal, published quarterly since 1940 (first as *Shane Quarterly* and since 1958 as *Encounter)*, has given permanent form to the texts of many of the important addresses that have been delivered in connection with the Seminary's history. *Mid-Stream,* the quarterly journal of the Council on Christian Unity of the Christian Church (Disciples of Christ), has also been the means that papers and addresses related to the history of the Seminary have been published.

The study also depends upon conversations and interviews in which I have participated and notes on some of the interviews are deposited in the Seminary's archives. Especially important as correspondent and conversationalist was Ronald E. Osborn, and a file of letters and notes of interviews is deposited in the Seminary's archives. My special thanks go to members of the Seminary staff, and especially those in the library, whose assistance and courtesies have benefited me in my work.

It is difficult to estimate the impact upon this manuscript of the undocumented memory of conversations, events, personalities, and meanings that have accumulated during the half century that I have been connected with Christian Theological Seminary. I am grateful to all of my friends, colleagues, and family members who have reviewed portions of this manuscript as it has been in progress. Although we have sometimes differed in our recollections and interpretations, they have prodded me in my efforts to develop a history that is faithful to the sources and fair in its presentation of this story. I appreciate deeply the freedom that has allowed me to develop this book as a work of independent scholarship; and it is with great satisfaction that I am completing it during the Seminary's seventy-fifth year.

Most of all, I give thanks to my wife, Billie, who has been part of this story all of these years, and to our children, Sharon, Marilyn, Michael, Carolyn, and Kenneth (Shortridge High School graduates, every one), who had the privilege of growing up in the Butler-Tarkington neighborhood of Indianapolis because their dad taught at Christian Theological Seminary.

Keith Watkins
All Hallows Eve, 2000

1
Stalemate in Indianapolis

The Struggle to Create a Central Training School for the Disciples of Christ, 1855–1921

Whether Catholic or Lutheran, Presbyterian, Methodist, or Disciples, the people who created new communities all across America built academies, colleges, and seminaries almost as quickly as they built their houses and barns. These institutions of learning were one of the key means by which people of religious conviction served the public good while at the same time providing a new generation of leaders for the religious communities themselves. The landscape of Indiana shows this determination. With Notre Dame, the Catholic Church served South Bend and the industrial periphery of greater Chicago; with DePauw, Methodists ministered to Greencastle and the rural heartland of the new state. The Quakers' Earlham College focused a specific religious tradition for Richmond and the adjacent areas of Indiana and Ohio. Presbyterians, Baptists, and other religious communions also created their institutions of higher learning in communities all across this state.[1]

The Disciples' School in Indiana

Early leaders of the Disciples of Christ in Indiana also were determined to create a seat of learning to serve the church and the world. Although they chose Indianapolis as the site for this school, they intended that it would serve the entire Northwest Territory and therefore named it North Western Christian University. They were ready with their new building to begin instruction in 1855, scarcely a generation after the founding of the city. Disciples already were firmly planted in Indiana; most communities, it seemed, had a band of Disciples meeting as a Church of Christ or Christian Church. In 1855 there may have been as many as 25,000 Disciples in Indiana, with Presbyterians only half that number and Methodists three times greater. The population of Indiana at that time was about 988,000.

The new academy-college soon outgrew its first location at Broadway and Thirteenth Streets in Indianapolis and accepted the invitation of the village of Irvington to move to a new location east of the city.[2] Irvington was a congenial environment for the University. A planned community laid out according to the most progressive ideas of its era, Irvington was attracting a civic-minded and educated citizenry. The town plan called for a college, and North Western Christian University established itself on that site. Because of the significant services of Ovid Butler, a prosperous Indianapolis lawyer and Disciples layman who had shaped the college's early documents and become its largest financial supporter, the college's board of directors voted to change the school's name to Butler University.

The founders of North Western Christian University were inspired by ideas that had been proclaimed by Alexander Campbell in his journal *Millennial Harbinger* and had become the organizing principles for their churches throughout the country west of the Alleghenies. Human society would soon come to its perfected state—the millennium—and the United States would be at the forefront of this new social order. The character of this perfect society and the outline of the united church that would bring it into existence were authoritatively presented in the Bible which was a public document that could be studied and understood by all who made the effort to do so. Colleges were basic to the redeemed society and to the churches which sustained it because in these schools the rising generation learned the arts, sciences, and religious ideas that they needed in order to be leaders in the church and society. One curriculum, based on the classics and featuring the Bible, would provide the foundation for all students, including those preparing for the ministry.[3]

Despite Campbell's position as the theological and institutional leader for Disciples across the entire nation, many people in the North were troubled by his willingness to tolerate traditional Southern mores and systems. North Western Christian University was designed to be an alternative to Campbell's Bethany College in Bethany, [West] Virginia,[4] its founders hoping to appeal to Disciples and others who wanted to study in a school located in a free state. In Indianapolis students attending this new

Disciples school would not be brought into contact with "the habits and manners that exist in populations where slavery exists."[5]

Despite this determination to found a school that was distinct from Alexander Campbell's college, Indiana Disciples continued to be influenced by his example. Now fifty-two years of age, Campbell towered over all other leaders of the movement. His monthly journal of opinion, the *Millennial Harbinger*, was read by people in most congregations, north and south; he also traveled extensively, thus maintaining personal connections with local leaders across the nation.[6] Bethany College, he believed, was still another way to shape the mind and work of the Disciples. His college was an undergraduate institution with five programs of study, each called a school: Sacred History and Moral Philosophy; Ancient Languages; Mathematics and Astronomy; Natural, Intellectual, and Political Philosophy; Chemistry and Belles Lettres. Some years later he added a sixth school, Hebrew and Modern Languages.[7] Students could complete all of their requirements for the Bachelor of Arts degree in each of these schools without "entering" any of the others.[8] All students were required to study the Bible and to participate in religious activities on campus. By the time that they completed this program, all graduates were to be properly fitted for leadership in the general society and in the church.

Because at this time Disciples were ambivalent about ministerial leadership, they doubted that a special program in ministerial study was needed. Campbell himself had denounced the traditional pattern of specially trained, salaried pastors—"the hireling clergy"—and in its place had recommended what he perceived to be the biblical model—a threefold ministry of evangelists, elders, and deacons.[9] Evangelists were by definition itinerant preachers who organized new churches, while elders and deacons were chosen by congregations from their own membership. In this system, no special ministerial education was needed—only the moral and academic training needed by serious Christians in any of the occupations. The classics curriculum at Bethany College and other schools built according to this model, including North Western Christian University—Butler University—in Indianapolis, provided exactly that kind of education.

Most congregations were not as well-favored as the Bethany Church of Christ where Campbell, others of his family, and several preeminent intellectual and religious leaders of the Disciples could serve as elders and take turns preaching. In his autobiographical notes J. W. McGarvey, who had become a dominant intellectual leader of the Disciples, described worship at the Bethany church during the years when he had been a student

(1847–1850). Alexander Campbell would often preach, as would W. K. Pendleton and Robert Richardson, two professors who were widely known across the entire movement. The richest Sundays were when Campbell preached "followed by Dr. R. in a talk of 5 or 10 minutes at the Lord's Table." These communion reflections were published in *Millennial Harbinger* and later, because of McGarvey's influence, republished in the book *Communings in the Sanctuary*. "Thoughtful reading" of that book, said McGarvey, "would greatly enrich the spiritual experience of the brotherhood. Preachers would learn from it how to better conduct services at the Lord's table."[10]

Across the country, congregations were looking for people who were "apt to teach" (1 Timothy 3:2) and could assume continuing leadership in the pulpit and become full-time, settled ministers of congregations. Since the traditional classics curriculum, followed by apprenticeship with experienced pastors, was failing to produce an adequate supply of pastors, the challenge for the colleges was to develop programs that would develop the ministerial leaders that the churches demanded. This need was the background to a report on the Disciples colleges that was published in 1896 by Albertina Allen Forrest, the executive in charge of the newly created Board of Education of the Disciples of Christ. She described the classics curricula in these schools and compared these programs with a standard that she had derived by examining the admission requirements of "nearly ten of the standard institutions of this country."[11] All of the Disciples schools were deficient at some point, with Kentucky University, Bethany College, and Christian University most problematic. Hiram College, near Cleveland, and Butler University were closest to meeting the standard at the point of admission. In all of the Disciples schools only one person had earned the Ph.D. degree. Butler had the highest number of people who had done graduate study of some kind. Eleven of the twelve persons listed had studied beyond their college degree, and ten of these had studied in Europe for periods ranging from one to seven years. These schools ranged considerably in enrollment, although the greatest variable was in the size of preparatory departments. Forrest's tables showed 498 persons studying for the ministry in the preparatory and collegiate divisions of these Disciples schools, twenty-four of them at Butler.

The Department of Biblical Philology

When Forrest made her study, Butler was experimenting with a new model of ministerial education in response to pressure from some professors and other leaders of the churches. Although the traditional classics structure was still in place, the University was making special provisions for the significant number of students whose intended use of this education was in salaried ministries of the church. Some of the University's directors hoped that the final gift that Ovid Butler had given the University, five years before his death in 1881, could be used to fund this new program, but others were convinced that the purposes of that last donation were more broadly defined.[12] In 1889 the University took an important step by establishing a Bible chair and transferring Professor Hugh Carson Garvin from another University post to develop a program of specialized ministerial study. Garvin was the son of a prominent Disciples evangelist; a brother and nephew were also prominent preachers among Disciples. He had taken his undergraduate degree under Alexander Campbell at Bethany College and for seven years had studied in Germany, without earning a degree. After teaching briefly at Franklin College (probably the Churches of Christ College in Nashville, Tennessee), he came to Butler where for seventeen years he occupied the chair of languages. Garvin preached in surrounding churches and alternated with other members of the faculty as preacher in the Irvington Christian Church, which was established soon after the University moved to this community.[13]

The following spring John Chapman Miller, an Indianapolis pastor who for many years had been "a powerful factor in the progress of the University, as Professor, Director, and active advisor as to faculty and courses of study,"[14] summarized a plan, "with hearty applause by the other members of the Board," that would add five people to the University faculty, two of them in Bible.[15] Because of an economic depression, however, the University had been forced to cut faculty salaries and the directors were unwilling to expand the Bible department until these cuts had been restored and new funds had been generated.[16] Two years later, before new funding could be secured, faculty president Allan R. Benton returned to teaching and joined Garvin in the Bible department. Scot Butler, who had followed his father as faculty president of the University, assisted them by teaching Latin. Thirty-nine pre-ministerial students enrolled as the program began.

Garvin's new program at Butler was called biblical philology and it showed the evidence both of his classical training and his studies in Europe. Students took the Butler classics curriculum, but would use elective hours for study that prepared them to become pastors. Initially the course was intended to be three years in length but a fourth year was added as the program developed. There were five parallel courses: Hebrew (Old Testament); Greek (New Testament); Latin (church history); German (theology and ethics); and homiletics. Each year students were to continue in this five-course system, simply moving forward in each of the disciplines being studied.

The most distinctive feature of this program was the intention that students would study and exegete the entire Bible in the original languages. In his description of the program, A. M. Hall, a Disciples pastor and reporter on academic matters for the church press, stated that "due regard was had for the opinions of commentators but, as far as possible, all preconceived ideas and prejudices were laid aside, and the meaning sought in the words and context." The interpretation of scripture that developed, Hall continued, "was not dogmatic, but, in free discussion, the opinions of all were heard and corrected. This gave exercise to the student's own thought. Every passage was taken in its broadest scope, unless limited by the writer." In their church history studies, students translated portions of Augustine's *City of God,* and read Fisher's history of the church, and listened to lectures. Theological studies consisted primarily of a thorough reading of the writings of Johann Tobias Beck. Hall cited the authoritative McClintock and Strong theological encyclopedia that ranked Beck as "one of the first Protestant theologians of the nineteenth century" and the "complete antipode of [F. C.] Baur, the father of the hypercritical Tübingen school. 'All modern novelties he treated with the silence of utter contempt, professing to know nothing but the Bible as the book of life.'" Hall expressed the Disciples conservatism in biblical studies when he continued his praise of Beck: "Having exactly our standpoint, and a vision cleared by a thorough linguistic training, by a pious and devoted life, and by a struggle with the greatest minds of Germany, his treatise on the God-head, the falling away into sin, redemption, and the final state of all things is the most complete of the present age."[17] Homiletics consisted of students developing sermons and preaching them in class where they would be subject to evaluation by students and professors.

Hall supported Garvin's program at Butler because it taught people to think and to base that thought upon the scriptural text rather than upon what the doctors said about the text. "When that Word comes not with narrow teachings, but with the grandeur of a great world plan, the solemnity of a sin-cured world, the sympathy of an all-wise Father, and the eloquence of a loving Christ, it fills the spirit with purer thoughts, greater trust and more humble submission." Hall believed that the Butler program gave students a strong spirituality and desire to preach the gospel because it brought them "abreast of the times" in their views "of the great Bible doctrines." The old dogmas were passing away, Hall stated, and new light was breaking. "We must advance, or soon we will be the narrow sect, while the present sects will be pleading with us to come to higher planes of life and light."[18]

This was a dangerous time, however, to start a new program of biblical studies and to speak about the passing away of old dogmas. During these same years one of the most important battles over biblical interpretation was taking place among Presbyterians, with Charles A. Briggs of Union Theological Seminary, New York, at the center. Briggs had advocated the adoption of the new methods of biblical study coming from Germany and as a result had generated intense opposition in his church. Although he continued to hold the traditional evangelical faith that was widespread among the protestant churches of the nineteenth century, Briggs believed that doctrines of verbal inspiration, literal inerrancy, and prophecy as prediction of specific events were barriers to the acceptance of the Bible by people of his time. The struggle over Briggs reached its climax in 1894 when the general assembly of the northern Presbyterian Church took formal action against him, resulting in the decision by Union Theological Seminary to withdraw from the Presbyterian Church and become an independent theological institution.[19]

At first, Disciples seemed to be protected from such battles because they had inherited from Alexander Campbell a commitment to study the Bible with the same principles of interpretation that were used with other ancient texts. Thus it might have seemed that Disciples could readily move forward with the modern approaches to biblical study that used a vigorous method of historical and literary analysis. Such was not the case, however, because the methods of historical study inherited from Campbell were based on the assumption that because God was the author of the Bible it was internally consistent and revealed certain facts about God and the redemption that God offered through Jesus Christ. Campbell believed that these "facts," as he called them, would be compelling except among people whose sinful rejection of these facts closed their minds to the truth.[20] Most Disciples continued to believe in this set of assumptions and therefore they could not follow newer scholars, like Baur, who no longer accepted them.

Another problem for Disciples as they dealt with new methods of biblical study resulted from the certainty with which they agreed with the conclusions that Campbell had reached half a century earlier about baptism, the Lord's supper, the ministry, and the polity of the church. This set of ideas, which some called "gospel order," had become the core of Disciples' self-identity; any approach to the Bible that questioned these ideas was rejected. The most important of these Disciples ideas was that "the one baptism" described in Scripture (Ephesians 4:5) consisted of the immersion in water of people old enough to believe in the gospel, repent of their sins, and confess their faith in Jesus Christ. Only people baptized this way, they believed, were numbered among those whom "the Lord added to the church" (Acts 2:47), and therefore they were the only people who could become members of Disciples congregations. The "pious unimmersed" could be received as brothers and sisters in Christ, even being welcomed to the communion table, but they could not be members of a Disciples congregation until they had "completed their obedience to the Lord."

Many Disciples were aware of the Briggs debate and the transformation in the study of the Bible that Briggs represented. Although a few pastors—mostly graduates of Yale Divinity School and, a little later, the Divinity School of the University of Chicago—were favorably inclined toward modern approaches to the Bible, most Disciples were opposed. Professors like J. W. McGarvey of the College of the Bible in Lexington and pastors like Z. T. Sweeney in Columbus, Indiana, became the leaders of the resistance to ideas that threatened their understandings of the Bible and its teachings about baptism, the Lord's supper, the ministry, and church polity. By 1893 Sweeney and other Disciples preachers in Indiana were beginning to suspect that Garvin's ideas were sympathetic to the new approaches to the Bible, and they were increasingly anxious about what would happen to the churches when young men he had trained were released into the ministry.

In the spring of 1894, a group of pastors and other church leaders at a district missionary convention in Crawfordsville, Indiana, passed a resolution rejecting certain doctrines, if they were being advocated, and urging that action be taken. This resolution, obviously pointed toward Garvin and Butler University, was reported in the secular press and caught the attention of J. H. Garrison, preeminent Disciples editor and opinion-maker at his post with the *Christian-Evangelist* in St. Louis. Shortly thereafter, the Disciples' state convention was held in Columbus where an even more serious course of action began to unfold. The spokesperson was Z. T. Sweeney, now retired from his Columbus pastorate.

The full text of the pertinent resolutions and correspondence was printed in the *Evangelist*. Sweeney wrote that it had been the feeling for some time "among the prominent preachers of the State that Prof. Garvin was not a perfectly safe and reliable head for the Bible Department, and many of us feel that we cannot conscientiously recommend young men to go there to fit themselves for the ministry, while he is at the head of that department." This feeling, Sweeney continued, "crystallized" at the state convention, which then appointed a committee of three persons, including himself, to develop the convention's response. The committee drafted a letter to Garvin, stating its belief that his teachings did not "fitly represent" the ideas of the people whom he was to serve and asking that he resign from the Bible department and ask to be transferred to another position in the University. The letter indicated that the preachers did not wish to abridge freedom of thought or speech, but they wanted the Bible position filled by someone in whom they could have complete confidence.

Garrison—who was national spokesman for theologically moderate Disciples—was disturbed by these reports and in his columns criticized Sweeney's group of pastors. What they had done was contrary to Disciples' practice for two reasons, he believed. Missionary conventions "should keep aloof from all interference with doctrinal questions or cases of alleged heresy" and Disciples should "adhere loyally" to their own "fundamental position, in allowing the largest freedom of investigation and liberty of thought consistent with faith in Jesus Christ and a Christian character."[21]

Garvin's opportunity to present his case to the churches came in the Indiana Disciples' annual Bethany Park Assembly in the summer of 1894 where he delivered a series of lectures. One lecture was later published in the *Evangelist*, which also carried other letters and columns about the dispute. Early in 1896 Garrison[22] stated his understanding of the real issue behind all of Garvin's articles—the belief that Disciples should "receive into their fellowship pious persons regardless of the question of baptism." When William F. Clarke, one of Garvin's former students, wrote to defend his teacher's ideas, he confirmed what Garvin's critics were saying. It was not that scripture was to be disregarded, as some had claimed that they were teaching, but rather that scripture did not teach that baptism by immersion in water was necessary. "Whoever, therefore, opens his heart to Jesus is, to the extent to which he opens it, in fellowship with Christ and a member of Christ's Church." In its "earthly temporal organization," the church "should embrace all those who are in any degree members of Christ's body, all those who have opened their hearts, though ever so little, to Jesus. We should not adopt any plan or system or dogma that prevents the harmonious cooperation of all such."[23]

Garrison regretted that these young men—Garvin's students "who probably want to do good in the world"—were being led off "into these vague, nebulous ideas and turning their backs upon a definite plea for the restoration of New Testament Christianity, which has demonstrated its providential character and the necessity for its existence in its wonderful growth and influence."[24] Every religious movement, Garrison asserted, had to have an agreement among ministers and churches concerning the principles of reform and their practical embodiment in the church. Garrison then offered his summary of what held together the churches of their movement:

> Suffice it to say, here, that among these principles are the inspiration and authority of the Scriptures, as our only rule of faith and practice, the Messiahship and divinity of Jesus Christ as the true creed of Christianity, and unquestioning submission to its authority in all that relates to church life and individual loyalty. This latter principle involves holding fast to the ordinances in the form and for the purposes which they have in the New Testament. It requires that churches shall be built upon the same faith and submit to the same baptism and be guided by the same principles as the New Testament churches. There is almost perfect unanimity among us that baptism (immersion) was submitted to by all believers as a condition of discipleship and church membership.[25]

Finally, the University yielded to the opposition, transferring Garvin to another department. A short time later he left Butler, becoming pastor of the Congregational Church in Eldon, Missouri, near St. Louis. There he wrote his connected view of the topics that were important to him, publishing them in a 280-page book with the title *What the Bible Teaches*. In the short, blunt preface Garvin asserted that the church was in a deplorable condition that could be traced to the quality of preaching it was hearing; the quality of preaching could be traced to the theological schools that had prepared the preachers. He rejected the idea that the return to orthodoxy would strengthen the church; for, even if orthodoxy in its full vigor could be restored, the church would again decline because "there were and are elements of decay in the church doctrines and therefore there can be no permanence." Some people, Garvin claimed, "think that the cure for all evils will be found in the holding of orthodoxy with such an easy and accommodating grasp that any part may be relinquished whenever the shifting views of the world may demand it."[26] He rejected this idea, saying that "if orthodoxy was not true in its full vigor, it will not be true anywhere on the line towards the vanishing point to which it is hastening." Only the truth can make the church free, he claimed, and that truth can be found in the Bible.

Although Garvin probably did not hold this radical a position when he established the Department of Biblical Philology, the conflict had pushed him to a point of view that could only with great difficulty be sustained within the Disciples of Christ of the time. He refuted the idea that God instituted rites, ceremonies, and sacraments as means of divine grace. At most, Garvin conceded, God regulated practices that emerged in the community for other reasons. Although a few of the most liberal Disciples may have held similar ideas, the overwhelming majority were convinced that their traditional understandings of baptism and church membership were fully scriptural and essential to the Christian life.

The debate over Hugh Carson Garvin revealed three important characteristics of the Butler program for preparing ministers of the gospel. The first was that the University's program in ministerial education was controlled by the church constituency—pastors like Z. T. Sweeney, lay leaders in Indiana like Joseph I. Irwin, and national leaders of opinion like J. H. Garrison. The University, which included a few liberal Disciples among its faculty and board, sought to protect Garvin from outside forces; but quickly their support was no longer strong enough to keep him in his position. Garrison may have been right when he criticized missionary conventions for speaking out as though they were ecclesial institutions, yet they had spoken the consensus of their participating members—and that consensus was that the Butler program was being led by someone whom they could not trust. Therefore, the University found that it had little choice but to change the leadership of the program.

A second conclusion was that the church constituency was still united in its views concerning the classic theological position of the Disciples movement. By this time tensions were developing within the movement because of differing ideas about the validity of missionary societies and the use of musical instruments in worship. Although these tensions would lead to a formal separation in 1906 of the Churches of Christ from the rest of the Disciples, the movement was still together during the Garvin years. With respect to ecclesiological issues, such as the relation of baptism to church membership, both branches of the Stone-Campbell movement continued to hold very much the same point of view, even after the division of 1906. Garvin's error was not that he had become a modernist, along the lines of Charles Briggs, but that he had dared to question the traditional position of the Disciples. Garvin's European studies had acquainted him with critical views of the Bible, and he used them to some extent in his program at Butler. Yet he had identified himself with the most conservative aspects of the critical movement in Germany and he depended upon text-books representing that conservative position.

A third conclusion was that despite their differences over baptism and church membership, Garvin, Sweeney, and Garrison were still representatives of nineteenth century traditional theology. They were ready to use a scientific approach in studying the Bible, but they could not imagine that the presuppositions of divine authorship and authoritative contents would be set aside. Garvin and others in this struggle were more like Robert Milligan, Disciples theologian of the previous generation, than H. L. Willett, a young Disciples biblical scholar at the University of Chicago, who represented the generation to come. For most Disciples, the point of the Bible's reliability was really twofold. They believed that the scriptures gave absolutely clear instructions about the nature and form of the church. They also believed that anyone who read the Bible according to good principles of exegesis would find the same ecclesial system and be persuaded to adopt it. What made Garvin so dangerous was that his reading of the Bible according to the agreed principles of interpretation led him to radically different conclusions about the church and its sacraments. Garvin's ideas threatened the Disciples consensus, and this threat the leaders of the churches could not tolerate.

Searching for a New Model

As the Garvin episode came to its completion, the University entered into a quiet time of respite, drawing back briefly from its effort to establish a training school for ministers. A new professor—Edward Scribner Ames—was called to its faculty in 1897 to teach philosophy and education at the undergraduate level. The son of a Disciples pastor, Ames grew up in small towns of the Midwest, took the standard Disciples college program at the recently established Drake University, and began to preach around at nearby churches. He then went to Yale for further study, including residence for the Ph.D. degree. Following his major professor to the University of Chicago, Ames wrote his dissertation there and was the first to be granted the Ph.D. degree by the University of Chicago. Ames stayed in Indianapolis only three years and then returned to Chicago as pastor of the young, small Hyde Park Church of the Disciples of Christ, which under his leadership was to be transformed into The University Church of the Disciples of Christ and the leading congregation of liberal theology among Disciples. While continuing as the pastor, Ames also became a regular member of the faculty of the University of Chicago. For a generation he was the commanding center of the Disciples Divinity House that was connected to his church, related to the University's divinity school, and the fountainhead of liberal theology among the Disciples.

Ames was deeply read in a newer range of post-critical studies, primarily philosophical and psychological. John Locke, William James, and John Dewey were the intellectual figures who shaped his mind. At Butler he was positioned in a chair that was not considered crucial by leaders of the church—the chair of philosophy and education. Almost as soon as he began at Butler, he was accused by a professor at Bethany College with "infidelity and pantheism and disloyalty to the cause." Yet, these charges published in the *Christian Standard* did not stir up the controversy that had swirled around Garvin. Ames suggested that the Indiana churches may have been tired of controversy by this time or may have ignored him because he was only a professor of philosophy. He was impressed, however, "with the marked difference between having the freedom of a tolerant academic position, teaching a subject like philosophy, as compared with teaching or preaching religion under the constraints of a conservative constituency."[27] Ames's description of his years at Butler was cordial and affirming of the life of the school. He described the practice of daily chapel for faculty and students. There was something about this assembly, he said, "uniting daily in songs, readings, prayers, and short talks, that built morale and college spirit."[28]

The events at Butler were part of a larger debate about theological education among the Disciples. They were maturing as a religious movement and along with Methodists, Presbyterians, and Baptists were beginning the transformation from sect to denomination.[29] Increasingly at ease with the prevailing social order, Disciples congregations wanted stronger pastoral leadership than the prevailing educational programs offered. One sign of this need was the growing interest among Disciples candidates for the ministry in Yale Divinity School even though Yale was not one of their own institutions. Yale began advertising in the *Christian-Evangelist* as early as 1891, and Disciples, drawn by Yale's "dedication to the education of a liberal and evangelical ministry,"[30] were responding. By 1900 nineteen Disciples, some of whom would become prominent leaders, had studied at Yale Divinity School.

Most Disciples, however, wanted a strong school of their own where their ministers could study. A prominent voice in this discussion was that of H. L. Willett in Chicago who believed that a Disciples school of higher learning would help the churches combat two problems. The first was that many ministerial students and congregations believed that ministers of the gospel did not need training beyond the first year or two of college. The second problem, sharply contrasting with the first, was that some students wanted to go on beyond the work that was available in Disciples colleges. Is it not time, Willett asked, for us to encourage all students to complete the prescribed courses of study already existing and for Disciples to provide a school of such advanced rank that it would attract our people who now go on to other schools and also encourage more of our graduates to want to attend Disciples schools?[31]

One way for Disciples to create such an institution was to strengthen their already existing Bible colleges in the hope that one of them would grow to sufficient strength that it would accomplish the objective. The problem with this approach, critics noted, was that several schools were vying for position, each of them hoping to become that one great seminary of the Disciples. One of the most vocal groups recommending this approach was supporters of Drake University in Des Moines, Iowa.[32] A second proposal was that Disciples create a new school for this purpose; but critics noted that it would cost at least $400,000 to start such a school, and that fund was scarcely enough to maintain an adequate program. (Butler at that time reported assets of slightly more than $400,000, divided roughly into equal parts for physical assets and endowment.) The third option was to establish a ministerial training program in connection with the Bible chairs such as those that Disciples had already established at the University of Michigan and Indiana University. Critics of this approach, however, claimed that the classes offered by the Bible chairs would not be accepted by the universities where they were based. Still another method was being developed at the University of Chicago, with Edward Scribner Ames and H. L. Willett at the center of the effort. Their idea was to create a Disciples institution directly connected with an already existing seminary. The Disciples' divinity school would provide nurture, financial support, and special Disciples courses, while the existing seminary would provide the main program of theological studies.[33]

As one of the strongest of the Disciples' universities, Butler University had to be interested in this debate concerning a theological school for its church. The University's spokesperson was Scot Butler, Ovid Butler's son who had become faculty president of Butler University.[34] He was aware that the Christian Woman's Board of Missions (CWBM) intended to contribute a significant sum of money to establish a Bible chair at the University of Michigan—because the need for a better educated ministry was great and because the CWBM had been unable to "secure a united action" in any of the existing Disciples institutions. President Butler corresponded with James B. Angell, his counterpart at the University of Michigan, and reviewed this correspondence in the Disciples' news journals. Despite Angell's positive response to the idea, Scot Butler concluded that there was a better way for the CWBM to invest its money if the women wanted to create a strong seminary for their church.[35] They could take control of Butler University, "free from all entanglements whatsoever." He cited figures given him that day by the secretary of the board of directors of Butler University, indicating its worth at $425,000. This University, said its faculty president, "for years, has been laid at the feet of the Church. Those who, in the discharge of duty, have been acting as its custodians, recognize that outside the Church it has no reason of being."

If, Butler continued, the CWBM "will invest in the capital stock of the institution the same amount that they will have to invest at Ann Arbor to even make a beginning—say $100,000—they can be virtual owners of a first-class college property, having the best location in the United States." With this contribution to the university, the university's worth would be $500,000, distributed as follows: $375,000 endowment and $150,000 in buildings, grounds, and apparatus. Because Butler was a joint stock company, and "$100,000 will elect its board of directors," it would then be possible for them to

> do what they choose with it. They could change its Board of Directors, its faculty, its name; they could change its whole purpose, making a purely theological seminary out of it if they so wish. And this without saying "by your leave" to any body. . . . In a word, the Christian Church, under whatever form of organization it may find it practicable to adopt, can have for its very own an educational institution, worth in cash $525,000, at an outlay of less than one-fifth such valuation.[36]

Even if President Butler had been serious in his proposal that the churches take control of his university, others on the Indianapolis campus were making plans that were significantly different. They sought to create an institutional framework that would unite several professional schools in the city into the University of Indianapolis, with Butler serving as the Department of Arts. Among the schools that were affiliated with Butler during the early 1920s were the College of Missions, the Indiana Law School, the Indiana Dental College, the Metropolitan School of Music, and the John Herron Art Institute. In such a framework an independent but affiliated theological school made sense, and University leaders began to discuss these possibilities with church leaders. The Board of Education of the Disciples' American Christian Missionary Society set up a committee of five pastors, four from Indianapolis, to confer with the University concerning the need for a program to prepare ministers.[37] Z. T. Sweeney—always a key figure in these matters—was a member, as was Burris Jenkins, the young, Yale-educated pastor of Third Christian Church, one of the strongest Disciples congregations in Indianapolis. Jenkins represented the more liberal urban constituency that would gradually assume greater importance in the University's affairs.

The result was that in 1897–1898 the Bible College of the Christian Church of Indiana was established. With its own board of trustees and controlling its own finances, this new school would be separate from but related to Butler. Jabez Hall, a Disciples pastor from Virginia who had studied under Alexander Campbell, was appointed head of the new Bible College. Joining him on the faculty were W. E. Garrison, son of the St. Louis editor who with his newly acquired Ph.D. from Yale was to become a leading Disciples intellectual, Burris Jenkins, and Butler veteran Allan R. Benton. The Bible College would use Butler's facilities, and Butler University students could take a major in religion from the Bible College to apply on their degrees. The Bible College was opened officially on October 3, 1898, and the first person to be graduated was Willis Judson Burner, who received his B.D. degree in 1901. It was, said Disciples historian Henry Shaw, "an innovation in Disciples educational circles, the first three-year graduate seminary in the brotherhood."[38]

A goal to raise $100,000 to endow the school was set up, with Joseph I. Irwin pledging $25,000 when the other $75,000 was secured. Nothing developed from this fund-raising effort, which was to be the churches' "Twentieth Century Movement."[39] While the Bible College was coming into existence, some of the University's directors took steps to assure that Butler would remain faithful to the teachings of the Christian Church. They tried to persuade Butler's board to approve the idea that the University's stockholders could "prescribe the religious beliefs and church affiliations of a majority of the board members." This effort was set aside largely because of faculty president Scot Butler's intervention.[40] Butler reminded the board of his father's intentions that the University provide a broad, religiously-based education for all students.

In 1900, after two years at the Bible College, W. E. Garrison left the faculty to do editorial work on his father's magazine in St. Louis. In 1902 the University's directors voted to discontinue its relationship with the Bible College, which promptly closed. Subsequently the University's catalog stated that while the full B.D. degree would not be granted until further notice, the University did intend to establish "a Graduate Divinity School" in the future. In 1904, following the retirement of Scot Butler, Garrison returned as faculty president of the University, but in less than two years, his health broken, he resigned. He was later to be appointed to the faculty of the Divinity School of the University of Chicago where he long reigned as a dominant Disciples intellectual.

The character of the theological debate between the two branches of the Disciples could be seen in a series of letters between Z. T. Sweeney and H. L. Willett of Chicago, published in the pages of the *Christian Century* in 1908 and 1909. Sweeney started the correspondence, responding to an editorial of Willett's that, Sweeney believed, undercut the significance of scripture, the nature of Christ, confidence in salvation, and the continuing viability of the Christian faith. Neither man was willing to accept the other's position or yield to the other's debating style. Willett was convinced that Sweeney's position depended upon a metaphysical interpretation of miracles that used words that were unscriptural and unacceptable to people of a modern mind. Sweeney believed that Willett's understandings went counter to the Bible and virtually the entire Christian tradition. His final letter was an impassioned plea that Willett, a man almost young enough to be Sweeney's son, turn from his ways while there was still time. "I have preached the simple gospel for forty years. My father before me preached it for seventy-five years, as likewise did his father. All my brothers have given their lives to it, and I love it with every heart pressure of my life." Sweeney continued his dramatic pleading. "I have seen hundreds of young men start upon the same premises you are now building, and invariably they have either disavowed them or gone into the rankest infidelity. If you are not one of these things, you will be the exception among thousands."

A Dual Approach to Theological Education

In order to offer a graduate program of ministerial education the University needed new leadership and new financial resources. The turning point was July 1903, when forty-four-year-old Hilton U. Brown was elected president of Butler's board of directors, a post he was to hold for the next fifty-two years. An Indianapolis native, graduate of Butler, active Disciples leader, journalist and editor, and civic leader, Brown was the kind of person who could bring "new forces into supporting position."[41] The directors immediately set out to raise $250,000, approaching Z. T. Sweeney to lead the new campaign, with Brown's active cooperation. Uneasy about Brown's hints that he would widen representation on Butler's board of directors, Sweeney responded to the invitation by offering the directors a "contract." He would undertake to raise the funds only if the University's directors would get a bill through the Indiana legislature to ensure that 80 percent of the board would always be members of the Christian Church. His contract also stated that no pledges would be collected until the entire amount of $250,000 had been pledged and that no moneys would be spent until at least $200,000 had been collected. Although the directors accepted his conditions, Sweeney did not conduct an active campaign, limiting it primarily to writing letters and contacting family members and church associates.

The drive was launched when Joseph I. Irwin, Sweeney's father-in-law, pledged $100,000. Two other Disciples also made substantial gifts, including $25,000 from Marshall T. Reeves, a Disciples businessman from Columbus, to establish a chair in religion to honor the memory of his parents. Despite this strong beginning, the campaign faltered and Hilton Brown moved to save Irwin's pledge by reaching outside of the College's church constituency, securing pledges from Andrew Carnegie and Indianapolis civic leaders. More than half of the $150,000 came from people who were not identified with the Christian Churches.[42]

In 1910, three years after Reeves funded the chair in religion, W. C. Morro was called from Kentucky University to the faculty to be the Reeves Professor and head of the Department of Religion. Since 1906 he had served on the same faculty with the foremost Disciples educator of the generation, the conservative J. W. McGarvey. When first approached by Butler representatives, Morro had declined the opportunity, but after much urging and with the assurance that he could build his own program, he finally consented.[43] Reeves and William G. Irwin, Joseph I. Irwin's son who was assuming leadership of the family's enterprises, pledged to pay the salaries for two more professors. Soon Charles E. Underwood, a Butler graduate serving as president of Eureka College, came to the faculty. Like Morro, Underwood had received his doctorate from Yale University.

The new Butler program was influenced by the simultaneous launching in Irvington of the College of Missions. The sponsor of this specialized academic institution was the Christian Woman's Board of Missions. The idea for a training school for missionaries had been proposed as early as 1884 in the columns of the *Missionary Tidings,* the CWBM's journal. Not until 1909, inspired by the centennial observance of the *Declaration and Address,*[44] did the project move forward, encouraged by the fact that in 1906 Disciples women in Indiana had begun to raise funds for a building that could be headquarters for the CWBM and a missionary training school. The building was dedicated August 18, 1910. Charles T. Paul accepted the call to be principal of this school which, two years later, became the College of Missions. Paul's title was changed to president and he continued as the central figure in this school throughout the life of the institution. Paul had operated a language school in Toronto, taught at the University of Nanking, and served at two different times on the faculty of Hiram College, where he had developed a missionary class that the *Christian Herald* described as the world's greatest mission study class.[45]

The College of Missions was located in Irvington not because of the presence there of a Disciples university but rather to be connected with the CWBM. The nearby location of Butler University was a further advantage to the purpose of the missionary school, which was to provide the specialized training needed by people preparing for missionary service, home on furlough, or interested in learning more about missions even though they did not expect to become missionaries. President Paul and his staff "sought from the first to bring the College of Missions up to and maintain it as a graduate school."[46] Since many of its students came without the needed amount of biblical training, the College established instruction for them in "the religion of Hebraism, Judaism and Christianity, courses in Old and New Testament, Christian apologetics, and the history and program of the Disciples of Christ." In keeping with guidelines developed by the World Missionary Conference, the College curriculum was divided into five departments of study for all mission areas of the world: the science and history of missions; the religions of the world; sociology; pedagogy; and the science of language, and the language required on the field selected by the student.[47] A notable feature of the College of Missions was its library, which was described as "the best working library in the field of missions on the western hemisphere."[48]

From its beginnings the College of Missions was broadly interdenominational, while still retaining its central Disciples identity, drawing students and faculty from across denominational lines.[49] Initially the College offered a diploma for two years of work but later it offered two degrees. The Master of Arts required two years of work plus a thesis of at least 15,000 words. The Bachelor of Divinity degree required three years, including at least two years of classical Greek and up to thirty hours of foundational studies in biblical and other subjects in addition to those required for the M.A. The first M.A. degrees (two in number) were awarded in 1919; there is no evidence that the College of Missions awarded any B.D. degrees.[50]

This program of theological and missiological study at the College of Missions was compatible with the graduate program in ministerial studies that W. C. Morro set forth at Butler University. Working quickly, he set forth a regimen of work that would lead to a B.D. degree, drawing both upon his Butler colleagues and upon the faculty of the College of Missions. In his first catalog (1911–1912), Morro listed three professors from Butler—William Charles Morro, head of the department and professor of New Testament text and interpretation; Jabez Hall, professor of homiletics and theology; and Christopher Bush Coleman, professor of church history; and three from the College of Missions—Charles Thomas Paul, professor of comparative religion and missionary history; Harry Clark Hurd, professor of anthropology and missionary science; and Fred Elmore Lumley, professor of sociology.

The curriculum listed thirteen areas of study in Butler's program, two of them offered in conjunction with the College of Missions, and in addition ten areas of study offered by the College of Missions. The range of topics covered was broad, with a strong leaning toward the more specialized work required by prospective missionaries. The Butler catalog said concerning the College of Missions that its admissions standards were practically the same of those of Butler; students of each school had access to the classes of the other school.[51] Butler's *Alumni Quarterly* reported activities at the College of Missions in the same way that it reported those of the University itself.

Early in Morro's administration the Butler program was upgraded from the Department of Ministerial Education to the School of Ministerial Education. The program took hold; in 1914, thirty-one ministerial students were enrolled and sixteen others were preparing for missionary work or other forms of religious leadership.[52] The College of Missions also began well and in its third year, 1913, enrolled twenty-seven students, the number growing steadily until it reached its high mark of fifty-five in 1921.

Despite the promising beginning of these coordinated programs of specialized theological education, both were to fail in less than two decades. Butler's program was the first to diminish. In the catalog of 1917–1918 Underwood's name was gone; he had died of cancer, working hard right to the end.[53] In the 1920–1921 catalog there was a major reduction in the program. In 1922–1923 the catalog no longer provided for a college or department of ministerial education, simply listing on two pages the courses in biblical literature and language. Although Morro was the highest paid member of the Butler faculty, well-liked by his colleagues, and popular among students, he failed to gain the support of church leaders who controlled Butler's program of theological education.[54] In 1924 he left the University, accepting briefly the respite offered by the College of Missions, and in 1927 he began a long and distinguished career at Brite Divinity School. The decline of the College of Missions began in 1922, and enrollment fell to eighteen in 1926. In 1927 teaching activities were suspended for a year, and a three-year agreement was made with the Kennedy School of Missions at Hartford, Connecticut. The College of Missions and President Paul moved to Hartford to continue their work there.

It is interesting to reflect upon what the preparation of ministers would have been like had the Morro-Paul ideas continued as the central character of the Indianapolis program. These men and most of their faculty colleagues were sympathetic to the liberal branch of the Disciples movement and to missions on the worldwide scene. They maintained historic connections with Disciples, but worked harmoniously with people from a wide confessional range. They combined classical theological studies with strong work in contemporary social sciences. Like Ames and Garrison before them, Morro and Paul brought an academic culture formed in the emerging universities of the new era, and for a while it looked as though their progressive vision would shape theological education in Indianapolis. Had their programs succeeded, the Butler-related theological center would have developed in ways that paralleled the post-1917 College of the Bible in Lexington, where the battle over biblical interpretation had been won by the liberal forces in the faculty and board of trustees.[55]

That these programs in Indianapolis collapsed was probably the result not of deficiencies within these two schools but rather of the harsh theological and organizational battles that were taking place among Disciples during the late teens and early twenties. Although the details had changed, the theological issues were much the same as during the Garvin episode—the methods of biblical study, the reliability of the biblical witness, the relation of baptism and church membership, and the functions of church-related organizations. During the Morro-Paul era, new issues were intensifying the conflict. In China, where Disciples missionaries were dealing with a tiny Christian minority in a culture with a radically different religious system, mission churches were moving toward the free exchange of members regardless of differences in theology and sacramental practices. Disciples missionaries concurred, and their superiors in the Indianapolis-based missionary societies agreed that on the field the right thing to do was to accept unimmersed Christians from other churches into the membership of the tiny Disciples congregations. These actions, however, violated the traditional practice in the Disciples congregations of North America. The voices in favor of open membership on the field seemed to be drowned by the outcry of those who opposed any changing of traditional Disciples practice.

At this same time, Disciples were working to consolidate several of their missionary and benevolent societies into one mission entity—the United Christian Missionary Society. Many Disciples would have opposed this development even without the challenge of open membership on the grounds that this kind of organization was unscriptural and therefore wrong for Disciples. The fact that the new missionary society was identified with people favoring open membership compounded the troubles. These were the kinds of issues that divided churches—and although the Disciples had prided themselves upon their ability to stay together during the Civil War it now looked as though they would break apart over these issues.[56]

One of the mediating influences during this struggle over missions and open membership was Z. T. Sweeney. He was a thoroughgoing traditionalist in his commitment to Disciples ideas, and totally committed to the vision of a church united upon these ideas. That Disciples should break apart into rival sects was scandalous to him, and he used much of his waning energy during these last years of his life to hold the Disciples together—but on terms that were consistent with the sacramental and ecclesial doctrines that he had preached throughout his life. He and others of like mind controlled the ecclesiastical relations of Butler University, and they were determined that Butler's program of theological education hold firmly to the Disciples tradition.[57]

With the collapse of three efforts to create a moderately progressive form of theological education in Indianapolis, it was clear that only a conservative program could be sustained. But what would be the character of this conservative alternative? And how could it command sufficient respect to be accepted by the progressive and city-minded members of the University's board of directors and faculty? These were the questions that had to be answered if the Disciples of Christ in Indiana were to have a seminary at Butler University.

2
More Religion—Less Theology

A Viable Plan for Ministerial Education at Butler University, 1917–1924

As the new century moved forward, Indianapolis was being transformed by the commercialization of agriculture and the growth of manufacturing. Wealth and culture were coming to town and the tight little colleges of an earlier period were becoming universities, many of them identified more with their cities than with the churches that had created them. From his newspaperman's desk at the center of civic life, Hilton U. Brown could see a new and grander Butler—full university character, broadened curriculum, and most important an expansive new campus. For this to happen, however, he needed the support of his church, which still provided a significant portion of the student body and generated major financial undergirding. Disciples in Indiana, however, were increasingly conflicted among themselves. Although the conservative Churches of Christ had largely split away, the remaining Disciples were still a major force in Indiana, fully capable of supporting his dream, if only they could work together. Brown's problem was that people at the University, Disciples leaders in the Irvington-based agencies, and pastors of some leading congregations were adapting to new currents of thought about religion and society, while the people who provided major financial support and controlled actions of the University's board of directors were Disciples traditionalists—people like William G. Irwin and Z. T. Sweeney. Brown had to find a way of satisfying both interests if he had any hope of developing the greater Butler University.

A Mediating Voice

The one person who could help him accomplish his goals was Frederick D. Kershner, who in 1917, at the age of forty-two, entered into the history of theological education in Indianapolis. He had studied with J. W. McGarvey, then the premier but traditional Bible scholar among Disciples, and later at Princeton and in Europe. After teaching in Pennsylvania, he had been president of Milligan College and Texas Christian University. He was well known among Disciples as a columnist in the church's popular theological journals. Kershner's commitment to Disciples ideas had been signaled by his book on baptism, first offered as oral presentations in 1912 to a conference of the Christian Unity Foundation of the Protestant Episcopal Church and the Commission on Christian Union of the Disciples of Christ.[1] "The goal of the Christian religion," Kershner declared, "is ever the Christian life, the life which realizes most nearly the ideas of Christ, the life which strives to embody Him as He embodied the Father in all He did while He was upon the earth."[2] Kershner distinguished between "formal religion" and "vital Christianity," affirming that "the church with its ordinances, its regular appointments for worship, its significant and impressive symbolism, affords the only possible means for the extension and preservation of vital Christianity." Kershner interpreted baptism as the initiating ordinance of Christianity and affirmed the necessity of believer's baptism by immersion, at the same time rejecting infant baptism. "What she [the church] should insist upon . . . is *the greatest possible freedom in regard to thought and opinion, and the greatest possible certainty in regard to action and ordinance.*" An ordinance partakes of the nature of a law; and the best laws are those which are most specific, and "admit of the least variation or equivocation in the process of administration."[3] Throughout this book and in his other monographs during this period, Kershner held steadfastly to the classical Disciples ideas about the church. Rarely did he identify them as the Disciples position, but instead, he presented these ideas as the central core of what all Christians believed and he subsumed them under what he called "vital Christianity."[4]

In 1915 Kershner was living temporarily in Washington, D.C., on leave from his work as president of Texas Christian University.[5] His advice was sought by correspondents from across the nation, and he was courted by people interested in his returning to Texas Christian University, or to the presidency of other Disciples colleges, including William Woods, Drake, and Bethany.[6] Late that year, even though he was a columnist for the *Christian Standard,* Kershner was invited to become the editor of the *Christian-Evangelist* in St. Louis, the strongest competitor of the *Standard* for the theological heart of the Disciples. From the beginning of his negotiations, Kershner's relations with the St. Louis staff were tense.[7] His appointment was lauded in a lead editorial in the *Standard,* whose editors congratulated Kershner for coming to this position at a time when people were reaching for "the great unities of our plea" and to a more positive movement. "No one known to us could swing the large constituencies of the *Christian-Evangelist* into line with greater unanimity than he."[8] Kershner's assumption that he had made a major career change was indicated in his good bye to his *Standard* readers in which he spoke as though he were severing relations with his lifelong work in higher education. The only reason he could make this change was the belief that in his new work he would do more for the ultimate good of the Restoration movement.[9]

While working for the *Evangelist,* Kershner exchanged several letters with Russell Errett and John Errett of the *Christian Standard* in which they referred to their concerns about trends among Disciples. The Erretts commended Kershner for his work at the *Evangelist,* praising him for bringing that paper around, but without giving details of what they meant. They talked of their meeting surreptitiously when one of the Erretts was in St. Louis. "This letter is of course written in the strictest confidence," he wrote to Russell Errett just before beginning his work in St. Louis. "I don't think I would have written what I have to any one but you. I have written not only because I trust you absolutely, but also because I wanted you to understand the situation just as it is."[10] Kershner's relations with his St. Louis colleagues remained tense and after only a few months of service at the *Christian-Evangelist* (December 1915 until July 1917) he decided to leave. He was rescued by his friends in Cincinnati who appointed him to be book editor of the *Christian Standard.*

In this new role, Kershner continued his interest in higher education among Disciples, publishing two articles in the *Standard* on the education of ministers. In the first article, Kershner noted that ministers stood in a long line that included Amos, Micah, Paul, Timothy, and Jesus. The prime characteristics of ministers in the New Testament period were "an unswerving faith in the divine message, a thorough knowledge of the ideals of their Master, an absolute fearlessness in proclaiming the truth as they saw it, and a completely disinterested attitude toward the claims of anything which did not appertain to the work they had in hand."[11] Dismissing much of what happened after the New Testament, Kershner discussed four characteristics of education that would be adequate for ministry in his time: "First, an emphasis upon the great spiritual realities; second, a similar emphasis upon the moral ideals of religion; third, the practical application of these principles to the immediate needs of the people; and fourth, the use of the thought culture of the age to serve the purposes of religion." Kershner spoke out against modern schools of divinity. "Instead of deepening the faith of those who enter their halls they seem subtly calculated to destroy what faith the prospective minister possessed before he sought their guidance."[12] He disparaged the idea of theologian, indicating that even Paul was not one. We need a practical message, Kershner claimed. "One of the reasons why our civilization is so filled with paganism is because we have had too much theological and formalistic preaching and not enough of the Sermon on the Mount." He granted, before finishing the article, that we do need to give attention to speculative theology, but only at the conclusion of the program and not as the beginning emphasis.

A year later Kershner published another article on "the Restoration College." He stated that an endowment of at least $200,000 was needed, and he noted that state universities and privately endowed colleges had endowments of from $1,000,000 to $28,448,701. The three reasons for church colleges to exist were to supply adequate intellectual and spiritual leadership for the church itself, to furnish a background of sympathy and support for the world mission of Christianity, and to foster a type of moral and intellectual fiber for the state that would not otherwise exist.[13] Although Kershner also corresponded with Thomas Carr Howe, faculty president of Butler University, this relationship seemed personal rather than professional. Although Howe suggested that they get together at meetings that they might attend in connection with college-related business, his reason was that the two of them could "get together in the back room of my library and try out some Cheroots which I have. . . . I am just aching to swap yarns with you."[14]

The Formation of a New Partnership

During this interim in his academic career, Frederick D. Kershner was developing plans for a dual project. He dreamed of creating a central training school for the Disciples of Christ that would bring together the theological intelligence of the Christian Churches and Churches of Christ and inspire a new generation of ministers to take the message of the Restoration Movement into the modern world. In order to fund this new seminary, Kershner proposed that an idea that had been taken up by several prominent financiers and several cities be embraced by the people of his church. They would create a national foundation that would gather funds for religious purposes, with primary emphasis given to education.[15] As these ideas took shape in his mind, a correspondence developed with William G. Irwin, who was rapidly becoming a dominant member of Butler's board of directors, second only in influence to Hilton U. Brown.

Born in 1866, Irwin was but seven years younger than Brown, and since the death of his father, Joseph I. Irwin, in 1910, had assumed the leadership of his family's business and educational activities. William Irwin had not married and continued to live in the family home with his sister Linnie and her husband, Z. T. Sweeney. They and the Sweeneys' children took their meals together and regularly discussed the full range of the family's affairs—in business, church, education, politics, the arts, and the community. Their custom was to exchange ideas freely until consensus was reached. In these discussions, Sweeney led the discussions concerning religion and Irwin those concerning business affairs. Both men were active members of Butler's board of directors. In their correspondence about a central training school and its supporting foundation, Kershner took the lead; but Irwin was an informed and active strategist who readily offered his suggestions and was ready to use his contacts to open the way for Kershner to follow up. They depended upon correspondence more than the telephone, sometimes writing to each other every two or three days. Their intention was to bring wealthy, committed Disciples from around the nation into the network that would support the foundation and the central school they intended to create.

These communications between Kershner and Irwin showed that they had already determined to create the school and foundation that Kershner was proposing, and that their intention was that it would be at Butler University. Because the letters say nothing about the program that W. C. Morro was heading, it can be concluded that Kershner and Irwin both assumed that the existing program would somehow be absorbed into the new graduate program that they hoped to develop. In July 1919 Irwin took a major step by providing a salary for Kershner (four thousand dollars per annum) and covering Kershner's travel expenses and other costs.[16] Kershner listed eleven duties that he understood to be his, and they included securing members for the board and faculty, organizing the school and providing for its catalog and curriculum, finding a place for it to meet, generating support among the churches, and recruiting students.

Kershner's role as mediator between conflicting branches of the Disciples was threatened, however, by his vacillating position in the increasingly bitter disputes over ecclesiological issues on the mission field and in North America.[17] The conservative reaction to these developments coalesced in a gathering called the Restoration Congress that met in Cincinnati for the two days prior to the 1919 International Convention of the Disciples. Kershner's name was published as one of hundreds from across the nation who "authorized" the call for this congress. He, along with Z. T. Sweeney and Marshall T. Reeves who were becoming Irwin's allies in the foundation-college enterprise,[18] were prominently listed on the front page of the *Christian Standard*. At the time that the call was published, however, Kershner's attention was focused on the recurrence of serious eye trouble. On June 16, 1919, he suffered a retinal hemorrhage similar to the one he had experienced in Hagerstown in the spring of 1905. He went to the same doctor in Philadelphia who had treated him earlier and the condition improved.[19] He was required, however, to use his eyes very little during the rest of the summer and did not see the call until much later.

When he saw the list of names, C. C. Morrison, editor of the *Christian Century*, wrote to find out if Kershner had intended for his name to be used for the call or if it had been used without his permission as Kershner claimed had happened in a similar incident the previous year.[20] Kershner explained his eye trouble and stated that because of this the call "had received wide circulation" before he had had "an opportunity to examine its contents." He did "not disapprove of a meeting held for the purpose of discussing the vital issues now before us," but he did not approve "any meeting characterized by an uncharitable spirit or which did not have in mind first of all the vital interests of the Kingdom." He deplored the "unbrotherly attitude of many of those with whose doctrinal position I agree." He told Morrison that he had resigned his position with the *Christian Standard* to take up work with a new school in Indianapolis. Morrison offered to write a veiled entry in the *Century* calling into question the integrity of the list of names, but Kershner disapproved of any reference being made and especially disapproved the idea of a covert reference.[21]

Negotiations with Butler University

Kershner's efforts reached a climax in the spring of 1919 when he met with a small number of people from Butler University to present the idea of establishing a College of Applied Christianity at their school. Present for the conference were Thomas Carr Howe, faculty president of the college; Hilton U. Brown, president of the Butler board of directors; W. C. Morro, dean of the Bible department of the college; and Allan B. Philputt, pastor of Central Christian Church in Indianapolis and Butler trustee. Kershner spent twenty-five minutes presenting the idea and the rest of the afternoon responding to questions concerning the academic standards of the proposed school, its relationship to Butler University and the effect of divorcing it from the ministerial work of the collegiate program, the personnel of the new institution, and its relations to the new plans under way for Butler. He found the people critical of the ideas during the first hour but fully persuaded and enthusiastic by the end of the discussion. He left the meeting with instructions to prepare a written draft of the plan and an outline of the charter to present to the Butler board at the earliest possible date. His comment to Irwin: "I really believe that we have these folks 'going.' " He was much impressed "by the language and attitude of Mr. Brown" who had come to the meeting "prejudiced against the whole proposition" but left "full of enthusiasm for it. I believe he will be a valuable factor in the future working out of our plans. I do not think he agrees entirely with the religious ideals we have in mind, but he is broad-minded enough to see that only along the lines we have marked out can there be a real future for Butler."[22] Kershner assured Irwin that he had "made no compromise, whatever, in my presentation of the type of school we have in mind and they thoroughly understand the whole scheme. They also understand that those who are behind this project mean business and that they do not propose to be sidetracked."

Kershner had in fact set a process into motion—but it would be careful and deliberate and he would not be privy to what was going on. The University's directors appointed a committee of five to consider this proposal further. Its members—James L. Clark, Z. T. Sweeney, Allen B. Philputt, Thomas Carr Howe, and Hugh Th. Miller—represented authority in the University and power in its church constituency. Miller was a strategic choice as chair of the committee because he was the son of Disciples minister and longtime Butler trustee, John Chapman Miller; Z. T. Sweeney's son-in-law; and William G. Irwin's business partner.[23] The committee wanted its new program in theological education to appeal to the full range of the Disciples' constituency. This would be difficult because both conservative and liberal forces were actively pursuing their interests. Howe's views were expressed in his ongoing correspondence with Miner Lee Bates, his counterpart at Hiram College. These two men worried about the attacks on the faculty at Transylvania College in 1917 and were concerned that this conservative force would threaten the effectiveness of the national fund-raising campaign of the Disciples called "Men and Millions." From his travels around Indiana, Howe had become convinced that a great many pastors and people were "growing more liberal constantly."[24] As he told the Butler directors, the University's goal should be scientifically trained men and women as well as soundly educated ministers.[25]

This concern about the conservatism was justified because in 1917 the directors had approved a resolution offered by Marshall T. Reeves in which they pledged the University to adhere to its original goals, oppose biblical criticism that would be "destructive to faith," and stay with the doctrines and practices of the Restoration Movement. Z. T. Sweeney's genial manner and breadth of interests, they knew, were attached to a strong commitment to a theological position similar to Reeves's. President Howe also was aware of the views of William J. Laymon, a Butler graduate who was dean of Drury College's Bible department, and C. C. Morrison of the *Christian Century*. These men, who represented a liberal voice among Disciples, deplored the signs that Butler would sell out to the highest bidder. They had no confidence in the motives of the monied interests from Columbus. Morrison's language in his *Century* editorial was especially pointed as he expressed his shock that Butler would consider a school funded by "ultra-conservative sources at Columbus, Indiana," and controlled "in the interest of reactionism in theology."[26]

Hilton U. Brown and an important number of directors were committed to the dream of creating the greater Butler University and knew that any actions they might take concerning a graduate program in religion had to be consistent with that vision. They also knew that in any case, the advances the University could make depended upon adequate funding. Although they were committed to a broad financial base for the University's relocation to Fairview Park and expansion of program, they also knew that they needed the support of wealthy Disciples from Columbus—including Reeves and the Irwin-Sweeney-Millers. William G. Irwin was a key to keeping the vision of the new Butler alive while also preserving the support of conservative church interests. Sweeney's commitment to solid education and conservative theology was known. Miller had once been on the Butler faculty and he, too, could be considered in favor of new developments at the University while at the same time being attentive to traditional Disciples connections.

Although the board of directors and the committee of five moved carefully, one factor seemed clear—that Kershner represented a moderate position: "sound" on Disciples theology, but neither reactionary nor radical, neither conservative nor liberal.[27] They reviewed Kershner's ideas and pushed forward in developing a constructive proposal that would satisfy the various concerns that the board was holding in balance. At a meeting of the Butler board on April 28, 1920, several directors had expressed their views fully. Brown was clear in his support for a school to prepare ministers—that would appeal to all of the brotherhood and be part of the University's efforts to reshape itself to meet modern needs. Only then, he believed, could the University uphold the church in a new era. Sweeney agreed with Brown and pledged to support with his heart and financial resources a venture that would prepare ministers with "correct" views, educate undergraduates to be good church members, and uphold standards as good as those in the best seminaries. It became clear that the board of directors as a whole could support a new development in ministerial education that was consistent with Disciples' traditional beliefs, fully a partner in the greater Butler, and adequately funded.

In June the committee of five reported a plan that proposed a school that would be part of Butler rather than independent. It would be overseen by five Butler directors who would report to the full board and it would receive a fixed share of the University's endowment. Although primarily a graduate school, it would offer limited work in biblical history and literature for Butler undergraduates. The school would have to be adequately funded, and here the committee was hopeful that new fund raising ventures would bring in the needed resources.[28] The deliberations of the committee of five were known to William G. Irwin. Hugh Th. Miller and Z. T. Sweeney shared the Irwin family home with him and matters like this were included in conversations around the family table. He also was part of the Butler board and regularly participated in its deliberations. The one person who seems to have been left out of these ongoing discussions was Kershner, who was puzzled and irritated by the delays that he experienced without any way of knowing why no action was taking place.

Kershner's Vision for a New College

Kershner's ideas about this new theological school had been well developed as he was preparing for conversations with Butler people. He had first written them out in pencil, with frequent erasures, and then, with a new typewriter provided by Irwin, he had transcribed portions of the manuscript and drafted bylaws for the college that he envisioned. Three considerations had prompted this plan: the need among Disciples for more trained leaders, the general recognition that Disciples currently lacked a central institution where special training could be received, and "the rapidly increasing emphasis upon the necessity for applied Christianity in our modern and religious life, as opposed to the older and more specifically speculative training afforded by the average theological institution." The memorandum continued with paragraphs dealing with name, location, organization and control, internal administration, physical equipment, and budget.[29]

Kershner arranged the academic program in five departments: Old Testament, New Testament, Christian history, homiletics, and religious education. W. C. Morro was one of the persons proposed for the faculty, as was Walter S. Athearn, a Disciples scholar moving into national significance in theological education. Two of the most influential, and conservative, Disciples pastors were also on the list: Z. T. Sweeney and P. H. Welshimer, the latter pastor of the Disciples' largest congregation.[30] Kershner estimated the cost of the college's first year, with a faculty of five, to be $25,250. It would in time need an endowment of $400,000 and additional funds for the building and a student loan fund. Kershner preferred an Indianapolis location, but if the Butler board would not go forward with this project, then another location would be chosen. The college would be self-controlled, with its own self-perpetuating board working in cooperation and harmony with the Butler board. "It will doubtless be true that a considerable number of the new trustees will be also trustees of Butler College, although no fixed regulation in regard to this matter will be made a provision of the charter."

Kershner's thinking behind his preferred name for the new school, the College of Applied Christianity, was implied in a series of articles that he published under the title "The Old Gospel and the New Age." Writing passionately of the transformation of the world, he declared that the imperialistic system of Rome, renewed by the Kaiser, had been destroyed and a new democracy of the people was coming into being. The result for the religious forces of the world was lessened emphasis upon metaphysical speculation and ecclesiastical forms and increased emphasis upon meeting the practical needs of humanity. "More religion and less theology, more spirituality and less formalism, more brotherhood and less caste, more practice and less theory—these are some of the unquestioned demands of the new order." Then, seeming to speak to Disciples, Kershner continued: "The church which flies in the face of these demands, and clings to old and outworn theologies and formalities, is certainly doomed to become a 'disappearing brotherhood.' It will have, and can have, no voice for the needs of present-day men and women, and must therefore pass away with the old order."[31]

Kershner's and Irwin's efforts to attract Walter S. Athearn to head the program of religious education in the new college revealed the spirit of their vision. Although neither of them knew Athearn personally, they had read his articles in the *Christian Standard*[32] in which Athearn had advocated education that was thoroughly Christian, church centered, and free from denominational control. There was a hard-driving conservative and independent sound to these writings. Their further investigations convinced them that Athearn was loyal to traditional ideas of the Disciples, conservative in his theology, and sympathetic to the position on these matters as laid out by the *Christian Standard*. They knew that Athearn's program of religious education at Boston University led the nation. Kershner told Irwin that only when professors of this caliber were called would they be able to establish the school they envisioned. Apparently Athearn was willing to consider an offer, for Kershner set up plans to meet Athearn, who was coming to Columbus, Ohio, to lecture.

During the summer and fall of 1919, Kershner tried to work out details for coming to Indianapolis and beginning the college. His primary contact at Butler was W. C. Morro, the head of Butler's existing religion department. The new school needed to be incorporated, but this discussion had to wait until Hilton U. Brown returned to the city. Kershner asked Morro to help write material for publicity for the new school and Morro agreed. Kershner kept in close contact with Irwin and reported important aspects of these conversations with Morro. They discussed names for the board of trustees and Morro objected to the name of P. H. Welshimer. Although Kershner stated that it would be awkward to remove that name now, this name soon disappeared from the list. Kershner explained to Morro that just as Welshimer's name caused difficulty for some of Kershner's supporters, so "Brother Philputt's letter endorsing the Christian Century . . . is giving me no little trouble on the conservative side." He concluded: "Personally I have no desire whatever to found a Christian Standard institution and I have just as little desire to found a Christian Century school. I want an institution which will seek the truth first of all and which will be as free as possible from any partisan bias."[33]

They discussed the name of the school, with Kershner noting that friends were suggesting the College of Religion or the College of the Christian Religion.

Morro tried to help the Kershners find suitable housing. Kershner, however, reported that housing in midwestern cities was very tight, and that they didn't want to move precipitously. He was ready to continue his residence in

Cincinnati and commute to Indianapolis. In all of these discussions Morro seemed businesslike and helpful, but there was little sense of enthusiasm for what was taking place. The conservative forces had won and his own plans to develop a mainstream Disciples seminary had been set aside.

The Christian Foundation

Despite these efforts to launch the new school in the fall of 1920, the venture didn't come together. The practical problems such as housing seemed manageable, but resistance of other kinds was not. In addition to the opposition discussed earlier, a second cause for delay was the opposition of the Board of Education of the Disciples of Christ. In one letter to Thomas W. Phillips, Jr., Kershner wrote: "I understand that the Board of Education has declared war on us and has voted to oppose our organization by every means within its power." He then commented that this opposition was the proof they needed that their project was a good thing.[34]

Kershner counseled Irwin that perhaps they should concentrate upon establishing the foundation while waiting for things to develop for the college. The two men had consulted with each other extensively about the creation of a foundation, with Irwin sometimes opening the door for Kershner's correspondence with wealthy Disciples around the country. They seem to have received positive responses from most of the people on their list—with the notable exception of R. A. Long, whose dedication to the Disciples was to be most fully expressed in his purchase of the St. Louis publishing company that J. H. Garrison had developed into an enterprise with a major impact upon Disciples. Long then donated this company to his church while he was leading in the process of its becoming the Christian Board of Publication. On April 1, 1920, ten men met in Indianapolis to organize the Christian Foundation: L. C. Brite, a Texas cattleman who had donated a significant sum to found the Brite Bible College at Texas Christian University when Kershner had been president; James L. Clark, Indiana jurist, trustee of Butler University, and member of the church in Danville where another Sweeney was pastor; H. J. Derthick; George W. Hardin, businessman from Johnson City, Tennessee, and active supporter of Milligan College where Kershner had once been president; William G. Irwin; Frederick D. Kershner; I. N. McCash, president of Phillips University; George B. Peak, insurance executive from Des Moines; Benjamin D. Phillips, Pennsylvania businessman and trustee of Hiram College; and Thomas W. Phillips, Jr., who in addition to his Pennsylvania business interests was a trustee of Bethany College. In addition to their support of other Disciples colleges, the Phillipses' support of the new college established in Enid, Oklahoma, had led the trustees of that school to name it Phillips University.

This list of interested persons showed part of Kershner's grand scheme, which was to create a central school at the graduate level that would appeal to graduates of all of the Disciples undergraduate colleges. The list did not include people who were coming into prominence because of their support of the Bible colleges that were just coming into the picture—schools like Cincinnati Bible Seminary. The time would come early in the history of Kershner's seminary when the Disciples' liberal arts colleges would largely drop out of the loop of his school while the graduates of the Bible colleges would make it their seminary of first choice.

Kershner was able to give these prominent Disciples a brief review of the history of foundations, beginning with the Peabody Fund, created in 1867 by George Peabody. Because the powers of that fund had been so narrowly defined, its potential had been severely limited, and later foundations were created with more broadly defined powers. Some of the most prominent businesspeople in America had been involved, and among the foundations created were the Carnegie Foundation in 1906, the Russell Sage Foundation in 1907, and the Rockefeller Foundation, established by an act of Congress in 1913. Kershner took special note of the work of F. H. Gore of Cleveland, who in 1914 had established the Cleveland Foundation, a new kind of fund to which many people could contribute; and he noted that twelve cities, including St. Louis and Indianapolis, had taken similar action. He believed that no one had yet adapted this idea to religious purposes, but was convinced that foundations could be used to combat sin and promote the gospel. Foundations provided a scientific method for social giving by establishing a board of competent and impartial persons who would determine the merits of the causes and institutions that would be supported. The Christian Foundation would be established with powers similar to those of the Rockefeller Foundation.[35]

On February 21, 1922, the Christian Foundation was incorporated by nine men who were also listed as the charter members of the foundation's board. In contrast with the national scope of the earlier meeting, this second conference consisted of Indiana men—four from Danville, where Z. T. Sweeney's brother, William E. Sweeney, was pastor and five from Columbus.[36] Four of the Columbus people signed the articles of incorporation. The board of trustees of the foundation was named as were officers of the board, and an executive committee. All of the members of the executive committee were also members of the board of directors of Butler University. Soon after the initial actions were taken, Hilton U. Brown and Marshall T. Reeves were also elected to the board of the Christian Foundation. In 1925 Brown was named president of the board, a position he was to keep until his death in 1958. Reeves gave the foundation its first major gift—a contribution of $144,500—and later added further amounts with a total by the time of his death in 1925 of $611,000.[37]

Between the organization of the Christian Foundation and its incorporation, the Butler directors took another step to regularize the financial structure. Even though the University's system of governance had been reformed in 1909, the University needed a new instrument to generate, receive, and distribute contributions. The Butler directors, therefore, requested the Indiana legislature to create a holding company that could receive funds and distribute them for the designated uses. The Butler Foundation was established in 1922, with William G. Irwin as its president.[38]

The theological agenda of the people who created the Christian Foundation were clear. The foundation was to receive, manage, invest, and distribute funds "according to the instructions of the donors. . . .or if not instructed by the donors then according to the judgment and determination of the Board of Directors *in promoting the realization in world activities of the ideas and teaching of Jesus Christ, and in furthering the progress of the Church founded by Him and made known through the New Testament scriptures*" [italics added]. The bylaws added further detail "in order that there may be no misunderstanding" concerning the meaning of "the Church of Christ." Eight elements were listed, including the authoritative character of the New Testament, the priority of Peter's confession in Matthew 16:16, the importance of immersion baptism of believers, and the weekly observance of the Lord's supper, the name Church of Christ, the necessary unity of the church, the freedom of the local congregation in the "larger unity of the universal brotherhood of the church," the New Testament method of conversion, and "unfeigned belief in the deity of Jesus Christ and therefore in His miraculous power as recorded in the New Testament." May 27, 1927, the Christian Foundation made its first appropriation to the Butler Foundation on behalf of the School of Religion and on April 19, 1928, its first contribution to Cincinnati Bible Seminary, which was especially favored by the Reeves family.

A Period of Uncertainty

By the time that these foundations had been created, Kershner had largely given up on the possibility of establishing his College of Applied Christianity at Butler University. In Indianapolis, he told Thomas W. Phillips, Jr., "I have met with nothing but opposition, distrust, and delay. It was always hard to put my finger on the source of the trouble, but the trouble itself was always there. I finally concluded that it would be wasting time and money to try to build up the kind of work which I desire under such circumstances." In the meantime, friends in Iowa were persuading him to consider Drake University—like Butler, a small Disciples college—as the place for him to teach. Kershner visited Des Moines twice, spending nearly a week on one of these visits, in order to ascertain the theological and institutional factors. One reason for his caution would have been the controversy that had been generated by the *Christian Standard* when Arthur Holmes had been nominated to the presidency of Drake. The editor, George P. Rutledge, was alarmed by the fact that Holmes claimed to be a Disciples progressive and was a member of the Campbell Institute, which was dominated by liberal Chicago Disciples. In response to an earlier request from the Drake committee for suggestions, Rutledge had suggested several names. Later, representatives of the Drake board met Rutledge in his Cincinnati office, trying to persuade him to endorse Holmes. Other contacts led Rutledge to believe that a concerted effort had been made for the purpose of "swinging Holmes into the presidency,"[39] and he remained firmly opposed to the appointment.

In his campus visit, Kershner became convinced that Holmes, whom he had not known previously, leading trustees such as George B. Peak, and the faculty of the Bible College were loyal to the Disciples plea and could be depended upon. The plans to raise significant amounts of money for the University impressed him greatly. He resisted Holmes's request that Kershner ask his own supporters, such as Irwin, to contribute directly to Drake since their support would come through the Christian Foundation. In Iowa Kershner found himself surrounded by pastors and other colleagues who valued his leadership and looked to him to help the Disciples recover their true nature. He was invited by churches to preach on Sundays and to lead revival meetings. Irwin—who knew much about the Butler workings that Kershner did not—had yielded reluctantly, noting in a letter to Kershner that the main desire of the Butler people "is to have a city school rather than a church school. The only object of having the church hitched onto it, it seems to me, is to get such funds as might be obtained through it. However, after the meeting next week, we can discuss the Des Moines situation."[40] When word leaked out that Kershner might move to Des Moines, opposition developed in Disciples organizations. H. O. Prichard of the Disciples' board of education went to Iowa to persuade Drake not to participate in Kershner's plan. Pritchard claimed that the conduct of Arthur Holmes, president of Drake University, was unethical because he refused to go into an interchurch campaign and instead launched a separate drive for Drake.[41]

In his final negotiations with President Holmes, Kershner stated that he was willing to settle in Des Moines only if his commitment to establishing a central school for the Disciples could be maintained and if his relations with Irwin (including financial support) could be continued. He indicated his willingness to make Des Moines the location of his new school,[42] and in the full intention that the new graduate school of the Disciples of Christ would be established at Drake University, Kershner moved to Iowa in time for the beginning of the 1920 school term. During the first two years that Kershner was in Des Moines, his family and the family of President Holmes developed a strong friendship. More important, these two colleagues found a deepening fraternity developing between them. All seemed to be going well until the spring of 1922 when Holmes abruptly left Drake and settled in Philadelphia in what was at first a limited relationship with the University of Pennsylvania. Whatever may have been the causes of Holmes's leaving Drake, Kershner found that Drake, even in Holmes's absence, continued to be a reasonable place for him to work on his mission of creating a central school for Disciples and developing the Christian Foundation.

While Kershner was settling into his new life in Des Moines, Irwin increased the level of activity at Butler University. Not only did he lead in establishing the Butler Foundation, but he gave his support to the drive to create the "greater Butler" and to relocate to a new campus on the north side of Indianapolis. He also used his influence to reshape the Butler board of directors so that it would be more congenial to the purposes that he and Kershner had developed. Irwin now believed that everything was on track to reestablish Indianapolis as the site of their new training school. Writing to Kershner, he reported: "Our board [Butler] is absolutely all right now. There are only three members that are not in entire sympathy with a most conservative policy in the church part of the school. The people of Indianapolis are giving evidence of a desire to cooperate in every way with the institution, particularly if the move to Fairview is made."[43] During these same years the committee of five continued its work to develop the outlines of a feasible graduate program in religion at the University. Irwin asked Kershner why Arthur Holmes had left Des Moines, questioning the believability of the announced reason, that he was not good at fund-raising. Irwin proposed that Holmes might well be the one who should succeed W. C. Morro, who, it was clear, would not have a place at the reconstructed theological program that Irwin was determined to establish at Butler.[44]

In November of 1922 Irwin wrote to Kershner, declaring: "I believe we have a very fine opportunity to offer to any one who will head the Bible department. It is a big program that we have on hand and I want as many big men behind us as possible." The question, however, was who would be the "big man" to head up the program. This topic came up frequently in the correspondence between Kershner and Holmes during a critical period of time beginning in September 1922. The letters dealt with family matters, intellectual questions, the situation among Disciples, activities and campus politics at Drake, and their advice to one another about career issues. Holmes urged Kershner to study for a Ph.D. degree, with Harvard the preferred location. Then he engineered a way for Kershner to do it in Philadelphia, studying at the University and serving as pastor at Third Christian Church.[45] Kershner, however, was cool to the idea of working for the degree, doubting that it would help him much in the work he wanted to do. He reported that Irwin would be willing for him to delay his other projects by a couple of years; but Irwin also seemed unenthusiastic. Kershner's dream continued to be the central school for ministerial training.

From late in 1922 until the spring of 1924, the relationships between Kershner, Holmes, and Irwin developed a new character. In their frequent letters to each other Kershner and Holmes insisted that the other man was the right one for the job at Butler, and they made similar claims in their communications with Irwin.[46] Despite his protestations about the position at Butler, Holmes met Irwin at a bank, probably in Philadelphia, and told Kershner that he found Mr. Irwin "to be a man of far more personality than I anticipated, good-natured, talkative, forceful, straight to the point." Holmes had begun the discussion with the observation that the brotherhood [the Disciples' euphemism for denomination], in the minds of some, was ready to disappear in the union movement; and that unless "we had a college turning out real preachers of our position who by their efficiency in their work, their ability and character exhibited in the community so as to win respect from leading men, could promote our work, we would disappear in ten years." Irwin agreed, at which point

Holmes had continued by saying that he was "not in sympathy with the ideals of most of our Bible colleges which seemed to aim primarily at becoming standardized theological seminaries." His preference was "to formulate an entirely new method of making preachers, bearing down heavily upon practical training for practical tasks!" Irwin "received my tirade in respectful silence, then said, 'I want you to come out to Butler and start such a preacher factory.'" Holmes said no and then recommended Kershner.

Responding to Holmes's letter, Kershner reported that Irwin had been well impressed with the interview and hoped that Holmes would accept. The overwhelming majority of our people want a strong university for the Disciples, he noted, but the leaders do not. Right now the possibility no longer remains at Drake whose board "sinned away its day of grace," but has swung back to Butler. Irwin and Marshall T. Reeves, who dominated the board, would be able to carry the project through, and Irwin believed that Holmes was the man to lead this venture. Surely, Kershner pleaded with Holmes, "to formulate the ideals of a group of over a million and a quarter people is quite as significant as to barely touch the fringe of things in one of our state institutions. I feel that we need you for this work and that you can find in it a field worthy of your best thought and attention."[47] In mid-January of 1923, Holmes reported that he had heard nothing more from Butler. A few days later Kershner wrote that he too had not heard from Irwin, but that he understood that Butler had withdrawn from the Disciples' board of education. On February 7, 1923, Kershner wrote to Holmes that Irwin was going to press forward and try to persuade Holmes to come to Butler; but Holmes responded in mid-February that while he was willing to meet Irwin again he could not accept the Butler position.

Despite these statements, Holmes allowed himself to be drawn more deeply into the negotiation, even to the point of going from Cincinnati "over to Columbus, Indiana," where he had dinner with Sweeney, Irwin, Philputt, Thomas W. Grafton, and one or two others about training ministers for our people. They had concluded that it would be good to consult with a number of able ministers about how to train ministers in a school of religion. He asked Kershner's suggestion about securing these ideas. Mr. Irwin, he reported, is interested in "making a certain kind of church, the kind I want to see made myself." Then Holmes reported: "I like him very much personally and feel at home with his type of mind and his purpose." Although no offer had been made, says Holmes, he intended to develop a plan when he was in Dayton over the summer (1923). Kershner responded positively and also reported that Irwin and Marshall T. Reeves were planning a meeting of the Christian Foundation for the summer.

Holmes developed a questionnaire, which he sent for Kershner's comment, and developed a financial estimate for Kershner's review which would be sent to the Butler people, calling for an endowment of $500,000 and a scholarship fund of $50,000. Building, grounds, and equipment would total $90,000, bringing the cost of establishing the school to $640,000. He proposed that the annual budget consist of $25,000 taken from the endowment and $5,000 coming from gifts. The expenditures budget of $30,000 included a salary of $7,500 for the dean, and $12,000 total for the professors. Kershner's response was to confirm these figures and to mention also the gifts of a million dollars received by Bethany and Culver-Stockton Colleges. He continued to hope that someone would care for Butler at a similar rate.[48]

Although Kershner and Holmes were largely agreed concerning the purpose for this new school and its conservative theological character, they differed in their ideas about the academic character of the new institution. Holmes was determined to create a school that trained ministers who were committed to the Disciples plea and who would be skilled at developing churches. He was willing to set aside all customary patterns of theological development in order to create a program that would accomplish his intentions. Kershner, however, pressed for a graduate school. He proposed that the undergraduate colleges could innovate in their programs, but that there should be one school for the Disciples to which the college graduates could come. He believed that this school should be genuinely at the graduate level, able to command the respect of all people. This was what he wanted to establish, at Drake, Butler, or someplace else.[49]

Z. T. Sweeney, whose name was rarely mentioned in the Kershner-Irwin correspondence, took the lead in continuing the negotiations with Holmes who continued to resist the offers, although stopping short of outright refusal. Holmes was thriving in his university position and did not want to risk that freedom and security.[50] In a letter to Kershner in February 1924, Holmes reported on his most recent exchange with Irwin. "I told him I had not seen any inducements that would lead me to accept the precarious position which my limitations would involve me in if I came to Butler. I made no offer to talk more. I did say that I myself would not think of a faculty at Butler Bible College without you. So the matter rests. I see no inducement that would sway me. Evidently they are not agreed upon their men."[51] In this same letter Holmes reported on having spoken that Sunday evening on the radio broadcast of the Sunday Evening Club "as an antidote to Fosdick who had been there a week before. Only my throng did not break down the doors to get in. Mine was a nice, gentle crowd—about 3000 instead of 5000! Think of Fosdick as an appealer to the MOB."

The Move to Indianapolis

During these weeks in the spring of 1924 the Butler-Columbus group also was communicating with Kershner about the Butler position. Apparently they had concluded that either Holmes or Kershner would be satisfactory to them, and they were working on both in hopes of securing one. Kershner was also considering an offer from L. C. Brite to return to Texas Christian University, recently the recipient of a $4 million gift. Holmes reported his fear to Kershner that this new gift would lessen the influence that Brite had previously wielded in Texas. In another letter to Holmes, Kershner seemed ready to consider the Butler situation but noted that "it all depends upon whether the Indianapolis people are alive to an opportunity or whether they are too slow or too parsimonious to grasp it."[52]

In a letter written a few days later, Kershner reported to Holmes that he had been summoned to Indianapolis by Irwin and had gone immediately from Des Moines. There he met the Butler committee in the college offices: Thomas W. Grafton, Allan B. Philputt, Robert J. Aley, John W. Atherton, and William G. Irwin. Z. T. Sweeney was in Florida and Hilton U. Brown was ill. They offered every inducement they could to persuade Kershner to come, but "failed to meet the only real proposition which I felt I could make them." This proposition was substantially the same as the one which Kershner and Holmes had discussed a few evenings earlier in Kershner's home. If the Butler situation was to realize its potential, "the brethren there must realize that it is up to them to make some sacrifices and to invest in the proposition, as you said, something on the scale which they would follow if it were a real business proposition. They must be willing to put in thirty or thirty-five thousand dollars a year if they want to develop a first class school for ministerial training. This they do not seem to be ready to do." [53] They tried to induce him to "take hold of things on a smaller scale," but this did not appeal to Kershner for reasons that he and Holmes had discussed. He had presented them, as if it were his own suggestion, a proposition similar to the one that Holmes had made, but he didn't know what they would do with it.[54]

In early March Kershner told Holmes what had been happening. Following the meeting in early February, Irwin had written Kershner insisting that Kershner undertake the work and pledging to stand behind him if he did. Kershner responded in a letter dated February 21, 1924, stating the four "conditions under which I would consider coming to Indianapolis":

> First, that the ministerial work should be organized in a separate college, after the plan of the Drake College of the Bible.
>
> Second, that I should be given the privilege of selecting my own faculty, subject, of course, to the approval of the Board of Trustees.
>
> Third, that an initial budget of not less than fifteen to twenty thousand dollars should be provided for the new school.
>
> Fourth, that my own salary should be fixed at five thousand dollars a year and that my moving expenses from Des Moines to Indianapolis should be paid.
>
> Until he received a reply from Mr. Irwin, Kershner continued, "there is nothing further for me to do."[55]

Apparently Mr. Irwin made a suitable reply because the Butler catalog published in the summer of 1924 listed Kershner as a member of the Butler faculty, and the next year the graduate College of Religion was founded under his leadership. At the same time that the College of Religion came into the picture at Butler, other dramatic developments were taking place. The school reclaimed the title of university, and it announced formal alliances with other schools in Indianapolis: the Metropolitan School of Music, the Indiana Law School, the College of Missions, and the Herron Art Institute. Irwin had convinced Brown, and with him other Indianapolis based trustees, that the new seminary was compatible with their hopes for a new university. Brown had apparently reached the conclusion that Irwin's participation in the development of the new university depended upon Brown's support of the new seminary. Although Brown was a lifetime member of the Christian Church, active in the normal pattern of lay leadership, primarily at the Downey Avenue Christian Church in Irvington, he was not "emotionally religious," to use a phrase from his own memoirs. His lifetime commitment was to make Butler a strong institution and he was ready to team up with William G. Irwin in order to achieve that goal. Irwin was one key to ongoing financial support and to the commitment of the Disciples community throughout Indiana, illustrated by the challenge gift of $300,000 that he and his sister Linnie Irwin Sweeney offered to

Butler on the condition that the University raise $700,000 to make up the $1 million that was needed to secure the move to the new campus.[56]

Brown may also have seen in the proposed new college a way of strengthening the academic program of the College and bringing in a strong contingent of students. By the time that Butler broke ground for Jordan Hall on the Fairview campus, Irwin and Sweeney had contributed $700,000 to this venture, their contribution surpassed only by the $1,000,000 given by Arthur Jordan whose name the building bears. In the events at the laying of the cornerstone, Hilton Brown stated that "none of this work would have been possible without the generous support of William G. Irwin, and his sister, Mrs. Sweeney." Later in the day another trustee, Arthur V. Brown, said that the Irwin-Sweeney gift of more than $700,000 was "only a small part" of their gift because "Mr. Irwin is giving of his time, day after day . . . in helping to formulate all the plans that are going on here."[57] Hilton Brown proved to be a sturdy friend, because he became a central figure in the Christian Foundation and School of Religion Committee for the rest of the time that the Kershner-Irwin partnership endured.

When Butler's new College of Religion was launched, according to the plans developed by Hugh Th. Miller's committee of five, several of the details differed from those that Kershner and Irwin had laid out initially. Its name was the College of Religion rather than the College of Applied Christianity. It did not have its own board of trustees, but a special committee of the Butler board acted as a board for the seminary. The membership of this committee was to be nominated by the Christian Foundation which Kershner and Irwin, with the help of Hilton U. Brown, had created.

In this way Kershner and Irwin were able to achieve their goal which was to create a school that would be determined by its church connections rather than by the administrative processes of the University. Although part of the University's program, the Seminary was independent from the University in every important aspect of its life—in its funding, its board of control, its selection of faculty, and in its power to determine its own curriculum. The Christian Foundation, which Kershner had proposed and helped create, was to underwrite virtually all funds needed to maintain the program of the theological school, but furthermore the Foundation also assumed a portion of the general university budget. Irwin served simultaneously as Butler trustee, member of the College of Religion committee, and as member of the boards of the Butler Foundation and the Christian Foundation. Hilton U. Brown's importance to the enterprise was signaled by the fact that he also served on the board of the Christian Foundation. This complex interweaving of persons provided power and understanding, and the point of it all was to be sure that the church portion of the University remained true to the church that Kershner and Irwin served. For nearly two decades until old age and death would overtake them, the partnership of these entrepreneurial, traditionalist Christians, often tested by circumstances and situations, made their school strong.[58]

3
Training Men and Women "of All Faiths" for the Christian Ministry

The Seminary's First Decade, 1924–1935

Frederick D. Kershner was moving to Indianapolis at a challenging time for leaders of the Christian Churches. Along with the people of other mainstream protestant church bodies and other mainstream organizations such as the Women's Christian Temperance Union, Disciples were contending with the changing social structures of American life. One of these organizations was the Ku Klux Klan which was rapidly rising in power, with Indiana at the epicenter. From 1922 through 1925, the Klan was at the height of its influence. Its membership mirrored mainstream society, both within the churches and outside of their membership. Church people, including large numbers of women, joined the Klan because its social policies seemed similar to those of the protestant churches: opposing the liquor trade, encouraging traditional family values, and seeking to protect older American patterns of life from the impact of Catholics, Jews, and immigrants. The Klan and the Republican Party were closely aligned, so much so that in 1924 the Klan virtually controlled state-wide politics.[1]

The Klan was represented in the churches, averaging 6 percent of the membership across the entire protestant church spectrum of Indianapolis. Disciples, at 7.7 percent, were above average while Baptists with 4.9 percent were below. Some clergy supported the Klan and others opposed it, often at great risk to their professions. During 1923 four Disciples pastors in Indianapolis were forced out of their pastorates because of their opposition to the Ku Klux Klan, which was rising to the high point of its influence with an estimated forty thousand members in Indianapolis. The first of the four to lose his position was F. E. Davison who quickly went public concerning the things that were happening in his church. He was quickly supported by the Christian Ministers Association of Indianapolis and then by clergy and laypersons from around the state. A second group of Christian Church ministers, however, the Central Indiana Christian Institute, disavowed that action.[2]

The most prominent Disciples layperson of the period was Edward L. Jackson, church member along with Hilton U. Brown at Downey Avenue Christian Church and an Irvington neighbor of the Klan's Grand Kleagle, D. C. Stephenson. In 1923 Jackson presided over sessions of the Disciples' International Convention meeting in Colorado Springs and in 1924, with Klan support, he was elected governor of Indiana. The Klan appealed to a broad spectrum of people, especially protestant church people, because it seemed to be "an ally in the struggle against the forces of evil and to keep America pure."[3] Many people in communities like Indianapolis who were not Klan members were quietly sympathetic to the Klan's goals, or at least unwilling to act in ways that would seem to be in opposition to the Klan. In his editorial responsibilities with the *Indianapolis News,* Hilton U. Brown spoke against the Klan; but it is probable that several members of Butler University's board of directors were among the people who quietly sympathized with the broad public goals that the Klan proclaimed.[4]

Like many others of his time, Kershner remained publicly silent concerning these issues. It is likely that his position was similar to one taken by G. H. Combs, the foremost Disciples pastor in Kansas City. In a column in the *Christian-Evangelist,* Combs disagreed with the militant and divisive approach to the issues the Klan attacked, while affirming the goals of the movement.[5] Kershner's attitude, however, can be perceived in his actions which included establishing his own connections in the city, not only with his colleagues at the University and in Disciples' circles, but also with religious and civic leaders in the wider community. One of the most prominent of these intellectual and professional colleagues, especially in light of the anti-Semitism of the Klan, was Morris M. Feuerlicht, rabbi of Indianapolis Hebrew Congregation and the preeminent leader of the Jewish community in the city. Feuerlicht was deeply involved in activities dealing with the well-being of children and youth, working both in the private and public sectors. He was a vigorous opponent of the Klan and he also condemned the Nazi government and propaganda. Twice he debated Clarence Darrow before large Indianapolis gatherings.[6] In 1926, Kershner appointed Feuerlicht to be lecturer in Semitics at the Seminary, and he continued in that position until 1951.

Soon after their friendship began, Kershner and Feuerlicht formed a partnership for intellectual discussion, with two other men joining them as charter members—Jean S. Milner, pastor of Second Presbyterian Church, and Frank S. C. Wicks, pastor of All Souls Unitarian Church. Calling themselves the Wranglers, they met monthly at the Athenaeum in downtown Indianapolis for dinner and discussion of political, economic, cultural, and religious topics. In a letter inviting Judge John L. Niblack to join the group, Kershner stated that it had "no constitution, no by-laws, no officers, no initiation, no dues, no formal speeches and no obligations of any kind except to attend its meetings and to pay for your dinner." Although the club began prior to 1930, Kershner's file on the Wranglers included materials from the late 1940s until his resignation in 1951, and the lists of participants were undated. They included other clergy, such as the Episcopal bishop of Indianapolis, educators from Butler and DePauw Universities, Disciples executives from Missions Building, and business leaders from Indianapolis.[7]

These activities were part of Kershner's larger work which was to organize the newly established College of Religion. With the help of Hugh W. Ghormley, a former student who had come with him from Des Moines, Kershner cared for the undergraduate students who remained from the Morro program. The more pressing duties were to convert the vision of a "College of Applied Christianity" into the reality of the "College of Religion, Butler University." The major elements that Kershner had insisted on were in place—structural freedom to operate, dependable financial backing, and theological control—but now he had do the hard work of developing programs of study, selecting and appointing a faculty, recruiting students, and raising money.

The First Steps

Kershner published the first full prospectus of his envisioned College of Religion in a sixty-six-page bulletin dated December 1924. The frontispiece showed the architect's sketch of the College of Religion building proposed for the Fairview campus, where Hilton U. Brown intended, with William G. Irwin's help, to relocate the University and create "the greater Butler." The sketch matched the architect's rendering of the administration building that was to house the major departments of the University on the north side of the city. Both buildings were collegiate gothic, in stone, rendered by architect Robert Frost Daggett. With a strong document such as this,

Kershner could confidently communicate his vision to people in the several educational and ecclesiastical networks with which he worked. They would be his recruiters.

Kershner's bulletin published an "Historical Sketch," which also appeared in the University catalog, in which he explained that the College of Religion had been established as one of the constituent colleges of Butler University by action of the Butler board of directors in the spring of 1924. The College of Religion was to be "directly administered by a Dean and Faculty of its own, acting under the immediate supervision of the Church Committee of the Butler University Board of Directors." Kershner listed the members of this committee, and while he did not identify them, anyone who cared about such matters would know who they were. The chair of the committee was Z. T. Sweeney, whose loyalty to the classic position of the Disciples was unquestioned. He was supported by William G. Irwin, equally loyal and also a key player in the larger affairs of the University. The University's interests were assured by the presence of Hilton U. Brown and John W. Atherton, who as city manager of the University (and Hilton U. Brown's son in law) also served as secretary of the church committee. The pastors of the two largest Disciples congregations in Indianapolis were also members—Thomas W. Grafton of Third Christian Church (1,803 members) and Allan B. Philputt of Central Christian Church (2,150 members). Kershner himself was also listed on the committee. The College had its own special endowment fund, and money could be given directly to this fund if donors desired.

The most important announcement was Kershner's statement of purpose for the new school: "The College of Religion is open to students of all religious faiths on equal terms. Its purpose is primarily to train men and women for the Christian ministry, and for allied forms of Christian service."[8] By the word "faiths" Kershner probably meant denominations or churches, rather than religions other than Christianity, and its inclusion in his statement indicates that Kershner's vision was for a seminary that would serve all of the churches. This statement was consistent with the preface to the University catalog, which said that its purpose was "to teach and inculcate the Christian faith and Christian morality as taught in the sacred Scriptures, disregarding as uninspired and without authority all writings, formulas, creeds, and articles of faith subsequent thereto,"[9] words that firmly echoed the leading ideas of the Disciples movement while allowing a nonsectarian interpretation. The broad scope of Kershner's educational vision was made clear by the comprehensive course of study that the bulletin announced—5 departments with a total of 128 courses, 13 in Old Testament, 14 in New Testament, 6 in church history, and 14 in Christian doctrine. The fifth department, practical theology, listed nearly half of the total number of courses that Kershner anticipated—21 courses in homiletics and practical ministries, 26 courses in religious education, 28 courses in fine arts and religion, and 6 courses in secretarial training.

One of the greatest challenges would be to find professors to teach all of these courses. From his earliest hand-written memorandum, Kershner had been thinking of the people he hoped to call to his faculty; but now he had to decide which persons would be best suited to the program, and then he had to persuade them to come to Indianapolis to join him in this cause. "We are having some difficulty in getting our faculty together," he wrote his friend and confidant, Arthur Holmes, in November 1924, explaining that since April he had been trying to persuade President Hilley of North Carolina to come but had finally been turned down. Kershner believed that one reason was opposition from secretary H. O. Pritchard of the Disciples' board of education. He and other officials of the United Christian Missionary Society "seem to have it in for Mr. Irwin, and do not hesitate, when they have opportunity, to puncture his program."[10]

Kershner needed to find people who were sympathetic to his purposes and capable of achieving the high quality that he believed to be essential if he were to achieve his goals. He could count on Irwin to support him, but that meant he also had to be sure that the persons he chose would be acceptable to other supporters in Columbus. The task was made easier by the fact that only a few of the courses were strategically important to the theological battle he was waging. A much larger group of courses was largely outside of this circle of sensitivity and could be staffed by people of competence even though they were not conservative Disciples.

Kershner's first catalog arranged his anticipated faculty into four groups. The most important was "Faculty of the College of Religion," which included the president of the University, Kershner as dean of the College, three other full-time professors and one part-time professor. These men included his brother, Bruce L. Kershner, one-time missionary in the Philippines who would come from Lynchburg College to teach New Testament and church history; Hugh W. Ghormley, Kershner's former student, who would teach Old Testament; H. Parr Armstrong, another of Kershner's former students, who would teach practical theology; and Guy I. Hoover, promotional secretary of the Disciples' board of education, who would teach practical theology part-time. Augmenting these professors would be half a dozen Disciples pastors who would offer classes in practical theology and church history.

This core faculty would be surrounded by three other groups of people whom Kershner listed as part of the teaching staff: seven Butler professors from the fields of education, public speaking, Greek, journalism, and history; seven instructors from schools associated with Butler—the Metropolitan School of Music and the John Herron Art Institute; and other special lecturers who would come for short periods during the year. The special lecturers for the year were a distinguished group of people, including major figures in the religious scene of that time: A. T. Robertson, Kirby Page, Henry H. Halley, Rufus M. Jones, and Arthur Holmes.

This first catalog stated that the College of Religion would provide programs of study leading to three degrees and two special diplomas, which were offered "particularly for the training of young women for efficient service as full-time religious workers." The secretarial diploma could be earned within the four years of a normal college program, but the program for ministerial assistants required at least one year of study beyond the baccalaureate degree. The most important degrees were the undergraduate Bachelor of Sacred Literature (B.S.L.), which was awarded upon the completion of 120 semester hours of work—seventy hours in religious disciplines and fifty in general studies. The Bachelor of Divinity (B.D.) was the major graduate degree offered at the completion of ninety semester hours of work done according to a fairly even division between Old Testament, New Testament, church history, Christian doctrine, and practical theology. Twenty of these hours were to be in New Testament Greek or Hebrew; and the program allowed about twenty elective hours. Following a widespread practice in American universities of the time, the final year of the undergraduate program could consist of courses that also would count toward the graduate degree.

It can be assumed that Kershner intended that all or most of these courses would be offered, and in subsequent catalogs he indicated whether a course would be taught in first or second semester of the year. The catalog also gave further guidance as to how these courses could be chosen to fulfill the requirements of the various degrees. The course descriptions indicated that some of them would be available upon demand. "Practical Church Pageantry," which would be offered by John Herron Art Institute for a minimum of fifteen students, would cover "the practical artistic side of Church Pageantry and Bible Dramatization." The Metropolitan School of Music would offer a course in "Chorus and Orchestra Directing" if "there is sufficient demand," with special reference to "work with choirs and other organizations within the church." Herron also offered a course in "Church Poster Design," again if there were sufficient demand. As in other courses, there were prerequisites, in this case a year-long sequence in the history of art, a course in design, and another in lettering.

The catalog also acknowledged the presence of the College of Missions, which was offering the degrees of Master of Arts and Doctor of Philosophy. Courses taken at the College of Missions could be credited toward the degrees of the College of Religion upon the approval of the faculty of the College of Religion. In sharp contrast to the catalogs during Morro's time at Butler, however, Kershner's catalog showed no interest in linking the program with the one at the College of Missions. It was noteworthy that his preliminary listing of faculty for the College of Religion made no reference to the distinguished group of teachers, most of them Disciples, who were working so close by.

The New Seminary Begins

Following a year of very hard work, Dean Kershner was ready to launch the graduate program of the College of Religion. Despite the promised support of the Christian Foundation, he had to give some of his attention to raising some of the funds the College would need during its first year. During the summer before the opening of the new graduate program, he traveled across Indiana, preaching in churches and talking with their members, with varying degrees of success. Neither fundamentalism nor modernism, Kershner noted, bothered the Hoosier farmer "half as much as the thought of a pledge coming due on the first of January. He fears starvation even when surrounded by plenty, and the idea of paying more than fifteen or twenty cents a week to the church he conceives to be the rankest heresy."[11] Even so, by mid July Kershner had raised some twelve thousand dollars; and later in the fall Butler received a bequest for thirty thousand dollars for ministerial scholarships.

The opening convocation was held at Downey Avenue Christian Church in Irvington on Sunday afternoon, September 13, 1925, with Z. T. Sweeney delivering the sermon. In what was to be his "last formal address," Sweeney based his message on 1 Corinthians 2:2: "I determined to know nothing among you save Jesus Christ, and him crucified."[12] The records give little information about the process by which students were enlisted for this program, but they came. At the end of his first year, Kershner listed ten graduate and thirty-nine undergraduate students enrolled in the College of Religion. An additional eighteen students from the College of Liberal Arts and the College of Missions also took work in the College of Religion. He noted that more than thirty students in the College of Liberal Arts had expressed the intention "to devote their lives to the ministry or to some other allied form of Christian service."[13] His professors were busy in their work, for class records indicate that in the first semester of the graduate program Armstrong offered four courses, for fourteen hours of credit, with forty-seven students enrolled. Ghormley offered four courses, for eleven hours of credit, with fifteen students enrolled. Bruce Kershner offered six courses with thirty-five students; and Frederick D. Kershner offered five courses, for thirteen hours of credit, with twenty-eight students enrolled. This pattern of enrollment continued in the early years of the Seminary's life.

"Chapel exercises" were held Tuesday, Wednesday, Thursday, and Friday at eleven A.M. in the College of Missions chapel, with attendance upon these exercises required of all students in the College of Religion.[14] The weekly schedule offered classes over the entire week, some meeting Monday through Friday, and others with varied patterns throughout the week. Evening seminars met from seven until nine on Tuesday and Thursday. Occasionally special examinations took place on Saturday. Many students traveled to congregations in central Indiana to conduct worship, preach, and perform other pastoral duties. Apparently they went by interurban or train, and were away from campus over Saturday night only.

One of the high points of the year for Kershner and the Seminary was a series of Bible lectures by Arthur Holmes, which he later published under the title *The Mind of St. Paul*.[15] One of the first Disciples to earn a Ph.D. degree, Holmes had previously published books in the field of child psychology. In his lectures on Paul, Holmes conveyed the sense that he trusted the biblical account and accepted a traditional understanding of God and reality. His psychology and his biblical interpretation were woven together into a smoothly constructed development that showed erudition and traditional faith intermingled. Holmes may have been more liberal in his biblical understandings than many of the students at the College of Religion, but he wrote in a way that would reassure them, describing Paul as "a towering genius" who shares our "common humanity." Yet "the arc of his life reaches out into the firmament of God beyond the tracing of human pen. While his hard-driven body was on earth, his soul was partly in heaven."[16]

While consolidating curriculum, faculty, student body, and institutional relations, Kershner was attentive to the death throes of the College of Missions nearby, noting the rumors and reports that came to him and speculating upon the members of the staff he would be willing to add to his own. Word came in 1927 that the College of Missions would suspend its operations in Indianapolis. That fall the College of Religion began its third year in facilities leased from the College of Missions, for the first time enjoying ample room for recitation and offices. Joining Kershner's faculty from the College of Missions were distinguished Disciples missionary Everard R. Moon, and the young Christian convert from Japan, Toyozo W. Nakarai, who would become one of the stalwarts of the faculty of the School of Religion. Although Nakarai's Ph.D. dissertation from the University of Michigan was on the *Odes of Kokin-shu* that he had studied at the University of Kokugakuin ten years earlier, he taught Semitics at the Seminary until his retirement in 1965.

The next year Kershner added Dean E. Walker to his faculty. This young man quickly became the most important member of the faculty other than Kershner himself. For twenty years Walker's ideas and gruff presence shaped the experience of most students who came to the College of Religion. The son of a prominent and conservative Disciples leader, Walker had done his undergraduate work at a small college in northeast Indiana and a little later became a history teacher at Rushville High School in a county seat town near Indianapolis. He became a student at the College of Religion and was appointed to the faculty soon after completing his B.D. degree.

As soon as Kershner arrived in Indiana, the new dean took an active role in the work of the Disciples in the state. His columns began appearing in the *Indiana Worker*, which was published monthly, and the work of the College of Religion was frequently reported. One of his most important actions was to establish a "ministerial bureau" in cooperation with Disciples district superintendents and the "state missionary headquarters." Card index files were being developed for ministers who would be suitable for Indiana congregations, and officers of the churches were invited to write to Kershner's Butler office when they were seeking a new pastor.[17]

The next year, in the fall of 1928, the College of Religion joined the rest of the University in its move from Irvington to the Fairview campus on the north side of Indianapolis. It occupied quarters in Jordan Hall, where it remained for more than a decade until moving to its own building. Since 1890 this 250-acre site had been a suburban park at the end of the street railway line. In addition to its wooded beauty, the park included amusements and others attractions to increase its usage. During the early years of the twentieth century, the largely rural sections north of 38th Street, which then was called Maple Road, were being subdivided for residential development. Houses of near-mansion proportions were being built along Meridian Street; in adjoining neighborhoods less expensive middle-class housing was developing. Churches were moving into this area, although the financial distress of the 1930s created severe problems as these congregations began their building plans.[18]

The Seminary's relocation seemed to increase its momentum. Midway through the second year in Jordan Hall on the Fairview campus, and in the fifth year of the Seminary's life, Kershner's reports to the School of Religion Committee of the Butler board and to the directors of the Christian Foundation described the School's achievements and outlined its needs. In five years enrollment had increased from forty-eight—twelve of whom were at the graduate level—to 142, forty of whom were graduate students. Thirteen were "African" and three were "of Mongolian or Malay type." He reported that more Disciples ministerial students were going to Butler that year than to Yale, Hartford, or Chicago for their graduate work. A professor from a college that the previous year had sent fifteen graduates to Yale had visited Butler and would henceforth do all that he could to direct graduates to Indianapolis instead of New Haven. This move to the front rank meant that the Seminary needed to add another full-time professor, erect its own building, and because of "competition with schools like Hartford, Yale, Chicago, and Oberlin," erect a dormitory where ministerial students could "be housed together under proper cultural surroundings at a living expense they can afford." To the Christian Foundation he also spoke of the need for a chair "in the history, ideals and teaching of our Historic Movement," along with a library for research. This kind of work could not be done in any of "the great graduate schools of America"; only lack of funds was keeping the College of Religion from achieving this goal.[19] Kershner also indicated that his teaching load of sixteen hours was more than deans of comparable schools were expected to carry.

As the student body and faculty grew, their experience with theological education also grew, with the result that revisions of the curriculum became necessary. The catalog for the fifth session, 1930–1931, published a revised pattern for the courses of instruction and the requirements for the undergraduate B.S.L. degree and for the B.D. degree. Hours in religious subjects were reduced and requirements in liberal arts and sciences and elective hours were increased. Fifty-eight hours of specifically required courses were listed. Most courses carried new three-digit numbers that indicated the level of instruction for that course and whether it was elective or required. While the catalog did not state for which degrees these requirements and electives held, there were other indications as to the way these courses could be taken for several degrees. Some courses were followed by the note that they were "open to Juniors, Seniors and Graduates." At the end of some departmental listings the note appeared that all of the courses may be applied to the B.D. degree if taken not earlier than the senior year of college.

This issue of the Bulletin listed graduates for the first four years and the roster of students in the 1929–1930 year. Ten people had received the B.S.L degree, seven the M.A. degree, and ten the B.D. degree. Among these graduates, four were to become members of the College's faculty at some point in the future: Alfred T. DeGroot, William F. Bacon, Dean E. Walker, and Harold F. Hanlin. Forty-two persons were listed as graduate students and 117 as undergraduates. After seven successful years, Kershner had every reason to be pleased with what had developed in Indianapolis. He had established a viable program of ministerial education at Butler University. What he had not accomplished, however, was to create the one school that would draw most ministerial students from the Christian Churches and Churches of Christ around the country. During these same years, other Disciples schools were also creating programs of graduate ministerial education. At about the same time that Kershner was publishing his statistics, Drake University listed 110 students in its College of the Bible, eighteen of them working at the graduate level; the College of the Bible and Transylvania University in Lexington reported seven graduate ministerial students, twenty-nine undergraduate ministerial students, and thirty-two special students studying for the ministry. Brite College of the Bible at Texas Christian University reported a total of ninety-eight ministerial students, but without identifying the number of graduate students. The largest program of all was at Phillips University with a total of 128 students preparing for the ministry, twenty-eight of them at the graduate level. Kershner could find some considerable satisfaction in the fact that the largest enrollment at the graduate level was in his program. He was holding his own when compared to the Disciples' Divinity House at Chicago, which in the decade from 1920 through 1929 awarded 11 B.D. degrees. Yale, however, continued to dominate the reports, awarding 89 B.D. degrees to Disciples during those same years.[20]

The Struggle to Preserve the Vision

Just as Kershner and his College of Religion seemed to be settling into a mature pattern of operation, new stresses developed that threatened the existence of Butler University, challenged the independence of the College of Religion, and alienated Irwin and his family both from the University and the College. The move to the new campus on the north side of Indianapolis took place during years when most people had become unduly confident about the economic conditions of the United States and the world. Butler's expansion had included plans for the University to become a major athletic power with the result that the University had built the fieldhouse as its first building on the new campus and committed itself to a salary schedule for coaches and athletes that it could not afford. As a result, the North Central Association of Schools and Colleges had removed the University's accreditation.

As one of the most important trustees, who had also been involved in some of the plans for expansion including the new corporation for the athletic program, William G. Irwin went to work to help resolve the problem. He turned for advice to a prominent Disciples theological educator, Walter. S. Athearn, who had left Boston University and was living in Washington, D.C., "engaged in research work in the Library of Congress and the Bureau of Education in the Department of the Interior."[21] Athearn's advice, based on his understanding of accreditation standards, was that Butler had to extract itself from the financial situation created by its exuberant expenditures for athletics. Irwin's response was to deposit $1 million in a special fund that could be used to restore the fiscal structure of the University. Irwin was drawn toward Athearn, inviting him to visit the family's summer home in Canada, a privilege which Kershner had never enjoyed. Irwin apparently had concluded that Butler's president, Robert J. Aley, would not be able to bring Butler back to its full strength and began to think of Athearn as the University's rescuer. In the early summer of 1929 Athearn visited the campus; he had spent an evening with a group of University trustees and the next morning had spoken in chapel, "in characteristically good form." In addition to reporting this visit to Arthur Holmes, Kershner reported his understanding that there would soon be a change in the presidency. He was staying out of the process because "experience has taught me that it is wiser for a teacher not to meddle in the deliberations of his board of directors. Whoever wins, there are some scars left and they are apt to reappear later under more or less embarrassing circumstances. I have confined my part in the matter," Kershner concluded, "to giving very carefully worded information when specifically questioned by members of the board. Whoever comes here will not have a sinecure and I want to do my part toward making things as easy as I can for him."[22]

The conversations between Irwin and Athearn about the presidency of Butler were kept at a confidential level. Even after the decision had been made, but before a public announcement was issued, Athearn maintained a "no comment stance." Apparently everyone else did, too. Kershner was aware of the ongoing conversation, but more as an interested and privileged bystander than as one who was directly involved in the process. Athearn's later description of his appointment to the presidency stated that a committee of the Butler board had urged him to come to Butler as president but that he had refused to consider the proposal until the University was at least tentatively restored to accredited status and there was a vacancy in the office of president. President Aley was provided a satisfactory retirement pension, agreed to the arrangements made with him, and retired after a decade of service. Only then, says Athearn, did he come to Indianapolis to negotiate with the Board to become the president of the University. Athearn reported that his coming to Butler was opposed by three of the board members with political power—the president of the board (Hilton U. Brown), the financial secretary (John W. Atherton), and the chairman of the standing committees of the board (who may have been Emsley W. Johnson). The fourth powerful member of the board held his influence through financial support. Athearn stated that "in an emergency, one man can control the whole university."[23] Presumably this fourth person was William G. Irwin.

During the summer of 1931 the confidential negotiations were finally completed, and in August Athearn came to Indianapolis to take up his duties as president, hand-selected by William G. Irwin to lead the University back into solvency and respectability among universities. Respectability would be achieved through the restoration of its accreditation and the development of a modern system of academic administration. Solvency would come through efficient administration and, one might suppose, through expansion of the sources of income.

It would have been difficult to imagine a better person to bring to leadership at this time. During his ten-year stint at Boston, Athearn had developed a strong set of ideas about the issues of higher education, especially with respect to colleges and universities that had been founded by or on behalf of churches. He expounded these ideas in a 500-page book, in the press at the time of the negotiations, which discussed the decade "of experimentation in the collegiate and professional training of Christian workers." The book, entitled *An Adventure in Religious Education,* had started out as a two-part report to the administration of Boston University concerning the program he had developed there.[24] Clearly too long and unwieldy for its primary purpose, the manuscript was sent to a wider public by its publication as a trade book. Athearn was ready to distribute it widely as a way of stimulating discussion concerning the issues of higher education.

Athearn was especially interested in the challenge facing church-related colleges that were becoming urban universities. "It can be taken as a general rule that, whenever a religious denomination undertakes to operate a university which attempts to make unnecessary the building of a tax-supported university in a city, the ideals and standards of the institution are apt to be determined by its municipal patronage rather than by the ideals of its founders."[25] This was exactly the situation with Butler University, under the strong and forward-moving leadership of Hilton U. Brown and the board of directors. The "Greater Butler University" was their goal for the future and they were reaching out to a broad metropolitan patronage. In contrast, the religious legacy of the founders was embodied in William G. Irwin, the principal financial supporter of the University.

Athearn's solution to this problem was the "isolated college," by which he referred to part of a university that was able to take responsibility for all aspects of the education of students in its keeping. Athearn was critical of academic organizations in which students did part of their work in one division of the school and another part in a different division that also certified their graduation. He was especially interested in the isolated college as a way to ensure high quality in the training of future Christian workers. The isolated college would be part of the larger university, but with a significant degree of autonomy. Although Kershner and Irwin had not used this term, their College of Religion functioned as an isolated college, carrying responsibility both for undergraduate and graduate professional training. Thus it could be ensured that the undergraduate students would be adequately prepared for the later, and more important, work that they would take at the graduate level. Presumably Irwin and Athearn had discussed ideas like this and were ready to advance the cause at Butler. Athearn's strong loyalty to a conservative vision of the Disciples plea would have endeared him to Irwin and given Kershner confidence in Athearn's integrity and dependability. Because of his extended career in academic institutions, Athearn could be expected to know how to move at Butler with skill and efficiency. The cordiality and candor in the initial correspondence between Athearn and Kershner shows that the dean of the College of Religion was happy in the choice of a new president.

Athearn's first year provided challenges for his administration, although Kershner reported that his work was commendable as far as the College of Religion was concerned. None of the Seminary's faculty, however, could have anticipated the direction that Athearn's administration would take. His interest in the public responsibilities of universities and his commitment to modernization of university forms, and the Great Depression, led him away from the very ideas that would initially have commended him to people committed to the ecclesial traditions of Butler University. The challenges of recovering accreditation and revising the University's procedures were foremost on the list for Athearn as he began his presidency. In his 1933 report Athearn listed ten points chosen from a longer list of criticisms brought by inspectors from the standardizing boards, including the inadequacy of the library and the undue emphasis upon competitive, intercollegiate athletics; loose administration of academic procedures; and the subordination of academic standards to other concerns. He listed and briefly described fourteen reforms instituted in the two years of his administration, including the creation of a system of health education, improvements in major aspects of academic administration, the reorganization of the colleges of education and religion, strengthened offerings in liberal arts, and significant changes in faculty and staff.

In all of these developments, Athearn claimed, he was guided by two interests. The more pressing was his desire to reestablish accreditation on a firm foundation. The second was the one with which he began his report—the development of a modern urban university. The rapid shift of population from rural to urban areas had created a new challenge to educators and other public leaders if the masses [Athearn's word] were to be educated. His response was that urban universities had to be created and that in Indianapolis Butler University was becoming the center of a cluster of educational enterprises. The result was that Indianapolis now had a "great urban university" similar to those that had developed "in New York, Chicago, Detroit, Syracuse, Denver, Los Angeles, Cleveland, Akron, Toledo, Cincinnati, Louisville, Dayton—to name a few of the American cities with successful urban universities." On the Fairview campus, Indianapolis was building "a city university with the high-grade cultural college of Irvington history at its very heart."

Although Athearn's goal of building an urban university coincided with the vision of Hilton U. Brown and some other trustees of the university, their respective methods of achieving that goal differed at significant points, the most important being the place of intercollegiate athletics. For Brown, Atherton, Irwin, and others, building the football stadium and the finest basketball pavilion in Indiana and recruiting strong coaches and athletes were at the heart of the venture. Athearn, however, believed that "the days of spectacular, competitive, inter-collegiate athletics have passed and will never return."[26] Perhaps the example of the University of Chicago was in his mind. He therefore set about to create a program in intramural activities which he believed to be the proper function of a university. In other ways, too, Athearn's methods of developing an urban university contrasted with those of trustees who shared the same hope for Butler.

When Athearn came to Butler for the opening of the fall semester in 1931, the business and economic depression was well under way. Thus, the new president faced the responsibility of helping the University respond effectively to cutbacks in income, especially those generated by student tuition. He addressed these issues straightforwardly, combining several methods, including: 1) reduction of the size of the faculty and systematic cuts in salaries and benefits of those who remained; 2) compression of some aspects of program, such as summer session; 3) cutting back of curricular offerings in the several departments and divisions of the University. The tone of Athearn's presidential communications about these matters was candid, careful, and commendatory. The faculty was addressed with cordiality and in the spirit of colleagueship. Despite the unpleasant nature of the communications, Athearn seemed to have understood the feelings and anxieties of the people involved. In his 1933 report, Athearn discussed the University's fiscal problems at considerable length and stated that he had reduced University expenses by more than $215,000. He implied that the most serious financial threat was not the business depression, but rather the complex financing of the athletic program which from the beginning had been unwise and inappropriate for Butler. Athearn asserted that most aspects of the University's financial operation were under the control of the city office and the University's financial secretary rather than under the control of the president of the University. "The economic conditions of the past few years, and the failure of the Board of Directors to consider seriously the advice of educators are at the bottom of Butler's athletic deficit. Business men, who are alone responsible for this unwise venture, should not permit educators to be blamed for their own conduct."

Whatever may have been the origin of Butler's financial distress,

Athearn's reforms were not enough to correct the problems. Irwin and his sister Linnie Irwin Sweeney made up the difference, in some years contributing as much as a fourth of the University's budget. Butler's board was increasingly dismayed by the financial crisis and angered by Athearn's manner. Even Irwin became convinced that Athearn's administration had failed. Furthermore, Irwin's ability to provide what seemed to be unlimited financial backing was being affected by the costs of his partnership with Clessie Cummins to develop a marketable diesel engine. As a way of easing Kershner's impatience with Irwin over fiscal matters, Edwin R. Errett, a stalwart friend of both men and an active member of the Butler board, suggested to Kershner that the high cost of developing the new diesel engine may have been the reason for Irwin's hesitancy—that inability rather than unwillingness may have been the cause of his financial caution.[27]

Even with these constraints, significant contributions from the Christian Foundation continued to be a major part of the University's financial mix, providing the major funding for the College of Religion. Irwin and Linnie Irwin Sweeney were the primary contributors, but so were other Disciples interested in preserving the traditional plea of their church. Kershner could appeal to Irwin for special financial needs or to support specific parts of the ongoing program of the College of Religion, and if Irwin agreed to fund a program that the University had not included in its budget, his offer of funds would reestablish the program. During these years the University and the Christian Foundation were intertwined through the device of common membership, especially at the high level of their respective boards, with Hilton U. Brown serving as president of the Christian Foundation and William G. Irwin president of the Butler Foundation. Although Irwin and other family members exercised strong influence upon the Christian Foundation, and could use it as an instrument for distributing funds to causes they supported, the foundation's board of directors made final decisions.

Reshaping the College of Religion

By the second year of Athearn's administration, the loyalty of the College of Religion faculty was waning. A major reason was that Athearn and the executive committee of the University board recommended changes in the operations of the College of Religion. Although Athearn justified these recommendations as ways of meeting the University's fiscal challenges and affirmed that other portions of the University were also being cut back, the

College of Religion faculty became convinced that they were being dealt with more harshly than were other schools or colleges of the University.[28] They began to wonder if Athearn intended to do away with the College of Religion. By the end of the second year, it was all that Kershner could do to maintain his support for the president and his policies. He wrote to Athearn explaining that his continued support was prompted primarily because it was necessary for the officers of an administration to maintain a united posture in their relations with the public.[29]

In the spring of 1933 the College of Religion faculty became alarmed when Dean Kershner received an unexpected communication from President Athearn, announcing the reorganization of the College of Religion. The actions that he reported were taken by the executive and finance committees of the University board on March 21, 1933. Athearn's announcement of these actions was dated that same day, and his communications to professors who were being discontinued were received on March 22. The first knowledge that Dean Kershner had of any of these actions was his receipt of the formal notice from President Athearn. Five actions were reported. The first was that at the close of the academic year the undergraduate program would be "discontinued from the College of Religion," which would thereafter be a graduate institution requiring for admission a four-year undergraduate program from an accredited college. The second was that the department of missions in the College would be discontinued until the depression was over. The third, fourth, and fifth elements related to the reduction of faculty. Kershner also was to discover that his private secretary had been dismissed. He did not want his rapidly failing vision to be known, and his secretary enabled him to do his work; without her services his capacity to accomplish the responsibilities of his office would be significantly curtailed.

Athearn listed the three full-time professors who would continue in the College—Frederick D. Kershner, Bruce L. Kershner, and Toyozo W. Nakarai—and named three other members of the University faculty who would be available to teach part-time in the College.[30] Although a part-time professor of homiletics would also be secured and stipends for two of the lecturers could be continued, the stipend for Rabbi Feuerlicht would end. Athearn's justification for these changes was that academic standards in the College of Religion were low and the broad needs of the student body were given too little attention because of the ministerial orientation of the program. He noted that athletes enrolled in these courses because they didn't have to pay tuition and because of the reputation that these courses were easy.[31] Later in the year Butler published a description of the new undergraduate program in religion. While acknowledging that one of its purposes was pre-professional background for further work in graduate schools of religion, the main emphasis would be upon broader social and personal purposes for religious studies.[32]

Kershner and the College of Religion professors saw this reorganization of the undergraduate program as a serious threat to their graduate program. No longer would they determine the purpose and curricular requirements for the baccalaureate degree. Instead, this degree which they used to give a strong foundation for studying at the Seminary's level would be controlled by the dean of the University and the faculty of liberal arts and sciences. Kershner believed that the result would be that many people would be lost to the ministry, and many who continued with that professional goal would come to their seminary studies insufficiently prepared for the program that he had developed. Kershner and his supporters were convinced that this effort to fold the undergraduate program into liberal arts and sciences constituted a serious threat to the very life and future of their College of Religion.

A second proposal from President Athearn and his executive committee, dealing with tuition, was also understood as an attack on the undergraduate program. Athearn recommended that students in the undergraduate program be charged the regular University tuition of $200 per year. The College of Religion faculty strenuously objected. The fiscal arrangements in force at the time apparently exempted undergraduate College of Religion students from the normal tuition and instead they paid fees according to the charges for particular courses taken. A detailed analysis of the financial results was provided in the response of the faculty of the College of Religion, demonstrating that the existing pattern of charges for College of Religion students brought in more revenue than the one proposed by the president and executive committee and at the same time was perceived by students to be easier to meet than the plan set forth by the president. The religion faculty proposed a compromise: that undergraduate students in the College of Religion be assessed tuition that was the average of what was paid in other Disciples undergraduate Bible colleges and departments of religion. The College of Religion faculty suggested that $50 a semester ($100 a year) would be reasonable. Their alternative was agreed upon and the threat momentarily overcome.

Kershner wrote strong letters to Linnie Irwin Sweeney, chair of the University's church committee, Hugh Th. Miller, and William G. Irwin.

His letter to Irwin was written with a caution that implied that these two men had drifted apart:

> Because we have been so intimately associated in this project in the past and because of its tremendous implications for our whole brotherhood life, I have felt that I must write frankly to you, notwithstanding my reluctance to trouble you with these matters. If you feel that you care to go into the subject discussed in this letter more in detail, I shall be glad to see you personally at any time. I leave this, however, entirely with you.[33]

Irwin's response two days later could bring only cold comfort to his onetime close associate.

> I have been giving thought to the same questions you have. I have felt for some time that there were people on the faculty of the School of Religion who were not of the value to us that others might be and for that reason, I have approved of the actions that have been taken up to this time. I shall be very glad to talk over with you the questions that you bring up but I would prefer not to have this talk until after I have some further information.[34]

Closely related to this growing distance between Kershner and Irwin was the precariousness of support from the Christian Foundation. On February 11, 1933, some six weeks before the devastating notice from President Athearn, Kershner had written the president asking for his support with the trustees of the Christian Foundation, scheduled to meet during the second week of April. Kershner knew that there would be "strenuous efforts" from other institutions to secure money from the foundation. Among them would be "non-conformist schools like Cincinnati and Grayson [Kentucky]." Because five of the nine foundation trustees were also Butler trustees, they "ought to be able to sit tight." Judge Clark, however, was infirm and the opposition was aggressive. Edwin R. Errett also taught at Cincinnati and tended to vote with that school, so here Athearn's special influence upon Errett could be very helpful. At the forthcoming meeting, Benjamin Phillips, Judge Clark, and William G. Irwin were likely to be absent. Of the six remaining trustees, Errett and Reeves "are generally very aggressive for Cincinnati appropriations. Neither of them is especially unfriendly to Butler, but in a choice between the two the preference is pretty sure to go to Cincinnati."[35]

However he might have responded to Kershner would have made little difference because Athearn was soon to be deposed from his presidency. The final crisis, as Athearn explained it, began in June 1933 when he discovered what he described as evidence of "an organized system of petty graft in which a number of persons were conspiring to defraud the University." His efforts to deal with this discovery led to conflict with the city office and John W. Atherton. Athearn recommended that a special committee chaired by Hugh Th. Miller be established to investigate, but the committee was not authorized. Despite the conflict with a small group of powerful board members, Athearn moved forward vigorously with a program to "sell Butler" to its own board. Athearn reported an enthusiastic beginning of the 1933 school year, with strong support from the city and from accrediting agencies. His campaign to sell Butler to its board was scheduled to begin in early November, but on the Saturday before it was to be launched, three trustees—Hilton U. Brown, Hugh Th. Miller, and Emsley W. Johnson—called on President Athearn to inform him that the board had removed him from office. He was not to reenter his office at the University. The committee refused to consider any extension of time or to give reasons for the action of the trustees. The fact that Miller was one of the committee of three indicated that Athearn had alienated himself even from the members of the board who had been his supporters.

Athearn did not leave quietly. He proposed methods for review and arbitration and, failing in this effort, he filed a suit of $50,000 against the University. He published his own report on his administration and the dismissal. Later, as Kershner told Holmes, Athearn had offered to reduce the suit to $30,000 if the board of directors would sign a statement indicating that "he is the greatest of living educators, that his administration was a success in every particular, and that he is mentally and physically in the very best possible condition."[36]

The College of Religion Continues to Develop

Despite these trials, Kershner and his faculty continued to develop their program to prepare ministers for the church. They worked over the structure of the B.D. program of studies, softening a little the requirements in Greek and Hebrew. They shifted the schedule of chapel services during the week and made attendance mandatory, defending their actions with this explanation: "Not only do the Chapel exercises furnish inspiration and intellectual culture, but their chief design is to assist in providing that atmosphere of personal devotion without which no institution for the training of ministers can accomplish successful work."[37]

Following the dismissal of Athearn, the College of Religion was able to rebuild its faculty. The 1934 catalog listed thirteen people, four of whom were full-time teachers at the graduate level. Temporarily missing from the list was Dean E. Walker, then on leave in Scotland to work on his doctorate. Despite the formal separation of the two levels of instruction, the undergraduate program continued to function in close relationship with the graduate program; the undergraduate professors of religion participated fully in the activities of the faculty of the graduate College of Religion. One of these persons—Elmer G. Homrighausen—would soon move to Princeton Theological Seminary, where he had a distinguished career in the field of Christian education, and the other—Ross J. Griffeth—served for several years as secretary of the College of Religion faculty, giving up that post when he left Butler to become president of Northwest Christian College in Eugene, Oregon.[38] In 1935, Arthur Holmes was appointed to the faculty in a part-time position as professor of psychology and philosophy of religion. His position at the University of Pennsylvania had been terminated, and responding to Kershner's urging, Holmes's coming to the Seminary had been approved. Despite this rebuilding of the faculty, the number of students at the College of Religion declined during these years of economic distress. In 1933, forty-one were registered at the graduate level of the College of Religion. In the previous commencement seven people had received the B.S.L. and one person the B.D. degree. Three persons with religion majors received the M.A. degree.

The success of the College of Religion during these early years was undergirded by the rise among Disciples of the expectation that their pastors would do a seminary degree in addition to the traditional baccalaureate degree. One step in this development was a conference of Bible teachers in the colleges and universities that were members of the Disciples' board of education. Held in Indianapolis in the winter of 1928, the conference also included prominent pastors and institutional administrators. It was called to discuss the content of Bible courses, the relation of these courses to other departments of the college, and the question of providing for graduate training of ministers.[39] One conclusion of the conference was that its members were united in discouraging the idea that an A.B. degree was sufficient preparation for ministers. They agreed that ministers should receive "graduate training" of from two to five years.

Not everyone agreed with these ideas. During this same period of time a new movement gathered strength—the creation of undergraduate Bible colleges with the primary purpose of preparing ministers for congregations. These schools made little effort to follow the patterns of traditional colleges and universities such as Bethany and Butler. Instead, they set aside most of the liberal arts and sciences in favor of concentrated study of the Bible, Christian doctrine, and the skills of ministry. The most challenging to Kershner and the College of Religion at Butler was the Cincinnati Bible Seminary, which was founded in 1924. At the center of this school's mission was the defense of traditional Disciples ideas. Its geographical and theological proximity to the Standard Publishing Company gave it considerable influence. Some of the Columbus people, including Marshall T. Reeves and T. K. Smith, pastor of the Christian Church, were favorable toward Cincinnati, as was Edwin R. Errett, who was a part-time instructor. Schools like Cincinnati Bible Seminary challenged Butler's College of Religion by proposing a different model of ministerial education and by advocating a more conservative ecclesiological position than Kershner's.

The other response of academic institutions to the recommendations from the conference of Bible teachers was to strengthen their own graduate programs of ministerial education. The College of the Bible in Lexington, Brite Divinity School at Texas Christian University, the Graduate Seminary at Phillips University, and the Divinity School at Drake University were improving their offerings and increasing their enrollments. In addition, Disciples continued to do B.D. degrees at Chicago and Yale. Between 1920 and 1929, eleven Disciples received that degree from Chicago and eighty-nine from Yale.[40] Further dilution of theological education among Disciples was the creation of a Disciples house in conjunction with Vanderbilt University's divinity school. This meant that Kershner's dream of creating one central seminary for the Disciples could not succeed. The challenge was to maintain its quality and to accentuate its distinctive characteristics so that students, with many places to choose between, would come to the College of Religion at Butler University.

4
Catholicity and Conservatism

The Bible, Unity, and Mission at the School of Religion, 1935–1944

By the time that the Athearn debacle had ended, Dean Frederick D. Kershner found the challenges of his work to be even more difficult than before. The conditions in the world around him and the changing balance of power in the church and the University meant that he could never rest easily in his labors to sustain the Seminary. The necessity of constant vigilance was confirmed in mid July of 1934 when Kershner discovered that the Columbus family had turned violently against his work. Believing that someone had carried misleading reports to Columbus, he suggested to William G. Irwin that a committee of three prominent and absolutely trustworthy pastors—P. H. Welshimer, W. R. Walker, and T. K. Smith—investigate the College of Religion and report to Irwin if it found anything out of place. A few days later Kershner noted that people of wealth were nervous, fearing that huge debts would be piled up, which they ultimately would have to pay. Believing that the threats against the College of Religion had subsided, he concluded that "the best thing to do is keep one's head, go on with one's work as far as possible and trust for better things at the earliest possible date. That is what I am trying to do."[1]

In Columbus, the Irwin-Sweeney-Miller family had much to discuss around the dinner table and in the library of the Irwin family home. As with all businesspeople, they were facing the ongoing depression. Their financial situation, however, was strained in a unique way because for nearly two decades the family had been bankrolling Clessie Cummins's development of the automotive diesel engine that would become the source of increased wealth for the family. The engine was ready to be manufactured on a large scale, which meant that the project had to move out of Cummins's machine shop into a modern manufacturing plant. Because manufacturing was a capital-intensive enterprise, banker William G. Irwin would have to take the lead in finding funds in addition to the family's resources to make this project go forward. The new company would need managers, and in 1934 the family selected Hugh and Nettie Miller's twenty-five-year old son, J. Irwin Miller, to take on that responsibility.[2]

The tensions between conservative and liberal wings of the Christian Churches were becoming much stronger, and the difficulty of keeping Disciples together was increasing. Theological debates over biblical interpretation continued to divide pastors and congregations. Battles over baptism and church membership were unresolved. These theological and ecclesial debates erupted into organizational division as a second convention was created as a rival to the International Convention of the Disciples of Christ, which had been created in 1917, following several years of trial and error concerning the form of the annual meeting of Disciples in the United States and Canada. The debate, in part, had been whether the convention should be a mass meeting open to all who wanted to attend or a conference of the delegated representatives of congregations and agencies. The idea that resolved the problem was proposed by Frederick D. Kershner, at that time editor of the *Christian-Evangelist,* and introduced to the convention by Z. T. Sweeney. Their idea was that a bicameral convention be established, with the main body continuing the mass meeting and a much smaller committee on recommendations consisting of delegated members. Despite the continued opposition of conservative Disciples, expressed primarily through the editorial pages of the *Christian Standard,* this idea was adopted at the Kansas City convention of 1917.

The debates over open membership and missions continued, however, with conservative Disciples ever more determined to find ways of asserting their convictions. The result was the creation in 1926 of the North American Christian Convention with the purpose of representing the principles that conservative Disciples believed should be determinative of life in their church. Sweeney died in the spring of 1926, prior to the creation of the rival convention, but already this possibility was being talked about. Fearing what might happen, Sweeney counseled his family shortly before his death that they never leave the International Convention, for "if you do, you will find yourselves sitting on the banks while the rest of the world goes by."[3]

Because the College of Religion had been created in the hope of transcending that tension, the increased intensity of the struggle was especially painful. For Kershner and his Columbus supporters, these tensions came into focus as people debated the merits of a graduate seminary in a university setting as contrasted with an undergraduate, unaccredited Bible college. Which was the better way to go—Butler University with its College of Religion or Cincinnati Bible Seminary? While for Kershner the answer to this question was self-evident, some of the conversationalists in Columbus were not quite so sure. In the Irwin home, full university level education was the right way to go, but in the Christian Church across the street, and on the board of the Christian Foundation, both Cincinnati and Indianapolis had their supporters.

Negotiating a New Future

In the context of this controversy among the churches of the Disciples movement, Kershner encountered a growing level of difficulty in his administrative work at the College of Religion. The economic distress of the business depression made it difficult to keep the college funded, and he pestered Irwin for contributions to pay for summer session or to provide stipends for lecturers—including Ludwig von Gerdtell, Ross J. Griffeth, and Emory C. Cameron, who were to become important members of the faculty.[4] Irwin's response was increasingly guarded and he indicated that he wanted to discuss the entire situation in regard to the School of Religion.

Kershner's troubles became far more serious on April 11, 1935. At a meeting of the University's graduate council, Kershner told Irwin, "a resolution was presented demanding that all the courses leading to the degree of Bachelor of Divinity, and in fact the entire control of the degree should be taken from the faculty of the College of Religion and placed in the hands of the general faculty, which of course means in the hands of the faculty of the College of Liberal Arts, as this group is overwhelmingly in the majority on the university faculty." Kershner reported that he objected strenuously, asserting that this control had been given to the College of Religion by Butler's board of directors and could only be taken away by the Board. He believed that if this resolution should be accomplished, the control of his program would be given to people most of whom were not affiliated with the church and had no knowledge of the church's work. "I think," he concluded, "that this would be practically destructive, so far as the College of Religion is concerned."

Kershner concluded this important letter with the recommendation that if the College of Liberal Arts was unwilling for the College of Religion to carry on its work, then the College of Religion should adopt the plan, modeled on the English conception of a university, that had been adopted at Texas Christian University. This would involve "a separate charter, endowment and board of control of the College of Religion."⁵ Irwin's response the next day should have greatly encouraged his beleaguered dean:

> I am surprised by the contents of your letter of the 12th inst. It has been my understanding all along that we were running the School of Religion as a separate institution, however allied with the University. I had heard that the North Central Association is demanding that it be regarded as a department and not a separate school. I can see no reason for such action on the part either of the North Central or of the graduate council. I think we should discuss this quite thoroughly. Certainly I can see no reason for the Christian Foundation making any further contribution to the school if it is to be under the control of people who are not in the least interested in what is trying to be done there.⁶

Irwin's letter ended with his statement that he wanted to meet with Kershner when he was in Indianapolis a few days later. Kershner's response repeated his belief that the control of the B.D. degree could be taken from him only with the consent of the board of directors. He was alarmed, however, by part of Irwin's letter and responded with some agitation:

> For the Christian Foundation to withdraw its support at this time, would play into the hands of the people who are opposing us. It would inevitably cripple our work and would largely destroy the value of the investment already made in the school. Moreover, it would encourage the surrender of the most strategic location for ministerial training in our brotherhood, to the very people who ought not to control it. I think this would be a tragedy for our entire movement. There is, however, no need for pessimism. If the Board of Directors will stand by us, we can win this battle and defeat completely the forces which are opposing us.⁷

The confusion and conflict within the University were severe enough that people began to talk of revising the University's bylaws. University president James W. Putnam and Kershner discussed these matters several times, with Putnam indicating, so Kershner told Irwin, that "he would be glad to change the by-laws in the light of my criticism." The resolution for the University to take control of the College of Religion, which Kershner had concluded "was a providential occurrence for us," had been introduced by the University's Dean Gino A. Ratti, and Putnam now realized that it had been a mistake to have it introduced.[8] By this time Irwin was interested in an even greater separation between the College of Religion and the University, and he regretted that he would have to be away most of the time until the bylaws were to be approved. Irwin told Kershner: "I think that there is every reason for a separation of the two schools and that your suggestion of last week to have a separate board and a separate institution is proper. I shall oppose the adoption of the present By-Laws unless a separate school is established for your work."[9]

At this point, Edwin R. Errett of Cincinnati took the lead in negotiations between the College of Religion and the University. As editor of the *Christian Standard,* Errett was a leader of opinion among conservative Disciples. He had been a longtime friend of the Columbus family, who found his editorials better than the rest of the *Standard,*[10] and a member of the Butler board of directors. Yet his office location in Cincinnati and his aggressively conservative theology made him a logical choice to be lecturer at the conservative Cincinnati Bible Seminary just as William Shullenberger's Indianapolis location (as pastor of Central Christian Church) and mainstream theology made him a logical candidate to be lecturer at the College of Religion.

Kershner, Errett, and Irwin began to talk with one another about the full separation of the two schools. Citing the example of Brite College and Texas Christian University, which he had set up more than two decades earlier, Kershner outlined the provisions he hoped that the Butler board of directors would approve: (1) a separate charter for the College of Religion; (2) a separate board of directors, perhaps following the Brite example of nine directors, six of whom were also on the university board; (3) separate endowment and financial management; and (4) separate building or buildings on land ceded by the Butler University board of directors to the directors of the College of Religion. Kershner concluded this part of his argument: "With these provisions, I believe that our independence and religious and financial integrity will be secure. This will remove us from the field of the North Central Association [of Schools and Colleges] and at the same time enable us to exercise a very profound influence upon Butler University."

Kershner reaffirmed the importance of the College having a building of its own. He believed that there was enough money on hand to provide space for administrative and instructional purposes, and that chapel and dormitories would have to wait. "Of course, we could carry out the legal steps indicated above without constructing the new building, but I think that it will become increasingly difficult to carry on here without a separate plant, after the legal separation has taken place."[11] A few days later he wrote to Irwin that the situation was moving rapidly toward separation. He reported, too, that a North Central examiner had said that it would not require the College to become a department of the College of Liberal Arts, although it favored that development. Kershner's conclusion: "Of course, what these people have had in mind all along is the destruction of Butler University and the substitution of Butler College (Liberal Arts) in its place."[12]

After this flurry of letters, with their indication of rising hopes for separation, nothing seemed to happen. In early August (1935), Kershner wrote to Irwin, expressing the hope that the old church committee of the Butler board, or a new committee to deal with the College of Religion, could function for the next year. If the College couldn't get its own building, then the situation in its current quarters needed improvement. In passing, Kershner noted that Professor Paul Tillich was being made available by Union Theological Seminary to lecture for $50 and spoke in favor of the invitation. Irwin's response, however, was that he would not be pleased with any one from Union because it had become so radical. "I would rather have some one of our own people, such as Welshimer, lecture to our boys than any one in such an institution as Union."[13]

Although quiet for a time, the interest in separation of the College of Religion was still present, and in the summer of 1936 became active once more, with Edwin R. Errett again the active negotiator. His conversations were with Hilton U. Brown, initially to see if the Butler board would be inclined to make this provision. Errett stated that full separation might not be necessary at this time. He suggested that Kershner might contact some board members in support of the proposal that the College have a separate board to receive the proportionate share of the endowment income already enjoyed by the College, a section of the campus deeded to the College for a building, and the funds already on hand for the College of Religion building.[14] Kershner's response was that he had talked with President Putnam and board member John A. Titsworth. They both were favorable to these negotiations. Then Kershner stated the core of the matter:

> I believe that the board will go to almost any length in order to meet proposals from the Irwin family which are really specific in the way of a definite gift. This was Mr. Titsworth's idea, and I believe he is fairly representative of the majority sentiment. Stating

the matter in the baldest way, the board is willing to strain a good many points if Mr. Irwin is willing to put up real money. Otherwise, I do not think very much can be done.[15]

The conversations made progress, for by early August Errett wrote to Kershner reporting that he had been appointed chair of a committee to develop the proposal. He wanted Kershner's ideas about the constitution. Errett then summarized his own ideas. The constitution should include a strong declaration of principles for which the school stood, and should indicate that the trustees would be sincerely devoted to these principles. He felt that the Butler board would want to name the first trustees of the new corporation but he would insist that they "be members of the church of Christ and sincere adherents to the principles for which the school stands." Errett asked whether there should be departments in the College and encouraged the idea that the charter include a provision for publishing books and magazines, thus preparing the way to develop a quarterly. He also asked about the name. Should it be called Butler College of Religion? He thought better of Butler School of Christianity or College of Christianity. The committee consisted of himself, Shullenberger, and Titsworth. Emsley Johnson and Crate Bowen were "attorney members in an advisory capacity."[16]

Kershner's response was that he had talked with Atherton who, it seemed to Kershner, would not object; he felt that others who might have opposed were moving toward the idea. He also believed that legal problems could be overcome, and that the constitution should be broad and simple. The declaration of principles in the charter should be strong but brief, with the details of the agreement in the bylaws. He cited the charter and bylaws of the Christian Foundation as an example and sent Errett copies. He wanted a self-perpetuating board from the very beginning. He acknowledged that there could be legal problems concerning ownership of a building and the naming of professors supported by the endowment that would stay at Butler but be used for the College. Some years earlier, he and Z. T. Sweeney had gone over names for the school with great care, including the one that Errett favored, and had selected the one they believed to be the best. Although the title they had chosen was not clearly stated in the letter, Kershner identified himself as Dean, College of Religion, Butler University.[17]

The legal issues continued to trouble the committee. Crate Bowen, one of the attorney advisors, suggested that they go to the Indiana legislature with a request that Butler's charter be amended so that it could set up an administrative board for the College of Religion, with "absolute powers both of self perpetuation and of control of the personnel and teaching policies, while the board of the university would be left to carry out the trusteeship of funds which the law lays upon them as an obligation."[18]

A few days later Mrs. Miller [Nettie Sweeney Miller] stopped by to tell Kershner that "two representatives of Phillips University had been at the house during the past week and that the family were very favorably inclined toward Phillips, unless the Board at Butler would meet their requirements." Kershner had responded that to abandon Butler would mean the loss of all that had been invested to this point, and that for our people to lose here would be "a failure of colossal magnitude for the future history of our work."[19] Errett's response must have been disheartening. Yes, they would have to act quickly, but if the Butler board did not yield soon, then he was in sympathy with the purpose of the Irwins to turn their resources "to other media for accomplishing what they have in mind." And, he was not convinced that Phillips University was so lacking in strategic value as to prevent building a worthwhile graduate school there. He still was hopeful that Crate Bowen's plan for the College of Religion could be accomplished.[20] A month later, Errett reported that a meeting of the committee on separation had been postponed. The current plan proposed by Bowen was that the amended charter would not grant the School of Religion power to collect or hold money on its own. This plan, he stated, was unacceptable to himself and the Irwin family.

A New Contract with the University

On June 8, 1937, Errett wrote Kershner that conversations had continued, and John W. Atherton seemed to think that developments were acceptable to the Christian Foundation. Errett took this to mean that the plan had developed as the outcome of conferences between Irwin, Smith, and Miller.[21] Errett had wanted to put the college relation into the center of things at the University, but would not oppose the revised document.[22]

Kershner's files have preserved copies of two versions of proposed bylaws between the Christian Foundation and Butler University, one version dated in 1937 and the second dated June 12, 1940, and signature lines for representatives of Butler's board of directors, the board of the Butler Foundation, and the Christian Foundation. Much of the language in these two generations of the contract was identical; the general character of the two documents was the same. Both were premised on the long-standing commitment of Butler University to maintain a College of Religion and on the need to expand the program of that College. Both documents acknowledged an existing fund of money intended to erect a building for the College and indicated that additional resources would be needed both to construct the building and to maintain the program of the College. Both documents indicated that the University was to hold title to the building but that the Christian Foundation was to provide the funds and to exercise full control over the continuing program of the College of Religion. Both documents named the architectural firm that was to be in charge of developing plans for the building. Both provided procedures for discontinuing the relationship between the University and the College.

Despite these major similarities, the second version of the contract included significant changes. Whereas the earlier draft stated a maximum amount of money that the Christian Foundation would contribute to Butler year by year, the later contract promised the monies to complete the building and also promised full support of the College of Religion and a prorated contribution to the University's administrative and general expenses. Not only did the later contract name the architectural firm, but it also specified the style of the new building—the "Early American style, which . . . has been used to some extent in the Divinity School of Yale University." The completed contract was to be in force for ten years, with annual renewals possible thereafter.

The most significant change was in the theological language of the drafts. The 1937 version included a lengthy theological and ecclesiological section that followed the general lines of the articles of incorporation of the Christian Foundation. The agreement would remain in force "so long as the teaching in said College of Religion is in accord with the teaching and purposes of the Founders of Butler University (then Northwestern [sic] Christian University) and of Alexander Campbell, Barton W. Stone, John Smith, Isaac Errett, and other leaders of the movement in the United States in the first half of the 19th Century to restore the faith and ordinances of the Church of Christ of apostolic days as the only logical and practical basis for the union of all Christians"[23] No such language appeared in the contract adopted in 1940. Instead, the contract clarified the full control of the College by a select committee of University trustees. Three of the five members of this committee were to be nominated by the Christian Foundation, whom the University "will cause to be elected to its Board of Directors." The other two were to be selected by the University itself, but even they were to be approved by the Christian Foundation.[24] There was little evidence to indicate that the College of Religion Committee acted in the early years. Instead, the real control over the College of Religion was exercised by the Christian Foundation, and in particular, by William G. Irwin.

This contract was an agreement between three legal entities, but only two persons were listed as principals and two others as witnesses. Hilton U. Brown was to sign as president of Butler University's board of directors and William G. Irwin as president of the board of directors of Butler Foundation. John W. Atherton, Brown's son-in-law, was to attest to these signatures in his capacities as secretary-treasurer of Butler's board and as secretary of the board of Butler Foundation. Brown also was to sign as president of the board of trustees of the Christian Foundation, with Frederick D. Kershner attesting in his capacity as secretary to the Christian Foundation. Brown, Irwin, Atherton, and Kershner had been central players in this drama for more than two decades; they continued to dominate the action.

The next year (1941) reports circulated that supporters of the School of Religion were requiring that the school approve a creed. In his columns in the *Christian-Evangelist* Kershner defended his school against the charge, but the editor of the *Evangelist* and C. C. Morrison of the *Christian Century* were not persuaded and spoke out strongly against the situation. The debate even reached the pages of *Newsweek*.[25] In one important regard the criticisms were incorrect. They were saying that wealthy, conservative Disciples had looked around to find a school that expressed their theological interests and then gave their money to support it. Instead, an entrepreneurial young educator, with the backing of these wealthy Disciples, had created the school, funded it, and managed its academic affairs. The new contract, even with its creedal language, changed none of that. With the contract these people intended to strengthen the school and enlarge its program, all within the framework already established. As trustees of Butler University, with specific responsibilities for the College of Religion, they were acting in ways that seemed consistent with their constituted authority.

The Bible, Unity, and Mission at the College of Religion

Once the negotiations got on track, beginning sometime in 1937, the relations between Kershner and Irwin took on a happier quality. There still were problems to work out—finding money to support faculty and special projects, providing support for African American students, developing scholarships to support students and to meet the competition from Yale, Chicago, and the other Disciples seminaries. Kershner and his faculty had to care for all of the routine of academic life, including revising the programs of study, teaching courses, conducting chapel, and dealing with the challenges of student life. In contrast to the sense of crisis that had marked the earlier years of the decade, however, everything now seemed unified. All parts of the Seminary's constituency were committed to common goals for the College of Religion in Indianapolis.

During these years, while the contracts were being renegotiated, the College of Religion was growing. The total registration for 1938–1939, including summer and without duplications, was sixty-six. In 1941–1942, the number was 119. Despite the doubling of the number of students the faculty remained the same in number, with eight regular members of the faculty and a small number of lecturers each of whom taught one course. In 1938, the Seminary's development was marked by its accreditation by the American Association of Theological Schools. The only other Disciples seminary to have achieved that distinction was the College of the Bible in Lexington. What may have been an even happier development was a gift to the Seminary by W. E. Garrison, distinguished Disciples historian who had briefly served as president of Butler University early in the century. Three bronze plaques, of Walter Scott, Alexander Campbell, and Barton W. Stone, "were designed and executed for the new College of Religion building," and matched the Seminary's duplicate of Garrison's plaque of Thomas Campbell that the Disciples of America had given to the Presbyterian Church of Ahorrey, Scotland, where the elder Campbell had been pastor before he came to the United States.[26]

By this time, Dean E. Walker had become the most important member of the faculty other than Frederick Kershner himself. When appointed to the faculty in 1928, he was only twenty-nine years of age and a decade later he was entering into the prime of his life. Because of Kershner's near blindness and other serious illnesses, Walker had taken on an increasingly heavy load of work at the College, and following his return from doctoral studies in Scotland, he set aside work on his dissertation because of these other duties. His power as a speaker was illustrated by the testimony of one of his students many years later who referred to him as "the Alexander Campbell of the twentieth century. . . . I first heard him speak at a Camp Leaders' Week at Lake James, in Angola, Indiana. I didn't wait until the lectures were completed to decide that where he taught was where I wanted to go to school. The very next Monday I was at the Dean's office enrolling at the Butler School of Religion."[27]

Like Kershner, Walker was interested in the Disciples' tradition and its potential as a force for unity in the church and the world. He presented his ideas in a series of lectures entitled "Adventuring for Christian Unity," which he first delivered to a British audience in the summer of 1934. The foundation for these addresses, Walker noted, was Frederick Kershner's book *The Christian Union Overture,* in which his former teacher gave an analysis of Thomas Campbell's *Declaration and Address*.[28] Moving beyond Kershner's exposition, Walker summarized Campbell's ideas in two principles. The protestant principle he described as "the Lutheran contention of private judgment, plus the Chillingworth statement of the Bible and the Bible alone as the religion of Protestants." To this was added the catholic ground of "the infallibility of the universal reason." Walker expanded upon this second principle: "A consensus of the majority of honest and intelligent and spiritual scholars does give the verdict of universal reason."

After discounting the value of ecumenical councils, Walker stated that "in religion, revelation, as interpreted by full and honest scholarship, is the last word; and that unity must rest on truth thus arrived at, or be forever despised of."[29] Walker stated that "the driving motive" of the Disciples was the longing for the Kingdom of God that, they believed, could only come about "through resting upon the authority of the New Testament." He reaffirmed the Disciples' assertion that the Bible as a book of revelation could be understood by ordinary scholarship and sanctified common sense. "This does not mean that they [Disciples] have opposed Biblical criticism—quite the contrary. If the New Testament is not true, they want to know it," and have welcomed light upon the text and its interpretation. "But they have consistently drawn the line between discovered facts and theories constructed upon those facts."[30]

This emphasis upon the Bible was reaffirmed in an address, "The Authority of the Word," delivered at an interseminary conference in 1949. In the address, Walker emphasized that God is personal and comes to humankind through Revelation, supremely in the Law and in Jesus Christ. To get these revelations into our minds, however, requires the use of language, and here Walker distinguished between four forms of the Word of God: The *Apostolic Word,* which is continued in the church today through the *Word Articulate,* which is Preaching; and the *Word Incarnate,* which is continued today through the *Word Incorporate,* by which Walker meant the

Church. All four of these forms of the Word, however, could be known only through the Written Word "by which we may try our understanding of the Word in its more active forms." All of Walker's published writings exuded confidence in the reliability of the Disciples' traditional interpretation of scripture and conclusions concerning the Christian life, the form of the church, and the patterns of worship.

Although Kershner was as committed as Walker to the Disciples position, his theological position was more supple than Walker's. His theological travels had brought him into contact with a wider range of Christian thinkers, and his ethical passion had given him a broader understanding of the relationship between unity and mission. Kershner identified four approaches to unity, rejecting two of them—"surrender to Rome" and federation—and showing that the other two were very much alike. The Anglican position, summarized in the Lambeth Quadrilateral, and the Restoration plea both agreed on the authority of Scripture and the importance of the two sacraments. Since Anglicans interpreted the ancient creeds with such liberality that there was practically no difference between them and Disciples with their emphasis upon Peter's confession, the one significant difference between them was in the realm of polity. Kershner stated that Protestantism at large, if given a choice, would choose democracy over monarchy as its ultimate form of church government. Therefore, he concluded, "there never was a time when the Restoration plea, if adequately presented, had the opportunity for acceptance which it has today."[31]

Despite this conciliatory attitude, Kershner later refused to be one of forty to fifty Disciples who would sign a response to the Lambeth Appeal. He believed that the Disciples' document seemed to repudiate the program for restoration of the New Testament church and accept the evolutionary theory proposed by Roman Catholic scholar Alfred Loisy. "Ultimately, it is my conviction that the Christian world will have to choose between Roman Catholic modernism of the type advocated by Loisy and [George] Tyrrell and the New Testament norm theory as advocated in essence by the Campbells."[32]

Yet Kershner was bothered by the attitudes and actions of more conservative supporters of the classic position of the Disciples. He addressed some of these issues in one of the most important addresses of his long career: his presidential address to the Denver International Convention, October 16, 1938, entitled "One, Holy, Catholic, and Apostolic Church." Kershner called attention to the distinction between the Particular and the Universal. Illustrating one tendency was the "fellowship that uses hooks and eyes rather than buttons," and its contrast with that age-old affirmation that the true church has the four marks identified in the title of his address.[33] New Testament unity, he affirmed, was illustrated by the doctrinal basis of unity in the proposed World Council of Churches—"Jesus Christ as God and Savior"—or its variant in the Federal Council. His own preference would have been one of the biblical phrases "Lord and Savior" or "Lord and Christ." It didn't matter which was used, however, since they meant the same thing. "They represent a pledge of loyalty to the Head of the Church without which no true union is possible."

Kershner offered an eloquent plea for the churches to be bold in their witness against the atrocities of the time. "A cringing church, a materialistic and selfish church, a church whose members cannot live and dare and die for their belief can no longer seriously move the world." He drew upon two statements by officers of the Association for the Promotion of Christian Union to create a list of the catholic elements that all should work for, but then said that what was important was not "the mechanical cataloguing of these details but rather the acceptance of the principle of catholicity. . . . The realization that no Particularity can be made a test of fellowship in a truly catholic communion is the all-essential consideration."[34] Even Disciples had to be careful lest Alexander Campbell become for them hooks and eyes.

Kershner dismissed proof-texting as a way of using the Bible because it was an "unscientific, unscholarly, and unscriptural method," and modern criticism of the Bible because it undermined the Bible's authority. He acknowledged that in the convention "denominational machinery" had to be dealt with, "things being what they are in this workaday world," yet the main purpose of the gathering needed to be to call the people "to the genius of our mission." The most direct statement of Kershner's conviction came near the end of the address: "The cry of a bewildered and broken humanity today is for the actual embodiment of the one true church in all its glory and power unhampered by trivial disagreements and by petty particularities. Loyalty to the Church Universal should be the passionate longing of every Christian heart."

How this might be done was demonstrated in the 1939 Butler Summer Institute that, said Professor Arthur Holmes, exemplified the spirit of the Seminary's dean. Four themes cut across the several days of the conference. "The Church at Work" dealt with practical subjects such as stewardship and evangelism. "The Problem of Christian Unity with Special Reference to the Universal Christian Council" was prompted by the actions that were to result in the formation of the World Council of Churches following the conclusion of World War II. "Democracy Versus Dictatorship" presented speakers who discussed major political developments around the world. "What Attitude Should One Take Toward the Problem of War?" included panel presentations using four speakers, with Harold E. Fey of the Fellowship of Reconciliation representing one extreme and H. L. Chailleux, Americanization Division of the American Legion in Indianapolis, representing the other.

One of the remarkable features of this institute was the wide range of leaders from the Christian Churches who took part. Well-known pastors from liberal and conservative churches, including Roger T. Nooe of Nashville and P. H. Welshimer of Canton, Ohio, editors from left and right, including C. C. Morrison (the *Christian Century*) and George P. Rutledge (formerly of the *Christian Standard*), the state secretaries and agency executives of the cooperative churches, and significant leaders among the churches inclined toward independent patterns of work. All were integrated into a full, complex program staged in the Butler University Field House, largest basketball pavilion in the state and an appropriate location for the "several hundred" people whom Martinsville pastor Wales E. Smith reported to be in attendance. In his summary of the institute, complete with careful statements of the themes of the addresses, Dean E. Walker stated that "500 brethren" attended.[35]

This spirit was also evident in the new theological journal that the School of Religion launched the following year.[36] *The Shane Quarterly*, announced editor Kershner, "represents the effort of a group of teachers to portray and interpret world conditions in the light of their own religious and spiritual convictions at a very crucial period in the history of human progress."[37] The first article, also written by Kershner, listed and commented on the twenty most notable events during the final months of 1939. All of them dealt with public affairs, such as the Stalin-Hitler accord, the death of Sigmund Freud, and the double defeat of President Roosevelt's policies by the U.S. Congress. Later that year the editor reflected upon the causes of the great trouble the world was then enduring and stated that material progress had moved more rapidly than had the forces of the social sciences, ethics, and religion.[38] He spoke of the necessity of a new international order to take the place of the chaos they were experiencing and cited the universalism that Paul proclaimed, asserting that missionaries such as E. Stanley Jones understood how things ought to be. "These men [the missionaries] recognize the necessity for getting rid of the anarchy of nationalism, tribalism and isolationism in order that war may be abolished and that the universal rule of peace in the true world community may begin." Then, said the writer: "It is time for the church at large to awaken to the necessity for proclaiming this message not incidentally, but constantly, persistently and with all of its unified power in order that humanity may be kept from slipping entirely into the abyss."[39]

Despite this grand vision of a united church renewing a fractured world, Kershner and his faculty colleagues were leaders in a church that was tearing itself apart. Disciples had grown rapidly, but they had also shown a contentiousness throughout the history of the movement with no way of holding things together. The harsh spirit of young Alexander Campbell, as expressed in his periodical *Christian Baptist*, sired a continuing zeal for truth at the expense of continuing relationships among the congregations and agencies of the Disciples movement. As soon as one crisis was resolved, usually by separation, another would develop. Another of these crisis periods was developing in the 1920s and, by the middle 1930s, was threatening another splintering of the movement for a united church. In the hope that division could be averted, the Disciples' 1935 International Convention authorized the creation of a commission on restudy of the Disciples of Christ "to overcome divisive tendencies within the Disciples of Christ."[40]

For nearly a decade Frederick D. Kershner and Dean E. Walker were at the heart of its operations, and joining them were A. E. Cory who taught on the faculty, T. K. Smith, Columbus pastor who lectured at the Seminary, and Edwin R. Errett from the *Christian Standard* who was a prominent trustee. R. H. Miller, a trustee of the Seminary, was a less active member of the commission; and during the last years of the commission's life Kershner's successor as dean of the Seminary, Orman L. Shelton, served as member and chair. Kershner, chair of the commission for its first nine years, was a logical choice for this position. Not only had he suggested that such a commission be created, but he also was known as a person able to talk with people in all aspects of Disciples' life.

The members of the commission were primarily mature pastors and editors and they ranged from Edward Scribner Ames on the theological left to Errett and William E. Sweeney on the theological right. In the margin of a paper being discussed at one meeting, Kershner categorized the people participating in that session. As liberals, he identified six of the thirteen people at the session, none of them significantly connected with the School of Religion. Professor Cory was one of two whom he marked as "center left," Kershner himself was the one person he identified as "center right," and all four whom he identified as conservative were connected to the School: Errett, Smith, Sweeney, and Walker. Three issues gave rise to the commission: the debate over higher criticism of the Bible and its impact upon the traditional Disciples' plea; Disciples' participation in the Federal Council of Churches, which seemed to conservative Disciples to mean that they condoned denominationalism; and the advocacy and practice of open membership, at home and abroad.

Members of the commission prepared, read, and discussed papers on a wide range of topics, made reports to their constituencies, and tried to bring about a reconciliation of the two conventions and the networks of agencies developing around the conventions. Although the conversation continued, there was little evidence that anyone was coming to a different point of view. The participants found themselves drawn to one another at the level of "spiritual fellowship" but they could not overcome the theological and organizational chasm that separated them from one another.

Finally, the Goal Achieved!

One of the most important topics that came up repeatedly at the Seminary during the latter half of the 1930s was the need for a building for the College of Religion. The North Central Association was urging that the College of Religion have its own facility. Kershner was finding himself ever more crowded and inconvenienced in the quarters allotted him in Jordan Hall. Errett pushed for getting on with the building, but Irwin seemed less ready to move forward. By the end of 1939, however, the project was under way. The faculty, with Toyozo W. Nakarai taking a prominent role, was developing an outline of the facilities that would be needed in the building, and these ideas were being forwarded to the Millers in Columbus. During the last months of 1939 and the first months of 1940 Kershner and the Millers corresponded frequently. Hugh Th. Miller was often away for medical treatments and Nettie Sweeney Miller took the lead. She sent Kershner an article about Eliel Saarinen who was developing plans for their church in Columbus and Kershner wrote back (November 30, 1939) that "it would be a very wonderful achievement to enlist the service of the one superior architect now living in this country." Mrs. Miller reported the Saarinens' deep distress over the plight of their native Finland, being threatened by Russia, and they agreed that the Indiana congressional delegation should be urged to support Finland's request for a loan. In mid

January Mr. and Mrs. Saarinen visited the Butler campus and Kershner's later note to Mrs. Miller indicated his pleasure at the visit. She suggested that the Saarinens' son, Eero, was only thirty, but was already achieving a strong reputation of his own. Kershner clearly was willing for the younger man to be selected as architect for their building. On January 19, 1940, the senior staff of the University and all of the faculty of the Seminary signed a letter to the Indiana legislators urging the action on behalf of Finland.

These efforts to secure a Saarinen as architect failed, however, and by later in the spring all references were to the firm of Burns and James. Instead of the reputation-making facility that Kershner and the Millers hoped for, they settled for the nice but utterly conventional building that soon was to rise.[41] Although Burns and James were known to specialize in the Georgian architecture that was used for the School of Religion, they could also do architecture that would have been more consistent with the rest of the campus, as was illustrated later that decade by the educational building they designed for North Methodist Church at Thirty-eighth and Meridian, in Indianapolis.[42]

A year later, as the plans moved toward completion, Kershner reported that W. E. Garrison had stopped by. He had assured Kershner that bronze doors something like those in the baptistry in Florence could be secured. He also offered to do four additional bronzes, similar to those already purchased, to be mounted on the second floor of the building. They would probably be of Raccoon John Smith, Isaac Errett, James A. Garfield, and Joseph I. Irwin. He would charge them little more than the cost of the bronze and the casting, which would mean about seven hundred dollars.[43]

As plans developed for the building, Irwin was again in the forefront and he and Kershner discussed its size and the merits of enlarging the plan before beginning construction. Kershner believed that they needed room for 250 students, but Irwin thought they should stay at 200. They had to negotiate a site for the building. Would they build a baptistry outside of the building, modeled after the baptistry in Florence, as Nettie Sweeney Miller hoped for? Or would they place it inside the building as Irwin preferred? Irwin won. When they laid the cornerstone for the building, June 8, 1941, Irwin made the statement:

> In the name of Jesus Christ I do now lay this cornerstone: that here true faith, the fear of God and brotherly love may abide: and that this place may be set apart for the teaching of the doctrines, ordinances and practices of the New Testament church, and the

worship of Almighty God. Other foundations can no man lay than that is laid, which is Jesus Christ.[44]

Fortunately for the Seminary, construction moved quickly so that the building was nearly completed by December 7 of that same year, when the bombing of Pearl Harbor propelled the United States into World War II. In February 1942, the College of Religion began the new semester in its own facility. The building was located on high ground north of Jordan Hall, facing east, with a wide expanse of lawn between the entrance and the Clarendon Mall. The west side of the building looked "out on the beautiful valley of White River."[45] The Seminary's library of nine thousand volumes, plus periodicals, occupied the south wing of the building and Sweeney Chapel the north wing. The main floor included the dean's offices, lecture rooms with wood tablet chairs lined up in straight rows, and a lounge with glass doors opening to a flagstone deck facing west. The second level of the building included a small museum, additional faculty offices, and seven seminar rooms—one for each of the departments of the curriculum. The walls of the seminar rooms were lined with bookcases so that important reference works in that area of study could be available to advanced students. The lower level of the building contained an auditorium underneath the chapel, a large club room furnished with leather chairs, a small kitchen, and recreation rooms. The building was conventional, solid, and suitable to a traditional academic program.

The Seminary's new stature, that its own building demonstrated, also was indicated by its use from this time forward of the name the *School* of Religion rather than College of Religion by which it had been known throughout the Kershner years. Although its administrative relationships with Butler University remained essentially unchanged, the Seminary's life began to drift away from the University within which its academic and religious activities had always taken place.

Kershner and Irwin talked of appointing a dean of the chapel, following the example of Riverside Church in New York City and Rockefeller Chapel in Chicago. Kershner's choice was R. H. Miller, who was well known to Kershner and Irwin and trusted by them. More important, Miller "was undoubtedly the outstanding minister in our brotherhood from the standpoint of popularity and forensic ability. He had achieved a reputation at Washington where Justice McReynolds and other distinguished men are among his closest admirers."[46] William G. Irwin had been one of the Hoosiers who had joined the train of prominent Disciples traveling to

Washington to create the National City Christian Church, where Miller was pastor, and Irwin had contributed to the building fund and served on the administrative committee.[47] University president James W. Putnam was willing to move in this direction; and Miller had indicated that he would be willing to consider such an appointment despite the fact that the salary that would be offered was but half of what he received from his church in Washington, D.C. Nothing was to come of this effort, however.

Finally, the dream of creating a graduate school for Disciples seemed to be reaching its fulfillment. The institutional connections had been negotiated, the financial undergirding assured, and a new building occupied. The dean and faculty, the primary benefactors, and conservative Disciples spokespersons were united in their hopes that the School of Religion could represent the traditional Disciples' ecclesiology in a way that would be appealing to people in other traditions, too. Instead of going east to Yale, or even to Hartford Theological Seminary, which Z. T. Sweeney had favored as the alternative to Yale, people could come to the School of Religion at Butler University.[48]

This description of the future mission of the School of Religion represented one way of responding to the challenge created by the fact that other churches had not been absorbed into the one church that the Restoration Movement had envisaged. Edwin R. Errett, who had become one of the most active of the Seminary's trustees, and Dean E. Walker, who was becoming the most prominent member of the faculty, were committed to a conservative interpretation of the historic plea of the Disciples movement; yet the continuing presence of the other churches (the denominations) could not be ignored. What was beginning to develop in their minds was that even though the denominations would not go away, some of them could become partners with Disciples like themselves in theological education.

Errett's wrestling with these ideas was suggested in addresses published in the 1941 issue of *Shane Quarterly*. In a paper that had been prepared earlier for presentation to the Commission on the Restudy of the Disciples of Christ, Errett spoke out of his experiences at the Oxford and Edinburgh Conferences on Faith and Order. His confidence in the Disciples plea was strengthened by these meetings, but his openness to the people of other churches was also strong. He seemed ready to join in common effort with all who were willing to work for unity upon the basis of "New Testament doctrine and order."[49] In his address at the laying of the cornerstone of the School of Religion building, however, Errett reaffirmed his unswerving commitment to the classic Disciples positions. "This college," he declared, "is to represent and to serve that group of people for whom Christ is the cornerstone of the church." Referring to the people who had begun this movement a century and a quarter earlier, Errett identified their central principle as "the doctrine that Jesus Christ is the central fact of Christianity, its sole creed and source of authority." He continued: "This school is to serve them by adhering to that principle in training their ministers and missionaries, their educators and editors."

Then Errett referred to his participation in ecumenical conferences and affirmed: "We must make this school the most practical instrument in the world by making it serve that purpose of unity upon Jesus Christ. It must bring the best of scholarship to serve the cause of unity by returning to the centrality and unique authority of Jesus Christ."[50] Such a school, he believed, would be attractive to conservative Christians from other churches, too. On May 4, 1941, he and T. K. Smith of Columbus spoke to some seventy-five Butler graduates, students, and friends at a gathering during the Disciples International Convention in Kansas City. The event was reported in the *Christian-Evangelist* under the headline, "Policy Announced at Butler Parley." Errett was quoted: "We shall try to get the very best of conservative scholarship into the school and make it a center of strong scholarship, not only for ourselves, but for all of Protestantism. . . . My conception is that there is no incompatibility between the best of scholarship and a conservative position toward the Scriptures." The final word from Errett was that establishing a strong conservative faculty that attracted students from "outside the brotherhood" would make the school "a center to spread our plea generally."[51]

It was right that these statements by Errett and T. K. Smith in the early 1940s be reported as *a new policy* for the School of Religion, for they represented a turning away from the catholicity of Kershner's vision toward theological conservatism. From his earliest writings Kershner had combined a cautious approach to contemporary theology and a traditional understanding of the Disciples' plea for the reunion of the church on the principles of apostolic Christianity. His hope had been that this combination would be persuasive to the people who encountered it. But Kershner's tone was different from Errett's. He was sometimes described as irenic, which implied that the difference between himself and the older Z. T. Sweeney and the younger Edwin R. Errett and Dean E. Walker was a difference of temperament. The difference, however, was more than temperament; it was a difference in understanding the mission of the

Disciples and of the Seminary. Kershner's vision was broader. For him, the catholicity of the faith through the ages was even grander than the Disciples' plea, whereas for Errett and Walker and the conservative constituency whom they represented loyalty to the plea was the primary consideration.

As the Seminary settled into its new building, there was good reason to believe that this conservative reconstruction of its mission would become the dominant line. While he was still active in his work as dean, Frederick Kershner was in his middle sixties and blind and soon would have to step aside; and Errett in his fifties and Walker in his forties were ready to take control. Although William G. Irwin was now past seventy years of age, he still exercised power in all aspects of the Seminary's life and, Errett and Walker believed, could be counted on to side with them in establishing the new policy of conservatism at the School of Religion.

Architectural rendering of North Western Christian University at Thirteenth and Broadway, Indianapolis, c. 1855. (Courtesy Christian Theological Seminary)

Z. T. Sweeney
(Courtesy J. Irwin Miller)

William G. Irwin.
(Courtesy J. Irwin Miller)

Butler University in the Irvington community of Indianapolis. The College of Religion met on this campus its first two years. (Courtesy Christian Theological Seminary)

Jordan Hall on Butler University's campus, 1928. The College of Religion was located here during most of the Kershner years. (Courtesy Christian Theological Seminary)

Clockwise from top left: Frederick D. Kershner, William Robinson, Orman L. Shelton, and Dean E. Walker. (All courtesy Christian Theological Seminary)

The School of Religion (now known as Robertson Hall) at Butler University, 1943–1966. Sweeney Chapel is in the foreground. (Courtesy Christian Theological Seminary)

5
In the Best Possible Hands

New Leaders and the Renewal of the Seminary's Commitments, 1943–1949

The opening years in the School of Religion's Georgian building were a brief interlude of peace for the faculty and students. The building itself provided a rich context of beautiful floors, paneled walls, and heavy academic furniture. Sweeney Chapel was an austere worship space with gray marble floors, white walls and ceiling, and white-backed walnut pews. The deep tones of the oriental rug in the reception area suggested elegance, and the bronze busts of the four early leaders of the Disciples reminded everyone of the heritage of their school. Frederick D. Kershner, Dean E. Walker, Toyozo W. Nakarai, and Arthur Holmes were the stars of the faculty; their convictions fired the imagination of the students and their eccentricities were the stuff from which legends were made. The professors took seriously the Bible and the classic ideas of the Disciples, and students responded enthusiastically to the work. Over the years the faculty had continued to revise the program of study, gradually evolving a system that made it possible for students to earn their B.D. degrees while coming to the campus only two consecutive days of the week. Thus, they could spend a large part of the week living in the field, serving as pastors of churches. The library featured the L R Room,[1] a section of the stacks behind a heavy wire screen, in which nearly everything that had ever been written about the Churches of Christ—Christian Churches—Disciples of Christ was being collected. These and all of the other books in the library bore the name-plate that stated "Property of The Christian Foundation."

The theological and ecclesiological character of the Seminary's academic life was consistent with the policy that Edwin R. Errett had been announcing among alumni—the traditional Disciples ideas interpreted in the language of conservative protestant theology. Most of the Disciples who held these theological ideas were called Independents since they no longer supported the International Convention and the Disciples agencies related to it. The Cooperatives—people who supported these agencies—generally held more liberal theological ideas. Although the relations between these groups had not yet hardened to the breaking point, the alliances were congealing. At the School of Religion the sympathies were definitely with the Independents, and the Cooperatives often found themselves isolated, their opinions demeaned. Some students from cooperative churches discovered that their soul mates were students from independent churches because they believed the old Disciples ideas and earnestly advocated them in their churches. In this context of faith, some of these students left their cooperative Disciples connections for associations with the Independents while others were angered by the attitudes of the Independents.

The tension that had developed in the 1920s between the Kershner-Irwin seminary and the emerging Disciples leadership was leading to the marginalization of the School of Religion among Cooperatives, some of whom scarcely acknowledged it as a Disciples school despite the fact that half of its students came from cooperative churches and upon graduation became effective pastors of cooperative congregations. For many Cooperatives, reliable theological leadership was sought from the College of the Bible in Lexington, the Disciples Divinity House of the University of Chicago, Yale Divinity School, Brite Divinity School, and traditionally conservative Phillips University.

These shifts in their ecclesial world and at the School of Religion were matters of concern in Columbus. Although the family members' ardent Disciples convictions had aligned them with theological conservatives, they were also committed to the organized life of their church. Furthermore, they were people in the cultural mainstream—world travelers, interested in music, the theatre, art, and architecture, as their new church building in Columbus demonstrated. All of this was in their minds as they talked with their friends Edwin R. Errett and R. H. Miller, who embodied the two sharply contrasting perspectives concerning their church. After the deaths of Z. T. and Linnie Sweeney, their daughter Elsie Irwin Sweeney had become "the spiritual leader of the family." She was troubled by their church's unwillingness to acknowledge the full Christian status of people in other churches who had been baptized in a way other than the Disciples' mode; her studies, beginning with her father's own sermons, had also left deepening questions in her mind about the baptismal nerve center of Disciples ecclesiology.[2]

The Search for a New Dean

While these issues were coming into focus, the Columbus trustees knew that the time was coming soon when a new dean would have to succeed Frederick D. Kershner at the School of Religion. His critical illness in 1937–1938, which had kept him from his desk for several months, had signaled to the Seminary's trustees[3] that they needed to find someone who could take over the responsibilities of guiding the Seminary, calling new faculty, and reclaiming the Seminary's place in the life of the brotherhood of Christian Churches. They began to collect names of persons who might be able to provide the active, vigorous direction that the School needed, and they had found out all they could about these people. To use the words of Z. T. Sweeney, they wanted someone with "the ability to see straight and think clearly."[4] They were aware that "not all of those whose convictions are sound have the tolerance and tact to make them widely effective, or the experience in administration required."

They had decided against the logical candidate from within the faculty, Professor Dean E. Walker, who was the right age, absolutely trustworthy concerning the theological concerns of the trustees, and the recognized leader of many students and professors. With financial support from the Christian Foundation, he had spent two years in Scotland completing the residency requirements for a Ph.D. degree, but since his return to Indianapolis the dissertation had languished. One student at the time remembered a gathering of students at the Walker home sometime after his return from Edinburgh. When the fact of his unwritten dissertation came into the conversation, Mrs. Walker broke into tears, saying that already he was doing much of the dean's work and that students were always around him, on campus and here at home. How could he be expected to write a dissertation? It was rumored among students that he had been invited to Columbus to talk about the deanship but that unpleasant personal mannerisms created a serious block to his advancement. More serious, however, than these faults was Walker's stiff attitude toward the theological issues that were important to the trustees and his growing alienation from the organized work of the Christian Churches. The "unity of our people" was an important concern for the trustees, and they concluded that someone other than Dean E. Walker would be needed in order to accomplish this purpose.

Among the people whom the trustees consulted were Frank Marshall, boyhood friend of Hugh Th. Miller and longtime dean of the Bible College at Phillips University, and R. H. Miller. Marshall spoke favorably of Orman L. Shelton who, following graduation from Phillips, had served the university as development officer and then had demonstrated unusual competence in three pastorates. Some years earlier, R. H. Miller had been pastor of the Independence Boulevard Christian Church in Kansas City where Shelton now was serving. He knew Shelton from their work in general agencies of the Christian Churches. Although the trustees considered other names, no one else seemed to possess the combination of qualities they were seeking. When the trustees were ready to move forward, R. H. Miller and Marshall agreed to go through Kansas City and invite Shelton into the conversation. Their visit was unexpected. Ruby Shelton remembered the day when Orman came home from his pastoral activities exclaiming "You'll never believe what happened today!"[5]

In early July 1943, Shelton met William G. Irwin in Indianapolis to begin conversations. Through the summer and fall they exchanged frequent letters and met several times in Indianapolis and St. Louis with Nettie Sweeney Miller and Hugh Th. Miller joining the Indianapolis sessions. Irwin discussed developments with Edwin R. Errett, who did not know Shelton, and arranged a meeting between them. In the letter to Shelton setting up the appointment, Irwin made this further statement: "We feel that you are equipped for this work better than any one else with whom we have discussed the question. Your experience in the college work at Phillips and in addition, your years as a successful pastor give a back-ground such as no other person of whom we know in the brotherhood."[6] Shelton and Errett met at a luncheon on October 13, along with Irwin and the Millers. The next day Irwin wrote Shelton to say that Errett had been very pleased over the talk. "I am glad," Irwin continued, "to hear his thought that with your help at the School of Religion we would be taking a long step towards the unity of our people. This has been our thought here as we doubtless have expressed it to you."[7]

From the very beginning Shelton asked for documents that could help him decide: an audit of the Christian Foundation, the budget of the School of Religion, the articles of incorporation and the bylaws of the Christian Foundation. He also was candid about the factors that would influence his decision. Believing that God had called him to the Independence Boulevard Christian Church, and having come with the intention of completing his ministry there, Shelton had to be convinced that it was God's will for him to come to the School of Religion. Thus, he was regularly in prayer about this decision. He was leading his church in a program to raise funds for renovation, and he could not leave until these matters were cared for.

Even before he made the decision, these conversations were influencing Shelton's pastoral work. During the fall of 1943 a young man from the Independence Boulevard congregation was in his pastor's study discussing his call to the ministry. Shelton encouraged him, and they discussed where he would complete his college education and then do his seminary studies. Several colleges were considered, but only one seminary, the Butler School of Religion. Shelton had the catalog and financial statements on his desk. Together they looked through the catalog and Shelton commented on the professors, indicating their strong qualities. He described the financial situation of the School of Religion and showed how advantageous that factor was for students. As far as he was concerned, there was only one seminary for the young man to attend. Following his military service, this man, Bill L. Barnes, did study at the School of Religion and some years later became its development officer, a position he held for more than twenty-five years.

On October 29, 1943, Shelton wrote to Irwin stating his readiness to move forward, when the time came, to "open consideration" with the intention to accept the position. He had studied the catalogs of "all our Bible Colleges and ten of the major theological seminaries of our country" and had concluded that there was "no reason why the School of Religion cannot become the greatest factor in the training of the ministry in our Brotherhood, and stand alongside the leading seminaries of the country." If he were to come, he would want to do just that. "We are desperately in need of it, and our Brotherhood cannot come to the power it ought in religious leadership in the world unless some of our colleges come to that standing." He had talked extensively with Dean Marshall, who agreed with him "that no seminary in our Brotherhood has the opportunity the School of Religion has." Shelton's second conviction was that "we must train our ministers in the most scholarly atmosphere, but it must be an atmosphere of sound and profound convictions." The professors must possess "rich and growing scholarly minds, but they must also have a profound belief in the deity of Jesus Christ, and the divine destiny of the Church." He stated as his third conviction that students should be trained "in actual situations" and be guided "in practical experience while they are in training." He indicated that other seminaries were moving in this direction, citing Oberlin and Chicago as notable examples. He believed that Indianapolis was well equipped to provide this practical experience.

Shelton's fourth conviction was that Bible colleges ought "to be permeated with the Spirit of Christ" and send out graduates "imbued with His Spirit whatever their relationships." Referring to his conversations with Irwin, Shelton affirmed that he believed they understood each other. "The principal business of a Bible College is to ground men in spiritual and intellectual foundations, and not become entangled in surface things. In so doing, as I have said, it would need to take a carefully chosen middle-of-the-road position, built on the revelation of God in Christ, so that it would contribute a sound theology which would in itself work a unifying influence in our Brotherhood." The fifth factor in Shelton's decision was the progress in his church. Funds were coming in and plans for renovation were well in hand. The war, however, necessitated that they postpone construction until the war was over and materials were available. A new pastor would have time to take over leadership before this phase of the project could be completed. Thus Shelton could accept the offer from the School of Religion. Shelton noted that steps would need to be taken to stabilize the School's financial situation, and he discussed his personal needs for salary and related considerations.

This correspondence made no reference to the larger body of University trustees, the directors of the Christian Foundation, or the University administration. Shelton indicated that the negotiations could not be made public until the spring in deference to his church. Despite the private nature of these discussions, a rumor developed that a change was going to be made in the deanship, and Dean Kershner asked to meet with Nettie Sweeney Miller in late fall. In a long letter to Shelton she described the conversation in the dean's office on a November afternoon. Kershner had stated that his age and ill health required a change in the dean's office. He also indicated that several professors were growing old and soon would need to be replaced. She had agreed with him and indicated that "they" had for some years had these matters on their hearts and in their minds. He suggested the names of pastors for them to consider: Virgil Elliott of Pittsburgh and Warren Hastings of Washington, D.C. Mrs. Miller thought that he sounded as though he had heard the rumor that had come to R. H. Miller, but she would not satisfy his curiosity. Kershner indicated his desire to continue teaching, but she had the impression that he felt "that it would be a relief to be free from the administrative part of the work."[8]

These negotiations came to their successful completion just in time. In its December 4 and 11, 1943, editions the *Christian Standard* announced changes in policy, which the editor, Edwin R. Errett, had opposed. Henceforth, the *Standard* would fight modernism and "efforts to preserve the fellowship of the whole Brotherhood."⁹ On December 14, seventy-three-year-old William G. Irwin collapsed and died in his office at the Indiana National Bank which he was serving as interim president. On January 29, 1944, Edwin R. Errett suddenly died, only fifty-four years of age. Two days later, when he heard of Errett's death, Shelton wrote to the Millers from a Des Moines hotel where he was attending a meeting. He noted that now there were two vacancies in the Board of Trustees of Butler University that needed to be filled by the Christian Foundation. They had to take steps to fill these vacancies and someone else had to be chosen "to act with Mr. Miller in doing the things we have outlined regarding Dean Kershner and the possibility of seeing Pres[ident M. O.] Ross and guiding the matter through the Board of Trustees."¹⁰ Apparently, much had to be done to formalize the decisions that Irwin, the Millers, Errett, and Shelton had taken.¹¹

Follow-up actions continued quietly. Not until spring was Kershner brought into the picture. Secretaries in the dean's office remembered a day when Mr. and Mrs. Miller came from Columbus to see Dean Kershner. These secretaries, including the man who was the Dean's personal aide as well as executive assistant, came away from the day concluding that the delegation had told Kershner two things he had not known before: that he would be retiring at the end of the school year and that Orman L. Shelton would succeed him. A few days later (March 22, 1944), Dean Kershner dictated a memorandum of the visit and the agreements that had been made.¹² In letters to his family he reported that "Brother Shelton is said to be a very fine type of Christian gentleman . . . and was chosen especially for his administrative and executive ability." The only person around the Seminary and University who knew anything about Shelton was professor Ross J. Griffeth, who had been a classmate of Shelton's at Phillips. Kershner said of his first meeting with Shelton that "he impressed me very favorably."

By early April Shelton's appointment had made its way through the *pro forma* processes of University approval. President Ross wrote him on April 13, 1944, with notification of the positive action by the Butler board of trustees, and Shelton responded two days later: "I deeply appreciate the action of the Board of Trustees, and shall do my best to fulfill the responsibilities to which I am called." His letter of resignation from his church was addressed to the board of elders on April 19, 1944. In the brief summary of his career that he sent to Ross, at the president's request, Shelton noted that during his four years on the staff of Phillips University, its campaign had raised $1,250,000. During six years as pastor in Ponca

City, Oklahoma, the membership of the church had doubled, with a total of 1,661 additions, 1,019 of them by baptism.[13] A pipe organ had been purchased and the church's budget had more than doubled. At Wichita Falls, Texas, the church had received 545 additions during Shelton's ministry and remodeled and enlarged the building. At Independence Boulevard Christian Church in Kansas City, there had been 707 additions, the budget had increased by 50 percent, an educational program using new audio-visual equipment had been inaugurated, and nearly $25,000 had been pledged for a postwar remodeling program. When he left Kansas City to move to Indianapolis, Shelton's congregation listed 2,679 members and was larger than any Christian Church congregation in Indianapolis, St. Louis, or Cincinnati; only a handful of Disciples churches anywhere were larger. The Columbus congregation listed 1,567 members.

The New Dean Takes Charge

Even before he moved to Indianapolis to begin his regular duties, dean-designate Shelton became directly involved in the affairs of his new office. In early June he visited the campus and conferred with Harold F. Hanlin, professor of New Testament, who was supervising the preparation of the annual catalog to be issued in September. Immediately after returning home to Kansas City he wrote to other members of the faculty about a variety of academic matters.[14] Shelton spent time during the following weeks in preparing descriptions of courses he would teach so that they could be approved by faculty and listed in the catalog. A little later Hanlin wrote him indicating that publication was being delayed because of two matters. First, President M. O. Ross of Butler University had not yet sent the names of the trustees who were to serve on the School of Religion committee. Ross's word was that the committee had been named tentatively and that he had asked "Mr. and Mrs. [Hugh Th.] Miller to approve it for the Christian Foundation, and that when they reply to his letter he will be ready to give [Hanlin] the names of the committee."[15] This naming of members was important because since the previous catalog had been published William G. Irwin, chair, and Edwin R. Errett had died and Crate Bowen had dropped off of the committee. The new committee consisted of continuing members Hilton U. Brown and Hugh Th. Miller and three new members: R. H. Miller, Errett's successor, who was named the chair; Nettie Miller, replacing her uncle William G. Irwin; and John R. Rees, manager of the Miller-Sweeney Farms, replacing Bowen.

The second reason for delay was the changed status of Ludwig von Gerdtell, who had been listed as lecturer in church history and Christian doctrine and who taught a reduced class load. Von Gerdtell's connection with the School of Religion had begun in 1930 when the German Evangelical Association was formed in the home of Dean E. Walker expressly for the purpose of assisting in the work of von Gerdtell in Germany. Kershner was the first president of this association which later was renamed the European Evangelistic Society. When first established, the association's purpose was "to form an alliance between Disciples in America and the new groups of Christians brought together by von Gerdtell."[16] Walker had met von Gerdtell and through Walker's efforts Kershner and Irwin had been persuaded that von Gerdtell should come to the Seminary's faculty. In 1944, however, his sponsors in the Christian Foundation decided that von Gerdtell should no longer be part of the Seminary faculty and arranged for his continued financial support on the condition that he no longer teach there.[17]

There is no evidence that Shelton was involved in either of these matters, but during the summer the seminary's accreditation was threatened, and here Shelton not only became actively involved but single-handedly resolved the problem. The American Association of Theological Schools (AATS) had reviewed the seminary's program and determined that the Seminary's number of cataloged books was insufficient for the M.Th. degree and that all references to it should be removed from the catalog. Dr. Gould Wickey, general secretary of AATS, had explained this problem to the faculty in a meeting on April 21, 1944. He had also raised questions about the relationships of the University registrar and admissions committee to the committee on admissions of the School of Religion. Most difficult of the AATS questions was one concerning the possibility of interference by the board of the Christian Foundation in matters that should originate with the faculty. This interference came at two points: the method of choosing and electing faculty members and the possibility that faculty members would have direct access to members of the board.[18]

Even though he had not yet begun his duties, Shelton was chosen to attend the AATS June meeting in Pittsburgh to resolve the issues that stood in the way of accreditation. At first Kershner was to be the second person in the delegation. Then it seemed as though Dean E. Walker, as a younger member of the faculty, would go with Shelton. Then, at the suggestion of Mrs. Miller and Brother Miller the nominee was Butler president, M. O. Ross. Finally, Shelton went unattended. He met privately with Dr. Wickey and Dean Sherrill of the AATS and agreed that this matter of the M.Th. would be dealt with as the AATS required. Shelton stated in a letter to Kershner that he didn't know how difficult it would be to remove references from the catalog but that "that was a condition of accreditation." There is no hint in the reports of the conference of other topics that may have been discussed by the dean-elect as he conferred with these seasoned academic administrators. Kershner responded immediately with gratitude. "Again I want to congratulate you most warmly and enthusiastically upon the way in which you handled matters at Pittsburgh. It was a real triumph for the school, and I know enough about such matters to understand how much we are all indebted to you for the part you took in the deliberations of the Accrediting Committee."[19]

Because the Kershners were buying the house in which they lived, the Sheltons needed a place to live, and the Christian Foundation purchased a residence suitable for the dean.[20] The Sheltons moved to this home at 445 Blue Ridge Road in Indianapolis in time for the beginning of the fall semester. Shelton was to be a teaching dean. His initial offerings were three new courses orienting students to graduate study and to ministry, which would give him contact with all students and express his commitment to their field experience.[21] By his second year, Shelton was listed as the teacher for courses in preaching, church management, community organizations, and religious education. His normal teaching load each semester became two regular courses in Christian ministries in addition to one of the orientation courses.

People who were on campus when Shelton began his work perceived that a new era had dawned. Many were anxious, convinced that this new dean was too liberal and that his leadership would take the seminary in a direction they didn't want to go. Some were uneasy because he was not an academician by training or experience. Even so, he started off well. An important indication of his success in establishing himself with faculty colleagues was the annual School of Religion dinner that took place in June following his first academic year as dean. It was held at University Park Christian Church,[22] at Twenty-ninth and Kenwood streets, where the Kershners had long been members and where the Sheltons had also placed their membership. The major event of the evening was the unveiling of the portrait of Dean Kershner that would be hung in the School of Religion. In his presentation speech, Dean E. Walker linked Kershner in a chain of names—Alexander Campbell, J. W. McGarvey, and Frederick D. Kershner—who "stand in succession in the unfolding quest to develop a ministerial leadership commensurate with the significance of what Campbell called 'the current reformation.'" All three, Walker stated, answered affirmatively the question: "Could a graduate school, centered about the Bible, oriented to the highest scholarly tradition, and committed to devoted Christian living, be created to serve the Churches of Christ?" He described Kershner's contribution to that cause, quoting a statement that he had often heard Kershner make: "My purpose as an educator has been to secure for the ministry first, a positive faith; second, a sound education; and third, a commitment to the advancement of the mission of the Disciples." Walker concluded his remarks by referring to the realization "that in Dr. Shelton reside those same basic qualities of devotion and integrity which we have esteemed in his predecessor. In the months passed, we have learned to trust and to love the purpose and person of our new Dean."[23]

In his "Personal Word" upon the unveiling, Kershner described the succession in which he stood and which he handed on to Shelton. He then gave this testimony to the work of his successor: "I want to say here that it has been the supreme joy of my experience to be able to pass on the torch to one who is so consecrated and competent as Dean Shelton. As I remarked in our faculty meeting last week, out of an experience of over half a century I cannot recall any one who in the course of a year has so thoroughly won the admiration and esteem of his colleagues." Then Kershner made this statement: "I am sure that this great educational enterprise which means so much for the future of humanity is *in the best possible hands* and this is a source of supreme satisfaction to me."[24]

Defining the Center of Authority

Shelton immediately found himself in the position of clarifying the relations with the University's administration and in the process making clear the authority of the School of Religion committee of the Butler trustees. Even so simple a matter as his installation became the occasion to test the relationship between the School of Religion and its University. President M. O. Ross was assuming that the installation would be worked out by the University's department of public affairs; but Shelton was recommending that the program be sent to chairman R. H. Miller. "This is another one of the things," Shelton said to R. H. Miller, "which fits in to the picture that I presented to you and indicates that we will need to stand for the integrity of your committee in matters which they supervise. I will let you know whatever else may develop."[25] Four days later Shelton addressed another letter to R. H. Miller saying that "it is altogether proper and appropriate for you to define with the president the standing and position of the School of Religion Committee, but I think I should like to talk with you about it before you do. We can clear this whole matter up if the committee and the dean stand together on a policy, which we clearly understand and believe to be valid." He indicated that Hugh Th. Miller had called a meeting of the School of Religion Committee at the Athletic Club in downtown Indianapolis at 11:00 o'clock on October 11. They would lunch together and then go to the meeting of the Butler trustees at 1:30. Shelton indicated that because he had matters regarding the budget to discuss with the foundation members, he would meet with them earlier.[26]

Shelton found himself in the center of a triangle of authority: the University administration, the School of Religion Committee of the University's trustees, and the Christian Foundation. Although the School of Religion Committee acted formally as trustees of the Seminary, it was weak in comparison to the two other authorities. The financial support and directions for the Seminary's policy came from the Christian Foundation which controlled appointments to the School of Religion Committee. Despite the contract of 1940 that established this relationship between the University and the Christian Foundation, the University was a continuing instrument of power. The Seminary's legitimacy as an accredited degree-granting institution depended upon its being part of the University. As such, the dean and its faculty stood in a system of authority that expected conformity. Furthermore, legal title to the School of Religion building and control of all of the grounds outside of the building were vested in the University.

Since Shelton and Ross were both new to their positions, and neither of them participants in any of the negotiations that had led to the seminary's independence and to the controversies over the erection of its building, both men were interested in testing their authority.[27] The arrangement that gave the Seminary free rein, according to the decisions of a small group of people outside of the University's system of authority and responsibility, was unique. By the spring of 1946, less than two years into his new position, Shelton was at work to clarify these matters. He wrote a document interpreting the arrangement and discussed it at least twice with the School of Religion Committee. R. H. Miller was already into the pattern of non-attendance at meetings, and it is not clear that he knew the details of the discussion. In October 1946, Shelton reported to R. H. Miller that the interpretation of the contract which he had discussed with "certain parties appears to be perfectly valid from the legal standpoint." He found it necessary, however, to defer action for a while.[28]

Shelton's conclusion about this contract was stated with great precision and force. It guided every aspect of his work throughout the rest of his administration and culminated in the creation of the new corporation of Christian Theological Seminary a little more than a decade later. "It was the purpose of the contract," Shelton wrote,

> to establish the School of Religion as an independent and permanent Graduate Seminary to train ministers for the Christian Church. It was intended that it should be independent of and free from the jurisdiction of the Board of Directors of Butler University. . . .The contract vested entire authority over the School of Religion in a Committee composed of members of the Board of Directors [of Butler University] and of the Christian Foundation. This was for the purpose of establishing its integrity and freedom as a separate and distinct institution, and at the same time relating it educationally to the University with which it wished to maintain a cooperative relationship, and financially to the Christian Foundation which furnished its financial resources.

Then comes the sentence which marked the cutting edge of Shelton's interpretation: "The Committee is to govern for both with powers definitely vested in it by the contract."[29] In this sentence Shelton sought to link himself closely with one of the three points in the triangle, seeing it as the means of overcoming the potential conflicts that could come as the three entities struggled for their rights.

Following the death of William G. Irwin, his nephew J. Irwin Miller was released from his position with the U.S. Navy; after returning to Columbus, he assumed his uncle's leadership of the family's enterprises. He soon was elected to the board of the Christian Foundation and quickly became the most prominent member of that board in dealings with the Seminary and Dean Shelton. On April 16, 1946, following a meeting of the Christian Foundation in which Shelton had discussed the need for clarifying relations with the University, Irwin Miller wrote to the dean. In four lines he agreed with Shelton that clarifying these relations was important; he also expressed his confidence that Shelton would be successful in doing so harmoniously. The rest of the letter, twenty-three lines of text, was devoted to the topic that Miller wanted to hear about—the dean's plans "for improving the quality of ministerial training which the School of Religion offers." He suggested that Shelton might face a dilemma. If he were "to analyze the aims, the functions, the duties, and the responsibilities of a Christian minister in today's world," and "to classify the varieties of learning and the kinds of skills that would contribute most successfully to the effective discharge of the minister's duties," and if he were to "construct a course of instruction designed to impart the learning and training desired," then he might end up with a course of study that "the powers that be would consider . . . so unorthodox that its completion would not qualify a person for a degree." Miller suggested that eventually Shelton would become "dissatisfied with the adequacy of even the highest accepted types of ministerial training and will feel the urge to strike out on a new path."[30]

Rather than accept Miller's challenge about the curriculum, Shelton turned to what was crucial for long-term success: the rebuilding of his faculty. Not only did he face the need of replacing aging professors, but he also had to prepare for the significant increase in enrollment that he was sure would come soon. Even more important, Shelton was determined to create a faculty that would share his dream of building the Kingdom of God in the postwar world and help the School of Religion claim its rightful place at the center of the life and work of the Disciples of Christ. When he began his work, the full-time faculty consisted of seven persons, including the dean himself, all members of the Christian Church, all white except Toyozo W. Nakarai, and all men except for Lucile Calvert.[31] The next catalog indicated that Calvert was on leave and L. Gray Burdin was teaching speech, but the next year Calvert's name had disappeared. By 1947 Harold F. Hanlin had left the faculty and his place was taken by S. Marion Smith. David C. Pellett was added in Semitic languages and literature. Frank J. Albert was listed in Christian doctrine and church history. While these young professors had come from traditional Christian church backgrounds, thus making them acceptable to the conservative members of faculty and trustees, they were doing graduate study at major research institutions—Smith and Pellett at Chicago and Albert at Harvard.[32]

Shelton had two criteria in his selection of candidates for the faculty. The first was promise in the particular field in which they were to teach. Although he gladly considered people with completed Ph.D. degrees, most of these early appointments were persons who had not yet completed their academic preparation and who were still young enough to have only a limited career record. Shelton's intentions were revealed in the efforts to appoint a professor of religious education when he asked R. H. Miller's opinions of Ronald E. Osborn, who was teaching religious education at Northwest Christian College. "A religious education man is what I want. He must be a man capable of becoming a Veath [Shelton is probably referring to Paul H. Vieth, at that time the foremost figure in that field] or someone like that at the top."[33] When Osborn withdrew from consideration, the name of James Blair Miller was recommended, even though he had done only a little academic work beyond the B.D. degree. It was clear in R. H. Miller's correspondence with Shelton that while the young Bethany (West Virginia) pastor had good practical experience, "he would have to complete his doctorate if he were ever to become a full professor."[34] Yet Vieth had recommended him highly and that recommendation carried the day.

In addition to competency in their fields of study, these new professors needed to be sympathetic to the ecclesial position of the new School of Religion. Shelton's early ideas about this side of things were illustrated in his observations about the calling of A. C. Watters to work with Abe Cory in missions. Cory had had a long history of association with the United Christian Missionary Society, having served in China soon after the close of the Boxer Rebellion. Thus he stood aligned with the dominant institution on one side of the divide that was breaking the Disciples apart. Although he was committed to the cooperative approach to missionary work (the organization side, as some would put it), Cory told students that he believed in comity without compromise. He was candid in saying that he knew that the School of Religion would train some people who would become independent missionaries, but that was okay with him.

By early 1948 Cory wanted help and Shelton had talked with Cy Yocum and Virgil Sly of the United Christian Missionary Society who found it difficult to come up with someone who they felt would be a good teacher. Finally, UCMS missionary Don McGavran had been proposed and Shelton had undertaken negotiations but then had backed away.[35] Then came the conversation with Watters, a member of the Churches of Christ in Scotland, a longtime missionary, and a man with a Ph.D. Said Shelton to R. H. Miller:

> I have tried my best to thoroughly investigate his attitude on brotherhood matters. He has always been cooperative and the best that I can fathom it, he has a distinctly and definitely cooperative philosophy. I think he would make a contribution to our school and in a larger area by bringing his philosophy to bear objectively

upon our brotherhood problems. I think, therefore, he would be a distinct asset in that area and that to me is a very vital matter.[36]

Candidates for the faculty would come to Indianapolis where they would meet professors, sometimes being taken from house to house to speak with professors who could be found at home. Campus visits regularly included a trip to Columbus to be interviewed by people there. One professor remembered J. Irwin Miller's questions about his research for the dissertation that was in process and Elsie Irwin Sweeney's conversation along a more general line. Shelton also asked R. H. Miller to write his endorsements of candidates to Mr. and Mrs. [Hugh Th. and Nettie] Miller and to Miss [Clementine] Miller. Shelton placed high hopes on the selection of these new faculty members. After five years of working on the challenge of rebuilding the faculty, he admitted that he had sometimes been discouraged "in the possibility of things working out as I thought they should." He continued his note to R. H. Miller by saying that "I am more encouraged now of the not too remote possibilities than I have ever been since I have been here. I am sure that matters are going to make notable and noticeable progress in the very near future." A few months later, his spirits picking up, he said that "if we can get any or all of the above mentioned men, we will have a team here that is not equaled anywhere in any school. Young men, with ability, growing in preparation, who in five to ten years will have come into the forefront of seminary work in our Brotherhood life. This would give us a position unequaled, I think, and I am anxious about it."[37]

The people whom Shelton was inviting to the faculty were aware of the long-standing orientation of the School of Religion toward independent causes. Some of them needed persuading even to consider an interview, and some came to discuss the possibilities out of friendship to Shelton as much as for any other reason. In the conversations Shelton would explain his visions for the future, tell about others who would be coming, and interpret the new future that the school was entering. His presentations often were effective in persuading people to come. Their response was as much because of their confidence in the new array of teachers as it was because of their belief that Shelton was right. The building of a faculty began with choosing the people who would make a good team. Once they came to the school, however, much more had to be done to make them into a harmonious and effective group of people. The Sheltons worked hard at this task. They made full use of the fine house that had been purchased by the Christian Foundation for the use of the dean, regularly entertaining professors and their wives. People remember the warmth with which they were greeted and sustained in their work at the School of Religion.

Studying at the School of Religion

The professors at the School of Religion during these transitional years made vivid impressions upon their students. Lucile Calvert was a spirited presence on campus. Her students remembered her as skilled at helping them overcome speech difficulties in their efforts to become good preachers.[38] Harold F. Hanlin was a good teacher of New Testament. Students experienced his successor, S. Marion Smith, as genial but not very sure of his Greek, and ready to restate ideas when challenged in order to make them more agreeable to traditional Disciples ideas. Arthur Holmes was an old man by the time these students knew him, and his class notes that he deposited in the Seminary library were out of date, but the impact of his spirit was strong on students. He provided a sermon outline that could be used on any occasion and with any text: "What is it? What's it worth? How can I get it?" Toyozo W. Nakarai was experienced by many as a highly competent scholar, deeply humble man, and ardent defender of simple New Testament Christianity. Others, however, found him narrow, inflexible, and prideful. His attitude toward Shelton was condescending because he believed Shelton to be unqualified for the position of dean.

People who studied with Frederick D. Kershner by this time recognized that he had long since passed his prime as a Christian thinker and was weakening physically. He was "blind, physically frail, really almost feeble. . . . If one were quiet, or drowsy—and it was easy to be so under the circumstances, one could perceive that Kershner felt he was talking almost to himself and his voice would trail off inaudibly." In conferences in his office, as people read their work to him, he would sometimes doze off. Despite his blindness, Kershner kept abreast of world developments, listening to world news every morning on shortwave radio and dictating his reflections about the news. Readers made it possible for him to keep in touch with current literature and to prepare reviews for publication. He dictated correspondence and other composition to one of two secretaries who typed directly from his oral dictation. His ideas were clear enough in his head and his memory keen enough that he could be interrupted for other business and then return to the exact place where he had been prior to the interruption.[39] Students found that an attitude of great respect, often love, developed in their relationship to him. In his last sermon in Sweeney Chapel he announced that he was going to repreach a sermon he had delivered forty years earlier on Blind Bartimaeus as described in Mark 10. When he had preached it before he could see; but now he, like Bartimaeus, was blind. "His voice was strong and clear and rang through the chapel as he held his listeners rapt for twenty minutes. There was scarcely a dry eye or a cough to break the silence in the room."

An important quality of the School of Religion was its missionary perspective. One student of the time described the breadth of that vision: "In addition to taking more seriously the mandate of Jesus worldwide, we could not but take account of the threat to life from the loss of Christian values and principles which was embroiling western culture in war. Living as well as learning in the shadow of terrible atrocities and conflict impelled us to ask, what Jesus expected of disciples to counteract the effects of this tragedy." This person then noted the impact of Abe Cory's coming to be professor of missions. "Out of his early years in China after the Boxer Rebellion, and long and intimate association with missionaries, beckoned still undiminished idealism, coupled with the reality of living out on the mission field the faith we profess."[40]

When his appointment was first announced to the student body, Shelton was described as an excellent administrator. This side of the dean was expressed in his book *The Church Functioning Effectively*, which he completed in his first year on campus. Shelton was confident of the ideas in the book because he had developed them in his pastorates in which some 280 men and women on church boards had helped create the model. One student, pastor of an Indianapolis church, was so enthusiastic about these ideas that he borrowed the galley proofs and found enough typists in his church that over one weekend they typed out a full copy of the text for their pastor to use.[41]

Students also found Shelton to be a man of spiritual depth, firm convictions, and sensitivity. All of them consulted with him one-by-one concerning their academic programs. They dealt with him in the general issues of academic and ecclesial life. Chapel was especially important. Services were conducted four days a week and students remember that most of them attended most of the days that they were on campus. The dean regularly prepared the order of service, often typing it himself and giving it to a secretary to mimeograph. Ordinarily he also presided over the service. He preached occasionally, but on most days other people from the faculty or wider religious community did the preaching. There was a dignity in his bearing and in the spirituality of the service that students remembered positively. Shelton was determined, however, to do everything he could to help students become acquainted with the cooperative life and work of Disciples. In part he did this by inviting leaders from Missions Building to be preachers in chapel. One of the students, who at the time was an officer of the student association, was asked by Shelton why attendance had dropped off. The student reported that so many church executives were preaching that students were losing interest. Shelton's response was to ask how people would ever learn about our brotherhood work if they never heard about it.

Beginning in 1945 one of the assets for worship was the hymnal *Christian Hymns,* provided by the Christian Foundation. As their church in Columbus was preparing to enter their new building, Clementine Miller and her mother Nettie decided to prepare a hymnal for their church and for other Disciples congregations. They developed a list of congregations across the country and solicited their help. The congregations sent them their Sunday bulletins so that the editors could determine which hymns actually were being sung. The Millers reimbursed the congregations for their expenses, and for about five thousand dollars were able to develop the data they needed. Clementine Miller and her church's minister of music, E. Wayne Berry, were general editors. Nettie Miller selected scripture texts for each of the hymns, Edwin R. Errett prepared responsive readings, Hugh Th. Miller edited and corrected the proof, and Nettie's sister Elsie Irwin Sweeney was one of the people who prepared the indices and checked proof. Eliel Saarinen, who had designed their church, designed the cover for the book. Because the Christian Board of Publication was also publishing a new hymnal, *Christian Worship: A Hymnal,* the Christian Foundation made no effort for broad marketing of its book. For more than a third of a century, this handsome blue book with chaste gilt lettering provided the foundation for worship at Sweeney Chapel.

For most students of this era, the dominant presence on campus was Professor Dean E. Walker. It was a frequent experience that persons thinking about graduate study for the ministry would hear Walker speak at some conference. The breadth of his vision for the church and the power of his personality would persuade hearers that he was the one with whom they wanted to study. On campus they found their expectations realized. He reaffirmed their confidence in the central ideas of the Restoration movement. Restoration was more than the renewal of the form of the church as revealed in the New Testament, important as that might be, but was the renewal of all creation. His sensitivity to people, according to one recollection, was expressed when he met two of his students at the 1944 International Convention of the Disciples meeting in Columbus, Ohio. Sensing that something was seriously wrong, he was told that the father of one had died and he didn't know how he could get back to the funeral. Walker immediately loaned him the money and arranged for him to fly directly from Columbus to his father's home several hundred miles away to the west.

The main cause of dissension between Shelton and his most prominent professor was the ecclesial orientation of the School. Would the School of Religion continue to be the champion of a traditional view of Disciples theology and polity, be aligned with the *Christian Standard* and the Bible colleges of the land, and support the independent churches and agencies? Or would the School become a strong participant in the full range of the Disciples' organizational and academic networks. Walker and Shelton had tried to move past this divide by serving together in the last five years of the Commission on Restudy of the Disciples of Christ.[42] When Shelton succeeded Kershner as chair of the commission, he and Walker continued to labor closely with each other. Throughout these years they both hoped that the breach could be overcome and the church be bound into a more closely knit fellowship. Their reasons undoubtedly differed; they were not in harmony with respect to many aspects of church life. Yet both wanted unity and hoped that this process would make that unity possible.

The records of the commission reported that warm personal friendships had developed among them despite their differences concerning the Christian Churches. Yet the issues they were debating pulled them apart in their real life in the churches and institutions where they worked, and tension was building on the campus of the School of Religion. Because divisions were developing in congregations concerning these issues, Shelton and his staff began to ask students to declare their orientation, whether cooperative or independent. This could help in placing them in student appointments and in giving recommendations when they were applying for pastoral positions following graduation. Most students were willing to make the declaration but some refused. One remembered Shelton's frustration when the student insisted that he was simply a Christian, neither cooperative nor independent. Faced with this insistence, Shelton relented and gave his recommendation, using the student's own self-identification.

Students during those years later reported that the divisive questions rarely were discussed in the classroom; one suspects that they rarely entered into formal faculty discussion, either. Yet the discussions took place in other settings. One undergraduate student whose full commitment was to the cooperative work of the Disciples waited tables at Butler's Atherton Center and was the server during occasional Tuesday evening gatherings of Professor Walker and students on the conservative side of these debates. The table talk on these occasions dealt with issues being debated among Disciples and on the campus. Toward the end of this period Walker's position would come out in the classroom as he made snide remarks about his minority position on the faculty. Another faculty person with strong loyalties toward the North American-Standard Publishing side of the debate was librarian Enos Dowling. "I could feel the school slipping away," Dowling said many years later, "and it hurt. Often I would go to chapel and pray for the school, hoping that it could be saved."[43]

Dean Shelton was aware of this dissension and knew that soon the struggle within his faculty had to be resolved. He may well have been emboldened in his actions by a packet that he received one June morning from Elsie Irwin Sweeney containing two papers that she had written. She began with the declaration that "for some time I have felt that our position regarding baptism is untenable," and proceeded to explain her conclusion that her father's vigorously held position on the relation between baptism, salvation, and church membership was wrong. The second paper was her own fifteen-page exposition of scripture passages that bore upon baptism, church membership, salvation, and participation in the Lord's supper. Her conclusion:

> While I am willing to belong to a church, which insists upon baptism for church membership, I feel I should not support a church which refuses to cooperate with other churches willing to accept unimmersed penitent believers into a working relationship. Such a refusal causes division in the fellowship of believers. Christ prayed for the unity and not for the baptism of His disciples.[44]

In the summer of 1949 Shelton wrote to R. H. Miller describing conversations he was having with individuals on the faculty. He was trying to make clear and definite an "understanding of relationships which are expected in the future. I think some readjustments can be made and if not, then major adjustments will need to be made."[45] During that same summer Dean Walker was also thinking seriously about his future. Serving on the teaching staff of a Christian Service Camp in Illinois, he shared a dorm room with a student from the seminary also on the camp staff. One night, as the student remembered it, Walker was very restless. When the student asked if something were wrong, his professor said that he was facing a terrible decision, whether to leave the School of Religion. By the end of the year his decision was made, with reverberations that continued many years afterward. Walker left the School of Religion in order to become president of Milligan College in Tennessee. This old-line Disciples school, where Frederick D. Kershner had once been president, was sympathetic with the conservative side of Disciples debates; this college could be happy with a president who believed the way that Walker believed. More important, the presidency of Milligan College provided Walker a platform on which to create a new seminary that would hold to the conservative traditions of the Christian Churches. The mission to recreate the School of Religion in exile had also been placed "in the best possible hands."

When Walker discussed the invitation to go to Milligan, Shelton gave him his blessing. The battle for control had been won—first with the University, then with the Christian Foundation, and finally with his own faculty. Now he could begin the next and more dynamic phase of developing a seminary to serve the Kingdom of God.

6
For the Sake of the Kingdom

The Decision to Become Christian Theological Seminary, 1950–1958

After six years of hard work, Orman L. Shelton could see his vision taking shape in the life of the Seminary. Now it was time to take it to the churches. The first step was a luncheon conference with J. Irwin Miller on December 15, 1949.¹ Miller started the discussion by telling Shelton that he wanted to develop an investment policy for the Christian Foundation, concentrating on the School of Religion rather than scattering its funds "with no particular purpose." He asked the dean what the School's objectives should be and the budget that these objectives would require. Shelton answered that he wanted to increase enrollment from the current 214 to 275 or 300, which would call for the budget to increase from $100,000 to $143,000. They agreed that this budget might go beyond the resources of the foundation and that the School would need to appeal to the churches, which "neither felt was necessarily bad." The fact that 85 percent of Disciples congregations cooperated in pensions and missions gave Shelton reason to believe that they would respond to the School's invitation. He observed that comity agreements among Disciples academic institutions meant that the School of Religion would have to limit solicitations to congregations in Illinois, Michigan, Indiana, and Ohio, but that personal gifts and students could be obtained anywhere.

They agreed that they should concentrate upon the graduate program but emphasize that graduate students should think of themselves as "future preachers, not just as future teachers." The School's objective should be "to develop outstanding men who are as well qualified to be ministers as are other members of the community to do their jobs." Miller shared his concern that ministers no longer had the influence they once enjoyed. Shelton's answer was that the drop in ministerial influence "was relative, rather than absolute," that better ministerial education would enable ministers to regain their influence, and that he intended to improve the School's curriculum and educational program. They discussed Harvard's model of providing seminars for businesspeople, and Shelton indicated that the three-week summer courses for ministers provided an effective format to extend training to ministers. He proposed expanding the topics covered to include subjects such as labor and religion, ministry in industrial areas, and ministry in rural areas. They also discussed pending faculty appointments and retirements and the pension supplements that each would need from the Christian Foundation.

Midway through the next year, Shelton launched a glossy four-page newsletter bearing the title School of Religion, and in much smaller letters, Butler University, Indianapolis, Indiana, which was published twice or three times a year until Shelton's death eight years later.[2] The themes presented in this newsletter were few in number but constantly presented and vigorously stated. Shelton championed the faculty, especially the newer members; quantified the seminary's growth in student body and number of graduates; described the growing need for an educated leadership for the churches; and urged congregations and dedicated individuals to become financial supporters of the School of Religion and its students.

New Professors and Their Work

In the second issue Shelton proclaimed the coming of three new professors and in successive issues continued to announce new people. Most of these new professors—such as Alfred R. Edyvean and F. E. Rector— were young men in the last stages of their graduate studies, and in some cases already experienced in some aspect of ministry. Others—like William Robinson and Walter Sikes—were seasoned scholars and long-time leaders in the life of the church. They came to the Seminary from widely differing places— graduate school, the military chaplaincy, service with ecumenical agencies, the United Christian Missionary Society, the pastorate, and academic posts. In every case these new professors were people whom Shelton believed would help him reshape the School of Religion according to the new design that was emerging in his conversations with J. Irwin Miller. By the 1954–1955 academic year the faculty had been transformed. Of the fifteen professors, only Nakarai remained from the faculty that Shelton had inherited ten years earlier. Eight of the people had already received their doctorates, and five more were to do so soon. Fourteen were Disciples, one a Congregationalist, and another a Presbyterian. Three (Watters, Robinson, and Edyvean) had been born in Britain and one (Nakarai) in Japan. Only two (Robinson and Watters) were as old as the fifty-nine-year-old dean and two others (Sikes and Nakarai) were close to the same age. The other eleven averaged 40.9 years of age. Shelton described this faculty to Miller, stating that it "is composed of men of deep and reverent faith. In the main they would be looked upon as conservative in theology and view point, except by those who are ultra-conservative, and with them, anybody who is not an ultra-conservative is a modernist. I believe that it takes men of real faith to teach and enrich the faith of men in a theological seminary, and I have been very greatly concerned that we nurture, expand and enrich the faith of each man who comes here."[3]

The impact of these new appointments was increased as Shelton reported some of the activities in which they were engaged. Ronald E. Osborn and William Robinson were to attend the Faith and Order Conference in Lund, Sweden, August 15–29, 1952, Osborn going as one of the six principal delegates of the Disciples of Christ and Robinson as the representative of the British Churches of Christ and the World Convention of Churches of Christ.[4] Following the assembly, Osborn traveled through Britain, visiting "every known spot associated with Thomas Campbell, and the early life of Alexander Campbell," and later delivered a series of lectures to Disciples chaplains in the European Theatre. Toyozo W. Nakarai's new book, *Biblical Hebrew,* the publication of which had been subsidized by the Christian Foundation, was heralded as having "many revolutionary features" and as "being received enthusiastically by teachers and students."[5] A. C. Watters and F. E. Rector would be working in a new program that had just been developed with Purdue University in which rural missionaries would receive training at Purdue and receive credit on their degree at the School of Religion.[6] In the summer of 1953 Walter Sikes led an eight-week-long travel seminar to Europe, which the School of Religion sponsored because of the feeling that "a contribution can be made to an understanding of our world and its problems under the guidance of an interpreter trained in religious and social implications."[7] The program was successful enough that it was offered a second time the following summer. Two professors spent summers in the Holy Land—Toyozo W. Nakarai in 1953 and S. Marion Smith in 1954.

Special lecturers often spoke on campus, including Disciples from the United States and Great Britain as well as some of the most prominent figures in American Christianity. Additional lecturers came as a result of the second Assembly of the World Council of Churches, which met in Evanston, Illinois, in 1954. Quoting *Life* magazine, Shelton described the assembly as the "World's Biggest Protestant Meeting" and said that the School had gone "all out" to "enter into and become a part of it."[8] More than 125 students of the Seminary and eight professors, including the dean, attended some part of the assembly, and "41 people from 11 countries, officially connected with the Second Assembly, have been the guests of the School and given one or more lectures during the past ten years."

The radical change in the Seminary's stance toward the debates within the Disciples constituency was revealed in the indirect confrontation of Ronald E. Osborn with his predecessor, Dean E. Walker. During the 1940s and 1950s, Christian Church congregations around the country had divided because of their conflicts over the interlocking issues of biblical interpretation, relationship of baptism and church membership, and the kind of organizational network Disciples should maintain. A new issue had arisen: the control of church property. People who were increasingly uneasy because of the theology and ecclesial developments among the Cooperatives would decide to withdraw from cooperative relationships. Some of the members, however, would insist on continuing these relationships. Congregations would divide into two warring factions; then the question was which one would continue to own the church's property.

One of these divisions had occurred in Oxford, Indiana, and the ownership of the church's property was to be settled in a case being tried in the Benton County Court. Dean Shelton asked Osborn to counsel with the Cooperatives; it was generally understood that Walker, now at Milligan College, was advising the other side. The courthouse was divided with one set of Christians occupying one side of the room and the other set on the opposing side; a Jewish judge presided over this fractured Christian congregation. During the testimony Osborn showed that the founding pastor of the congregation had been acting as an evangelist on the staff of the Indiana Christian Missionary Convention and was a vice president of the American Christian Missionary Society. Therefore the tradition of the congregation was to be part of the organized work of the Disciples. Although the other side argued that congregations were free to change their affiliations, it was demonstrated that the decision to separate from the Disciples' organized work had been made in a congregational meeting that had not been called according to the congregation's own constitution. The legal case was settled, but the spiritual legacy of a divided church continued.[9]

The one person to speak a mediating voice among Disciples was William Robinson, longtime leader of the British Churches of Christ, whom Shelton persuaded to come to the School of Religion in 1951 as Frederick D. Kershner's successor in the chair of Christian doctrine. Having studied with C. H. Dodd, Robinson was conversant with British and continental scholarship, especially in sacramental theology and ecclesiology. Like the contemporary theologians whom he honored, Robinson spoke in traditional language but entertained radical ideas about reshaping the tradition for service in the contemporary world.[10] He had been introduced to the College of Religion by Dean E. Walker, who had met him while doing his doctoral studies in Scotland. In 1947 the Seminary had brought Robinson to the United States where he lectured extensively, publishing his lectures in a book entitled *The Biblical Doctrine of the Church*.[11]

Although Robinson addressed many of the same topics as did Kershner and Walker, his way of developing his ideas differed dramatically. Robinson undertook a serious discussion of the full range of ecclesiological issues, engaging in conversation the leading English-language scholars of his time. In books such as *Essays on Christian Unity*,[12] Robinson rarely referred explicitly to Disciples. Knowledgeable readers, however, could discern both his advocacy of ideas important to Disciples and his critique of the errors that he perceived among his Disciples church people. The terms of the discussion were those of Robinson's time rather than of Alexander Campbell's, and Robinson's hope seemed to have been a new meeting of minds across the ecclesial traditions. He appealed to conservative Disciples because he so fully supported classic Disciples ideas and the Disciples as a church. What other theologian of the Disciples had said, as Robinson did, that this "is my mother Church, the one into which I was born, and to which I owe all that I am"?[13] Robinson believed that the Disciples' doctrine of conversion, which included their understanding of baptism, was their most important contribution to a uniting church. Because he believed that only people baptized by immersion as believers should be admitted to church membership, he was strongly affirmed by the more conservative members of the School of Religion community.

Robinson differed from many of his colleagues among Disciples in his use of the Bible, disputing their dependence upon the doctrine of the infallibility of the Bible and their assertions that unity could be found on the basis of an infallible text. He claimed that the first generation of Disciples leaders used the Bible in better ways than did his Disciples contemporaries. The unity that Christ sought for the church, Robinson explained, was organic and institutional, expressed in one body and safeguarded by three features: the authority of a common faith, the obligation of two common sacraments, and the recognition of a common ministry.[14] Robinson's work as a theologian was grounded in his pastoral activities in the churches throughout his career; this aspect of his ministry was highlighted in his writings on worship, especially the Lord's supper. He deplored the slovenliness of worship in many of the churches, affirmed a classic theology of the eucharist, and recommended a pattern for the Sunday service that conformed closely to the liturgies of other church traditions.[15]

Two of Robinson's younger colleagues on the School of Religion faculty—Ronald E. Osborn and Robert Tobias—were also developing new ways of understanding the Bible, Christian unity, and the mission of the church. Although they had been acquainted since student days at Phillips University, these two men had gone in different directions in their later education and ministerial careers, with the result that their theologies were quite different. As their ideas became known, other members of the faculty found themselves moving toward one person or the other in ways that would later lead to tension within the faculty.

Tobias came to the faculty in 1953 following eight years in Europe, where his ecumenical activities focused upon relief activities in east Europe, faith and order discussions, and renewal movements sweeping across the church in Europe. His metaphor for describing the church's mission was "a once great cathedral, bombed, gutted by fire, its walls crumbling, the remains taken over by weeds, rats, and undisciplined children." How could people talk of a renewal of Christian faith and hope when the institutional structures of their churches had been so completely destroyed? The answer from these friends in eastern Europe, Tobias said, was that "when publications, Sunday Schools, lands, power, social institutions, and prestige were gone, they behold the soul and vitality of a living Church. Behind the crumbling and looted walls of an ancient structure stood a mobile tabernacle—God among men. And our friends in the East are bold to say that the Church was never more alive."[16]

Serving part-time as professor of ecumenical theology, Tobias also was a member of the staff of the Disciples' Council on Christian Unity. He organized a series of theological commissions and edited a quarterly journal in which questions of the church's mission in the world were discussed. Other Seminary professors who worked with him in these ventures included James Clague, Joseph M. Smith, and Walter Sikes. Tobias's voice was the strongest as he stated that Disciples were but one small church alongside the others and should resist the tendency to become stronger institutionally; instead, they should work to be renewed. Disciples should "seek a common faith at a deeper level than present agreement," and be ready to lose themselves by becoming part of the whole Body of Christ's church.[17]

Although Ronald E. Osborn was also interested in issues of unity, identity, and mission, he approached them in quite a different way than did these colleagues at the School of Religion. He had had little contact with the European intellectual tradition and was more attuned to the inner processes of Disciples life. His metaphor for understanding the faith of the church was the ocean, with its three levels: surface, currents, and the deep. Academic theology, which corresponded to the surface, had little impact upon the people of the churches. More influential were the major theological currents—liberalism, fundamentalism, and neoorthodoxy—because over time they would stir the deeper waters of the enduring faith of the people. Osborn believed that already liberalism had begun that penetration and would continue to command the loyalty of the people. Its effort had been "to retain intellectual honesty in religion and yet to maintain the essence of the Christian faith," which he summarized as "God the Father, the law of love, Jesus as Lord, and the Kingdom of God."[18] Fundamentalism, he believed, could not succeed because it had failed to address the problems that had brought liberalism into being. He discounted neoorthodoxy because of its pessimism and its failure to proclaim the message of salvation with clarity.[19]

Until coming to the School of Religion, Osborn had had little experience with ecumenical Christianity, but found himself increasingly active as a Disciples representative in world council sessions and in conferences looking toward unity among churches in the United States. He traveled widely among Disciples speaking on topics dealing with mission and unity, sometimes drawing as many as a thousand hearers. At first, Osborn seemed awed by people from other church traditions, realizing that except for William Robinson Disciples had produced no one who was able to represent Disciples' ideas in the world arena. He observed that no Disciples theologian had been able to persuade other churches of the importance of the Disciples' understanding of baptism which had become one of the causes of division. Despite these feelings of the Disciples' inadequacy, Osborn concluded that his church did have a witness to make in the ecumenical discussion. His list had seven items, some of which continued traditional Disciples ideas about baptism, the Lord's supper, and lay responsibility in congregational life. His list also included the continued belief in the dignity of humankind as distinguished from the "gloom . . . characteristic of Calvin, Kierkegaard, and Barth."[20]

Yet Osborn also had misgivings about what was happening in America which he expressed in the final chapter of a book based on lectures about the American church that he had delivered at the Ecumenical Institute in Bossey, Switzerland. The "haunting question," he said, was this: "Is the present good fortune of the American churches a true revival of Christian spirituality?" His conclusion was that Americans were confusing Christianity with American culture, and he closed the book with a question that would trouble him and his colleagues at the Seminary in years to come. "As American Christians . . . we must ask whether our faith and our obedience are sufficient to the needs of this dread hour. We must seek the grace of penitence and of submission to the guidance of God."[21]

Irrepressible Growth

While his new professors were developing their somber critiques of postwar Christianity, Dean Orman L. Shelton was facing what seemed to be the irrepressible growth of the Seminary. Virtually every issue of the newsletter provided further information about the increasing student body, the growing numbers of graduates, the increased faculty, and the resultant stress upon facilities and financial resources. In 1940–1941 the School had enrolled 90 students; in 1944–1945 (Shelton's first year as Dean), 146; in 1950–1951, 280; and in 1955–1956, 447. At his first commencement, June 11, 1945, Shelton announced 14 candidates for seminary degrees, including 10 who would complete requirements for the B.D. degree either in June or August. A decade later he announced 79 candidates for seminary degrees, 53 of them to receive the B.D. degree. The line of development was so constant that Shelton felt secure in projecting continued growth, and a forecast of 650 students by 1960 seemed reasonable.

This pattern of growth was matched with forecasts of the need for leadership in the churches, which Shelton based on reports by Disciples agencies, projections from the National Council of Churches, estimates from secular sources such as the National Association of Manufacturers, and his own studies of the need for religious leadership in an expanding society. Concluding that by 1975 Disciples needed to graduate 771 persons a year to fulfill their part of the responsibility of building the Kingdom, Shelton then stated that "our accredited seminaries graduated 125 ministers last year. No seminary is now equipped to enroll more,"[22] but, he added, the

School of Religion was making plans to provide additional buildings, endowment, and faculty to handle twice the number of students currently enrolled.[23]

Who were these students coming to the School of Religion in such numbers? One group consisted of veterans returning home following the close of World War II, making use of the G. I. Bill. In the six years beginning in 1944, 62 different veterans had been enrolled. A second group was graduates of unaccredited Bible colleges related to the Christian Churches. Their connections with the School of Religion had been established during the Walker-Kershner era, and many of the professors in the Bible colleges were graduates of the School and recommended that their own students also study at Butler. In 1946–1947, 210 students (omitting duplicates) had been enrolled during the year of whom 79, nearly 38 percent, came from the unaccredited colleges representing the conservative side of the Christian Churches.[24] They came to the School of Religion for practical reasons such as free tuition and the two-day schedule, which made it possible for students with families to serve larger churches including congregations beyond daily commuting distance. They also came because the School of Religion carried the reputation of honoring conservative convictions and helping conservative students pursue graduate studies in a congenial academic atmosphere.

Another reason for growth was the realization among the churches and pastors that an undergraduate education was not enough for pastors. Shelton described ministerial training as a two-story process, with the first story, provided by the brotherhood's undergraduate colleges, consisting of "a broad, basic program of education which lays the foundation for 'professional' training." The graduate schools provided the second story, the "specific and particular training for the ministry and other forms of church leadership"—the Bible and church history at one end of the spectrum and hymnology, speech, and radio-television at the other. This need for a two-story approach to preparation for the ministry was confirmed by the rising of the general educational level in the United States. "In a day when the standards for all professional work has [sic] risen, the ministry must be well-trained for the greatest work of all." The minister who was once the best-educated person in the community "must bring higher intellectual attainment to his demanding task."

Nearly every article about ministry and education in the *Bulletin* ended with an appeal to the churches to share in the cost of educating the ministry. For their own sake in years to come, and for the sake of the Kingdom of

God, they needed to support the preparation of leaders for the future. Among the examples given of notable generosity were the five new buildings and $600,000 that Mr. and Mrs. J. J. Perkins gave to the Methodist seminary that would bear their name and John D. Rockefeller, Jr.'s lead-off gift of $1 million for the benefit of Harvard Divinity School. Shelton encouraged the churches to support the Seminary by describing its pressing needs. Although the academic building was crowded far beyond the capacity for which it was designed, an even greater need was housing for students because the Seminary possessed no place for students to live.[25]

Although these recommendations were bringing in new financial support, they were based on Shelton's experience as an institutional fund-raiser early in his ministry and as a pastor in rapidly growing congregations. By the middle 1950s, however, he needed new methods of institutional fund-raising that could produce the significantly larger sums of money that the Seminary required if its growth were to be sustained. In 1955, following two preliminary efforts to devise a comprehensive appeal, the School of Religion announced a "Ten Year $10,000,000 program of Expansion and Advance." Half of the new funds were designated for expansion of the campus and half for expanded program and endowment. The faculty and School of Religion committee (the portion of the Butler board of directors to which Shelton reported) had been studying these matters for two years. A plan had been developed and reviewed by groups of laymen, ministers, and the state boards of the Christian Churches in the Seminary's area of support. The Disciples' Commission on Budgets and Promotional Relationships had given full approval to the launching of the first step and the announcement of the entire program.

The first increment of the expansion program, needed in 1955–1956, was $1.4 million for additions to the academic building, dormitory-apartment building, and increased endowment. Shelton announced that nearly a tenth of the first goal was already in hand—from Nettie Sweeney Miller, $25,598.60; Elsie Irwin Sweeney, $17,622.89; Clementine Miller Tangeman, $62,349.21; and Mrs. and Mrs. J. Irwin Miller, $28,263.66—for a total of $133,834.36. It was expected that all of the funds for buildings and endowments would come from individuals and families; and that some had already inquired about named professorships. "We believe in immortality as a part of our Christian faith, but there is an 'immortality on earth' in providing for continuing service here on earth either in a building that stands for one's Christian witness, or in a 'named' fund."[26] Dean Shelton and Robert Lewis, director of church relations, met with ministers and state boards of Disciples in New England, Pennsylvania, Ohio, and Indiana to present these expansion plans; they reported enthusiastic receptions. The Seminary also recruited a staff to lead the expansion program. On July 1, 1957, D. Wright Lunsford left the pastorate of Central Christian Church, Wichita, Kansas, to become director of financial resources. During his eleven-year pastorate in Wichita, the church had received more than two thousand into its membership and had raised $1,350,000 for major building expansion, missions and benevolences, and local budget. A few months later, two more people were added to the financial resources staff. Ervin L. Thompson came from the pastorate at First Christian Church, El Dorado, Arkansas, and Jack E. Sanders moved from the pastorate of First Christian Church, Alva, Oklahoma. Each of these men was described as having served effectively in their ministries.[27]

If the dean and faculty of the School of Religion had any doubts about this continued growth, there was no sign of it in the *Bulletin*. Nor did these reports discuss the ways that the School was responding to the social, cultural, and theological tensions of the decades following the close of World War II. Dean Shelton was aware that the growth of the School of Religion differed dramatically from seminary trends in general and had reported these flattened enrollments in the fact sheet that he had prepared for use in discussions with the School's constituencies. The fact sheet simply reported these facts without interpretation and gave no explanation for the contrast between the record of the School of Religion compared to other theological schools. Shelton's assumptions on the fact sheet seemed to be that the growth of the American churches would continue uninterrupted and that the School of Religion would also grow regardless of what was happening in other theological schools.

A Seminary of the Christian Churches (Disciples of Christ)

The enlarging of the School of Religion required campus planning, and here the University became part of the conversation. Dean Shelton was accustomed to making his own decisions about the School of Religion's program, and as long as he stayed within the physical confines of his building, he could maintain this control. Outside of the door, however, he and the Seminary's constituents were at the sufferance of the University, and suffer they did. Their building had been placed at the crest of the bank that overlooked White River and the canal, with a small parking lot adjacent to the chapel and a walkway across the front of the building. Most of the people who worked and studied in the building or who attended functions in the chapel had to park along the drive to the parking lot or on the street some distance away. Since there was no walk to the building from the street, these people had to strike out across the grassy plain in front of the building or walk a considerably longer distance along the drive to the parking lot and then along the sidewalk. On the other side of the building a gravel service lane was kept open so that coal trucks could deliver fuel for the building. Since the University refused to allow the lane to be paved, it was always rutted and in inclement weather puddled with water mixed with coal dust. Even Hilton U. Brown, for half a century the man who dominated the University's board and still served as its president though so frail that he required two people to help him walk, could enter the building only by being driven through these grimy puddles to the back door. Dean Shelton and President M. O. Ross dispatched testy notes back and forth, but the University refused to relieve these problems because the University's master plan called for further building in the general area of the service drive.

The School of Religion's representative in new negotiations with the University had to be someone from the Christian Foundation since the agreements that controlled all the relations between the institutions, defined the flow of revenue, and formed the basis on which Shelton had claimed his rights for essentially autonomous actions had been established between the University and the Christian Foundation. Now the head of his family's business affairs and their chief spokesperson in matters dealing with Butler and the School of Religion, J. Irwin Miller assumed the negotiating responsibility. His first step was to invite James Irving Holcomb,[28] president of the Butler board, and M. O. Ross, president of the University, to lunch in Columbus on November 1, 1955.[29] After a tour through the bank and lunch at Union Starch and Refining Company, the three men settled into a two-hour discussion in Miller's office. They went through each item on Dean Shelton's fact sheet, including the three-step, $5 million expansion program for the School of Religion. Miller closed this phase of the conversation by saying that funds were already on hand for the first step ($1.4 million), which included major additions to the School of Religion building, the construction of a dormitory-apartment building, and increased endowment to admit fifty more students per year. Before the Christian Foundation could start this work, however, "it would be necessary to come to some pretty clear understanding as to Butler University." This would be a good time to review the contract (with which he was not familiar) between the Christian Foundation and Butler University and for an area of ground on Butler's campus to be allotted in a manner on which the School of Religion could count. Ross and Holcomb agreed.

The matter weighing most heavily on President Ross's mind was what he "many times" referred to as the "anomalous relationship" between the two institutions. When Ross stated that the North Central Association was opposed to this relationship, Miller sought clarification by saying that this relationship was in operation when Butler had been re-accredited and had not been a bar to accreditation. Ross "confirmed this fact but mentioned exception taken to this relationship in the report made to the North Central Association at the request of the Lilly Foundation." Ross questioned Miller concerning "the desire and intention of the School of Religion Committee," to which Miller responded that "the possibility of the School of Religion changing its basic relationship to the University had never been discussed by the members of the School of Religion Committee." He pressed Ross and Holcomb for their opinion, which he later summarized: "It is evident to me that they, holding no hope that the School of Religion may ever be willing to come under the jurisdiction of the University, prefer that it become completely independent." Holcomb's "two best points of trade" appeared to be his assumption that the University would have to pay the School only $100,000 for its building if the School were to leave and that the School would have additional expenses if it were to operate independently.

Miller believed that Ross wanted to see the two schools continue a relationship that Ross frequently referred to as a "federated faculty." Holcomb stated his opposition to a dormitory, but not to academic buildings, in the vicinity of the administration building, which led Miller to conclude that the University would be willing to provide land for seminary housing near the current women's dormitory and for classroom space near the School of Religion administration building, granting both on a long-term basis "to the School of Religion as an independent but affiliated institution." Miller's position throughout the discussion was "that the status of the School of Religion was more important to the University than it appeared to the University and that any suggestions should come from the party that wants it to change." They agreed that Ross and Holcomb would make a proposal describing the relation between the institutions that they believed to be desirable and a proposed allocation of land that "would be fair and generous for the long term plan of the School of Religion and fair to Butler." Miller stated that he would have no part in agreeing to a plan that would make the School of Religion a second-rate institution in its status or facilities and that they should not contemplate anything but "a first-class solution to the problem for all parties involved." Miller told them he previously had thought that there was nothing inconsistent with his having an interest both in Butler and the School of Religion "but that after hearing Mr. Holcomb and President Ross talk today, I had received a severe shock and hardly knew how to evaluate what I had heard."

Miller concluded that the School of Religion was a nuisance to Holcomb and appeared to be a threat to his beautiful campus. In one conversation with Miller, Holcomb had expressed his exasperation by exclaiming, "Why don't you take your seminary to Columbus and do with it what you want!" He concluded that Holcomb's only interest in the School of Religion was his hope for the family's continued financial support for the Butler library and other buildings. Ross, on the other hand, had a "better appreciation of the value of the School of Religion to the University" and wanted to preserve it, though as a separate institution. Miller was convinced that the University would do all it could to preserve the relationship other than make major concessions of land around the campus or of buying new land.[30]

On December 13, 1955, Miller came to the Butler campus to continue the discussion. President Ross stated that the present relationship was unique in the University; but that a semi-independent relationship between a theological seminary and a university was in keeping with current custom and had advantages for both parties. It would be a loss for both schools if they were to make a complete separation and that even then they could pool resources, as in building a library. He believed that the University should make some allocation of land available that "would justify the permanent investment by the Christian Foundation of major capital funds." He suggested that the Christian Foundation propose to the directors of Butler a new contractual agreement, a statement of the capital and endowment program of the School and the needs it was to meet and a lay-out of buildings proposed and location of land desired. Then a joint committee with members from the University and the Christian Foundation could study these matters with the aim of reaching a solution agreeable and satisfactory to all parties.[31]

By the end of June 1956, the joint committee had been appointed and was well into its work.[32] The School of Religion members of the committee were asked to consider using the University's eighty-acre tract across the canal, but if they continued on their current site to avoid the area in front of the College of Religion building where Butler had plans for buildings.

The eighty acres north of the canal, the foundation members of the committee concluded, was unsatisfactory because of the danger of flooding. A second site, however, seemed promising enough that they had asked architect Eero Saarinen to prepare drawings showing a possible location of buildings. The School of Religion building served as anchor, and eleven new academic and residential buildings would be developed in four stages along the hillside and wooded area between the developed part of the University campus and the James Irving Holcomb Botanical Gardens. The design would have placed School of Religion buildings on the brow of the hill soon to be occupied by the carillon that would be built in memory of Mrs. James I. Holcomb, forming an arc to a spot near the garden house in the Holcomb gardens. The Saarinen sketch kept many trees and suggested a campus that snuggled into the hillside and preserved much of the character of that wooded location.[33]

When the joint committee reviewed this sketch, President Ross stated that few urban campuses had a natural forest and "the thought had been to keep this area intact and make it an important topographical feature to supplement the garden area." Kurt Pantzer, one of the Butler committee members, spoke favorably of the idea of a consolidated campus and of the value to Butler of a graduate school of the caliber of the School of Religion but questioned this plan because it seemed to deprive the University of its forest area and its opportunity of expanding its arts and sciences courses in years to come. Pantzer stated further that he was opposed to granting this much space in the middle of the campus to an autonomous institution, although he could be more easily induced to do so if "it were subject to all regulations of the Board of Directors, the Deans, and the President." Miller stated that while the Christian Foundation wanted a solution that was good for the University and the School of Religion, its responsibility to the Disciples of Christ was of equal importance and the foundation's "first responsibility." The commitment for this first group of buildings, he continued, would establish "the site of the College of Religion for possibly the next 500 years and the decisions of the men who make the first decisions on location would bind the future generations."

While some of the committee, representing both University and foundation members, were dealing with this issue as a matter of allocation of space and control of financial resources, Ross and Miller kept more important questions in the discussion. Ross stated that there was one fundamental question: "Is it advisable for two institutions with such magnificent plans to attempt to live together?" Miller phrased his question this way: "Is this worldwide communion of scholarship that exists on the Butler campus of value to Butler University or is it not?" This question, he believed, should be decided by the University, the president, the faculty, and the board. During the summer and early fall the Butler committee considered these matters, ruled out the forest proposal that the foundation committee had proposed, and identified two other sites that offered possibilities. One was the Shooters Hill property on 42nd Street which was owned in part by the University and three fraternities. The other was the J. K. Lilly estate across Michigan Road, which Butler expected to receive as a gift from the Lilly family by October 15 of that year.

In a private memorandum to his sister, Clementine Miller Tangeman, J. Irwin Miller stated some of his personal conclusions and filled in further information that he had gathered from members of the Butler board. He was sure that Holcomb wanted the School of Religion to depart from the campus because its demands would "interfere with his plans for the Birds and the Bees." Ross would like for the School to be completely under his control but knowing that the Christian Foundation would never allow it had as his second choice that the School "be set up as a separate institution with its own president, board of directors, confer its own degrees, and have a relationship with Butler University like that of the College of the Bible to Transylvania." The remaining members of the Butler board, he was told by Evan Walker, Harry Ice, and Dick James, believed "that it would be very bad medicine for Butler if the School of Religion were to leave, and they are most anxious to solve the problem." Mr. [Ervin] Thompson, "of the Fund Raising outfit" wanted a solution that would keep the School on the campus because its departure, he feared, "would imperil the success of his money-raising campaign."

Miller wrote another "confidential memorandum" on November 9, 1956, reporting on a phone call to him by Bishop Richard C. Raines of the Methodist Church. Holcomb had called the bishop asking for his evaluation of the School. Raines promised that he would send Miller a copy of any report he might prepare, but also said that if the School were to leave Butler "he intended to make an all-out effort to persuade the administration of the School of Religion to move to DePauw." When Miller called Shelton with this information, the dean reported two additional pieces of information he had received from Evan Walker of the Butler committee. The first was that Holcomb was claiming that Bishop Raines called the School of Religion "a third-rate accredited school" because students could earn their degrees while studying two days a week. Holcomb had wanted to include this opinion in the report issued by the Butler committee but Walker had refused until the matter could be checked out. Shelton had countered by saying that regardless of the number of days on campus a student had to complete the full number of hours for the degree and that the School was fully accredited with no qualifications or exceptions. Holcomb also had wanted to include in the committee's proposal that Butler would make land available "provided the Irwin family make a sizable contribution to the Butler library," but said Walker, "the committee unanimously refused to put this in the report."

The conversations, explorations, testing of positions, and negotiations continued into 1957. The key to the final solution was the bequest from Mrs. Carrie Frances Robertson to provide a chapel on the Fairview campus. Although her will had been admitted to probate in 1941, the University had made no effort to erect the chapel that she wanted built in memory of her late husband, Alexander M. Robertson. The possibility of using this bequest as part of the solution to the School of Religion-Butler University problem was investigated by legal counsel and two ways of using that money were considered. One idea was for the School of Religion to relocate on Shooters Hill and build a new chapel on a portion of that land owned by the University but leased to the Christian Foundation for 999 years. The other idea was that the University use the bequest as part payment for the School of Religion building and rename Sweeney Chapel as Robertson Chapel. By late in the summer of 1957, the basic decisions had been made that the School of Religion would be separated from Butler University and that the two institutions would continue to cooperate with each other. The yet-to-be named School of Religion would acquire property on Shooters Hill for its new campus and the University would buy its building using money from the Robertson bequest. Although the negotiations would continue on through the winter, and the School of Religion had much to do in order to become a separate educational institution, they henceforth would live together in a new way.

These decisions were released to the public on Sunday, April 20, 1958. President Ross and Dean Shelton announced that these agreements had grown out of the development plans of both institutions to "meet the greatly increased enrollment anticipated in both university and theological students." Butler planned new buildings, the first of which would be a new library, and required the land surrounding the School of Religion building. The School of Religion would move to a recently acquired site, twelve acres on the northwest corner of Forty-second Street and Haughey Avenue, and continue its $10 million expansion plan that had been announced the previous July. "The School of Religion," said the press release, "will incorporate as a separate institution, but the institutions will function as a single academic unit by mutual agreement." A second release was prepared by Ross and Shelton for Monday, April 21, 1958, announcing a $3 million gift to Butler University and the School of Religion. The gift came from the Christian Foundation and the Irwin-Sweeney-Miller Foundation and was believed to be "one of the largest single gifts ever given to a private college or university in Indiana." The School of Religion would receive $2 million to launch its expansion on the new campus and Butler would apply its $1 million toward a new library.[34]

The next five months were occupied by the hard work of drawing up the formal papers that would establish the new corporation, define the continuing relations between Seminary and University, and provide for initial organizational procedures. The Articles of Incorporation of Christian Theological Seminary, according to the laws of the state of Indiana, were executed on September 17, 1958, by the seven men who were also named as the first board of trustees.[35] The document listed eight powers for this new corporation, beginning with: "To educate men and women for effective usefulness in the various ministries of the church and for service in the Kingdom of God." It also stated that "the Seminary is a seminary of the Christian Churches (Disciples of Christ) and, as such, is related to and serves the churches of the Christian Churches (Disciples of Christ) in providing leadership and other services within the scope of its purposes."[36] The charter stated that "no person shall be eligible for election as a Trustee of the Seminary, or shall at any time act as such, unless he or she is a member of the Christian Churches (Disciples of Christ)." Among the first actions of the newly constituted board of trustees was to elect J. Irwin Miller as its chair, Orman L. Shelton as first president of the Seminary and Beauford A. Norris as first dean.

The Faculty Design for the New Seminary

While administrators and trustees were negotiating a new form for the Seminary, the professors were developing a vision of what their school could become. One indication of their spirit was illustrated by their transformation of *Shane Quarterly* into an enlarged and revised format with a new name, *Encounter*. In 1953 representatives of the Disciples seminaries and other Disciples agencies discussed the possibility of creating a "joint scholarly publication." Because the plans "were not matched with the necessary resources," the project failed. Subsequently, the faculty and administration of the School of Religion decided to enlarge the scope of their own journal, and in the winter of 1956 they launched *Encounter* as the continuation of *Shane*. Their purpose for the new journal was to consider topics from the various intellectual fields represented by their faculty and in the broader range of the humanities. They intended to address their articles "not to specialists in those disciplines but to religiously literate readers unable to specialize in every field." They stated that while their journal would speak from the Disciples tradition it would not emphasize articles about Disciples. Instead their purpose was "to enlist the best scholarship of this tradition and other traditions in the consideration of the major issues confronting the whole Christian world."[37] Ronald E. Osborn, who had followed Frederick D. Kershner as editor of *Shane Quarterly*, was the founding editor of *Encounter*.

A more important indication of the faculty's sense of self-determination was a long process by which it designed the new seminary which it hoped to create. Beginning in the fall of 1954, the Faculty Discussion Club, chaired by Walter Sikes, met frequently to discuss the first reports from the study of theological education that was being conducted by the American Association of Theological Schools (AATS).[38] The professors also referred to reports that the AATS had issued concerning the School of Religion and to the reports coming from Samuel W. Blizzard, director of the "Social Science in Theological Education Project." Funded by the Russell Sage Foundation and overseen by Union Theological Seminary in New York, the Blizzard project was studying the graduates of five seminaries[39] in order to evaluate their theological preparation and develop recommendations for introducing "social science knowledge and concepts into the instruction and training of the minister."[40] The professors then prepared brief discussion papers setting forth the ideals and programs of the departments of the Seminary. Sikes started the series with an analysis of the history of theological education, beginning with Robert L. Kelly's study of 161 theological schools in the United States and Canada that had been published in 1924.

In September 1956, Dean Shelton appointed a Special Committee to Study Theological Education, chaired by assistant dean Beauford A. Norris, with Ronald E. Osborn and S. Marion Smith as the other members. He suggested that the committee take two years to do its work and bring its findings to the faculty "so that free discussion might ultimately result in decisions concerning the future of our Seminary."[41] The faculty's initial assumption was that their seminary would continue within the framework of Butler University, but before the first year had ended it was clear that the School of Religion would become a separate corporation. Thus, the special committee found itself leading the faculty in developing the full outline for an entirely new school. On January 16, 1959, after more than two years of painstaking and sometimes hostile work, the faculty adopted the committee's "Special Study of Theological Education." Remarkably free of the "kingdom-building" language that marked Shelton's writings, the document offered hints that some of the professors, and probably the faculty as a whole, were more cautious in their anticipation of the future than their dean had been. The "Special Study" presented a comprehensive set of objectives, statements about theological education, and recommendations for the future of the new seminary.

The faculty recommended Christian Theological Seminary[42] as the name for their seminary because it was consistent with the purpose and program of the School, free of narrowness, designed to have highest possible acceptance within their constituency, simple and in good taste, in keeping with the tradition of the Disciples, and "not associated with any particular benefactor." The name should also communicate that this was a "special school for educating ministers."[43] The faculty stated the relationship that the Seminary would have with "the universal church" and the Christian Church (Disciples of Christ). Referring to Paul's reference to preachers in Romans 10:15, the faculty spoke of the importance of seminaries as the centers where "the church" prepares its "missioners" to go into all of the world. "The seminary is a Christian community for study, worship, and fellowship where the church is at work."[44] The document stated that the Seminary would "function responsibly within the denomination presently known as Christian Churches (Disciples of Christ)." The faculty's goal was that their school could "serve within the universal church as a denominationally related seminary with an ecumenical spirit."[45] The Seminary would prepare ministers who were to be *servants,* of Christ and of Christ's church, whose "first responsibility" was to help people *come to know God.* They were to have *a sense of mission to the world,* a mission outlined in religious terms: preaching, loving and serving people, shepherding the flock, leading the church to worship God, seeking to reconcile all people to God, guiding the people of the church to accomplish through the church the work that God intended, and guiding people in all of life's situations "to love one another as Christ has loved them."[46]

The faculty affirmed the importance of continuing "cordial academic relationships" with Butler University because of the long denominational relationship, the fact that Butler still held funds prescribed by donors to be used only for ministerial education, and the Seminary's need for "a strong under-graduate department of religion close by where pre-theological education can be taken." They hoped that the Seminary would "maintain the strongest possible consultative relationship with the University pertaining to the development of the department of religion in the university, with regard both to faculty and to curriculum."[47] The professors also recommended that the Seminary "participate wholeheartedly in the work of the Association of Theological Schools, and make it our aim to keep our standards at the necessary level to avoid all 'notations' by the Association."

The faculty spoke in detail about the students they hoped would be in the Seminary. Their objective was "to prepare ministers who through unique spiritual depth and a concern for true scholarship will be able to give competent leadership, both without and within the church."[48] The faculty intended that the most promising students from the entire country should be enlisted, that the program of study would occupy their major attention, and that the full life of the seminary would help students grow in their relationship with God and their ability to lead the church. Professors were to be "constantly concerned to improve their teaching materials and procedures," and campus life was to provide a wide range of social and religious activities for students. In order to fulfill their objectives for educating ministers, the faculty proposed an entirely new program for the B.D. degree, the first radical change in several decades.[49] The curriculum would be organized in five general fields instead of eight departments, with certain required courses in each field: Bible, twelve; theology, nine; history, six; with one additional course to be chosen from a group of three; culture and personality, twelve; Christian ministries, fifteen; with one additional course from a group of two; internship (fieldwork), two. These requirements totaled sixty-two hours, leaving twenty-eight elective hours for students taking this degree. The faculty stated that there would be no thesis in the B.D. program. The professors wanted the curriculum to have unity despite its complexity, and they intended that it impart knowledge, develop the disciplines of scholarship, and ensure a well-balanced education for whatever kind of ministry a student might undertake.

The faculty also spoke of institutional matters. It endorsed recommendations for developing a staff for the new institution and the financial goals that the administration had already developed. It affirmed that the new campus should provide for six hundred students, and that it be "so arranged architecturally that future expansion can be made if succeeding generations think it wise," and it endorsed the idea that Eero Saarinen be employed to guide the Seminary in its building plans. The faculty expressed its "gratitude for and confidence in The Christian Foundation," but also suggested that the administration of the Seminary "make sure that the necessary safeguards are provided to insure the continuance of our income from The Christian Foundation, whatever changes of personnel might occur in the administration of The Foundation; and, to insure that the program of the seminary shall at no time come under the control of this or any other foundation."[50]

The "Special Study" provided a comprehensive plan for the new Seminary. The committee of three that had led their colleagues had been privately lampooned as "one to think, one to write, and one to say 'Amen,'" but they had done their work well. These eighteen colleagues could anticipate the new era with the sense that despite their many differences they were united in the broad plan of how their new school would begin. Their vision of the new Seminary was adopted by the newly created Board of Trustees of Christian Theological Seminary on May 11, 1959. Their sense of achievement, however, was dimmed because of the loss of the leader who had been the key to the years of growth and had inspired the decision to become a new school. Most of the faculty had come to Indianapolis because they trusted "The Dean" and believed in the vision he inspired in them. But their honored Dr. Shelton had been sick during the latter stages of their work on the design for the new Seminary. The survivor of two heart attacks, he was one for whom easing up meant doing the work of only two men. On March 3, 1959, two days after his sixty-fourth birthday, and after a long visit with Irwin Miller, their friend and leader died. Orman L. Shelton had lived long enough for Christian Theological Seminary to be established as a legal entity, but like Moses looking over the Jordan from Mt. Nebo, while Caleb and Joshua led the people to the promised land, he was forced by death to remain behind, leaving his kingdom building, and his seminary of the Christian Churches (Disciples of Christ), to the younger people whom he had inspired with his vision.

Shelton worked during the period when the historic protestant churches reached their climax stage; their place in mainstream American society was secure, their functions within that society valued. These churches were closely parallel in structure and linked together in their efforts to minister to the rapidly growing and changing life of the nation. The way that ministers and congregations could be faithful to Christ and to the Christian mission was to work efficiently within the network of agencies that had developed within each of these national churches and in their ecumenical relations with one another. Shelton believed that the organized life of the Christian Churches (Disciples of Christ) was a faithful and effective "embodiment of an idea," to use Kershner's own phrase from a different era. He labored to his death in the full expectation that the support of the organized life of the Disciples was the best possible way to fulfill the historic vision of a renewed church and a redeemed world.[51]

It was Shelton's good fortune to preside over the School of Religion during the happy years when the churches in the United States were on a rising tide. Everywhere, as the country was powered by the postwar economy and the reinvention of American society, the churches boomed as elements in this new life. Certainly this was true at the School of Religion. Not only were churches expanding rapidly, and sending their young into the ministry, but slightly older people who had served in the war decided to enroll in seminaries on the G.I. Bill. Enrollment at the School of Religion exploded. Shelton was proud of this growth in numbers, and he was happy to report that it was the largest Disciples seminary, enrolling more than a third of all graduate full-time students for the ministry, and that it was the fifteenth largest seminary reporting to the AATS. He rejoiced in the fact that the School had the largest concentration of Disciples in any seminary and yet, with twenty-one denominations in its student body, had the widest range of any Disciples seminary. "The School of Religion," Shelton reported to the Christian Foundation, "has and maintains a well-balanced ecumenical program so that its students may be world-minded churchmen to serve the needs of the present day. It is in the very front of American seminaries in that respect."[52]

Shelton's commitment to this enterprise was expressed in a letter to R. H. Miller in 1951 when he commented on his decision to stay at the School of Religion rather than become president of the United Christian Missionary Society (an appointment that subsequently fell upon A. Dale Fiers). When he was pastor in Wichita Falls, wrote Shelton, the Pension Fund had made an offer, and shortly afterwards Unified Promotion.[53] He turned them both down after much thought, because "I came to the conviction that the ground work for the Kingdom of God is made in the local church, and that one was building at the foundation in the local church.... When I went to Kansas City," he continued, "I went there to stay the rest of my life, but when this situation [the School of Religion] was presented it came with the appeal that having to do with growing the ministry is strengthening the foundation units of the kingdom, i.e. undergirding and determining the kind of local church which is the foundation of the Kingdom. . . . It was at that point that I decided to make what was a very drastic and a very great step."[54]

Six years later, in the final stages of the negotiations with Butler University, Shelton held that same conviction. "This is a most thrilling and challenging adventure," he wrote to R. H. Miller, "and at times it looks like it is impossible in proportion but it must be accomplished for the sake of the Kingdom, and whatever must be accomplished for the Kingdom I know there are resources somewhere to accomplish. So we are moving forward with faith and confidence in the people of the church to respond." The dean believed that his faculty agreed. In this same letter to his longtime friend, Shelton thanked him for his prayers, then said: "We had a meeting Friday noon with all the members of the faculty and had a prayer circle around the faculty for the program. It is a most inspiring and challenging thing when the faculty is such a solid unit in their love for one another and in their desire to serve the kingdom to the utmost. We have a wonderful faculty."

To this faculty, and to his trusted colleague Irwin Miller, Orman Shelton bequeathed his vision and his work.

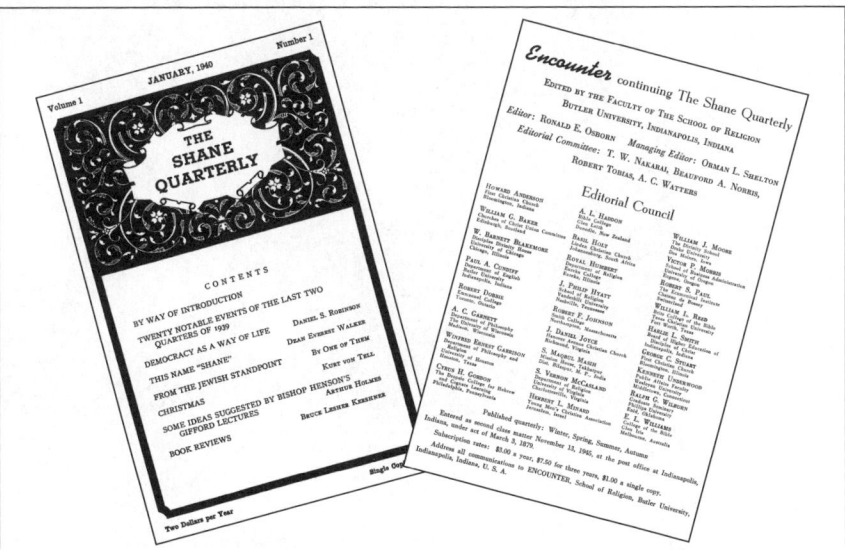

The Seminary's quarterly journal, *The Shane Quarterly*, begun in January 1940, became *Encounter* in the winter of 1956. Prices had changed also, going from sixty cents per copy to a dollar. (Both courtesy Christian Theological Seminary)

Top: The entering class at the School of Religion in the fall of 1953. In the front row are Vinton D. Bradshaw (third from left) and this book's author, Keith Watkins (eighth from left). (Courtesy Christian Theological Seminary)

Middle: The Seminary's office staff in 1955. From left: Donnette Gorman (Shelton's secretary), Barbara Culp, Sally Sheppard, Sharon Mart, Marsha DeWitt, and Laura Sheets (Norris's secretary). (Courtesy Christian Theological Seminary)

Bottom: Despite his many administrative duties, Dean Orman L. Shelton continued teaching, as with this church administration class in 1954. (Courtesy Christian Theological Seminary)

Left: Clementine Miller Tangeman presents President Beauford A. Norris with a resolution transferring $5.6 million in securities from the Christian Foundation to establish the Seminary's endowment, October 2, 1963. *Right*: Dean Ronald E. Osborn (left) presents a citation of appreciation to Sydney Steiman, rabbi of Congregation Beth-El Zedek and affiliate professor at the Seminary. (Both courtesy Christian Theological Seminary)

The faculty and executive staff of Christian Theological Seminary in Sweeney Chapel in 1963. Front row: Robert Tobias, James G. Clague, Calvin L. Porter, Frank J. Albert. Middle row: Alfred R. Edyvean, Lowell G. Colston, Walter W. Sikes, Lester G. McAllister. Back row: Franklin E. Rector, Bill L. Barnes. (Courtesy Christian Theological Seminary)

Left: Toyozo W. Nakarai, professor of Old Testament, near the end of his thirty-seven-year career at the Seminary, and Calvin L. Porter near the beginning of his thirty-seven-year career as professor of New Testament. *Right*: J. Irwin Miller, first chair of the board of trustees of Christian Theological Seminary, addressing the Seminary from the pulpit in Sweeney Chapel in 1963. (Both Courtesy Christian Theological Seminary)

7
Recklessly Committed to Christ and the Gospel

The New Seminary in a Decade of Cultural Crisis, 1959–1970

On October 28, 1959, Christian Theological Seminary was presented to the churches, colleges, and seminaries with which it would henceforth be associated. On this brilliant Indiana morning 105 representatives of religious and educational institutions joined students and faculty of the Seminary at University Park Christian Church for the inauguration of Beauford A. Norris as the Seminary's second president. The dual character of the event was stated by J. Irwin Miller who asserted of "this seminary and its leader" that "our responsibility to the Churches is to provide them with ministers recklessly committed to Christ and His gospel, and wise in the ways of witnessing, and to hold up to the churches a mirror of themselves as they are and a glimpse of what they may become."[1] The major address of the morning was delivered by Liston Pope, dean of Yale Divinity School, chair of the executive committee of the American Association of Theological Schools, and member of the central and executive committees of the World Council of Churches.

Accepting his office, President Norris stated that he could not "imagine a greater responsibility" than this and declared that "a readiness to cooperation and a deep concern for the unity of the church must direct much of the energy of the Disciple seminary executive." They had to be aware of their denominational heritage and the changes in the culture around them in order to provide leaders for tomorrow's church. "Will there be leaders enough?" Norris asked. "Will they be prophetic and dynamic in the leadership which they give or will they be lost in the real battles for men's minds and for men's souls?"[2] All of the speakers in the convocation referred to the century-old tradition of ministerial education at Butler University, a tradition being continued by Christian Theological Seminary.

The Crystallization of Plans and Aims[3]

The ebullience of these inaugural ceremonies masked "a series of events which sowed the seeds of unhappiness and discontent," including "the traumatic intra-staff and faculty struggle" that led to Norris's election as president.[4] Orman L. Shelton's final illness had begun in December, nearly three months before he died. As dean, Shelton had always kept his work to himself, allowing Assistant Dean Norris only limited access to major discussions, papers, and actions. In earlier times of illness Shelton had been strong enough that he could continue to direct the Seminary's affairs while recuperating. This time, however, he could do much less than before, and his return was increasingly doubtful. As the Seminary's second-ranking officer, Norris was responsible for the school and had to invade the privacy of the president's office in order to conduct the essential business of the Seminary. Upon Shelton's death, Norris was appointed acting president and David C. Pellett acting dean. With the help of Evelyn Hale, a student who had begun to work as secretary in the president's office, Norris began to organize presidential correspondence and other official papers that had been accumulating for some period of time and to determine the status of various negotiations and procedures in which the seminary was involved. Although the faculty had adopted their plan for the new seminary, it had not yet gone to the trustees. Furthermore, the process of disengaging from Butler and developing the Seminary's own structure had only begun.

As Norris worked at these tasks, the trustees completed their process for selecting Shelton's successor, a process that had begun a few weeks earlier when it had become clear that Shelton would not recover. Shelton had given his counsel to two members of the search committee—by phone to Theo Fisher[5] and in person to J. Irwin Miller who visited him on the day he died: "Beauford had developed well as an administrator and understood the Seminary's life; and the committee would have to look a long time before they could find someone better than Beauford to be president."[6] Miller had his own knowledge of Norris's abilities because for six months Norris had been the temporary pastor of North Christian Church in Columbus, which Miller and forty-three members of First Christian Church had established.[7]

At the April 3 faculty meeting,[8] Miller stated that the trustees hoped "to work out the most harmonious arrangements for mutual understanding and cooperation between trustees and faculty," and then he announced that the trustees "proposed to elect Dr. Norris as president." Norris left the room for the ensuing discussion. A motion that the faculty call a meeting, with acting dean Pellett presiding and Norris absent, to discuss the matter, lost by the vote of the acting dean who broke the tie, at which point Miller left the room. It was moved that the faculty concur in the trustees' action. There were no nays, but four abstained,[9] asking that their names be included in the minutes, and agreeing that the abstentions were "on grounds of procedure." Although shaken at first by this division in the faculty, Norris accepted the action of the trustees and decided to move straight ahead. "I am not going to apologize to anyone," he told people, "for being president of Christian Theological Seminary."

No longer acting president, Norris was free to act, and the situation required that he move firmly and quickly. He and President M. O. Ross of Butler asked the existing joint committee to continue during the interim until a new contract between the University and Seminary could be developed. They also agreed that the 1940 contract be terminated immediately in favor of an outline of working arrangements in which the Seminary, beginning September 1, 1959, would assume full responsibility for its business affairs.[10] The Seminary would henceforth purchase from the University special services needed for maintaining its building on the Butler campus and the University would assume full financial responsibility for its Department of Religion. The Butler Foundation would henceforth send funds for the support of the department directly to the University rather than to the Christian Foundation. It was agreed that this department would "continue to be regarded as the undergraduate school of the Christian Churches of Indiana for pre-ministerial education, and that financial support for this department be solicited from the Christian Churches of Indiana."[11]

Norris's effort to appoint a new dean, however, was constrained by activities already under way. Even before Shelton's death, Walter Sikes had been calling attention to Robert Tobias's stature and promise as a leader, perhaps intending that Tobias be recommended as the next president. Still the acting president, Norris assumed that Sikes's intention was for Tobias to be named dean and in a subsequent meeting of the Seminary's administrative council[12] made that proposal. When Tobias declined the invitation, Norris asked Ronald E. Osborn to consider becoming dean despite his commitment to teaching and writing; Osborn agreed. On May 11, 1959, President Norris recommended to the trustees that Osborn be elected dean, David C. Pellett director of summer program and graduate studies, and Henry K. Shaw director of publications. The trustees approved the recommendations but that evening in a dinner meeting with the faculty discovered that the faculty wanted a voice in naming administrative personnel. The next day the trustees rescinded the appointments and invited faculty comments. Norris received letters from eight of the faculty stating that Osborn was not the right person for the deanship, and in some letters there also were reservations against Pellett's appointment. On June 28 the trustees, after they had reviewed these letters, re-elected Osborn, Pellett, and Shaw to their positions of academic administration.

In this struggle with his faculty, Norris had decided that if he had to fight with the faculty over nominations, he would "be better off to fight it out first rather than last." He had conferred with Miller and Harlie L. Smith, president of the Disciples' board of higher education, himself a one-time college president, both of whom confirmed his feeling that it was imperative to establish the prerogatives of the president. Norris concluded that he would continue the tradition that Shelton had maintained of making decisions and staff appointments, in consultation with the trustees, and then announcing them to the faculty. Even candidates for the faculty were identified by administrative action rather than by open search.[13] Each faculty appointment was initiated by the president and dean, discussed with the field in which they would teach, and then invited to campus to meet the faculty. Upon confirmation by the faculty, the nomination was taken by the president to the trustees who would elect to office.[14] Ordinarily the initial term for an appointment was for three years, and the president and dean could recommend to the trustees that the term be renewed. The president and dean would monitor the professor's work and during the early years of service decided whether to recommend to the trustees that tenure be granted.[15] Little was said about procedures for evaluating a professor's work; but the trustees did establish mandatory retirement at the end of the academic year in which a professor turned sixty-seven years of age.

Norris called Cassius Fenton, a Methodist layman long involved in serving useful organizations in Indianapolis, to become business manager, with offices in the mansion at 940 West Forty-second Street on the new campus. D. Wright Lunsford was released, at the trustees' insistence, from his responsibilities as director of development, and on August 1, 1960, Bill L. Barnes began his work in this position.[16] Barnes had grown up in the Independence Boulevard Christian Church when Shelton had been pastor, graduated from the School of Religion in 1952, and since then had been pastor of a new Disciples congregation in metropolitan St. Louis. Soon after Barnes's arrival, the Seminary retained a consulting firm to advise the staff in their development program, with dramatic results in the Seminary's communications activities. Much of Dean Osborn's attention was devoted to activating the new curriculum and to making faculty appointments. Ten professors were added to the faculty from 1961 through 1968.[17] The faculty discovered that required courses were too large to conduct effectively and many of the elective courses were too small. Since the Seminary now had to conduct its own registrar's office, new procedures had to be developed.

Orman L. Shelton had been the "super pastor, coordinator, visionary and father-in-God" who had been able to blend "all those wild broncos from Sikes to Edyvean into a complementary team."[18] Norris and Osborn, determined to maintain a sense of common purpose within the faculty, encouraged the continuation of the faculty club for discussions of theology and theological education; they also established the annual retreat, an overnight working conference prior to registration day. The first retreat was held in early September of 1961 at Spring Mill State Park in southern Indiana. Despite the sweltering weather, the professors had to sleep two to a bed in rooms without air conditioning, wondering if perhaps this was too much togetherness. In succeeding years logistics were improved, and these gatherings became part of the annual calendar.

While Norris was developing his administration and Osborn his academic program, both guided by the faculty's "Special Study of Theological Education," the Seminary was faced with a crisis in two parts. One was financial, as the school was costing more than anyone had expected; significantly increased revenues were needed. Norris and Barnes responded by giving the first ever public reports of the Seminary's financial affairs, announcing in the *CTS Bulletin* of February 1961 that during the previous ten months income had been $401,000 and expenditures had been $370,000. Since the Seminary had to hold in reserve $56,000 of the $89,000 it had received from the Lilly Endowment, the operating deficit was more than $25,000. Whereas for most of its life as the School of Religion, the budget had been underwritten by the contributions from the Christian Foundation, this one source, even though it had contributed more than $190,000 during 1960, could cover just over half of the Seminary's operations. As the Seminary's officers gained experience, income from tuition, the churches, and other sources grew. Even so, the pressures to provide operating funds continued heavy.

Even more critical was the enrollment crisis. When the faculty had developed the "Special Study," they had understood that their decisions to be fully identified with the Disciples of Christ and to adhere to AATS standards would impact enrollment. They had not reckoned with the severity that these two decisions would have,[19] nor had they anticipated that the tailing off that had occurred at most other seminaries would also affect their school. On the opening day of the fall semester in 1961, the crisis hit them hard, for the final count for the day was under 200, less than half the number reported by Dean Shelton at the beginning of the last full year of the School of Religion. By the time that registration had closed, the number had risen above the 200 mark, but it was clear that the challenge of enrollment had to be confronted. The assured sources of students that had been key to Kershner's program and had continued to operate during Shelton's years, had now been compromised and new sources of students had to be discovered. Later that year, President Norris announced that Daniel D. Gilbert, a B.D. student, would join the staff as admissions counselor. He was to visit annually the four-year Disciples colleges and other accredited colleges in the Midwest, thus extending a program that had been begun by Professor Vinton D. Bradshaw.[20]

A Pre-Gothic Building

This dual crisis of finance and enrollment had an immediate impact upon the development of the new campus. Norris discovered that the Seminary and Eero Saarinen had not signed a contract and that Saarinen could not give this project the priority it needed if the Seminary were to meet its goal of moving into its new facilities by late1962. He suggested a small group of younger architects of promise whom the Seminary's building committee interviewed,[21] announcing in December 1960 that it had chosen Edward Larrabee Barnes, formerly design critic and lecturer at the Pratt Institute and Yale University and winner of architectural awards. Barnes began work that same winter, basing his design upon the faculty's "Special Study" and a newly developed architectural program for the new building. The Seminary decided to design a campus for an enrollment of 400, rather than 600, and to provide room for growth from the current enrollment which was reported, with a certain administrative generosity, as "about 260."[22] By the fall of 1961, Barnes had developed a flow plan for the campus, along with first efforts to arrange spaces on the campus for the major functions of the Seminary's life. Although he would modify the location of proposed units, the rambling, interconnected segments of the campus were already determined.²³ Later that winter Barnes and the building committee, in consultation with the faculty, revised the layout of spaces, settled on a floor plan, created elevations of the buildings, and prepared a model that could be viewed on campus and photographed for the Seminary's publications.

While all of this was taking place, Norris had been working with increasing frustration to complete the purchase of the intended site. The history of this tract of land had been influenced by the 1889 decision of the Citizens Street Railway Company to develop Fairview Park as an amusement center. A five-acre site south of the park, between Forty-second and Forty-third Streets, was dedicated as a mission for the use of the poor and a benevolent society called the Summer Mission for Sick Children was established. A house and other buildings were constructed, including a chapel very close to the place where Sweeney Chapel would be built a century later. In 1927 the mission property was bought by an Indianapolis business man and during the next half dozen years the rest of the site was purchased by three other families who incorporated their village and named it Shooters Hill, after an estate in Virginia that one of the families remembered.²⁴ In the early 1950s, three of the houses had been acquired by fraternities related to Butler University.

For a time it had looked as though the Seminary would have to revise its plans in order to build around one of the parcels whose owners were demanding conditions and payments that the Seminary was unwilling to meet. Not until November 1961 could Norris announce that the purchases had all been made and the architect released to complete his plan. The completed design was presented to the Seminary's constituencies. Barnes had used to great advantage the site on a bluff overlooking White River and open countryside to the north. He described the design as "pre-Gothic," stating that the edifice "has an affinity with the Middle East and the time of Christ," and noting that "the forms are plain geometric" and "the surfaces are simple."²⁵ The chapel was the dominant feature, even though its location was different from what some of the faculty—thinking of Marquand Chapel at Yale Divinity School—had hoped for. With its tower rising 130 feet above the great court and seating for 600, the chapel would be an element of such mass and magnitude that all of the rest of the campus would pivot around it.

While plans for the building were being developed, the challenge of paying for the campus was foremost in the work of Seminary administration. The $2 million grant from the Irwin-Sweeney-Miller Foundation and the Christian Foundation, along with some $777,000²⁶ of additional money, had made it possible to secure the thirty-six-acre site and begin architectural work. Still to be raised, however, was the $3,223,000 estimated cost for constructing the entire campus. President Norris and Bill L. Barnes consulted with Disciples leaders in Indiana in order to participate in a major capital campaign by the churches, and they gathered support elsewhere in a determined effort to generate funds in the hope that the entire campus could be erected debt-free. When construction bids came in, however, the cost of new buildings was significantly higher than had been estimated. Reluctantly, it was decided that only part of the master plan could be erected: the auditorium and common facilities, administrative areas, seminar and classrooms, and faculty offices. The chapel would be housed temporarily in the auditorium and the library in the lecture halls and lower level of the academic wing.[27] President Norris knew that the Seminary would have to approach donors another time and concluded that he would receive a better hearing if he were asking for a library and chapel rather than for an auditorium and lounge.

Ground was broken on a blustery winter day, March 10, 1964. In a service of thanksgiving in Sweeney Chapel, J. Irwin Miller answered his own question of why money should be spent on expensive buildings in a world of hardship by stating that "one of the great purposes of education is to bring to each generation the best that the previous generations have accomplished." He quoted Winston Churchill's declaration that "we shape our buildings, then our buildings shape us." Matthew Welsh, governor of Indiana and a Disciple from Vincennes, Indiana, affirmed that "the relation of the church and government is vitally important in our society—the church holds up the ideal we hope as a nation to achieve."[28]

Construction took nearly two years and on February 11, 1966, the faculty, staff, and student body moved from the traditional building on Butler's Fairview campus into their own contemporary academic complex on Shooters Hill. On a beautiful Sunday in May an open house was offered to the church people of Indiana, with great numbers coming to admire the new facility. A program in the nationally televised series "Look Up and Live" was broadcast from the Seminary's communications facilities. On April 13, the Seminary hosted a consultation on the arts, featuring an address by J. Irwin Miller. That evening the Indianapolis Symphony, conducted by Izler Solomon, performed a special "Salute to CTS" in the auditorium. The Seminary choir sang "Canticle of the Three Children," a work commissioned for the occasion and composed by Richard Weinhorst of Valparaiso University. A modern jazz oratorio of Psalm 22, written and conducted by Dave Baker of Indiana University, premiered to an overflow audience on July 22 and 23. In the fall the dramatic events continued with the world premier of a satirical musical revue, "Sure as You're Born" by Helen Kromer and Gene Benton.

The dedication of the new campus took place in two services on October 26, 1966, with some six hundred people in attendance. Speakers for the day included A. Dale Fiers, executive secretary of the International Convention of Christian Churches (Disciples of Christ), and James I. McCord, president of Princeton Theological Seminary. Fiers stated that many who had been watching this "magnificent complex of structures" take shape had an "unconcealed intent . . . to make this one of the truly great seminary centers of the world—ecumenically as well as denominationally, intellectually as well as spiritually, theologically as well as functionally." As chief executive officer of the Christian Churches (Disciples of Christ) and a trustee of the Seminary, Fiers stated that "a seminary today is inevitably doomed to second-class institutionalism when its overriding major purpose is to keep the label and preserve the sectarian aspects of its denominational heritage regardless of the consequences." The kind of change that a seminary needed to undertake "comes only with obedient response to deepening insights into the gospel and the church's mission in the world."[29]

Finally, on May 24, 1967, the Seminary conducted a Convocation on the Arts and Act of Jubilation. The speaker was Amos Wilder, emeritus professor of Harvard University, and the event included a liturgical procession through the campus as the Seminary gave thanks for works of art that adorned its spaces.[30] Although many disquieting things were happening in American life and in the world, and much else was happening on campus, these liturgies of thanksgiving and celebration of the arts dominated life at Christian Theological Seminary during the first half of the decade of the 1960s.

Encounter with Tomorrow

The transformation of the Seminary in Indianapolis was taking place in one of the explosive decades of American history. A cultural revolution that had been developing for more than half a century, but which had been held off by two world wars and a world-wide depression, was finally triggered by the Vietnam conflict. The political environment was determined by the cold war between eastern and western bloc nations, with their reliance upon

Marxist and capitalist ideologies. Always conservative in its politics, Indiana was usually suspicious of anything that seemed soft on communism and consistently favored a hard line on international relations. When the nation voted for John F. Kennedy in the 1960 presidential election, the mood on the Seminary campus favored Richard Nixon. One student sat in his car on the street in front of the seminary building "weeping for the fate of the nation," and many others on campus felt the same way.

Popular culture was shifting significantly. The Beatles and Elvis Presley were transforming the people's music. In his movies James Dean from Fairmount, Indiana, became the exemplar of a new style of being young; while in their writings Kurt Vonnegut and Dan Wakefield, both graduates of Shortridge High School in Indianapolis, were portraying a new spirit of life that was strange to the traditions of Midwestern culture. Turning her anthropological attention to western culture as well as to New Guinea, Margaret Mead announced that whereas in the past the young had always learned from the old, now the process had been reversed. Reviewing the dramatic shifts in religious practice around the world, Thomas Luckmann concluded that a new social form of religion was developing. Whereas the development of a moral consciousness had always taken place within a social context, now this process was occurring without institutional guidance.

The mood of this period was captured in a paragraph that Susanne Langer had published in 1956 and republished in a collection of essays in 1962. She spoke of "our age" as an anxious time of transition from the age in which Europe and "Christendom" had been ascendant, to a new age that could not yet be discerned: "We feel ourselves swept along in a violent passage from a world we cannot salvage to one we cannot see; and most people are afraid."[31] Although these interpretations helped people to cope with the overturning of everything they had known, they were little consolation in the times of crisis—the torching of the cities, the trashing of universities, and the increasingly violent confrontations of youth and older people.

This widespread social upheaval was expressed in three social currents that washed over the Seminary during these years. The civil rights movement made sense to the administration, faculty, and a large part of the student body who agreed with the justice of the movement, rejoiced in the religious base of the appeal and leadership of the movement, and eagerly watched its struggles. Eight students participated in the Theological Students' Vigil in Washington, D.C., in the spring of 1964 and a few persons, including Dean Osborn, participated in other events such as the march on Selma as an expression of solidarity with the people who followed Dr. Martin Luther King, Jr.'s nonviolent struggle.

Most members of faculty and executive staff lived in the Butler-Tarkington neighborhood immediately surrounding Butler and the Seminary and their children had attended School 43 or School 86 and Shortridge High School. Thus the faculty was inescapably interested in protests by African American students at Shortridge in the spring of 1969. Twenty-one students left the building in protest to actions by school administration. At nearby "Dignity Unlimited" (a bookstore that had become a meeting place for African Americans), they were counseled by Luther Hicks, a Methodist minister on the center's staff, to return to the steps of the school where they sang songs of protest. The students and several adults who had joined this peaceful protest were arrested by Indianapolis police, but the indictments were later dropped and the people were released. Among those protesting the city's actions were sixteen members of the Seminary faculty whose letter was quoted at length in the press. An ad hoc citizen's committee, including President Norris, was appointed to address the issue. Two members of the staff of the Church Federation, one of them a recent Seminary graduate, set up a tutoring program for the students that met for a time in the Canfield room on campus. Later, a detective from the Indianapolis Police Department consulted privately with members of the ad hoc committee, warning them that the protests had been the result of communist infiltrators, a warning that they did not believe, dismissing it as a sign of the paranoia of the times.[32] During these years that included the 1970 killing of students at Kent State University and a few days later at Jackson State University, people from the Seminary participated in rallies and special services despite the fact that the Indianapolis police were alarmed and warned against holding these events. The participation of Seminary people in these events, however, did not overcome the tension between these "white liberals" and leaders of the Black community who wanted them to be more confrontational.

Despite an earlier history of restrictive policies toward enrollment of Negroes at Butler University, the School of Religion always had been receptive to their enrollment and had graduated several of the Black leaders of the Disciples. Even so, it was obvious that the trustees, administration, faculty, and student body of the Seminary were mostly white, with most people of color being international students rather than American. Recruitment of African American and Hispanic students was increased as were other efforts to increase the visibility of people of color. One way of doing this was to recognize African Americans by awarding honorary degrees to people like Charles Spivey, who had been dean of Payne Theological Seminary and then had joined the staff of the National Council of Churches, and Duke Ellington. For most of the Seminary's history, Toyozo W. Nakarai had been the only person of color on the faculty. The first efforts to bring African Americans to the regular teaching staff had included conversations with half a dozen persons, some of them Disciples and some from other churches. The first successful overture, however, led to the call of Willie White, who in 1971 joined the faculty as professor of theology. Despite these efforts, the impact upon the Seminary was slight. To many people the Seminary's ethnic identity seemed the same as the prevailing color of the interior walls of the new campus—white.

The liturgical movement came to the seminary in two forms. The stronger and enduring form was the worldwide reform of worship that included the century-old renewal of Roman Catholic worship that culminated in the *Constitution on the Sacred Liturgy* of the Second Vatican Council and the several Protestant expressions of similar character. The more ephemeral form of the liturgical movement was an effort, especially in old-line Protestant churches, to replace existing music and ceremonial forms with those that were shaped by popular culture. Organs were to be replaced by guitars, classical music by the songs of Simon and Garfunkel or Bob Dylan, and preaching by consciousness-raising actions. For a time in the latter 1960s students pushed the faculty to loosen the professors' firm control of chapel and to allow experimentation to take place. At first, interest in Seminary worship was heightened, but by the close of 1968 there was a dramatic falling away. For the first time in the Seminary's history, campus-wide worship was reduced from four days a week to once a week. By now, it was clear that the auditorium was not a satisfactory environment for worship, and room 122 was made the temporary chapel. The little Holtkamp organ was moved there from the auditorium, and Seminary worship was conducted in this satisfying room until the construction of the library made a larger space available to be the provisional chapel.[33]

The more enduring impact of the liturgical movement was the form that gathered strength in most churches of the West and culminated in the publication of a significant group of modern books of worship. Keith Watkins was beginning his work on the faculty as this movement was getting under way. Through his participation in a series of Protestant-Catholic conversations on spirituality and the Commission on Worship of the Consultation on Church Union, he was becoming acquainted with the full range of the liturgical movement and with the scholars and writers who were generating a new set of liturgical systems and books. In his teaching and writing, and in his work as director of the chapel, he sought to find a way for worship to be catholic in substance and protestant in spirit. During these same years James R. Carley continued his leadership of sacred music, representing the classical music tradition in ways that gave it a bright depth. He conducted an annual children's choir festival that provided suggestions and encouragement for children's choirs in churches across central Indiana.

The ecumenical movement was the third way that the social upheaval of the 1960s washed over the Seminary. The National Council of Churches and the World Council of Churches were still gathering strength, and people from the Seminary were exercising leadership. Robert Tobias and Ronald E. Osborn, and others on faculty, continued their leadership in the conciliar movement around the world. The notable new development, however, was the election of J. Irwin Miller on December 8, 1960, to be the first layperson to serve as president of the National Council of Churches of Christ, for a three year term. Miller's interest in the National Council was shared by his mother, Nettie Sweeney Miller, and her sister, Elsie Irwin Sweeney. These two women had learned about the National Council from Harold E. Fey and Golda Fey because the Sweeney family and the Fey family had long owned adjoining farms in Rush County, Indiana. Because of his prominence as one of the leaders of the protestant establishment in mid-century, Fey had received tickets to give to observers at the ceremonies when the National Council was created and three of them had been used by the trio from Columbus. The Sweeney sisters had long been strong advocates of both the National Council and Church Women United and their families had been financial supporters of these organizations.

During Miller's presidency of the National Council, the Russian Orthodox Church applied for membership in the World Council of Churches, and in connection with this action a delegation of American church leaders, headed by Miller, visited the churches of the Soviet Union. Upon their return, Miller gave a report at the Seminary in which he discussed the many religious and political questions that were raised by the trip. He affirmed that the active presence of the church in the United States was one of the critical differences between the two societies, but pointed out that "the church makes this difference only because it is an active church— vocal, critical, courageous, influential in speaking to the evils and imperfections of individual persons but also of groups and of the whole society." If people want the church to stick to religion and keep its nose out of politics, he continued, they should study the Russian church. That is what it did before the Revolution, which is one reason why the Revolution came; and that is what the Communist government requires of it now.[34]

In 1963 a group of Russian church leaders returned the visit, with one of their stops being Christian Theological Seminary, an event that was one of the most colorful moments of its history. The cordial reception that the Seminary was offering to these representatives from on the other side of the Iron Curtain aroused the conservative instincts of many Hoosiers, including some from the political community. On March 7 Sweeney Chapel in the red brick building was filled with worshipers for the prayer service and a sermon by Archbishop Nikodim entitled "The Expression of Christian Love."[35] The ensuing discussion period in the student lounge on the lower floor, with its ramshackle leather chairs, filled the room to its capacity, with some students sitting on window sills.

This same lounge and Sweeney Chapel were also the locations in which Protestant and Catholic seminarians became acquainted with each other. Because of the new spirit of Pope John and the Vatican Council, the gates that had been closed between Catholic and Protestant seminaries creaked partway open. A series of annual visitations was held between Christian Theological Seminary and St. Meinrad School of Theology in southern Indiana. Each year a topic was chosen and students from both schools prepared papers on that topic. A delegation of students and professors would then spend two or three days on one or the other campus; the papers were read and discussed, the visitors would participate in worship, and there was ample opportunity for extended conversation long into the night. The topic for one of the years in Indianapolis was the meaning of the Lord's supper, and each side presented a paper that represented its tradition. The discussion was stiff with little evidence of rapprochement until Dean Osborn introduced a different line of thought. When he described a way of understanding the Lord's supper that drew upon the "mystery theology" of Odo Casel, as it had been mediated by C. H. Dodd and Gregory Dix, the confessional protectiveness of the Catholic and Protestant students disappeared and the rest of the evening was an experience of convergence that could not easily be forgotten.

Among the Protestant Churches of the United States a major focus of the ecumenical movement during these years was the Consultation on Church Union that had been brought into being by two of the most visible Protestant leaders of mid-century: Presbyterian Eugene Carson Blake and

Episcopalian James Pike. The Consultation soon became the cause that brought together the official representatives of ten protestant churches, including three predominantly black denominations, along with observer participants from Lutheran, Roman Catholic, Quaker, and Baptist churches that were not part of the Consultation. Ronald E. Osborn and Keith Watkins were included in the Disciples' delegation to the Consultation and brought their reports to the Seminary. The mood of the Consultation in those early years was wonderfully exhilarating and hopeful. By 1963 the Consultation had declared its intention to form a church that would be truly evangelical, truly reformed, and truly catholic.

Reflecting upon these ideas, Osborn developed a series of lectures that he delivered to various audiences and in 1965 published in an Abingdon Press book, *A Church for These Times*. In his concluding paragraphs, following (though unwittingly) the example of his colleague Robert Tobias, Osborn referred to a bombed-out cathedral in Europe. The Church of St. Katherine in Frankfort had been destroyed by Allied bombers during the war, and with the rest of the city had been reconstructed. All around the cathedral were acres of "modernistic aluminum and glass buildings, an island of contemporaneity girdled by residential structures from centuries long previous." The cathedral, however, had been reconstructed stone on stone to recreate the past. Yet this church was not the museum to antiquity that one might think; rather, upon entering one "will be stunned by the modernity of the interior." Osborn's conclusion was that the church in America was also "stirring with new life. Movements of reform and renewal are at work for the strengthening of her spirit, the stirring up of her mind, and the stimulation of her energies to meaningful Christian mission in our time."[36]

Perhaps this hopeful spirit was present in the faculty as it sought the right ways of responding to another aspect of the cultural revolution. The breaking down of traditional faith was expressed in the "God is dead" movement that was strong enough to lead the news magazine *Time* to print a cover using words without pictures for the first time in its publication history. In the secular and religious press, this movement took two forms. The soft form held that the reality named God existed, but that the theologies and liturgies that had previously expressed that reality no longer made sense to people. The hard form insisted that there was no such reality behind the word God. This theological movement was a remarkable contrast to the neoorthodoxy that professors Tobias, Walter Sikes, and Joseph M. Smith had learned from Reinhold Niebuhr at Union Seminary.

One by one, however, these men had left the faculty in the early years of the Norris-Osborn administration,[37] and by the latter part of 1965 the faculty was interviewing candidates for a vacancy in the field of theology. Gathered in the faculty lounge at Atherton Center, with the portrait of Hugh Th. Miller smiling benignly upon them, they asked candidate Clark M. Williamson about the death of God, and he answered by recounting a conversation with a parishioner while he was serving as pastor of University Church of the Disciples of Christ in Chicago. "When was the last time that you seriously mentioned the word God in a conversation other than in church?" he had asked her, to which she had responded, "I can't remember a time." "That," Williamson had told her, "is what it means to say that God is dead." When Sikes retired in 1964, Gabriel Vahanian, one of the best known writers on the cultural death of God, had been invited to campus for a lectureship so that the president and dean could consider whether to explore a faculty appointment with him, but their decision was that even if Vahanian would consider coming, his interests would not be consistent with those of the Seminary.[38] Instead, they invited Harold E. Fey, who was retiring as editor of *The Christian Century* to come as Visiting Professor of Christian Social Ethics.[39] Fey was one Disciple who for most of his career had been actively involved in the social witness of the churches. Sometimes wrong, as in his vigorous opposition to the Roman Catholic Church, Fey nevertheless represented the progressive, liberal, socially active character that was developing in this new seminary.

In the midst of this period of active development, the Seminary's chief administrative officers received another confirmation of their work. Clementine Miller Tangeman, president of the Christian Foundation, informed President Norris that in its meeting October 2, 1963, the foundation's trustees had decided to transfer the funds that served as the Seminary's endowment to Christian Theological Seminary. In a special convocation in Sweeney Chapel, Tangeman presented the resolution by which the foundation relinquished ownership of securities valued at $5.6 million and transferred them to Christian Theological Seminary. Earlier contractual agreements had guaranteed that 100 percent of the distributions from the Christian Foundation would go to the Seminary; for the current year that source had supplied $270,000 toward the $637,000 budget. Tangeman's statement in the convocation must have heartened Norris and his staff. Under the leadership of Dean Kershner, Dean Shelton, and President Norris, Christian Theological Seminary "has become, as we believe, the leading theological seminary of our brotherhood. Nor has its ecumenical witness escaped our notice. We are proud of every step that has been taken here in the cause of Christian unity." Her statement continued by citing "the eminent faculty" and their publications, leadership, and influence; and she stated that all of this "has given our Board cause for confidence in the future of the Seminary." Tangeman concluded: "We shall continue to watch the Seminary with keen interest and affection and we assure you that our Directors will always be numbered among your strongest supporters and most loyal friends."[40]

Stewards of a Tremendous Opportunity

During the next decade there was much to watch as Christian Theological Seminary continued to develop. The management of ongoing academic life was in itself enough to occupy the energies of the administrative staff and faculty. Students had to be recruited and guided in their studies. Because of the continuing difficulty to sustain enrollment, new ventures were tried, including sponsoring conferences on the ministry for college students. The development staff was enlarged and responsibilities for recruitment were added to the already heavy duties of raising operational and building funds and representing the Seminary in many community and church-related activities. The degree programs with Butler had to be cared for, and here David C. Pellett was especially valuable. The one member of the faculty whose connections with the University were heartfelt and cherished, he served as a strong connection between the old-line administrative staff at the University and the people at the Seminary.

New ways of serving the churches were tried out, including a non-credit Lay School of Theology developed and guided by Professor Lester G. McAllister. In 1968 the Seminary established a short-lived partnership with Central Baptist Theological Seminary in which Seminary professors offered courses that would be accepted for college level credit at the Baptist school. While the program would be open to everyone, "most of those enrolling are expected to be mature Negro men."[41] The Seminary's annual lectureships were consolidated into a week of lectures with a strong invitation going out to pastors across the Midwest, but with disappointing response. A more promising development was the decision of the Indiana Pastors' Conference, which for many years had met at DePauw University, to relocate on the Seminary campus. With its own board of directors and staff support from the Indiana Council of Churches, and an additional lecturer provided by the Seminary, the Pastors' Conference seemed to be a way to make the Seminary's new campus a theological center for all of the churches of the central Midwest.

Following the lead of a few seminaries around the country, the faculty developed a Doctor of Ministry (D.Min.) program to be launched in the fall of 1969. At that time no other Disciples seminary had made similar plans. This program provided for study in both theological scholarship and ministerial practice; while not intended as preparation for college or seminary teaching, the CTS D.Min. required students to do twenty-four hours of work in academic subjects, twelve hours in tutorials in ministry, and projects in ministry. In ambiguous language, the announcement referred also to "competence in working tools such as statistics and languages as needed in the applicant's proposed course of study."[42]

A significant part of the activity during these years was energized by a small group of entrepreneurial professors and funding from the Lilly Endowment and other sources of what later would be called "soft money." During the middle 1950s Alfred R. Edyvean and F. E. Rector had been consulting with the staff of the Church Federation of Greater Indianapolis in order to develop coordinated approaches to their common interests. Radio was already widely used by churches, and television was coming onto the scene as a way of communicating with the larger community. Although his longtime love was theatre, Edyvean had developed a keen interest in the broadcast media. The TV stations were interested in public service broadcasting, including religion. The Church Federation, a strong voice for Protestant churches, was interested in being a constructive partner in whatever might develop. The wording of the grants required that the federation join with the Seminary in planning, staffing, and conducting the projects. Rector was a sociologist by training, interested in demographics and their use by churches. At a time when urban communities were growing rapidly, with new neighborhoods emerging faster than at any other time in American history, it seemed to him that a coordinated approach to locating new churches would be important for shaping greater Indianapolis. Leaders of the churches agreed.

In 1958 these two professors were joined by another entrepreneurial spirit, Lowell G. Colston, who had come to teach pastoral care and counseling. At this very time, as hospitals around the country were arranging for chaplains to serve on their staffs, the medical institutions in Indianapolis were moving forward rapidly. Methodist Hospital, the Indiana University Hospitals, and Central State Hospital were in the process of appointing well-trained supervising chaplains to their permanent staffs.[43]

Clinical pastoral education was emerging across the country as a new way to help seminary students learn about themselves and become skilled in the caring ministries. All of this was coming together in a challenging way.

These openings called for funding well beyond that which could be provided by the Seminary's normal income from its endowment at the Christian Foundation. The senior staff of the Church Federation had already brought Dean Orman L. Shelton and staff from the Lilly Endowment into the discussion of these new ventures, and later President Norris continued the discussion, adding one more program, the seminary library. All of these interests came together in decisions by Lilly Endowment to fund these programs. In February 1961, Norris and Bill L. Barnes announced that the Lilly Endowment had awarded the Seminary $194,750 with which to purchase radio and TV equipment and IBM automation systems, to provide stipends for interns, and to meet other needs for their programs. Two years later an additional $138,275 was awarded. In 1966 a grant of $60,000 for planning and research was announced and a year later the endowment awarded $70,000 to help launch a repertory theatre in the Seminary's new auditorium.

The library's portion of the first grant, along with money from the Sealantic Foundation, had been used to evaluate the seminary's holdings, prepare recommendations for future development, and draft the architectural program to be given Barnes as he designed the new campus. Because pastoral care and counseling continued to grow nationwide, and the Indianapolis programs were so vigorous and well directed, this aspect of the Seminary's life continued with increased energy. Despite a succession of serious health problems, Colston's imagination and energy seemed limitless and his move through the ranks of national counseling organizations was swift. In 1968 he was able to attract a $232,000 grant from the National Institute of Mental Health to fund a five-year program that would train pastors to provide community-wide leadership in mental health. Initially Colston would direct the program with the assistance of Paul E. Johnson, who had come to the Seminary faculty on a part-time basis after retiring from his teaching post at Boston University's School of Theology.[44]

The first opportunity to assess this rapid development of Christian Theological Seminary was the accreditation review by the American Association of Theological Schools that took place in 1962. The Seminary prepared a self-study document for use by the accreditation team headed by Joseph Quillian, dean of Perkins Divinity School. During the team's campus visit, the faculty felt that they had learned more about Perkins and less about

CTS than they had hoped for. Nevertheless, the positive report from this first accreditation team following the Seminary's becoming an independent institution was reassuring.

At the same time that the Seminary was dealing with accreditation, President Norris was preparing his "Decade Planning Report." The report, which he intended to revise every two years, contained basic assumptions for long-range planning, major program objectives for the decade, and financial projections. In their May 1967 meeting the trustees adopted the forty-eight-page "Master Plan 1967–1977," which was Norris's answer to the question that J. Irwin Miller kept asking, "What would it take for the seminary to go first class?" It was shaped by Clementine Miller Tangeman's counsel: "Never start by asking, can we afford it? The answer to that question is always, no. Begin with the question, what does God want us to do? Then ask, how can we find the resources to do it?"

The report began with a list of presuppositions concerning excellence, improvement, and growth. It affirmed that the Seminary would continue as a seminary of the Christian Churches (Disciples of Christ), but it noted that it also would strengthen its relation with other churches. A set of four "targets" provided a concrete way of becoming first class: First, CTS would, during the next decade, gain recognition as the outstanding Disciples seminary; second as ranking with the outstanding seminaries of the Midwest; third as ranking with the outstanding denominational seminaries across the country; and fourth as ranking with the outstanding denominational and interdenominational seminaries.[45] This could come about if CTS would move forward aggressively to its potential as a seminary of four hundred students, faculty of twenty-eight, and fully developed facilities and resources. At the same time, the Seminary would seize the opportunity just developing to become one of the twenty-five to forty centers for theological study in the United States that the AATS was forecasting. The financial estimates were presented in eleven pages of small type that were likely to bewilder all but the closest readers. The vision was grand in scale but blurred. President Norris's spirit was clear, however: "As stewards of the Gospel we are also stewards of a tremendous opportunity in the church's history and mission."

Responsive to the New Age

Despite the plodding dullness of the "Master Plan," the Seminary moved forward in exciting ways, and in the tenth year of its new life, everything seemed to come together. The burden of indebtedness had been lifted when the Irwin-Sweeney-Miller Foundation had taken on the responsibility of paying the nearly $2 million that the Seminary owed for its new buildings. Clementine Miller Tangeman's challenge grant of $125,000 to finish up a few things, such as air conditioning, had generated a fund of $284,000 that cooled the building and cared for other incidental needs. Bill L. Barnes and his staff worked doggedly at the annual fund and while it was a struggle every year for the Seminary to operate in the black, the financial base seemed secure. New sources of money were undergirding several aspects of the Seminary's life. In addition to the ongoing stream of grants from the Lilly Endowment, the Seminary was receiving program grants from the National Institute of Mental Health and on-going financial aid through the college work-study program of the Department of Health, Education and Welfare.[46]

The board of Trustees was functioning well. Its first members had set the example of investing significant blocks of time in their trusteeship, and the term limits meant that new people were being recruited to work for the Seminary. The bylaws of the Seminary were changed, setting aside the requirement that only Disciples could serve on the board, which opened the door to new strength from other churches. Efforts to recruit people of color had brought John Compton, a rising leader among Disciples, Charles Spivey, staff of the National Council of Churches, and Frank P. Lloyd, a leader of the Indianapolis community, to its membership.

Furthermore, the student body was becoming stronger, and the promise of a brighter future was evident. Ever since the dramatic collapse of enrollment in 1961, the staff had labored to develop new ways of attracting students to Christian Theological Seminary. For most of the decade enrollment was in the low 200s, but in 1966 and 1967, fall enrollment had been 225. In the fall of 1969 the number reached 256, which while only one person higher than in the two earlier years, had fewer non-degree students. Fourteen of the students were enrolling in the new D.Min. program, and a few, the faculty believed, had come to Seminary rather than risk going to Vietnam; yet they contributed to a lively student body. The 1960s had been hard years in American life, with academic institutions in the center of the turmoil. CTS had come through these years with little disruption. Under the leadership of development staff member Herbert Gearhart, a series of conferences on the ministry for college students brought people from around the country to the campus to think about church vocations. In February 1970, a record 160 students from sixty colleges and universities spent two days on campus. The previous May, Gearhart had also conducted an invitational conference for black students, with 27 students participating. Although progress was too slow to believe that the goal of 400 would be reached by 1975, it now seemed achievable.

President Norris and Dean Osborn could take pride in the development of their faculty. Everyone who had opposed their leadership had left the faculty, and the teaching staff now consisted of people who were glad to be at CTS and who were content with the fact that Norris and Osborn were the leaders. Continuing from the Shelton years were Beauford A. Norris, Ronald E. Osborn, David C. Pellett, S. Marion Smith, Alfred R. Edyvean, James Blair Miller, James R. Carley, Henry K. Shaw, Vinton D. Bradshaw, and Lowell G. Colston; coming during the current administration were Keith Watkins, Lester G. McAllister, Calvin L. Porter, Donald R. Wismar, Edwin L. Becker, Clark M. Williamson, Charles B. Ashanin, Harvey Lord, Richard D. N. Dickinson, Jr., and J. Gerald Janzen. Already selected to join them in 1971 as their first African American faculty colleague was Willie White. These professors were working hard at their teaching and relations with students. They also readily participated in campus activities and in the affairs of the churches. They traveled and lectured, held workshops, and served on church and community committees. They were serious in their efforts to publish in journals such as the Seminary's *Encounter,* and a small number were beginning to break into book publishing.

After ten years of hard work, the Seminary was becoming established in the city of Indianapolis. Trustees like J. Irwin Miller and Harry T. Ice had already been known, but now others were joining them, including former governor Matthew Welsh. An advisory council of Indianapolis business and professional leaders was formed and some of the most prominent citizens of the city were now becoming involved in the Seminary's activities. The repertory theatre, with support both from the Seminary and Lilly Endowment, was becoming widely known across the city. An educational TV station was being developed and plans were under way for the CTS production facilities to be used by the soon-to-be-established educational TV channel.[47] The counseling service at the Seminary was becoming known as a place where people could receive help in dealing with the turmoil in their lives.

The Seminary's success in reaching out to the city was recognized when President Norris received a letter from the Metropolitan Plan Commission of Marion County asking the Seminary to plan, conduct, and host an urban forum on four dates in the fall of 1969. Leaders of the conference were to include internationally known authorities from the United States and abroad, as well as Richard Lugar, mayor of Indianapolis. In explaining why the commission had asked the Seminary to spearhead this effort, which was expected to draw as many as two hundred people, the letter said that it was because of "the great concern for and interest in the people of the Indianapolis area demonstrated by the Seminary."[48]

With all of these achievements in his decade of leadership, Beauford A. Norris, now sixty years of age, could feel that his administration had achieved much. Despite his quiet manner and ordinary gifts, he had expressed a reckless commitment to Christ and the gospel, and much had been achieved. The sense of achievement was shared by the faculty, executive and administrative staffs of the Seminary, and spouses who gathered for a dinner honoring Beauford and Shirley Norris on April 21, 1969. The evening was "marked by good humor and sincere appreciation" of his presidency. A letter from a professor on leave and away from the campus echoed the feelings of the people at the dinner. After stating his appreciation for Dr. Norris' leadership "in these changing and disturbing times," and for his president's "deep sense of commitment . . . to the mission and ministry of the church," this professor concluded: "I am continuously stimulated by the statemanlike leadership you represent: unwavering commitment to seminary education with genuine responsiveness to the entirely new age in which we must learn to live."[49]

8
The Liveliest Place in the Area

The CTS Ethos Emerges, 1965–1974

The 1960s and 1970s were difficult for universities and seminaries, especially those located at the centers of American cultural power such as Columbia University and Union Theological Seminary in the east and the University of California Berkeley and Pacific School of Religion in the west. The student revolts had taken control of campuses and brought about major, although temporary, changes in governance. The aftermath of these events in the 1960s was diminished enrollments and revenues at many seminaries, which resulted in the consolidating or closing of programs. Union Theological Seminary, for example, had sustained average enrollments of about 700 students throughout the 1960s but then experienced a rapid decline, falling to 456 in just five years. In 1970–1971 Union's inclusive faculty list, including adjunct and visiting professors, was fifty-five, but in 1974–1975 the comparable figure was thirty-five.[1] Because of significantly reduced enrollments in its School of Sacred Music, in which the late Robert S. Tangeman had taught, Union Seminary decided that it would discontinue this program. With significant new financial support from the Irwin-Sweeney-Miller family, however, the school was transferred to New Haven, becoming the Yale Institute of Sacred Music. In her letter to Yale's president, Clementine Miller Tangeman, widow of the deceased music professor, expressed ideas that characterized her family's attitude toward their support of educational institutions. She stated vigorously their Christian convictions; but at the same time affirmed that they did not intend to "bind the University" or to "lay a dead hand upon future generations." Rather, their aim was "to suggest a broad, and, one might even hope, timeless purpose to the enterprise, while recognizing that succeeding generations will choose to carry out that purpose in a variety of ways."[2]

The Disciples-related Drake University decided that it could no longer maintain its seminary. About the same time Oberlin College also decided to discontinue its school of theology; but in contrast with the Drake method of simply shutting things down, Oberlin was interested in merging the residue of its seminary with a theological program somewhere else. When news of the Oberlin decision reached Indianapolis, CTS invited Oberlin to become part of the new theological complex that was developing on Shooters Hill. Oberlin decided, however, to accept the invitation from Vanderbilt University instead of the one from Indianapolis, and this hope died. More promising were conversations between Beauford A. Norris and W. A. Welsh, who had become the president of Lexington Theological Seminary in January of 1965. At breakfast, during a meeting of the Disciples board of higher education, they talked in a carefully oblique way of uniting their two schools. They were pushed by the feeling among Disciples leaders that the consolidation of Lexington and Christian in the east and Phillips and Brite in the west would strengthen theological education among Disciples.

A committee consisting of six representatives from Indianapolis and six from Lexington met several times in motel conference rooms in Jeffersonville, Indiana, and exchanged campus visits.[3] Having moved into the new campus, the faculty and staff of Christian Theological Seminary were brashly confident of their future, and their self-interpretation to the Lexington committee was excitedly future-oriented. In contrast, the Lexington delegation had just celebrated a century of theological education at the College of the Bible, now Lexington Theological Seminary, and their self-interpretation focused on the 1917 debate over biblical interpretation that had "won the battle for academic freedom for the Disciples of Christ." The ethos of the two schools differed dramatically, and neither could imagine moving to the other location. The idea that they could effect a corporate merger but retain both campuses and programs, with a dean who traveled back and forth, was recognized as unworkable. Lexington people were convinced that if they were to move to Indianapolis, a new Disciples seminary in the southeast would soon be created. Although Lexington had just discovered a serious accrued debt in operational funds and CTS was deeply in debt for the new campus, neither school believed that its financial situation necessitated merging away its identity. Thus, this venture in growth by corporate merger also failed.

The Foundation for Religious Studies

During this same period the American Association of Theological Schools recommended a new policy to the seminaries of North America. Believing that the many small, usually free-standing, seminaries were insufficient and should be closed or consolidated, AATS executives proposed that some twenty-five to forty clusters of theological education be developed, each in close association with a strong university and, in most cases, in a major metropolitan center. The purpose of accrediting associations had always been to guide and exhort member schools, but at this time the AATS was becoming increasingly aggressive in its hortatory stance. To Beauford A. Norris and Ronald E. Osborn it seemed as though Jesse Ziegler, the executive director of AATS, was especially zealous in pointing out the shortcomings of their seminary. With J. Irwin Miller's push-pull on one side and Jesse Ziegler's goading on the other, they were caught in a vice that constantly tightened. The idea of clustering schools around their Seminary seemed to be a way to satisfy both of their friendly accusers. Although Butler could not be considered a major university, it did provide some of the elements that were needed, and the determination of the Millers for art, culture, and business to thrive in a remote place like Columbus, Indiana, already called "the Athens of the Prairie," gave further reason to believe that a theological center could rise up in Indianapolis, the city that some people called "India-no-place."

In mid 1965, Norris received communications from St. Maur's Priory located on the one-time Shaker community grounds at South Union, Kentucky. This Benedictine priory had been founded in 1949 by St. John's Abbey of Collegeville, Minnesota, in order to "exemplify the meaning of the Mystical Body of Christ in stark outline and underscore the teaching of St. Paul and St. Benedict that 'There is neither Jew nor Greek; slave nor freeman; for you are all one in Christ Jesus.'"[4] St. Maur had created a seminary which in 1963–1964 listed thirty-seven students in its four-year program, nine of them from Indiana. In the spring of 1964, St. Maur created the Institute of Race and Religion for the purposes of religious education and social action. The St. Maur *Bulletin* stated that twenty-six American Catholic Bishops and twenty-three Jewish and Christian social agencies had come to the support of the institute. Early in 1965, persuaded that the purposes of the seminary and institute could better be achieved in an urban setting than in rural Kentucky, St. Maur decided to relocate its enterprises in Indianapolis. It acquired an extensive tract of land on the floodplain across White River from the CTS campus on Shooters Hill and in December 1965 incorporated the Catholic Seminary Foundation of Indianapolis. Its "Preliminary Agreement" invited "other interested theological seminaries to share with us."

In November 1965 the CTS board of trustees passed a resolution expressing its delight in the St. Maur decision and affirming their desire to help in every way possible and their readiness "to work out all possible program interchanges" between the two schools. Beauford A. Norris wrote a proposal, dated January 24, 1966, to Bishop Johannes Willebrands, secretary of the Vatican's Commission for the Promotion of Christian Unity in which Norris described CTS as "an ecumenical school of the Protestant Religion."[5] The prior of St. Maur, Bernardin J. Patterson, and J. Irwin Miller met Willebrands and discussed the proposal with him, after which Augustin Cardinal Bea, head of the commission, sent formal notice of these developments to Paul Schulte, Archbishop of Indianapolis. Bea commented that this ecumenical development was consistent with the *Decree on Priestly Formation* and the *Decree on Ecumenism,* but he also stated "that the concrete course to be adopted here rests upon the local episcopal authorities."

Catholics in Indiana, including the Archdiocese of Indianapolis, had maintained a long and strong connection with the Benedictine community and educational institutions at St. Meinrad in southern Indiana. Here most priests of the archdiocese had been trained, and the "local episcopal authorities" saw little reason to change that pattern. A cool reception was given to the Catholic Seminary of Indianapolis, just enough for the school to operate, but little more. Nevertheless, negotiations continued and in November of 1966 President Norris announced that the Catholic seminary would open on the CTS campus the next fall "under a plan for a vast theological center for theological studies" that would include at least five protestant seminaries and "many Catholic orders," all of whom would be collected during the next ten years on a 155-acre site adjacent to the CTS campus.[6] While building its own facilities, the Catholic seminary would use classrooms and other portions of the CTS campus, expecting to enroll about sixty students its first year. These plans were presented in an enlarged joint catalog for 1971–1973,[7] its cover featuring a surrealistic view of *Sphere #6* in bronze color against a magenta background in which all detail disappeared. The eroded, gear-like surface of the sculpture, breaking the polished surface of this polished bronze sphere, intensified the impact. The guiding principle for this new venture was stated in the first paragraph: "Believing that theological education should be essentially ecumenical rather than sectarian, the two schools have cooperated in various ways while the necessary academic and ecclesiastical arrangements were being worked out." Later the fact that a Catholic seminary was the first to join with CTS was underscored as "taking a major ecumenical step at the very beginning."

When the Catholic seminary began its work on the CTS campus, few professors and students appeared. Instead of the anticipated sixty graduate students, only fourteen enrolled in 1970 when CTS enrollment reached a new record of three hundred. Of the professors who would enrich the intellectual life of the campus, only two maintained a regular presence, and they were persons without previous connections to St. Maur. Gerald W. Conway, with an S.T.D. from Gregorian University, Rome, was at first associate professor of doctrinal theology, and later president of CSF. A diocesan priest rather than a Benedictine, he dressed in non-clerical attire and conveyed a broadly secular demeanor. Sister Teresa A. Mount, from St. Mary-of-the-Woods Convent near Terre Haute, was listed as dean, registrar, and assistant professor of religious education.[8] She brought grace and strength that were consistent with her profession in the Sisters of Providence and changed the understanding of faith and piety for many of the CTS professors and students with whom she worked.

Meantime President Norris was developing the institutional framework for this consortium and in March 1969 announced the formation of a new corporation with himself as president. The Foundation for Religious Studies would have its own board of twenty-five trustees,[9] an executive director, and new funds for supporting its program. In addition to seminaries such as the Catholic Seminary Foundation of Indianapolis, the foundation hoped to attract other church-related organizations, especially those involved in research, planning, and training. The Ecumenical Center of Renewal and Planning, Inc., had already moved from Merom, Indiana, to the CTS campus; and its director, Donald W. Zimmerman, Ph.D., was firmly established in an office on the faculty floor. Soon thereafter the Seminary encouraged the repertory theatre at CTS to become a separate corporation with its own board of directors, and in 1971 the Repertory Theatre at Christian Theological Seminary became the first member of the Foundation for Religious Studies.[10]

During this period of spiraling hopes, Ronald E. Osborn was preparing for a year's leave, to be based at the School of Theology in Claremont, California. The decade had been a heavy but productive one, for in addition to all that he had done in his work as dean, which included creating the academic life of the Seminary and taking the lead in calling ten people to the faculty, Osborn had been deeply involved in major ecclesial developments. He had been at the center of the Disciples' delegation to the Consultation on Church Union and had used his extensive drafting skills for COCU's benefit. Osborn had been one of the leaders in the work of the Disciples' Panel of Scholars, a group of seventeen people who during the early 1960s developed a three-volume series of essays for the purpose of assessing the current state of the Disciples and proposing a course of action for the future.[11] When the agencies of the Disciples cooperating with the International Convention of Christian Churches decided that a major restructuring of their organized life was necessary, Osborn had become one of the most active members of the Commission on Brotherhood Restructure. At one of the early meetings of the commission, he had delivered the lectures that became the theological vision for the restructured church.[12] His point of view, as he developed these lectures, was that "theology and practical wisdom must interact in the work" of the commission.

In the 1967 International Convention Osborn had been chosen president for the following assembly, and in 1968 he presided over the last International Convention of the Christian Churches and the provisional general assembly of the Christian Church (Disciples of Christ).[13] In addition to all of these activities he had used a year's research leave to write a substantial book on the doctrine and function of the Christian ministry.[14] Since the summer of 1968, Ronald and Naomi had been grieving over the accidental death of their only child, Virginia, after her first year in college. The hard work of the decade and their continuing grief were enough. When he came back from Claremont, he told the president that he wanted to be free from the burden of being dean. Accepting the resignation, Norris moved quickly and nominated David C. Pellett to the trustees as the new vice president and dean. During this hopeful period, the trustees instructed President Norris to devote his major attention to the development of the consortium, and they created a new position, executive vice president, to handle the ordinary operations of the president's office. Professor Edwin L. Becker accepted this position.

Despite the dedication and competence of these two colleagues, Norris's ability to lead was diminished by the loss of Osborn from the leadership team. Over a period of fifteen years these two men had worked together with the imaginative power previously exercised alone by Shelton and

Kershner. Now Norris had to do his presidential duties without the insight and spirit that Osborn had provided. His presidential leadership was further diminished by J. Irwin Miller's easing away from the center. For twenty-five years Miller had been the most prominent advisor, challenger, door opener, and financier of the Seminary. During these same years he had been the central figure in the emergence of Cummins Engine Company as one of the major industrial corporations of the United States; he had also been involved in a wide range of cultural, religious, business, and political affairs. Since the Seminary's bylaws permitted trustees to serve only two consecutive three-year terms, Miller, who had chaired the board since its beginning, relinquished his membership at the close of the annual meeting in the spring of 1965. His close business colleague, Richard B. Stoner, succeeded him as chair, thus insuring that Miller would continue to be involved as consultant and challenger. Miller's friendship was genuine but never easy, and his leadership had been constructive and exacting, shaped by his commitment to excellence and his managerial style that never seemed to release the pressure to perform. For him to step back meant that Norris was left in an exposed position just when he needed all of the help that he could find.

Norris pushed forward to develop the Foundation for Religious Studies. He traveled constantly to present the dream to seminaries and institutes throughout the Midwest. The anticipated growth of the program called for new facilities for overnight guests and other kinds of activities. Therefore, Norris was authorized to consult with Edward Larrabee Barnes to revise the plans for completing the CTS campus and residential facilities. The costs escalated, but the new institutions would bring new resources and the result would be an ever grander consortium for theological education. The harder he worked for the Foundation for Religious Studies, the less Norris had to show for his labors. He shared projections for the future with the faculty and invited their comments about revising upward the plans for completing the campus buildings. Norris proposed a restructuring of Christian Theological Seminary so that its campus and endowment would be assigned to the Foundation for Religious Studies and the Seminary made into one of the participating schools. Despite Norris's efforts, the consortium in Indianapolis was not developing. The Catholic seminary had remained a marginal institution, and only one other seminary, the Anderson School of Theology, had showed any indication that it would move to Indianapolis. Its parent church, however, had refused to allow that action to occur.

It seemed to the faculty that their president was risking all that CTS had achieved and so far he could show nothing to justify the risk. With concern for their school, they asked President Norris and Dean Pellett to meet with them informally to share their growing anxiety about the future. In a tense meeting at the home of Richard D. N. Dickinson, Jr., they told their president of their fears. By this time, Norris was himself less confident. Despite his buoyant temperament and his grit that had enabled him as a 145-pound high school student to play winning football, despite his early years of achievement as president, he was unsure about what to do now. After a conversation with Norris, one of the Columbus trustees wrote an internal memorandum to J. Irwin Miller about this sense of discouragement, noting that Norris hoped that there might be some word in confirmation of his efforts.

A New Faculty Takes Hold

The confirmation of Norris' administration was already emerging, even if he could not see it at the time—the coming to life of a new seminary. The first of his achievements was to gather a band of new professors who created a distinctive theological climate at the Seminary. The last "President's Report" before Beauford A. Norris retired was published in November 1973. The faculty pages pictured twenty people, including Norris, who was soon to leave, and Thomas J. Liggett, who would succeed him as president. Also pictured was William G. Dever, who was temporarily listed as a member of the faculty although his primary work was with the American Schools of Oriental Research in Jerusalem. Of the seventeen regular members of the faculty, only Vinton D. Bradshaw, Lowell G. Colston, Alfred R. Edyvean, James Blair Miller, and David C. Pellett remained from the Shelton years. Eleven of the professors on his faculty had come to the Seminary since Norris's presidency had begun.[15] Most of them were still in the first half of their career, with a rising tide of interest in their disciplines and in their competence as teachers. In a series of installation addresses and essays published in *Encounter* these new professors began to articulate the themes that would develop into a new theological and spiritual ethos for their Seminary.

One of these themes was the transformation of biblical studies, and the first pronouncements by Calvin L. Porter and J. Gerald Janzen made it clear that finally the Seminary's approach to the study of the Bible had moved beyond the theological traditionalism that had dominated biblical studies at the School of Religion.[16] While Porter depended primarily upon theologically oriented writers, specifically Karl Barth and Rudolf Bultmann, Janzen built his thesis out of materials quarried from an essay on poetry by John Hall Wheelock. Both men quoted playwrights or poets, but for Porter they were incidental while for Janzen they provided the main structure of his address. Both men were fully aware of the tradition of technical, scientific biblical study, but both were determined to help students find the deeper religious meaning of these ancient texts.

Three of the new professors published materials that had implications for the study of church history and the articulation of a strong theological message for the churches. Lester G. McAllister[17] continued the Seminary's tradition of including someone with a strong interest in Disciples history; and Charles B. Ashanin[18] continued the tradition of including an historian with interests in the ancient ecclesial traditions. The relevance of historical studies for contemporary life was affirmed by Ashanin. Had the churches in East Europe, he suggested, been more knowledgeable of the church in the Roman Empire, they might have fared better in their struggle with communism. "It was this loss of historical knowledge which left the church so utterly unprepared to face Communism and the secular spirit of the modern world." In his conclusion he noted that the Christian religion teaches that we should have warm hearts for responding to God and one another and cool heads to guide us in our response. Instead, many Christians "have substituted hot heads and cold hearts, and this is the reason why much has gone wrong in the past of Christianity." Although his field was theology, Clark M. Williamson was also interested in the intersection of the church's intellectual tradition and its life in the contemporary world. In his initial lectures on campus and elsewhere, he offered technical expositions of the relationship of theology and history, with special reference to Ernst Troelsch and Alfred North Whitehead. He concluded his installation address with the assertion that "if redemption is to take place in history, then history must come within the sphere of God's tender, fatherly care; hence, only a supremely relative God can 'act' redemptively in history."[19]

Others of the new professors also expressed their strong interest in ways that the church and society intersected. Edwin L. Becker used the discipline of sociology as his way to reflect upon this connection. In his early addresses and in the classes that he introduced into the curriculum, he showed how the sociology of religions can help the church "to describe and make the world truly present to those whose ministries are to the whole man and the whole world."[20] Richard D. N. Dickinson, Jr.,[21] based his work on the discipline of social ethics and he insisted upon the importance of hard empirical data. His illustration, developed in a nuanced way, was American and Christian responsibilities in economic development in the poor countries of the world. Dickinson concluded that "it is by participation, involvement and sacrifice that we progressively discover our own real identity, our own meaning, our own humanity—as churches, nations and individuals called to oneness in Him." Keith Watkins began his work in the field of worship by focusing upon, first, the relationship between catholic substance and protestant spirit in worship and, second, the relationship between the church's worship and the church's effective witness for the gospel in the world. He concluded one of these essays by affirming that "when the church truly worships God, the rampant individualism of secular life is replaced by Christian *koinonia,* a foretaste of the true community which God intends for all mankind."[22] Donald R. Wismar focused his installation address upon the possibility for the rebirth of preaching in the contemporary world, basing his affirmations upon recent neoorthodox proclaimers and some of the assertions emerging in the liturgical movement.[23]

One by one, these teachers were developing new possibilities for the theological and spiritual life of the Seminary. All of them were articulating the ideas that were becoming the focal points of their future work and at the same time they were presenting themselves to their new colleagues. They may have felt a kinship of spirit, but at this point they had not yet reached a convergence that would establish a sense of unity in the intellectual spirit of the Seminary. Questions were still to be answered: How do the continuing faculty and the new faculty blend together into one? How do the ideas of all who are teaching at CTS blend into one coherent theological ethos? How can this faculty help the churches and their students deal with the new questions that were emerging in the revolution of the 1960s? How do all of these ideas come to expression in the academic life of Christian Theological Seminary?

In the spring of 1969 Dean Ronald E. Osborn began the process of creating faculty consensus by addressing a memorandum to the faculty describing the context of their work under the headings of the crisis of faith, negativism toward institutions, and confusion regarding ministry. The faculty responded by devoting a day to discussing these matters, using short papers by four of their colleagues as the focus.[24] As challenging as were these papers and the ensuing discussion, however, the faculty found that it was difficult to get hold of the ideas and the implications. Their day together ended with a feeling of frustration which they resolved, in part, by agreeing to continue the exploration at the retreat that fall, using as their theme "the coming shape of the church."[25]

The faculty felt the excitement of their work and were convinced that they were supported in their labors. Although their salaries were lower than the salaries in many other seminaries, the professors enjoyed two benefits that helped to compensate for financial struggles. The Seminary paid the costs for attending one scholarly meeting a year which made it possible for professors to establish professional connections with their colleagues around the country. The Seminary also established a policy for research leaves that at first provided the possibility of a year's leave, at full pay, after each six-year period of service, and later was amended so that a semester-long research leave could be taken following a three-year period of teaching. Most professors availed themselves of these research leaves, returning to campus with new angles of vision on their work, and usually with some kind of published material forthcoming from their time away from normal duties.

Professors grumbled at the tedious detail of committee work that took time away from their own study, writing, and teaching; they chafed at the process of triple discussion—first in committee, second at the academic council, and third in full faculty. Yet, they accepted their administrative burden because it provided them a strong voice in the policies and practices of the Seminary. The professors discovered that the administration supported them even when it was difficult to do so. Soon after he began his work as professor, one of these new appointees had been interviewed by a reporter from an Indianapolis newspaper and the resulting article may have misrepresented the professor but it grabbed public attention. Despite an uproar from readers, including some of the trustees, Norris and his staff were firm in their support. The professor wrote a brief statement clarifying his views which was included in letters to trustees, reporters, pastors, and church members who wrote to the Seminary about the article. Because most members of the faculty, including the one who had caused the flap, had not yet received tenure, they were reassured by the way that their president had stood by one of their colleagues.

As they worked together during those years, the members of the faculty and executive staff came to care for one another. Many of them went to church together, at Northwood Christian or University Park Christian, and their families were drawn together. During these years most faculty children attended the racially integrated Indianapolis public schools in their neighborhoods, including Shortridge High School with its student body that was three-fourths African American. One reason that this spirit could develop was the homogeneity of the faculty, since nearly all were white, male, American, married, Protestant, and middle class. Only later would a greater degree of heterogeneity contribute to the dissipation of the social cohesion of the faculty. This care for one another was strengthened as they shared the excitement of weddings and the grief of illness and death. Faculty and staff grieved with the Osborns at the death of their daughter, suffered with the Beckers and Edyveans during the illnesses and deaths of Georgia and Dorothy, and stood with their colleagues as memorial groves of trees were planted on campus. They accepted illness within their own ranks, including Lowell G. Colston's succession of major health problems and the loss of hearing suffered by S. Marion Smith and James Blair Miller. The faculty picnics at the Feys' farm in Rush County at the end of the school year were times when the growing children of these families played and the parents were drawn together in still another way.

A Lively Student Body

The positive energy of the faculty was translated into the student body. Although students moved through their years on campus and then went on their way, an ethos developed that was communicated to incoming classes and gradually deepened in the student body. Even before the move to Shooters Hill, the process began as some commuting students camped out for two or three nights a week in the 1040 and 1050 mansions on the new campus.[26] These houses that had been grand homes for the Hollidays and O'Neals were not well-designed as dormitories. Several students were assigned to each sleeping room and they shared common spaces for a little cooking, eating, and studying. Most of the commuters were men whose families stayed in the field where their churches were located. During the evenings in the dorms, as these pastor-husband-fathers studied, prepared sermons, and discussed the broad issues of faith and life, they found themselves drawn into friendships destined to last a lifetime. After the new campus was occupied, the shabby character of these living quarters stood out even more, and students demonstrated their discontent before administration and trustees. The initial plans for campus development had included housing facilities west of the academic buildings, and Edward Larrabee Barnes had prepared preliminary plans. It was with considerable disappointment that the president and trustees decided that the dormitory, which had eluded Orman L. Shelton years before, would also have to be set aside by Beauford A. Norris.

The good spirit of seminarians was communicated, in part, by the hilarity of opening activities each school year. The student association sponsored cookouts on the patio outside of the new dining room and for some years performed their interpretations of seminary life starring "Sammy Seminarian," set to the music of "Lit, lit, lit-urgy," parodied from *Mary Poppins*.[27] Because the academic schedule was arranged so that nearly everyone was still on campus on the last day of each semester, there could be splendid celebrations of the end of school. A series of Christmas parties in the common room, with every space filled, brought all of the staff, most students, and many family members together for carols, conversation, the visit of Santa Claus, and lunch in the dining room. For many of these years the last day of school in the spring reached its finale with the faculty-student softball game on the grounds in front of 1040. Faculty and staff members were still young enough to field the ball, clear eyed enough to bat well, and able to run the bases with abandon. Year after year, perhaps by strength and perhaps by the judiciousness of students waiting for their grades, the faculty and staff won those games. The one time that students won was when softball was rained out and a version of volleyball using a balloon was played in the common room. One of the events of the spring semester was the golf tournament using a sponge ball and with holes positioned in odd places throughout the long corridors of the campus.

Students also became involved in more serious issues of their time. They participated in demonstrations for civil rights both in Indianapolis and in cities of the South where many of the confrontations were taking place. They engaged in fierce debates with one another and with their professors concerning the whole range of issues that were being debated throughout American society. Although their demands and tactics were more subdued than those on many other campuses, CTS students also demanded changes in the internal life of the campus. They were granted participation or presence on committees of the faculty and on the academic council. They requested observer status on the board of trustees and were granted that right. Previously, the meetings of the board had been open only to trustees and the officers of the Seminary, who were to sit around the room in an outer circle able to speak only when specifically addressed. Now, a small number of students received the red books of docketed materials and freely discussed these matters with one another, to the consternation of professors who were never afforded the opportunity to see these materials. Students requested, with considerable urgency, that they have a larger part in preparing and leading chapel.

Students worked hard in their classes, often frustrated by the demands placed upon them by their professors. Some courses, like "The Church in Faith and History," often drew harsh criticism from students, yet many of these same students found that the work in their classes opened up new possibilities for their faith and life. They would find unexpected support, as one student testified twenty years later. While he had been a seminary student his father, a Disciples pastor, had died suddenly. The son could not understand how God could allow so young and good a man to die, and had he not been taking Williamson's class in process thought, he believed he would have lost his faith. Across the entire range of the curriculum students from all kinds of backgrounds found that their professors cared for the Christian faith, cared for the church, and most of all cared about their students.

One place where this experience was especially strong was in the students' field education. Early in his career Professor Vinton D. Bradshaw had been converted to the idea that work students did in the churches should be primarily educational and only secondarily remunerative. He studied the developing programs of field education in other seminaries, and set out to develop a strong version for CTS. Recognizing that most CTS students preparing for the ministry would work in churches throughout their time on campus, both to answer their calling and to generate financial support, Bradshaw developed SCOFE (Supervised Concurrent Field Education) specifically for them. Because he believed that practicing pastors could serve as mentors, he tried various ways of connecting students and these pastors in the field. One method was to create clusters of students with field assignments near one another and connect them with mentors in churches in the same area of the students' field assignments. When it became clear that closer supervision was needed, the seminars were moved to campus. When Bradshaw, with Norris's concurrence, decided that he had to earn a doctorate, he enrolled in the professional Th.D. program at the Boston University School of Theology and focused his entire program upon SCOFE, using his new academically acquired insights to evaluate and strengthen his program at CTS. Week after week his office received a steady stream of students interested in his counsel as they sought to overcome the challenges of their work in the churches. He had the ability to converse with businesspeople and farmers in the towns and villages where these student-churches were located; and as time went on Vinton Bradshaw was probably better known across the ecclesiastical Midwest than any other member of the faculty.[28]

During these years, the student body gradually grew larger and also increased in average age and diversity. The fall of 1970 was one of those moments of significant recognition because ten women embarked upon the M.Div. program. Although women had become increasingly evident on campus, most had enrolled in counseling, education, or music programs rather than the M.Div. When combined with the five women, four of them Disciples, who had begun their work in 1969, this new group of ten, mostly Disciples women on the basic degree program seemed to be a new beginning for the Seminary.[29]

The presence of Methodist students was also a factor of growing importance. As far back as people could remember, Methodists had been the second largest group on campus. Although some came from the two Indiana conferences, the students from the Central and Southern Illinois conferences made the larger impact. Many of them were mature adults—what later would be called "second career students"—and favored CTS over United Methodist seminaries because they found greater compatibility between their mild evangelicalism and the theological climate in Indianapolis. By 1970 the number of United Methodists began to increase. The average Methodist enrollment during the five years beginning with 1970 was fifty, and during the next five years the average increased to sixty-three. The Seminary provided courses in Methodist history, polity, and doctrine that the Conferences required for ordination; and appointed as lecturers the persons whom the Indiana Area of the United Methodist Church nominated.

The structure that connected all of these factors together was the curriculum, and especially the program of studies that led to the basic ministerial degree. Historically, students earned the Bachelor of Divinity degree, the B.D. In the 1960s, however, a few seminaries, led by Chicago and Claremont, experimented with other programs. What gradually emerged as a result of their first ventures and hard work within the accrediting association was a new degree, the Master of Divinity (M.Div.) Initially the AATS was determined that this degree would have to require more work than the B.D. After wavering in this regard, the CTS faculty decided to make a straight-across shift. Beginning with the commencement of 1967, the standard degree would be the M.Div., with no significant change in requirements from the previous B.D. Furthermore, the Seminary developed a procedure by which graduates could get a new diploma with the new degree terminology.

The name of the degree, however, was less important than the requirements for earning it. Here the faculty seemed always to be at work, sometimes tinkering with the details of the curriculum and sometimes making major changes. Their intention was to balance the church's theological tradition with the gospel imperative to be effective witnesses in the world for the increase of the love of God and neighbor. Their statements of purpose articulated these hopes. "From around the world," one statement began, "young people . . . are turning to Christian Theological Seminary . . . because they find the Seminary's balance of academic disciplines and involvement in human problems conducive to an understanding of man and society."[30] Yet their efforts seemed always to revert to the frustrating work of arranging and rearranging the courses and requirements. Their mood was well expressed in a comment that wise, tired S. Marion Smith exclaimed one day, "No matter how much you change the curriculum, as long as you have the same old faculty you have the same old curriculum."

These efforts at curricular reconstruction were efforts to arrange and rearrange four factors of curricular design. The first was the structural issue between a program that covered the full field in a general way and one that concentrated upon certain topics or practices of ministry. The second was the distribution between the classical disciplines of Bible, church history, and theology and the practical disciplines of sociology, psychology, and ministerial skills. The third factor was distribution among the fields. Some said that each field was equal in importance to the rest and therefore all requirements should be evenly distributed; whereas others said that the distribution needed to be determined by the relative importance of courses in their application to ministry. The fourth factor was the question of required versus elective courses. How much freedom should students have as they developed their programs of study? Each time the faculty revised the M.Div. curriculum it rearranged these factors.

During the late 1960s and early 1970s, however, the newly enlarged faculty sought to restructure its basic program, developing a system with two segments. The first was a thirty-six-hour component consisting of two semesters and a summer of full-time work with very little field engagement, followed by a forty-eight-hour component consisting of four semesters of academic work with more extensive field engagement. Although the catalog did not state the underlying rationale, the intention was to make a three-year M.Div. degree possible for CTS students by encouraging them to be in full-time residence as students for the first year and then to diversify with field education, clinical pastoral education, and other broadening aspects of work. The small reduction of total hours, from ninety to eighty-four, would also help. What the Seminary could not do, however, was to offer financial aid that would have permitted students to study without gainful employment. The M.Div. requirements made no reference to the five fields of study but instead described "four approaches" to theological study: "The Christian Faith, The Contemporary World, The Church and Its Institutions, Christian Engagement with the World."[31]

Within five years, however, the curricular issues were complicated by the creation of the Doctor of Ministry degree. The faculty sought to provide a basic program of studies that would be common to both degrees and then to provide two patterns for completing degree requirements. The M.Div. would require a total of eighty-four hours while the D.Min. would require one hundred semester hours of work and a doctoral project and paper. The intention was to offer two programs that, in effect, would offer regular and extended preparation for ministry. Most work would be the same whichever program students chose. This catalog made explicit what was implied in earlier descriptions of the revised degree: that a different system for assuring breadth of studies and depth of comprehension was now in place. Previously, the faculty had depended upon a large number of hours in specifically required courses. Now, the faculty would depend upon broad distributions in four of the fields combined with comprehensive written field examinations. Only the field of Christian Ministries would continue to achieve its objectives by requiring specific courses of all students on the M.Div. and D.Min. programs.

Two problems came to the fore, however. The first was that students had trouble passing the field exams with the minimum grade of B. Even when they consistently earned top grades in their courses, students struggled to earn a C on their field exams, and most students had to try a second or third time to earn a grade of B or higher. Once this pattern became established, the anxiety levels among students increased, heightening the probability of poor performance. The professors were unwilling to seek counsel from experts in testing, and over the next several semesters found themselves increasingly on the defensive concerning their administration of field exams. There was no answer that satisfied students and faculty alike to the question of why students who could do excellent work in courses failed the field exams. The second problem related to admission to the D.Min. track. Although the faculty had tried to avoid making the Doctor of Ministry a program for high academic achievers and the Master of Divinity for the rest, they admitted students as though this distinction were in place. When students finished their sixty hours of basic work and their four field exams, few were accepted for the D.Min. Professors had trouble accepting the idea that most of their basic degree students were actually performing at a doctoral level no matter how one defined doctoral studies. This faculty reluctance was shown by the fact that only four persons were allowed to graduate with this "in-course" version of the D.Min. degree.[32]

During these years the faculty tried to simplify its system of degrees. There never was any doubt about one fact: that the major program of study was the three-year degree that prepared for ordination. Long called the B.D., it had become the M.Div., and most students were enrolled in it. This program defined the work of most of the faculty. For much of the Seminary's history a two-year program with a major in Christian education or church music had also been offered for people who were not preparing for ordination. The Seminary had also offered work beyond the B.D. or M.Div. In conjunction with Butler University, students could take a Master of Arts or a Master of Science degree in an area of specialization that presumably offered greater depth to the students' professional studies. The Seminary also offered a one-year master's degree of its own—the S.T.M.— and a two-year master's—the Th.M. By the early 1970s, however, the system had become confused.

One reason was that a growing number of laypersons were interested in theological study and a second reason was the Seminary's intention to offer several distinct programs of study. The 1971–1973 catalog presented a newly rationalized system of degrees. It began with the M.A.R. (Master of Arts in Religion), which provided a one-year program of post collegiate study as an initial exposure to theological study. If students completing this program chose to continue on with another seminary degree, the work done on the M.A.R. could be transferred over. The M.Min. (Master of Ministry) degree was offered as a two-year program with specializations in Christian education, church music, communication, pastoral care and counseling, and community ministries. A different version of the M.Min. was offered as post-M.Div. or post-D.Min. studies, taking the place of the S.T.M. and M.Th. programs. Although the system made a certain sense on paper, faculty were soon to discover that students didn't understand or like the M.Min. designation; and further, the effort to use one degree for pre-ordination and post-ordination studies seemed unsatisfactory.

In 1969 the Seminary began an urban intern program that placed students in offices of business, labor, and political leaders of the city. With encouragement from Mayor Richard Lugar and his staff, the program was accepted by leaders in Indianapolis and students were invited into offices.

They met weekly in an action-reflection seminar to evaluate their work and answer the question "How do these decision-makers address issues of justice in our community?" This was one program, however, which Lilly Endowment was not willing to support since its religion department during this period consisted of persons who were interested in supporting conservative religious movements. Although they politely listened to the Seminary's presentation, they gave no encouragement to the program.[33] When Edwin L. Becker yielded responsibility for this program in order to become executive vice president, C. Harvey Lord was called to the faculty to oversee it and following his resignation from the faculty Robert S. Bates continued the work.

One of the reasons that students enjoyed life at CTS was that several groupings within the larger student body provided companionship and support. One group of students clustered around the theater. Many were studying for a master's degree in communications; but others were persons in the M.Div. program who were drawn by the excitement of the theater and the friendship that developed as they worked on productions each year. In its first seasons, the director Alfred R. Edyvean, the theater's staff, the seminary, and Lilly Endowment were finding their way, trying to establish the right mix of script and audience. Controversy over plays like Hansberry's *The Sign in Sidney Brustein's Window* threatened the continuation of the theatre, while others like Wilder's *Skin of Our Teeth* and Ibsen's *A Doll's House* brought acclaim and a growing audience of people from the churches and the general community of central Indiana. Being part of the theater, even as set builder or ticket taker, made people feel that they were part of an important new way to communicate the gospel.[34]

Another large group of students was focused on the programs in pastoral care and counseling. Some students were taking the master's programs in counseling, others were M.Div. students specializing in counseling, and still others were students on various degrees taking clinical pastoral education in the hospitals, with CTS credit. The students in pastoral care and counseling were more diverse than in the ministerial degree programs—Roman Catholics, Jews, Unitarians, humanists, and people from a wide range of protestant traditions could work happily in this program because it drew less upon theology and more upon psychology than did the M.Div. programs of study. Their studies and counseling activities helped people who were dealing with the deep issues of faith and life, and they found themselves indirectly exploring the mysteries of life and the reality of God. For many years Lowell G. Colston provided the energizing spirit that marked the programs in pastoral care and counseling, but he had developed a staff that consistently held similar qualities and developed them among the students.

During these hard days of the cultural revolution students were struggling to define who they were and to hear a calling to a way of life and work that could command their allegiance. Often impatient with their professors, they argued about chapel, complained about the curriculum, and accused their mentors of being insufficiently committed to society's struggles for justice. Feeling the need for a deeper spirituality than they were finding in the organized life of the campus, some created their own parallel structures, including a noon-time eucharist, evening prayer cells, and expressions of solidarity with leaders of the civil rights movement in Indianapolis. Yet on graduation day, they brought their spouses and children, their parents and church members, crowding the auditorium with people proud of the achievements of these seminary students.

Reaching Out to the Indianapolis Community

A third feature of the seminary that developed during the Norris years was a strengthened linkage with the Indianapolis community. Although previous leaders of the Seminary had been active in church affairs and had known some of the prominent people of the city, a new effort was begun under the leadership of the development department headed by Bill L. Barnes. Norris became a Rotarian and Barnes a Kiwanian so that week by week they would meet prominent business, professional, and political leaders of the community. They created the CTS Advisory Council as the instrument for establishing a closer relationship to Indianapolis leaders. Its function was "to counsel the Seminary administration regarding relationships to the greater Indianapolis community and recommend how the Seminary can be of service to the community."[35] Membership on the advisory council sometimes led to a later appointment to the board of trustees. This development of the Seminary's board was consistent with the pattern that was widespread across American religious and educational life. The same people who decided what kind of cars we should drive and cereals we should eat also shaped the policies of the churches and institutions of higher education. Near the end of Norris's presidency the board of trustees consisted of twenty-two persons in addition to president Norris. Nine were clergy serving as pastors or in other ecclesiastical posts, one was a layman serving as president of a Disciples college, and two were attorneys, including one who would become governor of Indiana. One trustee was director of research at a major hospital and the other nine were in business, most of them in highranking positions in companies like Upjohn, Eli Lilly, General Motors, and Cummins.

As new people came into the circle of friends and supporters, they developed a momentum that brought others into the circle. Cities have their own rhythms of public interest, with some organizations and activities coming to the center while others drift out of focus. By the middle 1970s CTS was moving into the center, with new trustees Thomas W. Binford, P. E. MacAllister, and Frank P. Lloyd as leaders. Each of these men was at the center of power in the economic, cultural, and political life of Indianapolis, and, significantly, none was a Disciple. Lloyd, the one African American, was Episcopalian, MacAllister was Presbyterian, and Binford was not identified with any church. They were able to attract other prominent community leaders to the board; their energy, connections, and skill were major factors in the Seminary's ability to move forward in its program.

While the recruitment of city leaders to the Seminary's board represented an important way of reaching out to the larger community, Project Understanding was an effort to minister to one of the most troubling aspects of American culture: the relations between the dominant white culture and the culture of African Americans. The Seminary's participation began in the spring of 1972 when Joseph Hough, the director of the specially funded, national program, invited CTS to come into the venture even though it was already under way elsewhere. With some reluctance, Richard D. N. Dickinson, Jr., agreed to be the CTS director, provided that Professor Robert S. Bates be asked to "be part of the team." The program was designed to combat white racism, and it called for the linking of churches and synagogues in local clusters with seminary students serving as program staff in these congregations. Racial tensions in Indianapolis at that time were shaped by the litigation concerning segregated public schools in Indianapolis and the certainty that some kind of busing would become necessary. Pastors knew that they had to make some kind of effort to respond to this areawide distress and therefore initially responded positively to the Seminary's invitation to participate in Project Understanding.

Funds were provided to give stipends to eight seminary students who would work with the clusters of congregations. Two of these clusters were formed, one called the Far North Cluster and the other the Meridian-Kessler Cluster. Meridian-Kessler had been a premier residential community on the north side of Indianapolis from the early 1920s onward. Until after World War II, like the Butler-Tarkington neighborhood immediately adjacent, it had been white and wealthy. After World War II, it had also experienced demographic changes, although most of the churches were predominantly or almost exclusively white in their memberships. At the same time that Meridian-Kessler had been changing, the newer suburbs to the north came into being; they became increasingly the residential communities chosen by white, middle and upper middle class residents of Indianapolis. Early in the process, it became clear that the pastors of the congregations in these communities were uneasy about becoming active in such highly divisive matters; and members of the congregations were mostly uninterested or unwilling to become engaged. In one of his quarterly reports, one intern noted that while the membership of the congregations in his cluster totaled eleven thousand people, the most they could persuade to attend a Sunday evening session was one hundred. Although the faculty's participation in Project Understanding had been encouraged, there was little interest among professors other than the people with official duties to the project. Before Project Understanding had been undertaken, the Seminary had already appointed a committee to explore matters related to racial issues in the city and at the Seminary. The two ventures seemed to be competing for time and attention.

When the program ended in 1974, the Indianapolis team for Project Understanding met in retreat to discuss its experience. It reaffirmed the assumptions of the national program which were that white racism had to be addressed directly, on institutional as well as attitudinal levels, and through religious congregations. Conclusions about the effectiveness of the project's work in Indianapolis, however, were guarded. Because of their late start and other challenges, they had achieved only a small part of what they had hoped could be done. Even so, Project Understanding broadened the Seminary's contact with some the strongest religious communities on the north side of Indianapolis. Its purposes continued after the project was formally closed as the Seminary used the impetus of this program to push forward its own efforts to overcome white racism at the Seminary itself. The faculty and trustees developed new procedures for faculty searches and they sought out new ways for African American students to find church-related work opportunities in Indianapolis. New efforts were begun to rethink the Seminary's curriculum so that the needs of black students would be more fully satisfied and so that white students would become "more informed by the phenomenon of white racism."[36]

A New Architectural Environment for Theological Education

The radical newness of Christian Theological Seminary was symbolized in the fourth legacy that Norris bequeathed to his successors: the campus itself. Although unfinished when he retired, the pre-Gothic campus had become known as one of the most important examples of contemporary architecture in Indiana. Many people who had only the vaguest understanding of what happened inside the building knew of the structure itself and admired it for its post-modern style. Just as Eliel Saarinen's First Christian Church and Eero Saarinen's North Christian Church had given these two congregations in Columbus national reputations, so Edward Larrabee Barnes's CTS campus was making a relatively unknown seminary a noteworthy part of the larger world.

Visitors to campus were astounded by the scope of the campus. From any one viewpoint on the outside, only a portion of the serpentine structure could be seen. As they walked the length of the cloister walk, stopping to look at the seminar rooms, going up the steps to the faculty area, walking through the administrative wing, and then into the common room, visitors realized how expansive the structure actually was. Then they would continue to the auditorium, unprepared for the oak-lined chamber with seating plunging to the thrust stage below. The vistas of glass on one side of the corridors, the gray floors, and the white walls and ceilings throughout the building conveyed a mixture of serenity and coiled energy. The space throughout the building absorbed people so that even when activities were at their height during the academic year, visitors were amazed at how little activity seemed to be taking place. One visitor to the campus soon after it opened exclaimed that she hoped one of her children would choose to enter the ministry so that he or she could have the privilege of studying in that building.

Part of the character of the building was the art that had been placed at important places throughout the campus. Victor Vasarely's *Quazar* dominated the entrance to the Common Room, suggesting by its multi-hued combinations of blue the cosmic scope of the gospel. Ben Nicholson's *Mycenae-axe-blue* in the Goodwin-Gemmer Board Room was striking to the eye even though its message was well interpreted in a sermon by Professor Harold E. Fey with the one word "judgment." Arnaldo Pomodoro's *Sphere #6*, in the main entrance to the campus, was described as depicting the tension between machine-age perfection and man's inner doubts; and successive generations of children have continued to rub the polished brass with their hands. George Ortman's banners of the cross in the seminar rooms and construction of the cross in the common room connected the seminary with its theological past; although they conveyed a static sense that could be a warning against freezing the gospel at any point in its history.

As remarkable as the new building was, it had significant defects. The heating and cooling system was complex and inefficient in heating and cooling the campus. Because the roof leaked in many places, the white plaster walls soon were water stained, and portions of the common room ceiling fell to the floor. The precast stone panels crumbled at the top and when laid horizontally at the entries to the campus deteriorated because of weather. Some of the furniture was more stylish than functional. Students and faculty often complained about the building. Having worked in conventional places, they had trouble becoming accustomed to a structure built to the scale of this new campus.[37] Yet, no matter how conventional or circumscribed the religious experience and theology of people who came to campus, they were opened to a new world by the physical environment within which their theological study took place.

A Moment of Equipoise

As Norris's retirement drew near, he and Bill L. Barnes continued their efforts on behalf of the seminary. One piece of good news came in one of the last phone calls during his presidency. As he prepared for his retirement celebration, an officer of the Krannert Charitable Trust called with a confidential report that Krannert would underwrite the new library, which Norris and Bill L. Barnes had been discussing with the trust. The Krannert trustees would wait to announce the decision after the new president had begun his work, but they wanted Norris to know as he went into retirement that the library was assured. Hearing this news, he rushed out to his cherry-red Karman Ghia automobile, stopped by the president's home to pick up Shirley, and drove the few blocks to Barnes's home. He had to tell someone the good news.

The spirit of CTS that had emerged during the Norris-Osborn years was expressed in statements by J. Irwin Miller at Norris's retirement dinner. This long time friend and colleague of President Norris affirmed that the Seminary had been wholeheartedly a part of the ecumenical movement while preserving the unique contribution that the Disciples make to the movement. He summarized the Seminary's improved financial support and campus—probably the best of all seminaries; and the growing strength of library holdings, faculty, and student body. Even more important, he said, "is the quality and spirit of the institution" for "through these years CTS has been the liveliest place in this area. It has pioneered in religion in drama; it has brought to Indianapolis the significant personages of our time; it has involved itself with sensitive issues when the Christian imperative called it to do so; and it has thoughtfully considered and responded to the needs of students."[38]

As its contribution to the honoring of their president, the faculty prepared a special issue of *Encounter* with essays by thirteen of their number. In his editorial, "Homage to a President," editor Clark M. Williamson noted that Norris had been called upon to serve in "one of the most turbulent and exciting decades in recent American history." Throughout this period, he continued, "Dr. Norris's steadfastness of character and breadth of vision enabled the seminary to step into the always uncertain but promising future which God holds out to mankind."[39] In his essay, J. Gerald Janzen affirmed that in life we crave to be educated "for earth and sky, for knowledge and imagination." The concrete experiences of ordinary life are transformed in moments of artistic experience, which are like that moment of equipoise at the top of the arc of a swing. Suppose, he continued, that

> God takes into Himself the raw materials of the whole world at any given moment, in all its concrete weights and colours, its sounds and textures, its joys and sorrows. Suppose that God literally bears the world in all its weights and specific gravities; and that in Himself He reconciles the world in that inclusive balance of all burdens, that deep harmony of all contrasts, which is His Peace. All disequilibrium, all discord, all inequity, is resolved; and the gravity of the world is transformed into His grace.[40]

For many people, this was happening during their years at Christian Theological Seminary. They brought the gravity of their life in the world and in the church with them to the classroom and chapel of the seminary. There a new kind of artistry worked its mysteries upon them and they went away transformed.

The administrative wing. (Courtesy Christian Theological Seminary)

Left: The Gordon Pipers lead the academic procession through the new campus on the day of dedication and consecration, October 26, 1966. The piper on the right is David I. McWhirter, a librarian at the Seminary. *Right*: Four professors in a faculty office in the new building, 1967. Seated: James Blair Miller and Edwin L. Becker; standing: Keith Watkins and David C. Pellett. (Both courtesy Christian Theological Seminary)

Conductor Izler Solomon leads the Indianapolis Symphony and the Seminary Choir in Shelton Auditorium, April 1966. (Courtesy Christian Theological Seminary)

Seminarians weather the snow as they prepare to leave for the Montgomery March, March 24, 1965. From left: Heung Ho Kim, Larry Gray, Jim LeSueur, Professor Lowell G. Colston, Nelson Scott, Dennis Short, (man in beret unidentified) and Joann Ford. (Courtesy Christian Theological Seminary)

Teresa Mount, S.P., dean and professor of religious education of the Catholic Seminary of Indianapolis, leads a chapel service in 1972 in room 122. (Courtesy Christian Theological Seminary)

Affiliate Professor John R. Compton with one of his classes in the late 1960s. (Courtesy Christian Theological Seminary)

Patrice Ramga and other students in the Seminary's common room during the 1972 arts festival. (Courtesy Christian Theological Seminary)

9
Coping with Adversity

Hard Times and the Deepening of Faith, 1974–1978

The decade of the 1960s had been a revolution in American culture. By the early 1970s the storms had abated, and it was time for all segments of the society to take stock of what had happened and then to move forward. Because the revolution had been focused on the Vietnam War, most people failed to realize that the deeper issues were the nature and forms of American culture. Even after the war was over, the reconstruction of life in the modern world would continue. Most vulnerable in this time of change were institutions such as mainline protestant churches. Strongly aligned with the dominant culture of middle America, they were shaken by the ideological and social violence of the 1960s. Yet, when the struggles abated, the churches could move forward almost as though nothing had changed. They soon were to discover, however, that the alignments had been changed. Secular forces were taking control of society and traditional religious forces were losing their grip. Churches that previously seemed to have little access to the hearts and minds of Americans—such as the Assemblies of God—surged in strength while the mainline protestant churches—such as the United Methodist and the Disciples—began to lose members.

Every church and church-related institution soon would be faced with the challenge of responding to this reversal of fortunes. At CTS this response took two forms. The more pressing, because the very existence of the Seminary was threatened, was the institutional and fiscal response, led by the new president, Thomas J. Liggett. In the longer period of time, the theological response of the faculty was more important because the professors were seeking to restate the Christian gospel so that it could continue to be effective in the post-revolutionary world that was taking shape all around them.

Survival the Goal

When Beauford A. Norris announced his plans to retire, the Seminary's trustees appointed a search committee to find his successor. Its choice was Thomas J. Liggett, who was president of the United Christian Missionary Society, the major mission board of the Christian Church (Disciples of Christ). Thomas J. and Virginia Liggett were lifelong Disciples and both had studied at the two respected Disciples' institutions in Lexington, Kentucky: Transylvania University and the College of the Bible. After further study at Union Theological Seminary in New York,[1] they had returned to Kentucky where T. J. served as pastor for three years while they awaited appointment to the mission field. In 1946, the appointment came through and they went to Medellin, Colombia, for a year's language study, followed by nearly a decade of work in Argentina. T. J. was then appointed president of the Evangelical Seminary of Puerto Rico, and during the eight years that he served in that position Virginia was the seminary librarian. Reluctantly, they left their work in Puerto Rico to return to the United States, where T. J. worked first as mission executive for Latin America and then as president of the United Society. From 1967 until 1972 Virginia Liggett served as reference librarian at the Seminary and then became an associate regional minister for the Christian Church (Disciples of Christ) in Indiana. In 1973 T. J. was a nominee (along with Kenneth Teegarden and Jay Calhoun) for the position of general minister and president of the Christian Church (Disciples of Christ), but after five and a half hours of voting the general board of the Christian Church elected Teegarden to that post.

The breadth and energy of Liggett's sense of mission were vigorously stated in a book he published shortly after becoming president of the United Society. "The whole course of history," declared Liggett, "is thus the context for mission. Economic development, political structures, social patterns, changing ideologies, new styles of living, international relationships and the emergence of new institutions are all caught up in the broad purpose of God." His evangelical spirit was revealed when he continued: "Christ died for the entire world and not for the Christian community alone. . . . The mission of the church, therefore is, through its total life, to bear faithful witness to God's love for the whole world and to seek in relevant ways, in the context of particular peoples and in particular places, to make this love tangible."[2]

Liggett was talking with the CTS search committee early in Richard

Nixon's second term as president of the United States. In the confidence of his reelection, Nixon had moved the Vietnam conflict into its final stages, developed new initiatives in foreign policy, and begun to reshape domestic policies according to conservative convictions. Despite several efforts to deal with the erratic performance of the economy, however, Nixon was unable to bring it under control. In 1973, when Liggett and the Seminary's trustees were in conversation, the inflation rate was 11 percent. In October oil producing nations in the Middle East announced that they would halt all oil shipments to the United States, with the result that prices of petroleum products increased sharply and the nation experienced an energy crisis. The stock market dropped sharply.

Even so, the Seminary's principal fund manager consistently reported that the endowment was producing far better than most other funds. Attracted by that fact, Liggett had asked his financial officer at the United Society why they couldn't do that well; and the answer had been that no one could produce that kind of income. The financial puzzle was intensified by the fact that despite such good earnings, the value of the Seminary's endowment was dropping rapidly. Stocks had to be sold at significant losses in order to maintain the payouts that the Seminary's budget required. In fact, the value of the endowment had dropped from $7.2 million at the end of 1968 to $4.4 million at the end of 1973 (and the spiral downward was accelerating, for by the end of 1974 it reached its low point of $2.7 million). The feeling was widespread that the Seminary was in serious financial trouble, but no one understood why.

Hardly had the new president taken his place at the president's desk in February 1974 when he received a call from an executive of the Krannert Charitable Trust asking if he intended to build the library. This phone message was the first word to Liggett about the Krannert promise to fund the library, and he didn't know how to respond. It was clear that the library had outgrown its temporary quarters; but no plans had been developed for immediate construction. More important, Liggett wondered how he could talk with the Seminary's constituents about new construction when he had to give an even higher priority to finding enough money to survive.

While the president pondered this question, a member of the finance committee of the board of trustees came to see him. Puzzled by good returns and shrinking endowment, he had painstakingly gone back over financial records and finally had discovered the problem: for several years the Seminary's principal fund manager had been providing erroneous information. Moneys being transferred to the endowment were being described as earnings on invested funds rather than as new capital. Instead of earning high returns on investments, the Seminary was having the same troubles that were inflicting other investors. Thinking that they were doing better than they were, the Seminary actually was selling off its assets in order to preserve the current operational budget. The trustee's message to the president was simple. After expressing appreciation for all that Liggett was doing to cut back on expenses, he stated that Liggett was "cutting off the rat's tail an inch at a time, but since the rat was going to die anyway," he concluded, "it would be better to develop some exciting new program and then go out of existence in a flash of glory." At the first meeting of the Seminary's board of trustees that Liggett attended as president, senior officers of the investment company explained the error to the board, apologized for their mismanagement, and resigned so that the Seminary could retain advisors in whom it could have confidence.

A few days later, Liggett was visited in his office by J. Irwin Miller and Richard Stoner, vice chairman of Cummins Engine Company, active member of the Seminary's board, member of North Christian Church in Columbus, and a prominent figure in other aspects of Indiana life. Miller started the conversation by reporting on the actions being taken by the Ford Foundation, Yale University, and Cummins Engine Company, on whose boards he served, and by Stanford University as reported by a friend who served on that board. In every case, he explained, the one goal was survival. After explaining that he shared this information in order to establish the context within which Liggett had to work, Miller asked the president what he was doing to face the crisis. Liggett responded by outlining the measures that he was setting into motion. Despite the high rate of inflation, the Seminary would reduce significantly the amount that it withdrew from the endowment. In order to shrink the deficit in operations, he was reducing expenditures dramatically on three fronts: stringent controls on utility usage; reductions in program, which also meant that the number of employees would decrease; and a virtual moratorium on salary increases. At the same time the Seminary's staff was increasing its efforts for the annual fund and anticipated several unrepeatable gifts that would help during the first year.[3] After listening to this report, Miller looked at Stoner and announced that they might as well go back to Columbus. "The Seminary's going to make it."

By this time Liggett was beginning to understand the squeeze that the Seminary was feeling. The budget that had been adopted in the spring of 1973 had authorized a withdrawal from the endowment of $50,000 a month during the 1973–1974 fiscal year. Even in 1973, that large a withdrawal was more than twice the amount that prudent institutions ordinarily would have taken, and with the rapid decline of the market during 1973–1974, the continued removal of funds at that rate was devastating. It soon became clear that a more radical approach to solving the problem had to be devised. As he worked on this problem, Liggett's guide—his Bible, he called it—was a book published by the Carnegie Foundation on the management of the endowments of educational and benevolent institutions so that they could have some assurance for the future. He was ready, in principle, to agree with the finance committee as its members developed new policies for managing the Seminary's endowment.

The new approach was based on a spending policy that "safeguarded the real value of the endowment so as inflation moved up, we allowed the endowment to grow."[4] The average yield of the New York Stock Exchange, rather than the earnings of the CTS portfolio, and the average annual real growth of the S & P 500 were two factors used by their fund managers. The income, as adjusted by this formula, was then split between growth of the endowment and current budget. The trustees were determined to achieve the goal of using not more than 5 percent of the endowment's value for budget support. Since the withdrawal that had been set prior to Liggett's coming was 12 percent, they decided to reduce the amount by 1 percent of the value each year, which meant that each year the budget would necessarily be reduced a corresponding amount.

Even though the recovery of the endowment's strength was given high priority, Liggett and the trustees also were attentive to the ethics of investing. These matters were discussed with their fund managers and procedures were developed for consultation with Seminary officers as the managers considered purchase of new stocks. The Seminary cooperated fully with the Center on Corporate Responsibility in New York City and voted its stock in support of socially sensitive issues, including employment, environment, and South Africa. Liggett acknowledged that they could not be "purists," using as his illustration the time when he had written to five companies in which the Seminary owned stock, asking questions about these matters. One of the companies wrote back saying that by asking these questions investors were "dabbling into business they didn't know anything about." The Seminary immediately sold its stock in that company. Another company, however, reported that one of its vice presidents did nothing but address these matters and sent Liggett a list of the things it was doing to respond to the ethically sensitive issues. The Seminary kept its stock. Both the board of trustees and the faculty were kept aware of these actions.[5]

Equally important to the Seminary's financial recovery was the trust that developed between the president and the Seminary's faculty and staff. Although they knew little of the detail, they sensed that the Seminary's financial problems were severe. They found themselves coming to trust their new president and therefore responded favorably to his initiatives. Larry Beloat and his staff of building engineers developed new ways of managing the facility. Although the building was too warm in the summer and chilly in the winter, they made such dramatic reductions in energy usage that the Seminary was awarded a citation by the city of Indianapolis for the achievement. Secretaries were willing to accept increased work loads as some of their number left to take other positions.

The reductions of staff affected the faculty as well. It became clear that there would be a lag between retirements and the calling of new professors which meant more work for those remaining behind. Most painful was the president's announcement as the first step of the tenure process that there was no longer a financial base for the position whose incumbent would soon be eligible for tenure review. The position was therefore terminated, and at the end of the academic year the professor left the Seminary's staff. Despite the straitened conditions, the faculty and senior staff held firm. Even with salaries frozen, several turned down offers to move to other schools or positions. Their determination to stay together, although never discussed among themselves, was one of the reasons why the Seminary could keep going during the period of crisis. There was a closing of the ranks of the people who worked at the Seminary. At the end of the second year of frozen salaries, there was a small surplus—enough to give a 2 percent increase—which the trustees decided should be given out as a one-year bonus that would not affect the next year's budget. Liggett's proposal, which the board accepted, was to give all employees a 1 percent bonus on the basis of their current salaries, which meant that those with the highest salary would receive the largest increase, and to divide the other 1 percent equally among everyone "so that the cook and the president would get the same amount." The impact upon morale and the stability of the employees, said Liggett, "was amazing."[6] As the crisis eased, the Seminary was able to make an appointment to the faculty—Edgar A. Towne in theology—because of the faculty's conclusion that the integrity of the M.Div. program required another person in this field.

While all of this was taking place, the funding package for the new library and a major revision of the master plan for the campus were being developed. Although complete working drawings for the library had been prepared in the early 1960s, these plans had to be revised significantly. The obvious reason was that the site plan had placed the library near the chapel on the edge of the bluff overlooking White River. The two facilities had to be built at the same time in order to use heavy construction equipment. A second reason was the need to develop a building that would be more efficient in operations than the parts of the campus built earlier. The master plan and all detailed drawings had been designed prior to the energy crisis when few people were anticipating the environmental issues that had come into prominence. The challenge facing Edward Larrabee Barnes was to relocate the library so that the chapel could be constructed later and to redesign it to meet new environmental and fiscal realities.

Liggett knew that the funding of the new library had to be done in a way that would not negatively impact the rest of the Seminary's program. This meant that he needed to preserve the original Krannert grant of $1.8 million, spend it for construction and endowment, and use it to generate additional funds. His first step was to negotiate with the Krannert trustees and gain their support for revising the plan for expenditures—$1.2 million for construction and $.6 million for endowment to support the library. He then talked with representatives of the Irwin-Sweeney-Miller Foundation who earlier had made a one-for-one challenge grant to the Foundation for Religious Studies. Liggett asked if they would reassign the challenge to Christian Theological Seminary and accept the Krannert gift as the amount that their challenge was to match. Their positive answer assured the Seminary that the gifts from these two foundations would provide $3.6 million for the library—a third of it to be used for construction and two thirds for endowment.[7]

The first announcement of the Krannert grant was made at the inauguration of President Liggett and Dean Richard D. N. Dickinson, Jr., on October 16, 1974; the completed facility was dedicated three years later on October 5, 1977. During these months the *CTS Bulletin* regularly described the need for the library, the basis for its funding, and the progress toward designing and building. This infusion of new money to the endowment increased its value significantly just at a time when the economy began to improve, so that the erosion of the Seminary's permanent funds came to an end.

During these same years the Seminary frequently reported other good news about its financial affairs. Scholarship and financial aid funds were being set up by congregations and individuals throughout the Seminary's service area. Even before the 1975–1976 fiscal year had been completed, contributions for scholarships for that year alone had increased by $87,479. Contributions to the annual fund were increasing. Lilly Endowment demonstrated its continuing interest in the Seminary with a grant of $300,000, which would be used as a supplement to normal operations in support of continuing education, field education, and improved teaching skills in general religious education. The Irwin-Sweeney-Miller Foundation stimulated new contributions to the CTS endowment by giving three dollars to the endowment for each new dollar received from other sources. In the year ending June 30, 1977, the foundation's matching contribution totaled $195,390.

The good news continued; on Commencement day, June 4, 1978, President Liggett announced another major grant, again from the Irwin-Sweeney-Miller Foundation: $1 million would be contributed to the Seminary's endowment designated for support of faculty salaries. As impressive as this gift sounded, however, the impact upon the budget would be modest. The Seminary's goal was to draw only 5 percent of the endowment for budgetary use, which meant that this gift would add about $50,000 per year to the salary line. With sixteen full-time professors, the increment per person helped make up for the years just passed when the salary scale had not kept up with inflation, but it would not be enough to close the gap between CTS salaries and those in many other seminaries.

One aspect of the forward momentum was the modest revision of building use that the construction of the library made possible. Opened up for new uses were several rooms that the temporary library had occupied: a lecture hall designed to seat 150 persons, another that would seat 75, two rooms each of which would seat 50, and the lower level that had been used as library stacks. Economies in construction and income from short-term investments of construction funds had created a small fund that could be used for renovating these areas; faculty and staff were asked to participate in the decisions about redesigning them for new uses.

Since few of the professors liked the one lecture hall that had been in use from the beginning, it was quickly decided that the newly opened space should be redesigned. The largest room would become the provisional chapel. The level floors in two of the lecture halls would be retained. The larger one would be furnished with movable chairs for larger classes and the smaller one would be the choir rehearsal room and studio for the professor of church music. The other small lecture hall would be reconfigured into a specialized teaching-learning area. The basement would be used as a student lounge.

The faculty was united in its determination that the provisional chapel would have a level floor and reluctantly Edward Larrabee Barnes agreed. A simple oak chair manufactured in Indiana was selected by a committee of faculty and staff, and the architect was invited to select the color for the upholstery. He chose a gray suede that maintained the quiet tones of the room while adding to the sense of simple beauty. Although the Seminary community had found Room 122 a happy location for worship, the provisional chapel was even better. It was larger and more eloquent in its proportions, and it was located at the heart of the academic section of the building, close to seminar rooms and close to faculty offices.

While the Seminary watched the library take shape, faculty and staff were conducting a self study in preparation for the periodic review of its accreditation by the Association of Theological Schools (the name had been shortened from the American Association of Theological Schools) and the North Central Association of Colleges and Schools. In his section of the report, which was to assess the Seminary's fiscal viability, President Liggett stated four criteria: conservation of assets, deficit-free operations, responsible allocation of funds in light of the purposes of the Seminary, and future possibilities. After describing the actions during the previous four years, his conclusions were that the Seminary had made significant, short-term progress on all four criteria, but that new ventures and new resources would be needed soon in order to sustain that progress. "So the judgment about the future prospects is cautiously optimistic, tempered with awareness of the continuing limitation with which the seminary must cope."[8]

A Future Bright with Possibilities

While President Liggett was coping with the Seminary's fiscal crisis, he was also facing challenges in his academic responsibilities. One of the positive results of the fiscal struggles, he reported in the 1977 self study report, had been the clarification of the primary purposes of the Seminary. All programs essential to the degree programs had been maintained, and "in some ways there has actually been increased strength and vitality which, paradoxically, emerged in the midst of adversity."[9] Even before Liggett had taken up his presidential duties, he had pointed to the importance of clarifying the Seminary's purpose and increasing its vitality. In an address to his faculty, sharing his vision of the years they would work together, he had chosen the word "continuity" to describe his intended leadership. He was proud of the record of the Seminary and wanted it to continue in the same direction. "I hope that all of us will see my joining the team simply as a new stage or new chapter in a process that is one of continuity and not of discontinuity." He spoke of the importance of vision, the sense of interdependence, and a growing sense of common priorities. Liggett identified "certain values at CTS which are shared in its recent history and which I would like to endorse": the Seminary's ecumenical stance, its academic freedom, its ideal of academic excellence, its sense of appropriate roles for all sectors of the CTS community, and the importance of maintaining a healthy combination of theological education and ministerial training.

Liggett's understanding of "continuity," however, was dynamic rather than static. He had concluded his 1974 remarks to the faculty by describing five values that "while present in the CTS situation, I would like to strengthen": the relationship between the church and the Seminary; interdisciplinary efforts between departments and between the Seminary and other institutions of higher learning; international horizons, which included bringing to the campus "a growing number of distinguished theologians from the Third World"; the relationship between "wisdom and instinctive knowledge that is often held by common people" and "the profound insight of high scholastic erudition"; and "a higher sense of self consciousness as a Christian community for ourselves and for the churches that we serve."[10]

From early in his administration, Liggett 's closest colleague in realizing this vision was Richard D. N. Dickinson, Jr., whom he had chosen to succeed David C. Pellett as vice president and dean of the Seminary. Even before Liggett had begun his work, Pellett had told him privately that health factors had led to the decision that he would step down from the deanship at the end of the academic year. Knowing that budget problems mandated that the payroll be reduced rather than enlarged, Liggett had announced to the faculty and trustees that the new dean would come from the ranks of the current faculty and that he as president would make the selection after consulting with the faculty and others. In his first weeks on campus he visited each professor in the professor's office, and one of the topics for discussion was the deanship. What qualities does the Seminary need at this time in its life? Who among the professors would be the right one to appoint to this position?

There was little discussion among the professors, either in public meetings or in private conversations, about the process or the merits of their own colleagues for the position. Although no one acknowledged an interest in the position, it was assumed that three or four of the professors would be willing to serve if asked. Yet, by late afternoon of the day prior to the faculty meeting when a choice would be announced, no one had been approached by the president. When asked by a colleague if he had been chosen, Richard D. N. Dickinson, Jr., responded by saying that he had not been asked and implied reluctance to accept if he were. A little later in the day, Liggett asked Dickinson to become the dean and gave him until the next morning to make his decision. When the announcement was made that afternoon, most professors were surprised but willing to give him their support. He was known to be innovative in his teaching methods, deeply committed to the church and to theological education, a producing author, and active in national and international activities of the churches. Furthermore, Dickinson had taken the lead in the faculty's resistance to the Foundation for Religious Studies.

By talking with all of the professors in this way, Liggett had involved them in the process more fully than had his predecessors. Shelton had chosen Norris without consulting the faculty and Norris had chosen Osborn prior to asking the advice and counsel of the professors. Much of the animosity that existed in the first years of the Norris-Osborn administration was caused by the way that the dean had been chosen. Norris's choice of David C. Pellett had included even less conversation with faculty than had earlier choices, but the faculty sensed that this was a long-term interim appointment more than the establishing of new academic leadership, and they trusted Pellett to manage the academic procedures with practical efficiency.

At the beginning of a new presidential administration, however, the choice of a dean was more critical to the long-term direction of the Seminary and working relationships of the faculty. While there was no outward opposition to the choice, the faculty's existing tendencies toward passive resistance were strengthened. During the next years, continuing debates over academic matters sometimes seemed motivated as much by the antagonisms established by the selection of the dean as by the actual factors pertinent to the issues under debate.

On October 16, 1974, when Thomas J. Liggett and Richard D. N. Dickinson, Jr., were inaugurated to their positions, each man described his vision for the future of the Seminary. Renewing statements that he had earlier made to the faculty, the president stated that one of his intentions was to exercise "a responsible trusteeship of the legacy of the past combined with a fundamental posture of commitment to the future." The dean, while referring both to the past and the future, warned against the tendency to "cling to past securities" and asserted that we should "accept the new as challenge."[11]

Before the Seminary could move forward into the future, it was necessary to respond to several academic matters left over from the past. In the 1973 accreditation review, the team representing the American Association of Theological Schools (ATS) and the North Central Association of Schools and Colleges had posed five questions to the Seminary's administration and identified two weaknesses. The questions dealt with the quality of the student body, the coherence of the academic program, governance, and fiscal matters, all of which could be improved through the normal processes of academic administration. Five years later, in his letter to another accrediting team, Liggett was able to report progress on all of the issues that these questions had raised.

The two weaknesses required a fuller response. The first was the Doctor of Ministry program, which was three years old when the 1973 accreditation review had taken place. Previous to this visit the Seminary had submitted its program to the ATS for evaluation and it had received preliminary accreditation. In 1974 the ATS reviewed all D.Min. programs with preliminary accreditation, including the one at CTS. Late in the year the ATS had again studied the CTS program and in June of 1975 continued preliminary accreditation and assigned two formal notations: one questioned the adequacy of the integration of classical disciplines with professional training and the other the adequacy of the goals and objectives of the program.

The faculty was frustrated by these notations because from the beginning it had wanted a program that would be strong in its academic character. In contrast to some of the other D.Min. programs developing around the country, CTS required students to do most of their academic work on campus in courses that met every week during the regular semesters. A special group of courses that met only one day a week was created for this purpose. The faculty was determined that both classical and professional disciplines would be included, even for students who wanted to concentrate in pastoral care and counseling. Goaded by the ATS critique, the faculty continued to revise the program, with the result that in January 1976 the ATS granted full accreditation to the CTS D.Min. program, although continuing the notation on the need to clarify goals. The faculty also yielded to the demand of prospective students for a version of the degree that provided a higher concentration of work in counseling, announcing this revision in 1976. Initially the faculty planned to limit admissions to the D.Min. degree to twenty persons per year. At first, enough people applied to maintain this level, but by the middle of the decade interest declined.

The second weakness was the library, and here Liggett could report significant progress in the five years since the previous visit. During that time the new library building had been constructed and occupied, which meant that physical needs were well cared for. The library's budget, however, had remained essentially flat because of the financial stress under which the Seminary had been living. Even so, special gifts had been secured to augment that budget so that the number of new books ordered each year had remained fairly constant. New procedures for selecting books had been adopted, and the librarian had been granted tenure. All of these measures, Liggett believed, constituted an appropriate response to the concerns that the 1973 accrediting team had raised.

During these years, the Seminary also had to struggle with the challenge of maintaining a student body. Recruitment was the primary responsibility of one of the senior members of the development department; despite this person's hard work, enrollment continued soft during the first years of the new administration. In addition to submitting detailed reports to faculty and trustees, Dean Dickinson regularly interpreted their meaning for the trustees. More important to the faculty and administration than the total registration was the breakdown. How many credit hours were these students taking? Was that number shrinking or expanding in relation to total enrollment? How were the students and their semester hours of work distributed among degree programs? Because it was agreed that the basic ministerial degrees, and especially the M.Div., were the focus of attention, the dean frequently expressed his anxiety as the number of registrants declined.

Together faculty and administration examined the student body and their own work, using surveys of students, alumni, and professors in order to evaluate what was taking place. All of this they reported to the accreditation team that came to campus in 1978. The fall enrollment in 1967–1968 was 225, and in 1976–1977 it was 289. During the decade the highest fall enrollment had been in 1970–1971 when 300 persons had registered; the average over the decade had been 264. Although the total registration had remained steady, the M.Div. enrollment had declined from 136 in the first year of the decade to 121 in the last; over the ten years the average had been 122. The number of women in all of the degree programs had increased from 22 in 1967–1968 to 55 in 1976–1977. In the first year 120 of the students were from the Christian Church (Disciples of Christ) and 47 were from the United Methodist Church. In the last year 98 Disciples and 66 United Methodists were included in the count.

In his interpretive comments to the trustees, the dean noted that "many of the more conservative seminaries are experiencing considerable growth, while seminaries of the mainline denominations are on a plateau, or experiencing only incremental increases."[12] The difficulty of making generalizations about enrollment trends, however, was evident in the statistics reported by the ATS. From 1969 to 1976 the enrollment at CTS increased 17 percent while the enrollments at Chicago Theological Seminary, Garrett-Evangelical, and Union in New York decreased, in two of them by a third. Yet the other Disciples seminaries all increased at a higher rate than did CTS, with Phillips Graduate Seminary outpacing the others with a growth of 75 percent. Vanderbilt, Yale, and Pacific School of Religion all grew as much or more than CTS. The dean's reference to the significant growth of evangelical schools was confirmed by Gordon-Conwell that increased to 622, an 85 percent rise; while Fuller exploded from 382 students in 1969 to 1,551 in 1976, an increase of more than 300 percent. In his October report, the dean confessed to the trustees that it was "a sobering fact to realize that only 121 (42 percent) of our students are working on an M.Div., with an additional 66 (23 percent) students working on continuing education professional degrees for pastoral ministry."

In the first and last years of the decade twelve overseas students were registered at the Seminary, but in 1971–1972 the number had reached a high of twenty-eight, with a decade-long average of seventeen. Although the table for the decade included a column for reporting the number of "U.S. Blacks" in the student body, there are only two entries—fourteen in 1974–1975 and eight in 1976–1977. Again, Dean Dickinson revealed his concerns in his report to the trustees. Noting that the number of "American blacks" had dropped still further, and that only half the number were enrolled as had been five to seven years earlier, Dickinson suggested several reasons for the small enrollment. The Seminary had no full-time black teachers and few courses specifically for black students. The Seminary had been more realistic in interpreting to prospective students the difficulties that the Seminary encountered in helping them find field positions, offering adequate financial aid, and assisting them in finding post-seminary jobs that paid at an adequate level.[13]

The faculty wanted to assess the impact of its program upon students and developed questionnaires and administered surveys to current students and recent graduates in order to find out. Questions about instruction at CTS were all answered with high scores, and in most answers current students and recent graduates were similar in their evaluations. Ninety-six percent of the current students and 81 percent of recent graduates agreed or strongly agreed with the statement that course objectives were accomplished. The scores were lower and the variation greater, however, to the statement that courses helped meet my goals: 84 percent of the students answered with "agree" or "strongly agree," compared with 67 percent of the graduates. Their perceptions of student-faculty relations were generally positive. The statement that faculty are genuinely concerned with students and actually helpful was answered "strongly agree" by 41 percent of the students and 31 percent of the graduates, and "agree" by 53 percent of the students and 68 percent of the graduates.

A different survey taken of graduates three and five years after graduation in 1972 and 1974 revealed that two-thirds of those responding were serving in parish ministry. There were no courses that stood out in the memories of these graduates as having been especially good, but eight courses were mentioned by two to five respondents: medical ethics, theology, theology of American culture, Tillich, process theology, personality and the Christian faith, preaching, and communication for the ministry. These graduates stated that the courses had been less than adequate in the arts, church administration, comparative religions, membership recruitment, evangelism, stewardship, preaching, and community leadership.

At the time the survey was taken, the Seminary conducted the chapel service of worship once a week. Faculty, students, and graduates were asked about frequency, with 61 percent of the professors, 77 percent of the students, and 63 percent of the graduates indicating that once a week was adequate, and most of the others indicating that more frequent services were desirable. Questions on spiritual formation while in seminary were asked: 62 percent of the faculty, 45 percent of the students, and 28 percent of the graduates said that corporate worship at the Seminary was important. The importance of spiritual disciplines was indicated by 54 percent of the faculty, 39 percent of the students, and 32 percent of the alumni. When asked about a "central tendency" as being most meaningful to people at the seminary, respondents mentioned twenty different items, with "intellectual development" the most frequently noted.[14]

With these and similar findings before them, the faculty concluded that "the vital signs" were strong. "A diversified program of instruction takes place, students are maturing in their faith and pastoral competence, and faculty-student relations are healthy." The faculty was drawing upon another body of evidence for the conclusions—personal experiences with students in classroom, chapel, and elsewhere on campus. Interviews with five of these students were published in an issue of the *CTS Bulletin* in 1977, the same year that the Seminary was doing its self study. Representative of the five was the comment by one student that during her years on campus her personal faith had been deepened "almost in direct proportion to the expansion of my theological horizon." All reported that their time at CTS had helped them understand theology and themselves with the result that their future work in the life of the church was clear.[15]

Yet the faculty was uneasy. "Some of the readings are marginal enough to indicate that faculty, staff, and students need to revise current patterns of life in the seminary."[16] Furthermore, a rapidly expanding body of literature provided critical histories of theological education, critiques of theological schools, and recommendations for reconstructing the programs of theological study. The faculty used four methods for revising patterns of theological study at CTS: incremental change of current activities, curricular reformulation, continuing education for themselves on methods of teaching, and the creation of special programs. Incremental change grew out of the painstaking care of the ordinary detail of campus life. Throughout this period of time, professors and administrators worried over every aspect of academic affairs. Even though the number of professors and administrators had declined because of the financial struggles, the amount of work continued undiminished. Despite their grumbling, the professors conscientiously kept going in the hope that their school would keep getting better. The faculty continued to fine-tune the programs of study, partially because of the demands from ATS and partly because of their own sense that improvements were needed. As in former times, the M.Div. program received the most attention.

The professors continued to improve their knowledge by taking research leaves, which continued to be granted by the trustees even during the period when financial pressures had been most difficult. The results of their work were expressed, in part, in a growing list of publications in scholarly journals and books. The professors also set up conferences and workshops for themselves on teaching and learning. The most important was the Alverna Faculty Retreat, a four-day event in January 1974, held at the Alverna Retreat Center on Spring Mill Road in Indianapolis. All of the professors participated, except the two on research leave, and president-elect Liggett attended briefly. The faculty invited three people to come as leaders—Prudence Dyer, professor of education from Drake University; Browne Barr, pastor of First Congregational Church, Berkeley; and Victor Neufeld, professor on the faculty of medicine of McMaster University. The conference focused on the character of a seminary, methods of teaching and evaluating work, and the religious and professional formation of students. By the end of the week the faculty had identified five topics for continuing work: strengthening ties of Seminary and church, redefining the Seminary's character so that it is more like the church and less like a school, finding a new model for the January term, reorganizing the Seminary's structure, and exploring methods of evaluation and counseling of students and professors.

They participated in tenure review teams that also aimed at strengthening the Seminary as a center of serious scholarship on behalf of the church and the larger community. Gradually, however, the earlier sense of élan had diminished and the teaching staff felt the burden of their work. They knew that despite their hard work and good performance, their salaries were depressed. In their report to the accreditation team in 1977, the faculty compared the average salary, including all benefits, for a full professor in all accredited seminaries, $23,521, with that of full professors at CTS, $19,897, pointing out the $3,600 disparity. Something more interesting than fine-tuning the current operation had to be devised.

Special Programs

Some of the excitement was generated by special programs that the faculty devised to express their widening interests, diversify opportunities for students on campus, and bring pastors to campus for continuing education. One of these was Project Experteach, developed by James Blair Miller in 1973, with funding by Lilly Endowment. Its purpose was "to experiment and provide experiences in creative teaching within the educational ministry of the parish church." During the three or four years that the program was in operation, Project Experteach conducted workshops in thirty congregations from six denominations and included two large celebrations in the CTS auditorium, with 200 to 300 people attending.

In April 1975, the Seminary celebrated the fiftieth anniversary of service to the church and the community with a series of lectures, featuring Peter Berger, a prominent sociologist of religion, and William Ruckelshaus, an Indiana politician who had established a national reputation as a conscientious and bold public servant. As the nation looked forward to the bicentennial of its founding, to be celebrated in 1976, the faculty developed a two-week seminar for the January interterm. Seventy-five people participated in a two-week seminar titled "The Rebirth of Religious Experience in America," and the response was so positive that the faculty decided to follow up the next January with another special seminar. During the spring semester, the faculty presented a series of popular lectures to the Indianapolis community on topics related to the development of religion in American life; and in the summer climaxed the emphasis with a series of essays in *Encounter* on civil religion in America.

During these same years the Indiana Pastors' Conference, which for a generation had met on the campus of DePauw University, relocated to the CTS campus. Although the conference was managed by an interdenominational board of pastors, Grover Hartman, longtime executive director of the Indiana Council of Churches, was the real organizer and spirit of the conference. Over the years, however, this annual gathering had dwindled, and even the move to Indianapolis did not halt that gradual loss of strength. Yet, the annual visitation of 125 or more clergy, many of them from smaller communities distant from Indianapolis, brightened a dull time between semesters.

Among the most memorable of the special events was a daylong retreat led by Henri Nouwen on December 1, 1978. At that time teaching at Yale Divinity School, Nouwen had become one of the best known interpreters of theology and spirituality in the United States; his coming to Indianapolis was due, in large part, to the friendship that Professor James Blair Miller had established with Nouwen while Miller had been on research leave at Yale.

These were years of strength in the Repertory Theatre at CTS. With funding from Lilly Endowment, the silent subsidy provided by the Seminary, and rising ticket prices, the theater was able to mount productions that attracted a growing audience from across the metropolitan area. In 1977–1978 the theater set a record: seven major plays, eighty-three performances, and 27,244 persons in attendance. The Indiana Committee for the Humanities funded a discussion program related to performances under the title "Matrix for Discussion." During that year, Matrix groups for Ibsen's *Wild Duck* averaged eighty-two participants.[17] During these exciting years, the Repertory Theatre contributed to the life of the Seminary in several ways. It expressed one aspect of the Seminary's ongoing interest in the arts. It brought interesting students to campus and provided parttime and fulltime staff who also contributed to campus activities. The theater's outreach into the community was extensive, both as it attracted people interested in working in the theater and many more who attended its performances.

The counseling program continued to gain strength despite the significant decline in the health of Lowell G. Colston. The National Institute of Mental Health awarded the Seminary a second grant, this one to focus upon the pastoral care of older people. Sue Webb Cardwell, who had come to the Seminary's staff in 1961, had been developing her academic and professional credentials and now directed the Pastoral Counseling Center. Professor Donald R. Wismar carried a heavy administrative, teaching, and counseling load during these years, thus compensating for Colston's diminishing capacities.

This emphasis upon ministry with the aging was intensified at the beginning of 1980 when the National Center on Ministry with the Aging was established on the CTS campus, under the leadership of Donald Clingan. Formerly a member of the staff of the Disciples' Division of Homeland Ministries, Clingan came to the CTS campus when the Seminary and the National Benevolent Association of the Christian Church created this jointly sponsored new program.

One of these special ventures, which signaled the emerging intellectual partnership between two of the Seminary's newer professors, was called a "working conference" on process philosophy and biblical theology. Since coming to the faculty, theologian Clark M. Williamson and Old Testament scholar J. Gerald Janzen had found each other to be a strong conversation partner as each one was developing the broader framework of his own discipline. Concluding that the conversation they were enjoying with each other would be beneficial to others, they invited some two dozen other scholars, including their colleagues Calvin L. Porter and Edgar A. Towne, to join them for several days of intense discussion. Two of Williamson's professors from the University of Chicago and two CTS graduates were among the participants who represented seventeen seminaries or universities, including Disciples-related Brite Divinity School, Lexington Theological Seminary, and Transylvania University. A follow-up to the event was a working group on process hermeneutics that began meeting in conjunction with annual meetings of the American Academy of Religion.

The working conference was shaped by the premise that "a new frontier of realism" was sweeping the western world.[18] One form of this new frontier was the neoorthodox movement, but after a short period of influence neoorthodoxy had diminished and a second form of theological realism—process thought—was gaining strength. By establishing a working relationship with this new wing, Janzen declared, biblical theology could "break fresh ground in the task of interpreting the biblical ethos for the coming age."[19]

Janzen saw in process philosophy a new metaphysics, a new set of general ideas, grounded in modern scientific developments. It was a *logos* alongside the Bible which was a *mythos*. Mythos and logos were alike because both cut away the "welter of sheer detail" and revealed the lines in nature and life. The one was concrete and the other abstract; and both modes of analysis and exposition were necessary to the full exposition of experience. Metaphysics, including process philosophy, served biblical theology by providing general ideas and as a critical control on inconsistencies between basic metaphors and "theological trajectories in the Bible." The Bible served metaphysics because the Bible itself was part of the evidence that the general ideas had to take into account, and served as a critic of the metaphysical tradition when it becomes "shallowly empirical" and "so tends to overlook some of the evidence in favor of a thin consistency."

Janzen's preliminary conclusion was that metaphysics and biblical theology "stand in a reciprocally constructive and critical relation to one another; and it is only when this relation is sustained in tensive balance that either can achieve maximum results."[20] Process philosophy had to be used in ways that were consistent with its own philosophical methods and principles of adequacy, and the full witness of the Bible had to be accounted for in the final synthesis. When faced with seemingly contradictory emphases, as in the Bible's interpretations of the nature of God's power, Janzen believed that the principles of process philosophy required that the two ideas be modified and then fused together into a new interpretation.[21] In this essay Janzen included a brief exposition of the Book of Job which had already become his most popular course and which would lead, a few years later, to his first published commentary.[22] In this book, throughout the rest of the Bible, and especially in the theology of Paul, said Janzen, life is experienced both as a structure of wrath and as a structure of grace. Human beings know this, he asserted, and an adequate metaphysical scheme will account for both aspects of this experience—both wrath and grace.[23]

Whereas Janzen's new frontier was defined by the two coordinates of process philosophy and biblical theology, Williamson's included both of these and also a third—the theological and ethical import of systems of thought that were closely related to Christian theology. During his first research leave (1972–1973) he had spent a semester at the Graduate School of the Ecumenical Institute at the Château de Bossey in Switzerland where the theme had been "dialogue on salvation among persons of living faiths and ideologies." The seminar that Williamson conducted dealt with a topic of particular interest to him at the time. It was titled "Salvation as Justice through Revolution: Christian-Marxist Dialogue." In his oral presentation to faculty colleagues, he stated that he was interested in the relations of Christian thought to its two closest companions—Marxist thought on the theological left and Jewish theology on the theological right.[24] At the time of the working conference, he was still developing his understanding of Marxist ideas, using them to develop his theological framework, and publishing in that field.[25]

Quickly, however, the focus of his work shifted. His interest in Marxist thought died and his interest in Jewish theology was transformed into a powerful desire to establish a new relationship with Jews and to come to terms with biblical studies, Christian theology, and ethical practice in a post-Holocaust mode. One result of this new interest was the decision in 1975 to team up with Rabbi Sydney Steiman to offer a new course, "Dialogue Between Christians and Jews." Williamson's growing interest in Jewish thought and related topics resulted in a joint effort between the Seminary and the Jewish Community Relations Council. In 1977 they sponsored a statewide conference, "The Moral Implications of the Holocaust," with such positive results that the collaboration continued in later years.

This focus of Williamson's theological power and ethical passion was expressed in his book, published in 1982, which showed the interconnection of three coordinates: the biblical text, process thought, and the Jewish-Christian relations. The theme of the book was expressed in the title, *Has God Rejected His People? Anti-Judaism in the Christian Church*. In his preface Williamson stated that the book was "an introduction to the history of the relationship between Judaism and Christianity, focusing on the ideology of Christian anti-Judaism," and that its purpose was to describe this relationship and ideology and to make practical and theological proposals for how it might be overcome.[26] While devoting extensive sections to interpretation of scripture and review of historical developments, the book was essentially an ethically informed theological exposition.

Looking to the Future

Despite the many activities between 1974 and 1978, the primary achievement during these years was stabilizing the Seminary's course by overcoming the fiscal crisis, maintaining an adequate student body, and extending the campus. The morale of faculty and staff was strong, exciting events kept life interesting, and students were challenged by the excitement of study at this building so filled with light and energy. The continuity that President Liggett has affirmed at the beginning of his administration had been maintained. The faculty and staff had worked creatively so that the campus had become a lively place, even more so than it had been when J. Irwin Miller had called it the liveliest place around. A succession of speakers from the third world, several of them longtime colleagues or friends of the Liggetts and the Dickinsons, had given international relations a high priority, but this too was continuity with the past rather than change.

The time had come, Liggett realized, when they had to look more to the future than to the past. A new vision that would capture the imagination of the entire Seminary was what needed to be developed. At his inauguration he had spoken of "a responsible trusteeship of the legacy of the past combined with a fundamental posture of commitment to the future."[27] Now that he had faithfully conserved the past, it was time to turn his attention to the future; and in so doing he could fulfill another of the hopes that he had expressed to his faculty as he took up his labors, which was to strengthen the Seminary's relationship with the church community from which the people of the Seminary received their financial support and students, and their own spiritual formation, and to which they sent their graduates to serve.[28] The way to move forward was to talk with church people all over their service area and to develop new goals for the life of Christian Theological Seminary. Staff at Lilly Endowment agreed and provided a fund of thirty thousand dollars to enable the study to take place.

10
The Finest Institution of its Kind

A Center of Theological Education and Reflection, 1979–1987

President Thomas J. Liggett moved swiftly to develop a plan for the Seminary, involving the faculty and executive staff in "the initial description of the planning process," some of the gathering of data, and midcourse evaluations. He and an assistant, whom he hired with funds from his Lilly grant, conducted most of the interviews and sifted through the studies of economic, cultural, and ecclesial developments across the nation. The president did many of the financial projections himself and, partly because secretarial staff was still depleted, he also typed the manuscript on his office portable.

The first draft, entitled "Christian Theological Seminary Looks to the Future," presented nearly twenty pages of "relevant background information," interpretive comments, and conclusions. Liggett believed that the economic and social stresses in American life would continue and that the basic life of churches and seminaries would stay largely the same although modified by new conditions. Denominations would continue in place, and regionalism would be more important as a practical factor in patterns of enrollment and usage of seminaries. He believed that seminaries would need to enter into creative arrangements with other institutions and need to develop more diversified programs for people who lived in geographical proximity. The president reflected upon the Seminary's purpose, concluding that the statement in the articles of incorporation remained valid but needed a more explicit articulation. His proposal was that the Seminary see itself "as a center of the theological life of the Church, committed to provide programs of ministerial education and theological reflection which are called for in the fulfillment of the Church's mission." This would mean educational service in five areas: basic ministerial education, continuing education for clergy, theological education for laity, "wrestling" with theological and ethical issues facing the church and the world, and services to enrich and shape the life of the church.

A notable feature of this report was Liggett's determination to move forward despite studies by Lilly Endowment and the Hartford Seminary Foundation projecting a surplus of seminary-educated ministers within twenty years. Liggett's response was that Christian ministry was first a vocation and only secondarily a profession. The projections that there would be an oversupply of ministers in later years were based on institutional rather than religious criteria. Referring to Jesus' declaration that the harvest was plenteous and the laborers few, Liggett declared that "Jesus would have us define the 'need' in terms of the world, and not in terms of the church." His conclusion, echoing Orman L. Shelton's rhetoric, was that "effective ministerial enlistment must begin with a recovery of a Biblical perspective of God's Kingdom and the urgent need for massive response to God's calling."

Referring to a position paper by the Carnegie Foundation, Liggett concluded that CTS was "well positioned to deal with the problems and opportunities of contemporary theological education." He cited "a strong academic program, firm rootage in the life of its sponsoring denomination but with a clear ecumenical stance, positive relationship with the principal religious bodies in the larger Indianapolis metropolitan area and . . . an open posture toward innovative program." The Seminary could look to the future "with positive hope and anticipation."[1] While "present realities and trends must be taken seriously, . . . the future is always more than can be projected from the present. . . . Future possibilities must be a combination of that which present realities indicate as probable and of that which faith declares to be possible."[2]

After listing concerns the Seminary needed to address and a wide range of programs that the Seminary would offer, Liggett turned to implementation. He listed eighteen components of campus, staff, and program, stating that nine were being cared for adequately and nine needed attention. Finally, Liggett developed financial projections for the five-year period that this plan covered: new gift income of $216,965, new endowment of $8,764,766, improved physical facilities, mainly student apartments, of $1,575,000, and costs for a financial campaign of $175,000, for a total of nearly $10.8 million. By the end of this period the Seminary would have "advanced significantly toward its objective of becoming the finest institution of its kind ever developed by the Disciples and of moving toward eminence in Indianapolis and the central region of the United States as a center of theological education and reflection."[3]

The faculty and executive staff were overwhelmed by the boldness of the president's plans to move forward despite all evidence to the contrary, and unnerved by his seeming disregard of the factors that indicated major changes in the cultural and ecclesiological context. They were uneasy with his financial projections, doubting that his figures were high enough, nor could they imagine that the Seminary could raise even the amounts he projected, let alone the larger amounts they imagined that this program would require. After listening to his colleagues' reactions to the plan, Liggett revised it and the faculty, with growing enthusiasm, embraced the vision and recommended it to the trustees. The trustees then devised their response, which was to develop financial resources so that the seminary could add six persons to the faculty and executive and professional staffs, increase salaries to recover part of the loss of purchasing power in previous years, build residential housing for students, and generate new endowed funds.[4]

A Daring Initiative

During the early years of his CTS presidency, Liggett was developing a board of trustees that more than at any time in the past linked the Seminary with the leadership system of Indianapolis. His manner of working with these prominent people was illustrated by the conversation in which he invited a prominent Indianapolis leader whom he did not know to become a trustee. The candidate told Liggett that if he were to come to the board the president needed to know that he was a conservative Republican who spoke his mind. Liggett assured the man that this was okay, but then he added that if the candidate were to become a trustee, he needed to know that Liggett was a liberal Democrat who spoke his mind.[5] Recognizing that they were both men of conviction, faith, vision, and energy, they agreed that they could work together for causes in which they both believed even though they might disagree on political issues.

The distinctive characteristics of Liggett and this board were revealed in the decision to move forward with a major capital campaign. A premier fund-raising company was retained to do a feasibility study, following the normal method of interviewing persons who represented major donors. These conversations indicated that there was little chance for the Seminary to raise the funds that it hoped for, and the written report to the trustees expressed this conclusion. On the morning that the report was to be given to the trustees, however, the representative of the fund-raising company phoned Liggett at his home and told him that one conversation had led him to conclude that the Seminary should not let the negative report deter them from moving forward. Liggett shared this private communication with P. E. MacAllister, chair of the trustees; together they decided to encourage bold action by the trustees.

After careful planning, the Seminary was ready to announce its plans for a $10 million capital funds program. The key to this campaign was the support that it was to receive from two foundations. When Liggett met with officers of the Krannert Charitable Trust of Indianapolis, which already had funded the library, he discovered that it had responded unfavorably to the discussion by the New York based fund-raising people. Yet it had decided to contribute $2 million to a campaign by the Seminary and asked for Liggett's counsel on how to announce it. They agreed that it would be given in the form of a challenge grant, with Krannert contributing two dollars for every three that the Seminary raised. Then it was time to ask J. Irwin and Xenia Simons Miller and Clementine Miller Tangeman for their support. Liggett was nerved by their statement that rather than asking them what they would give he should tell them what should be expected from them. By the time that the conversations were completed, the Christian Foundation had committed itself to match the CTS-Krannert contributions dollar for dollar. Thus every three dollars contributed to the Seminary by regular donors would generate seven additional dollars from the two foundations. P. E. MacAllister and C. Richard Petticrew, who chaired the campaign committee, pledged the first 10 percent of the $3 million goal that the Seminary had set out to raise, and the faculty and staff of the Seminary oversubscribed their thirty thousand-dollar goal by 50 percent. Every member of the Seminary's faculty and staff made a pledge or contribution to this "daring initiative," as Petticrew termed it. By January 1982, half of the $3 million had been subscribed.

One device for encouraging contributions was the opportunity to name professorial chairs. A gift of $300,000 would be matched with other campaign funds to create an endowment of $600,000 to support one faculty chair. The first to be endowed under this provision was the MacAllister/Petticrew Chair of Old Testament, honoring the two trustees who were leading the Seminary during this creative period. Shortly thereafter, the Seminary announced the William G. Irwin Chair of Church History and the Nettie Sweeney and Hugh Th. Miller Chair of New Testament. The following June (1983) Disciples churches in Ohio were moving closer to their goal of raising $300,000 to endow the Herald B. Monroe Chair of Practical Parish Ministry, honoring their longtime regional minister. Another chair would later be named the Lois and Dale Bright Chair of Christian Ministries, honoring a Disciples family who donated their Iowa farm to the Seminary.

The campaign went over the top in the fall of 1983. The CTS luncheon at the Disciples' General Assembly in San Antonio was chosen as the occasion to announce the achievement. When C. Richard Petticrew, campaign chair, announced that $10,018,483 had been subscribed, and that nearly three-fourths of it was already in hand, he received a lengthy standing ovation. Honored guests at that same luncheon were Beauford A. and Shirley Norris, whose faith in the Seminary was confirmed by the remarkable achievements of the decade since they had moved into retirement. Later in the month a victory celebration was held in the common room on campus with a victory cake for everyone to enjoy. An even stronger sign of the campaign's success was the architect's model for the thirty-six-unit apartment buildings that the campaign would soon make possible.

There was other good news. Because the Lilly Endowment's policies did not allow contributions to the capital campaign, it had indicated its ongoing support of the Seminary by making significant contributions to innovative aspects of the Seminary's program. In the spring of 1984, Liggett announced that new grants by the Endowment would extend for three more years its support of continuing education and the Lilly Visiting Professors; and it would support two new initiatives—a program to develop planned giving and a research project focused upon the "black community" with the goal of "laying the groundwork for reaching black churches."[6]

The success of these financial efforts was due, in part, to the skilled work of the Seminary's development staff. As the capital campaign came to its close, the Seminary honored Bill L. Barnes, who for a quarter of a century had served as the Seminary's development officer. At a reception on campus, the president announced that during the years of Barnes's leadership the Seminary had received $35,935,929 in gift income. Barnes told the gathering of students, staff, friends, and family that while he had regretted leaving the pastorate when Beauford A. Norris had called him to this post, he had "been able to do more for the church's ministry here than in any other manner of service."[7]

Getting on with What Is Possible

While the president and trustees, with the help of the executive staff, were recreating the Seminary's institutional structure, the reshaping of its theological, spiritual, and educational life was the responsibility of Dean Richard D. N. Dickinson, Jr., and the faculty. They did their work, to use words of the dean, with "a strong commitment to getting on with what is possible and to living faithfully in the midst of an unpredictable world and church."[8] Staff and students, the dean observed, were aware of "the burdensome and complex issues which we face on the national and international levels," and sensed that "the eighties will bring many unpredictable questions and certainly some almost overwhelming difficulties." Yet, he sensed "a strong resilience among faculty, staff and students." Despite being "heavily burdened with more work than it is possible to do well," they moved forward, anticipating creative possibilities for the future. They were united "by a basic mutual commitment to make CTS the strongest possible center for theological education and the enlivenment of the witness of the church."

By the middle 1970s, the faculty knew that it had to work hard on the central focus of its work, the M.Div. program. The reviewers for accreditation had reported that the purposes of the degree seemed unclear, and the relationship of theological and professional studies was not well defined. Professors were aware of the continued efforts by church leaders and by the ATS to assess the readiness of students for the ministry but had repeatedly turned down requests from ATS that the Seminary participate in the ATS "Readiness for Ministry" program. As the dean reported to the trustees in May 1979, less than half of the seminaries were in the program. CTS has its own reservations—the program would be costly in terms of time and money; there was doubt about the scientific validity of processes used in the development of the instruments; the faculty was uneasy about the predictive or normative quality of the instruments; and the faculty didn't want the use of this project to be a factor in later accreditation reviews of the Seminary. Several members of the faculty stimulated the conversation by circulating personal statements about curricular reform; after a few months of this informal discussion, the professors concluded that curricular revision would require a concerted effort.[9]

They committed themselves to a four-day working retreat in early January 1980, and chose the venerable resort of French Lick Springs in southern Indiana as the place for their reflections. Surrounded by the decaying splendor of the rambling structure where Franklin Delano Roosevelt had once campaigned for the Democratic nomination for the presidency, the professors and their colleagues on the executive staff approached their work in their normal fashion—by preparing papers for extended discussion. They dealt with an interesting array of topics: the needs for ministry in the next twenty years, spiritual formation, preaching, pastoral care, the arts, the kinds of learning needed in the M.Div. curriculum, and field education. They reviewed the programs of study in other seminaries, considered the approach to theological education in Orthodox seminaries, and assessed their own program. The schedule included periods of worship, generous blocks of time for splendid meals, and opportunities to enjoy recreational possibilities at the resort, which gave the participants a feeling of delight as well as of responsibility. A strong sense of well-being developed with the conviction that something new was coming into being

Despite the faculty's enthusiasm following the French Lick retreat, the efforts to create a new curriculum became an exercise in frustration. Because the consensus was a unity of spirit that had not yet developed a body, the first step following the retreat needed to be the drafting of a consensus statement that recorded the spirit in such a way that the embodiment could develop. No one was assigned this task and the spirit of French Lick gradually dissipated. Even so, the M.Div. committee worked energetically upon the task of reshaping the curriculum in keeping with the discussions of that exhilarating week, and a little later in the spring came forward with a diagram that suggested a new way of giving form to the work that students were to do. To longtime professors, however, the diagram seemed vague, with few handles to get hold of, such as required courses and hours distributed among the fields. The committee looked to the dean for help, but he too seemed unclear about ways of moving from conception to curriculum.

The dean made regular reports to the trustees, interpreting the provisions that the faculty hoped to include in the revised degree and explaining the delays. In May 1981, more than a year after French Lick, he told the trustees that Nelle G. Slater, who had recently come to the faculty as professor of Christian education, had become chair of the M.Div. committee. By that time an M.Div. Task Force had been created to do the work and during that spring it had been making regular reports to the faculty. Its proposed model, presented for discussion in the regular meeting of the faculty in June 1981, was built on the assumption that "the student holds as objectives the desires to: 1. Discern One's Christian Vocation; 2. Claim One's Vocational Identity; and 3. Actualize Ministerial Leadership." These objectives were understood to be present throughout the entire program but "in a spiral fashion each one builds on the previous one with special attention being directed toward each in serial order." The proposal gave descriptions of courses that would be the major units in each of the three phases and outlined a process of assessment and advice for students at the close of each phase.[10] It took another year, until the fall of 1982, for the faculty to complete its work. The new curriculum was finally introduced in the fall of 1983, more that three years after the French Lick retreat.

The dean noted with favor that it provided two tracks for achieving the purposes of the degree, which was in itself "an important advance over the previous curriculum." Track one was recommended to all students. Despite the imaginative beginnings soon after French Lick, what now had been created was a new listing of required courses, and a heavy regimen that all students were to take. By the time that these requirements were completed, little time remained for anything else, including the Biblical languages that their church required of Presbyterian students. Track two set aside most of the requirements and allowed students to design their own programs in the light of their previous work and their vocational intentions. The M.Div. committee, however, found most track two proposals to be insufficient, and the time spent in evaluating proposals and counseling students was more than the committee could take. Finally, the faculty worked over their new requirements and, abandoning all efforts to base the curriculum upon new principles of curricular design, reverted to its previous principles for constructing the program of studies—required courses distributed evenly across the fields of study, with the intention that nearly every professor teach a required course. Yet the memory of French Lick continued in the hearts of the professors and in their dreams. Fifteen years later, as one of the newest professors observed, French Lick had taken on "legendary proportions."

Despite the modest character of the reform, certain important elements became part of the new program. Team teaching was embraced as a way to increase the excitement and effectiveness of teaching. A new course, which was instituted as part of the curriculum, developed remarkable staying power—X-815 Christian Ministry, taken by students in the first semester of their final year. Under the direction of a team of two professors, a different team each year, the students were to develop papers on the church and their ministry within it. Much of the work would be done within the framework of small groups so that students could have the benefit of peer review.

Toward the end of the semester the professors also reviewed the papers and recommended revisions. The final step was an oral examination by a team of three (later two) professors. Students found that the course developed a high level of anxiety; and yet it was strangely affirming. Still another of these developments was the "inner city internship program," which began in the fall of 1982. Special funding made it possible for a small number of students to be assigned as workers in inner-city churches. Although the hope had been that white students could work in black churches, most applicants were African American students.

Vitality of Academic Life

Despite the trials of developing curriculum, these were exciting years at Christian Theological Seminary. Some of the longstanding programs were continuing and new program initiatives were developing. One of the most far-reaching of the new programs, called "Metropolitan Church Leadership," was announced in the spring of 1981. During President Liggett's fact-finding conversations with church leaders, the need for continuing education of clergy and laity frequently had been discussed. A faculty task force then developed a plan for "action-research," which won a grant of $461,000 from Lilly Endowment. During a three-year period, these new funds would support students and other church leaders who were doing research in church and social concerns that would result in changed programs in churches, especially inner city congregations. The Seminary was to call a new professor who would devote a significant portion of his or her time to developing the program. D. Bruce Roberts accepted the Seminary's invitation to move from Scarritt College and become the first director of this program.

As the program developed, the action-research model was eclipsed by the more common model of short-term, noncredit theological study. From the beginning, the program was received positively by pastors, lay persons, and judicatory personnel. After four years, when a second grant from Lilly Endowment was on its way, Roberts reported that the Seminary had conducted forty-nine events, with a total of 1,658 participants, an average of thirty-four persons per event. In addition, the continuing education staff assisted the Seminary in some of its other activities. Because the director constantly sought out cooperative relationships with other religious organizations, including congregations, the Seminary's connections with the entire religious community were strengthened.

Another venture—the Chrysalis program—reshaped the Seminary's long-standing commitment to ministry overseas. For many years members of the faculty had been active in ecumenical and international activities of the churches, and this participation had reached a high mark in the work that Liggett and Dickinson did on behalf of the National and World Councils of Churches. Early in his deanship, Richard D. N. Dickinson, Jr., developed a program that was intended to bring this international and ecumenical experience to the Seminary in a much fuller way. The people whom he hoped to attract as students were church leaders, especially staff members at the regional or diocesan level, and he wanted through them to bring about a much greater awareness among the churches of the development and social-justice needs around the world. His plan called for bringing world scholars and students from the third world to campus for two major purposes: to provide them the opportunity of studying and teaching in the United States and to make it possible for CTS faculty and students to have significant contact with these scholars from abroad. He had to work for several years to develop funding so that he could launch the program, and then he discovered that it was difficult to secure the commitment of students from overseas and across the country to enroll.

Nevertheless, the program was launched in the fall of 1981, and during the next four years a continuing stream of internationally acclaimed professors from Latin America, Asia, and Africa came to the Seminary to teach for short assignments or for full semesters. Twelve professors from Asia, Africa, and Latin America took part in the program, including some of the most prominent theologians from the Third World. The major disappointment in the program was that few of the denominational leaders came. Most could not take that much time away from their work; the level of interest was lower than Dickinson had expected. The Chrysalis classes were taken by some students on degree programs who were especially interested in the worldwide work of the churches. Other students on the M.Div. and D.Min. programs took Chrysalis courses in order to satisfy the needs for courses in ethics and culture, with the result that an internationalist perspective became a major factor on campus.

In his summary of the program, Dickinson listed ten semester-long courses that were directly tied to Chrysalis and thirty-nine students (not including M.Div. students) whose programs of study were directly shaped by Chrysalis. A thorough evaluation of Chrysalis was prepared by Professor Edwin L. Becker in which he noted the importance to the program of having several international professors on campus. "Their ideas could not be brushed off as idiosyncratic. . . .They confronted students with the embodiment of the church and the gospel as a fresh and inescapable reality."[11] The objectives of Chrysalis were extended by a series of travel seminars during the four years that the program operated and in later years using unexpended Chrysalis funds. In these two-week ventures, students, professors, and trustees experienced Puerto Rico, Nicaragua, and India from a justice-oriented perspective.

A second of the new entrepreneurial programs was developed, in part, by Clark M. Williamson. It placed a strong emphasis upon Jewish-Christian relations, which renewed and transformed the witness that had begun in 1925 when Rabbi Morris M. Feuerlicht of the Indianapolis Hebrew Congregation had begun his work as lecturer at the Seminary. Following Feuerlicht's twenty-six-year service with the Seminary, there was an eighteen-year period with no direct connection with the Jewish community. In 1968–1969 Rabbi Sidney Steiman of Congregation Beth-El Zedeck was listed as lecturer in Old Testament and in 1975 he and Williamson began team teaching a new course, "Dialogue between Christians and Jews."[12] In 1979 the Seminary cooperated with the Jewish Community Relations Council in sponsoring a statewide conference on the moral implications of the Holocaust." In succeeding years, the Seminary and the council continued their joint sponsorship of an annual forum on Jewish-Christian relations, bringing speakers of national reputation to the campus to speak on appropriate topics. These annual assemblies developed a constituency so that each year attendance filled the common room to its capacity.

Two of the new initiatives were related to the field of Christian education. Soon after she succeeded James Blair Miller as professor of Christian education, Nelle G. Slater developed the Christian Education Resource Center in order to serve students and leaders in the churches. With funding from Lilly Endowment, she was able to provide a center on campus where a wide range of currently available resources for Christian education could be reviewed. The staff was also trained to serve as consultants at the center and in the churches. As with most other grants, the Seminary was expected to generate new financial support to take over the ongoing costs of maintaining the program; and Slater frequently spoke to representatives of the churches to solicit their support. Although most of the faculty gave little attention to the center, many students used its materials in their fieldwork in congregations.

A second program in Christian education, with Slater as its director, was developed as the result of initiatives taken by Lilly Endowment. Robert

W. Lynn, the endowment's vice president for religion, had taught in the field of Christian education, and with leaders in that field around the country had begun to anticipate a dearth of well-qualified people to become the next generation's leaders in that discipline. The result was a program called the National Faculty Seminar on Christian Education which brought together an interdisciplinary group of eleven scholars from around the country for the purpose of evaluating the discipline of Christian education and discovering resources for its renewal. One hope of the conference was to identify younger scholars who could be encouraged to direct their future work specifically toward careers in Christian education. The seminar met from 1982 through 1986, with some of the most creative theologians, educators, and biblical scholars in the United States participating. Its work culminated in the publication of two volumes of essays on the theme of citizenship and discipleship.[13]

Another initiative during these years was taken by President Liggett, who had concluded that a greatly strengthened CTS bookstore would render a service both to the campus and the larger community and thereby become economically viable. Funding from Lilly Endowment allowed him to hire a manager and increase the inventory of books for the expanded operation. Upgrading of the campus following the completion of the library included the renovation of space near the common room for the store, which opened during the 1980–1981 academic year. Just as Liggett was developing these plans, an Indianapolis pastor, Edward A. Steele III, was taking steps to realize a longtime dream of managing a theological bookstore. He and Liggett discussed the possibilities for a new kind of bookstore in Indianapolis, with the result that Steele, although he had no business experience, was hired to develop the new facility. Throughout his years as a pastor, Steele had maintained an interest in serious biblical studies and therefore was interested in displaying a strong collection of commentaries and scholarly reference materials. He also believed that the bookstore's appeal and usefulness would be increased if it were to stock serious books from across a wide theological spectrum. The result was that he created a unique specialty bookstore that drew people from the entire metropolitan area and represented a far broader spectrum of theological conviction than usually came to the campus. Sales immediately rose dramatically, which confirmed the importance of the bookstore to the campus and community.

In order to provide training opportunities for students in counseling courses and to assist persons in need, the Seminary created a pastoral counseling center which, under Sue Webb Cardwell's administration, was to become an important agency in the city. During the 1980–1981 year, students and staff of the center conducted 3,478 counseling interviews, an increase of 51 percent over the previous year, and in a typical week some two hundred persons came for counseling. The program used a fee schedule graduated according to income and was the only program of its kind in the city where persons with low incomes could receive long-term counseling.

Renewing the Teaching Force

These exciting academic ventures were coming into the Seminary's life at a time when the faculty and executive staff had been reduced in size to meet the financial pressures that had threatened the Seminary's existence. The full class schedule could be maintained only by the use of lecturers whose pay continued to be low and of visiting professors whose support came from special funding. Liggett and Dickinson drew upon their many years of experience in the international networks with which they had been connected and invited former colleagues from around the world to serve for brief periods at CTS. Among them were José Miguez-Bonino of Argentina, a president of the World Council of Churches and professor of systematic theology and ethics at the Union Evangelical Theological Seminary in Buenos Aires. R. Pierce Beaver, eminent missions scholar, retired from the faculty of the Divinity School of the University of Chicago, spent a semester. Like some of the other short-term professors, he participated in a full range of campus activities, including the student-sponsored weekly eucharist, and by his suggestions for the service demonstrated the depth of his interest in the church's liturgical tradition. Lucius Walker, an African American scholar who was director of the Interreligious Foundation for Community Organization, Inc., Washington, D.C., enriched the campus by his participation for a semester. On repeated occasions the Chrysalis program was enlivened by the presence of Theo A. Mathias, S.J., priest, educator, and labor relations expert from Jamshedpur, India, who was the author of two books and more than one hundred articles on education, development, and social justice.

Another visiting professor was suggested by members of the faculty: Norman Pittenger, retired Anglican scholar from Cambridge, England, whose theological orientation was formed by process theology.[14] In addition to participating regularly in the student-led eucharist, he regularly ate breakfast in the CTS dining room where he was joined by a table of regulars—students, staff members, and an occasional faculty colleague—in an on-going early morning conversation about life in Indianapolis and the world. J. Clinton Hoggard, Bishop of the African Methodist Episcopal Church, with offices in Indianapolis, also lectured regularly. A grant from Lilly Endowment underwrote a series of visiting professors, the first of whom was B. Davie Napier, formerly professor at Yale Divinity School and Stanford University, and later president of Pacific School of Religion.

While the many part-time, short-term teachers added to the excitement of study at CTS, there was a negative aspect to this practice. The regular faculty, the dean told the trustees, carried a heavy load of "non-instructional work," and the need was pressing to call additional full-time professors. In addition to relieving the overload on current professors, the Seminary intended to enlarge its offerings in continuing education of clergy and laity, and it hoped to contribute more fully to the shaping of church and public policy. By expanding the full-time faculty, the Seminary could offer instruction in important areas of work it was not able to cover and it could increase the diversity of its teaching staff.[15] The challenges of maintaining a teaching staff were increased as some longtime members of the faculty retired—James Blair Miller in1979, after serving at CTS since 1951, and Edwin L. Becker in the summer of 1981 after 16 years at CTS and 12 at Drake Divinity School in Des Moines.[16] The retirements continued— Lowell G. Colston in 1983, after 25 years of service; Lester G. McAllister later that year closing out 21 years with the Seminary; Alfred R. Edyvean in 1986, with 35 years on the faculty; and Vinton D. Bradshaw in 1987, completing 30 years in field education. Donald R. Wismar, with 22 years at the Seminary, left the faculty in 1985. This group of professors included the last teachers remaining from the faculty that Orman L. Shelton had assembled, and together they had taught some 175 years at the Seminary.

As professors left the faculty, new people were brought to the teaching force. By the 1980s, however, the challenge of selecting people had increased significantly as was illustrated by the search for Edwin L. Becker's successor, which lasted for three years and frequently was discussed in the dean's twice yearly reports to the trustees. Even though more than forty applications had been received and five applicants had been interviewed, an appointment had not yet been made. Some of the conversations had been discontinued because of salary and housing issues or the employment opportunities for a candidate's spouse. More important in explaining the delay were other reasons that Dickinson identified as "our commitment to an open search, our efforts to bring greater diversity into our total faculty, [and] our concern to weigh the advantages of maintaining a clear Disciples' identity." He continued to search aggressively for prospective candidates, "especially from minority communities, and women." While stating that no stone must be left unturned in the effort to "add competent, strong, and possibly young, candidates with these kinds of backgrounds," he also referred to the Supreme Court's statement in the Bakke case,[17] that these should constitute "additional qualifications," not substitute qualifications. He sensed that "our faculty and administration generally concur with the conviction that we need to bring that kind of diversity to our life."[18] After an initial appointment as a visiting professor, Rufus Burrow, Jr., was appointed to a regular term in this position. He had done his Ph.D. studies at Boston University and prior to coming to CTS had been director of the Young Adult Conservation Corps for the Pontiac (Michigan) Area Urban league.

Sue Webb Cardwell's election to the faculty illustrated another of the challenges facing the Seminary in calling new teachers. After serving on the staff of the counseling program in several capacities, Cardwell had completed her Ph.D. in 1978, and a short time later was offered a faculty position at another seminary. When she told President Liggett of her opportunity, she also reported that her preference would be to stay at CTS. Liggett concluded that it was to the Seminary's advantage for her to become a member of the faculty and he announced to the faculty his intention to dispense with the open search and ask her to meet with the faculty as a candidate to be a professor.

Most of the appointments, however, followed normal procedures. K. Brynolf Lyon, a young Disciples scholar who had just finished his doctoral work at Chicago, and Brian W. Grant, who had at an earlier time directed the program funded by the National Institute on Mental Health, were called to the counseling faculty. D. Newell Williams, associate dean of Brite Divinity School, Texas Christian University, was called as associate professor of modern and American church history. Janet Johnson Riley came as the new director of field education. Ronald J. Allen, initially appointed for the academic year 1982–1983, was the first person on the faculty to focus upon preaching since Donald R. Wismar had been transferred from preaching to pastoral care. Allen had earned his Ph.D. degree in preaching and New Testament, and then had served as co-pastor with his wife Linda McKiernan-Allen, in Grand Island, Nebraska. In 1983, the trustees extended the appointment for an additional two years. Another person who came first as a visiting professor and then was given a regular appointment was Michael K. Kinnamon. Previously he had served on the executive staff of the Faith and Order Commission of the World Council of Churches in Geneva, Switzerland, where he had been directly involved in the preparation of *Baptism, Eucharist and Ministry,* one of the most important ecumenical publications in the latter part of the century. V. Gayle Sarber was appointed adjunct professor of sacred music in 1983. In that same year George A. Boyle became part-time director of training for the CTS pastoral counseling center.

In April 1983, the dean commented on the president's report to the trustees that searches for people to fill four and a half faculty positions were under way. While making these searches, they were cognizant of the fact that the faculty was "under-represented" in the categories of younger scholars, women, minority persons, and Disciples of Christ. A year later, in his comments on faculty expansion, the dean noted that nine persons had been appointed during the previous five years—three of them were women and one from a racial minority. Two of the four criteria for faculty development had been achieved—youthfulness and significant Disciples leadership. The next appointments would need to focus on the other two—women and minority representation, "with more attention to the need for seasoned church leadership."[19] No one, of course, would be called who did not exhibit by previous work or promise for the future "an exceptional level of competence (teaching, scholarly and creative, church leadership, etc.)."

The dramatic change in the composition of the faculty was especially evident when within a twelve-month period five people were called—Ronald J. Allen, Rufus Burrow, Jr., Michael K. Kinnamon, K. Brynolf Lyon, and D. Newell Williams. Three of these people had been advanced to regular faculty appointments following a year of faculty service as visiting professor, which was to cause dissension within the faculty during the next several years. The faculty relations document provided detailed instructions concerning faculty searches; and in these instances, along with the election of Sue Webb Cardwell, these procedures had been bent. In two of the appointments, President Liggett had recommended the persons to the faculty without a national search because of factors that were unique in each case. In another of these appointments, a search had been conducted but the appearance was that the person already serving had the inside track and the impartiality of the search was questioned. This discontent over procedures was wide-spread enough that the student association commissioned one of its members to present their opposition to the board of trustees. After listening to their statement, the chair of the trustees asked this question: "If you have a chance to secure a star professor, but have to violate your procedures to do it, you would rather stay with the procedures and lose the star. Is that right?" The student representative could not respond because she, and most of the other students, wanted to keep the star.

The discomfiture among the faculty had a different character. Some professors concluded that a process was developing whereby the president and dean could, in effect, make their own choices by this two-step process. The visiting professors were chosen by the administration without a search and often with little or no consultation with the rest of the faculty; their presence on campus would neutralize any search that would take place thereafter.

While these changes in the faculty were taking place, another key member of the Seminary's staff—Cassius Fenton—died suddenly only a few weeks prior to his retirement as business manager and treasurer. He was succeeded by J. Stuart Mill, II, an active Disciples church leader with training both in theology and business.

When Liggett had begun his presidency the regular, full-time faculty consisted of seventeen persons, other than himself (Ashanin, Bates, Becker, Bradshaw, Colston, Dickinson, Edyvean, Leslie R. Galbraith, Janzen, Liggett, McAllister, Miller, Pellett, Porter, Watkins, White, Williamson, and Wismar). By the time that he retired only seven of them remained (Ashanin, Dickinson, Galbraith, Janzen, Porter, Watkins, and Williamson). They had been joined by twelve new colleagues (Allen, Burrow, Cardwell, Grant, Kinnamon, Lyon, Riley, Roberts, Sarber, Slater, Towne, and Williams). With this great a change in the personnel of the faculty, one could have anticipated a reshaping of the theological and spiritual character of the campus. Yet the remarkable fact is that the Seminary's central character remained essentially unchanged.

Perhaps the most important reason for the resilience of the existing faculty ethos was that the core of the continuing faculty consisted of a small group of professors who had come to the Seminary at about the same time and had formed the consensus that had come to characterize the school. By 1980, having served together for more than a decade, they were coming into their prime years and exercised their leadership in assertive ways. Even though the new professors had come in a relatively brief period of time, they were not able to form a cohesive force for change. Two of the three new people in pastoral care and counseling had previously been associated with the program and thus continued much of its character. Similarly, one of the appointments in theology also had taught briefly at CTS at an earlier time and returned, ready to reinforce the faculty's commitment to contemporary theology. The second appointment in theology, who represented a divergent point of view, soon left the faculty. Two of the appointments were in low status positions and these persons were unable to overcome this difficulty. Two of the new professors found themselves largely in accord with the prevailing ideas and reinforced them. The final two found that their efforts to create a dialogue that could have led to change were not able to hold back the momentum of the longstanding members of the faculty.

Another reason for the continuity of the existing ethos was the increased diversity in its faculty. Although all of the new professors were American, one was African American, four were women, six were significantly younger than their continuing colleagues, and five were non-Disciples. Because they brought different ideas about what should happen in American life and churches, they could not quickly come to agreement about a new direction. Richard D. N. Dickinson, Jr., told the trustees it was "particularly gratifying" that in addition to her other work Nelle G. Slater had taken the lead "in raising the consciousness of the community on issues pertaining to women's rights and roles," and the result was that she was bringing "a measure of coherence and direction to concerns which relate to women's roles in society and churches." A parallel role with black and minority students was being played by Lucius Walker during his semester as a Lilly Visiting Professor and the impact was confirmed by the three Third World scholars on campus as part of Chrysalis. "As a result, the theological curriculum cannot but be influenced by sustained and serious reflection on the relationship between the Gospel and oppressed communities. This growing awareness and questioning is one of the most significant aspects of theological education at CTS."[20] Coupled with increasing diversity among students, this increased diversity within the faculty made the preservation of some center of meaning and purpose seem more desirable than it would otherwise have been.

During these years the student body finally began to grow, gradually moving toward the four hundred mark. While the president would enthusiastically recite the numbers, the dean would analyze them, pointing out to the trustees in meeting after meeting that these statistics were never as good as they looked. As one of his faculty colleagues commented: "For the dean every silver lining has a cloud." Contrasting ways of thinking about things were evident in the president's and dean's reports to the trustees in the spring of 1983. While President Liggett had reported increased enrollment, Dean Dickinson wanted to be sure that the trustees did not become unduly optimistic about the future. Approximately a quarter of the persons enrolled that semester were non-degree and forty-two of the students were registered for audit only. Even though the total enrollment was increasing, the number of hours taken for credit had not increased, which suggested to him that "we should be cautious in any optimism about increased enrollments." He was concerned about enrollment on the M.Div. degree, because students were taking somewhat longer to complete requirements than they had taken twenty years earlier. One hundred twenty-five students now would not produce as many graduates per year as the same number had produced in 1960. This semester was also the first time in the Seminary's history that any other denomination had as many students at CTS as did Disciples—exactly the same number of United Methodists as Disciples.

Whether one viewed the statistics optimistically, or pessimistically, the numbers were growing, and so was the diversity. In the early 1980s, the dean calculated, average enrollment was 30 percent above the average of the 1970s and 54 percent above the average of the 1960s. He noted the increasing number of African American students, women students, and "second career" students. The proportion studying on the M.Div. degree had stabilized. Not only had the numbers increased, but these students had developed a tradition of active participation in campus life. During the late 1970s and early 1980s, the student association sponsored a series of fine arts festivals. The festival that took place from March 26 to April 6, 1979, included a musical play written by a recent graduate, a series of lectures on the relationship of the fine arts and theology, the spring concert by the CTS choirs, and an art showing and competition by artists.[21] In March 1980 the student association sponsored the study "Christian Perspectives on Homosexuality," a daylong conference with leadership by CTS professors J. Gerald Janzen and Edgar A. Towne and guest leaders from Chicago, Kentucky, and Indianapolis. Nearly one hundred persons registered.[22] Other functions of the student association included helping at registration of students for seminary classes, sponsoring the annual campuswide Christmas party and other social events, publishing a newsletter, providing financial assistance to international students, and sponsoring a lunch time lecture series.

With the move to its new location in the academic portion of the building, the Seminary chapel took on growing importance as a focal point for the life of the Seminary. The main service each week took place midway through the morning, when a large proportion of the M.Div. student body was on campus. The choir room was just outside the chapel doors so its members had time to robe and rehearse the music before the procession into the chapel. For a time, President Thomas J. Liggett was himself the coordinator of the chapel, and later Ronald J. Allen, followed by Keith Watkins. Although these three directors exercised their leadership in ways that differed from one another, all of them and their committees—along with the musicians—were determined that Chapel services be carefully planned, skillfully conducted, and experientially strong. The room itself was faithful to the model that was recommended by Edward Sovik, who had become one of the best-known church architects in mid-century. He encouraged congregations to build "centrums," large, gracious rooms that could be used for many public activities, including worship.[23] The provisional chapel had proportions, light, and character, all of which made it the environment in which people could find themselves addressed by the Living Word who came to them through the scriptural word that was read and preached. Worshipers developed a style of communal prayer that combined the sentence prayers that many of them had learned in their protestant Sunday schools with responsive prayers that were characteristic of churches with formal prayer traditions.

With the completion of the apartments across Haughey Avenue, the sense of community was significantly strengthened among students.[24] The units were attractive and comfortable, and they were close to the classrooms, library, and chapel. For the first time in the Seminary's history a significant number of students and their families lived in facilities that nourished their friendships and helped overcome the tension that usually existed between students, their families, and their schooling.

Designing the Chapel

The most visible sign that the Seminary was reaching a mature phase of its life was the construction of the east wing and chapel. Early in the capital campaign, Clementine Miller Tangeman had first told Thomas J. Liggett that she and her family wanted to complete the master plan for the campus. The president had asked her to delay the announcement until the completion of the $10 million campaign. As soon as its success had been assured, Liggett focused his attention upon working with Tangeman and her family to create the chapel and complete the east wing of the campus. The master plan developed twenty years earlier had included the design for the chapel, but in two decades three factors had changed. The redesign of the master plan when the library had been built, and the Seminary's experience of using the entire complex, created implications for the design and placement of the chapel. During these years the liturgical movement in Western Christianity had developed extensively, with direct implications for the design of worship space. Furthermore, the Christian Foundation had not specified how much it was willing to contribute to the completion of the project, which meant that the design of the building and the devel-opment of a budget for construction and endowment would be intertwined.

Liggett appointed a task force of faculty and staff, trustees, and donors to meet regularly with the architect in order to plan the new structures. In addition to himself as chair of the group, Liggett appointed Dean Dickinson, Keith Watkins, who was professor of worship and the member of the faculty most knowledgeable about liturgical developments, P. E. MacAllister who was chair of the trustees, and Richard DeMars, head of a prominent Indianapolis construction company and chair of the building and grounds committee of the board of trustees. Representing the Christian Foundation were Clementine Miller Tangeman and J. Irwin Miller. It was agreed that Marilyn Keiser, head of the organ department of the School of Music at Indiana University, would be retained as consultant for the design of the organ and that the Holtkamp Organ Company of Cleveland would be the organ builder. Space for music, including practice rooms, and offices for the chapel staff were included on the lower level. A second major entrance to the campus, with parking area, would provide easy access to the chapel, the bookstore which would move around to the east wing, the counseling program which would also have new quarters, and the library.

Early in the process, Edward Larrabee Barnes came to the campus and described his hope that the revised plan could tighten the chapel design and move it slightly toward the west, partially closing the open leg of the quadrangle. In this way the campus would develop a more intimate sense and the three-hundred-year-old oak tree on the edge of the precipice would be given greater prominence.[25] The task force actively debated the arrangement of major spaces in the chapel, its acoustical properties, and the use of light. In each of these instances it yielded to the architect's recommendations, except in his early proposal that the ceiling of the chancel be covered with gold leaf. They reached a compromise in their debate over seating. Whereas the faculty, through its members on the task force, urged that chairs or easily moved short pews be used, the architect and nonfaculty members of the task force strongly supported fixed pews. The solution was long pews that would ordinarily be arranged according to the architect's recommendation but that with premeditation and hard work could be rearranged.

All agreed with the main elements of the design, which provided a large chancel with starkly simple furniture and with organ and choir on one side of the chancel, facing major windows. They wanted the chapel to be able to accommodate as many as 450 people while at the same time suitably serving congregations of 50 to 75. The resolution to this challenge was to provide seating on the main floor for 125, and a large balcony that ordinarily would not be used. The space under the balcony would be left open, but chairs could be brought in for special occasions. A stone bench would be built around two walls where a surprisingly large number of people could sit if they chose.

Watkins urged that a baptistry be added to the plan because he had found in his teaching that access to such a facility was important, especially in a seminary related to the Disciples of Christ, whose sacramental practice included adult baptism by immersion. After initially questioning the value of this addition, the task force agreed that Barnes should design a baptistry; the Millers arranged for Mr. and Mrs. Barnes to visit their church in Columbus in order to study its remarkable baptistry chapel. As the design began to take shape, the task force recognized that the baptistry could be used as a meditation chapel and space where small liturgies could be performed. Although some people questioned the location of the baptistry away from the main sight lines of the congregation, the wide arch that connected the two spaces, the murmuring of the water, and the vertical cutouts in the entry to the chapel overcame this objection.

Barnes developed sketches for the chapel windows in the long wall that was oriented toward the northwest. Although some members of the task force were urging windows that worshipers could see through, Barnes's first recommendations proposed glass similar to that which he had used in the Roman Catholic Cathedral in Burlington, Vermont—an opaque glass with sinewy landscapes in greens and blues. At that point he became acquainted with the pioneering work of James Carpenter, who combined artistic imagination with a command of the structural properties of large panels of glass. Carpenter proposed that the windows be made of three-dimensional structural glass with metallic film embedded in the horizontal members. This dichroic glass, as he termed it, would reflect sunlight in shades of gold and refract sunlight in shades of blue, the result being an ever-changing pattern of color across the chancel wall. Yet worshipers could see outside. A sample of Carpenter's proposal was manufactured and stationed at the Seminary. The response was so positive that the task force approved the design even though the orientation of the building would mean that the sun would bathe the windows during the afternoons rather than during the morning hours when chapel services ordinarily were conducted.[26]

As plans took shape, Liggett consulted with Barnes, Richard DeMars, and J. Irwin Miller to establish a budget and guidelines that could contain the costs. These decisions made it possible for Liggett and the donors to decide upon the amount of money they needed to provide in order to construct the east wing and chapel and endow the maintenance of the chapel. It was clear throughout these discussions that Tangeman, whose gifts to the Christian Foundation would provide the major source of this grant, would endow the building and its upkeep, but the Seminary would need to find other ways to fund the chapel staff and program. One of President Liggett's final actions related to the chapel was to recommend to the trustees that it be called Sweeney Chapel, thus continuing the name that had been used at the School of Religion building on the Butler campus. While not requesting that this name be used, J. Irwin Miller had written a letter to the president discussing chapel names, suggesting that some of the best-known chapels in the land—such as Rockefeller at the University of Chicago and Duke in Durham, North Carolina—bore the names of persons. Liggett's recommendation to the trustees was that the chapel proper be named after Z. T. Sweeney and that the tower carry the name Irwin. Clementine Miller Tangeman drafted the inscription in the tower to include others in the family line who had carried the Irwin name, and the family proposed the citation for the chapel itself, sifting through a set of scripture texts that they considered possibilities until choosing the one that is engraved in the memorial plate:

> Make every effort
> to supplement your faith with virtue
> and virtue with knowledge
> and knowledge with self-control
> and self-control with steadfastness
> and steadfastness with godliness
> and godliness with friendship
> and friendship with love.
>   For if these things are
> yours and abound
> they keep you from being ineffective
> or unfruitful in the knowledge
> of our Lord Jesus Christ
>   II Peter 1:5-8

Ground was broken for construction at commencement in 1985 and construction began later in the summer. All through that next year the attention of everyone on campus was captured by the monumental work taking place on the bluff. In the summer of 1986, when the Liggetts brought their work to a close and moved to California, construction was still in process, but Liggett's careful management of the entire process had established the framework for the successful completion of construction.

Early in the fall of 1987 the Seminary community moved from the intimacy of the provisional chapel to the grandeur of Sweeney Chapel. Despite their gradual acceptance of the stark whiteness of the campus as a whole, they were not ready to accept that same quality when blown up to the scale of this new place of worship. Since their services took place in the mornings, before the colors of the windows would flood the room with ever-changing patterns and intensities of blue, yellow, and green, the room overwhelmed worshipers with its whitewashed appearance and echoes so strong that they confounded tongues and baffled ears. Faculty, students, and guests had to learn a new way of speaking if they wanted congregants to understand them; in the process they discovered that their modest efforts to interpret the word of God often sounded like great preaching. The organ was a powerful presence in the room—visually against the side wall and aurally strong whenever it was played. The choir sounded very good, especially in the Advent service of Lessons and Carols. The baptistry was experienced as a peaceful place—because of the simplicity of the room, the sound of water, and the perfect flow of liquid over the rounded stonework all around the pool. The arc of the pool and the matching arch between the baptistry and the main chapel were the only curved lines in a room with straightness on every side. Edgar A. Towne preached a sermon soon after the Seminary began using Sweeney Chapel in which he suggested that these curved lines were the "grace notes" in an otherwise austere space.

The Seminary introduced the chapel to the churches and people of the larger community with Choral Evensong on a beautiful Sunday afternoon, the dedicatory service a little later on, and a winter evening concert by the Indianapolis Opera Chorus, made possible by P. E. MacAllister. In order to acquaint graduates and other Disciples from around the country with the chapel, two services of the eucharist were celebrated on Sunday morning during the Disciples General Assembly in Indianapolis in June 1989.

The most important of the opening events was the evening of November 15, 1987, when the Holtkamp organ was dedicated, because on that occasion Clementine Miller Tangeman made her last public statement on campus. She began by declaring that "religion and the arts have always had a close relationship," and then spoke of the fact that for thousands of years artists of every kind have used their finest talents to construct buildings worthy of the worship for which they were constructed. She then spoke extemporaneously of her research the previous evening on the history of the organ and the congregation joined in laughter as she told them that since the organ had been used in gladiatorial combats the early Christians had believed that it was not suitable for use in the church. Later the church's ideas changed, said Tangeman, and the organ has come to be the premier instrument for use in worship. Returning to her prepared text, she concluded by again speaking of the rich treasure that the arts bring to our faith. Her statement, which lasted scarcely five minutes, was delivered in rich full tones, with confidence and hope. For her, art, religion, worship, and God were tied together in a continuum, with the arts, and especially music, the medium that held them together. After the completion of the liturgy, Marilyn Keiser, professor of organ at Indiana University, played the dedicatory recital.

In this evening of celebration, a long tradition was reaching a climax. Thirty years after it was first conceived and twenty years after the first construction, the pre-Gothic campus of Christian Theological Seminary had finally been completed. It was significant that the member of the Irwin-Sweeney-Miller family who spoke on that occasion was a woman. Through the many years when William G. Irwin had been the public leader of his family, his sister Linnie Irwin Sweeney and his nieces Nettie Sweeney Miller and Elsie Irwin Sweeney had been strong participants in religious, charitable, and cultural affairs; these women had been leaders of the family's support of Butler University and the institutions of the Christian Church. During the years when J. Irwin Miller was the prominent member of the family in Seminary affairs, his wife Xenia Simons Miller also was a strong participant, later serving as one of the trustees in her own right. For more than half a century, Clementine Miller Tangeman was a significant leader in civic and cultural affairs, especially in music, religion, and education, in New York City, New Haven, and the Midwest. She, too, served as a trustee of the Seminary. Because her husband, Robert S. Tangeman, had been professor of church music at Union Theological Seminary, she had lived in the midst of a theological community and understood the rhythms of its life.

From the 1940s onward, she drew upon her own financial resources to challenge and encourage the Seminary in its mission. Throughout her lifetime she maintained a keen awareness that both of her grandfathers had been ministers in the Christian Church, and she wanted in every way that she could to continue the traditions that they had represented so fully. She often spoke of her mother's active life on behalf of the church and its institutions; the similarity of spirit was evident. Although she refused suggestions that her name be used in buildings on the campus, Clementine Miller Tangeman was for half a century one of its principal advocates and benefactors.

With the dedication of the new Sweeney Chapel, the material form of Christian Theological Seminary was finally complete and its program of theological studies had reached full maturity. Many of its graduates were serving as ministers of congregations, missionaries, and executives in the many agencies and organizations of the churches. Other graduates were finding their vocations as counselors, teachers and professors, and leaders of social service agencies. The Seminary's mission of being a center of theological education and reflection for the entire community was within reach. Many would have said that the objective that Thomas J. Liggett had announced eight years earlier had been achieved—that CTS had become "the finest institution of its kind ever developed by the Disciples."[27]

Left: Trustee C. Richard Petticrew at the Disciples General Assembly in San Antonio, fall of 1983. *Center*: Professors J. Gerald Janzen and Clark M. Williamson, whose interest in process thought made relational theology to be a central component in the CTS ethos. *Right*: Professors Alfred R. Edyvean and Lowell G. Colston at a convocation in 1983. (Courtesy Christian Theological Seminary)

President Thomas J. Liggett and Clementine Miller Tangeman, in the library of the Irwin family home in downtown Columbus, Indiana, conferring on specifications for the chapel and east wing. (Courtesy Christian Theological Seminary)

The Seminary bells await installation in Irwin Tower. (Courtesy Christian Theological Seminary)

Left: Architect Edward Larrabee Barnes presents plans for the new chapel in 1984. *Right*: Thomas J. Liggett surveys progress while the chapel is under construction. (Both courtesy Christian Theological Seminary)

J. Irwin and Xenia Simons Miller at their home in Columbus, Indiana. (Courtesy J. Irwin and Xenia Simons Miller)

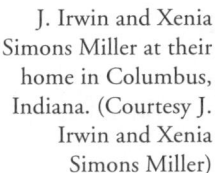

President Richard D. N. Dickinson, Jr., in the president's office. (Courtesy Christian Theological Seminary)

Students gather around Pomodoro's *Sphere #6*, 1991. (Courtesy Christian Theological Seminary)

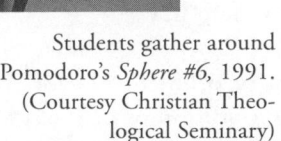

The Seminary community at worship in Sweeney Chapel. (Courtesy Christian Theological Seminary)

11
A Spirit Ever Restless

An Ecumenical Seminary of the Christian Church, 1987–1997

When Thomas J. Liggett announced his intention to retire, the board of trustees began a study process designed to assist the board in selecting a new president. One of the actions was to ask three of its members with strong Disciples connections[1] to develop a report that would "reaffirm and undergird the historic relationship between the seminary and the Christian Church (Disciples of Christ)." Upon their recommendation, the board revised the Seminary's bylaws. A majority of the trustees and "a significant portion of the faculty" were to be active participants in the life of the Christian Church (Disciples of Christ); and all trustees and professors should be "generally active participants in the worshipping tradition of their own denomination." The revisions replaced the requirement that the president be a Disciple with the provision that

> the president shall be a person of ecumenical spirit who actively participates in the worshipping tradition of his/her denomination and is committed to the maintenance of the historic relationship between Christian Theological Seminary and the Christian Church (Disciples of Christ) and will provide leadership for fulfilling the seminary's covenantal relationships with the Division of Higher Education, Regions related by comity agreements, the Council of Ministers, and other institutional ties.

The document added a balancing statement that "the Dean of the Seminary shall be a member of the Christian Church (Disciples of Christ) if the President of the Seminary is a member of another denomination."[2]

By July of 1986, when the board of trustees had adopted these revisions, President Liggett's announced date for retirement had come. He and Virginia had both experienced serious illnesses and they moved to their retirement home in California. Since the trustees had not yet chosen his successor, they asked Dean Richard D. N. Dickinson, Jr., to serve as acting president. A year later, with strong support of the faculty, the board elected Dickinson to be the fourth president of Christian Theological Seminary. As a member of the United Church of Christ, he was the first non-Disciple to serve as dean and as president of the Seminary. With the concurrence of the trustees, Dickinson appointed Professor Michael K. Kinnamon to serve as acting dean and three years later, following a national search, he nominated Joe R. Jones to become vice president and dean of the Seminary. A theologian and former seminary dean and university president, Jones had significant credentials as a leading Disciples educator and church leader.

Confirming Academic Life

As the new administration moved into place, a major focus of attention was given to the basic processes of Seminary life, beginning with the recruitment of students. Financial aid and scholarship support were restructured to increase the Seminary's effectiveness in attracting students.[3] Elaine Amerson was appointed to a new full-time position of admissions counselor, funded by the Irwin-Sweeney-Miller Foundation. Amerson traveled to many schools, proclaiming the excitement of study at Christian Theological Seminary. She invited college students to visit the campus where they discovered that her descriptions were correct; returning on registration day, they increased enrollment and reduced the average age of the student body. These students became active in ways that added to the excitement of life on campus. One of their concerns was the policy of apartheid in South Africa, and they successfully urged the Seminary's board of trustees to follow the lead of many educational and cultural institutions and divest the Seminary's endowment of stocks in companies that continued to do business in South Africa. Students also developed organizations for encouragement and support, including a women's caucus, a black caucus, and a group for gay and lesbian persons. A small group of students, most of them with ties to Phillips University, called themselves The New Oak Society, invoking the memory of the old oak tree that had blown down the previous year.

Dean Jones and the faculty devoted much attention to revising academic policies and practices. One reason was the changing cultural climate that increased awareness throughout the society to issues of justice. The Seminary developed policies for using inclusive language in the chapel and classrooms, adopted a policy statement on sexual harrassment and consensual relationships, responded to new federal guidelines concerning confidentiality of student records, and developed a new manual for employees that seemed to stiffen relationships. Because of changes in federal law, mandatory retirement of professors at age sixty-seven was discontinued. At the same time, processes for peer review were strengthened in order to encourage all professors to continue their work at high levels of academic productivity.

New appointments were being made to the faculty during these same years, both to fill vacancies because of resignation or retirement and to extend the range of persons in the Seminary's group of teachers. Special attention was given to increasing the number of women and persons of color. Between 1988, when Joe R. Jones became dean, and 1994, nine persons were called to the faculty—five women and three African Americans.[4] Each time that the Seminary conducted a search, the administration and faculty had to contend with the potential conflict between the desire to attract women and people of color and the commitment to bring people of high academic potential without regard to gender or race. Dean Jones developed a statement on tenurability and diversity to help the Seminary make these appointments. Tenurability was defined to mean that "prospective faculty should have either demonstrated or show promise of excellence and effectiveness in teaching, scholarship, and church life." Diversity was described with respect to church traditions, gender, race, and culture; the principle was declared that this kind of diversity "positively enhances the prospect of a rich, complex, adequate, and truthful instruction in, grasp of, and enactment of the Christian faith."[5] The document proposed a method for holding these two principles in close relationship whenever new professors were sought. It also proposed goals of eventually recruiting a faculty that would be approximately equal in numbers of men and women, with approximately 30 percent being people from non-Caucasian racial groups. Special attention was to be given to African American and Hispanic representation.

As always, the preparation of leaders for the church was at the center of the faculty's interest. In the early 1990s several cross-disciplinary courses were established to help students internalize their learnings and adapt them to life in the churches. A course early in the M.Div. program, titled "Spirituality, Autobiography and Christian Ministry," was described as "a theological reflection on the journeys and communities that [had] brought students to their common experience of entering CTS." Another change was the combining of field education and basic instruction in congregational analysis, leadership, and administration into a yearlong course that could only be taken concurrently with placement in a field position and participation in SCOFE—Supervised Concurrent Field Education.

A yearlong sequence in systematic theology was introduced in which students were to encounter "the church's central beliefs" and write a "constructive statement of their understanding of the content of the Christian faith." It was to be team taught so that students could encounter the central claims of the gospel from various perspectives. Several years after the course was established, Joe R. Jones, having given up his post as dean, indicated that he would be willing to teach the course in the future but by himself rather than as part of a team. Remembering the work of professors during his student days at Yale, Jones developed a two-volume typescript as a road map of the ideas and convictions of the Christian faith, thus continuing the work that he had published in *Encounter* on the theme of "God's salvific work in Jesus Christ."[6] With his grounding in Barthian theology and the postmodernist theology that had been characteristic of Yale, Jones provided a strong counterpoint to the Chicago school of process thought that had dominated the Seminary's faculty for a quarter of a century.

Church officials were also interested in what was happening with students during their seminary years, and they continued to ask the Seminary to assist them in assessing the readiness of students for ministry. Over the years the faculty had steadfastly held to the principle that the Seminary's responsibility was the academic preparation of students while the churches were responsible for moral and spiritual preparation. Yet church officials were insisting that seminaries had to do more than prepare students on the intellectual level. Not only should the professors work at shaping the moral and spiritual lives of students, but they should share information on a confidential level with representatives of the churches. In a new policy document the Seminary pledged itself to counsel students about readiness for ministry and to assess them annually with respect to a set of ten criteria. Students would be asked to sign waivers to allow communications between the Seminary and a judicatory named by the student. A "committee on counsel" would oversee this process and, if the committee deemed the action appropriate, ask students in its care to withdraw from the Seminary. The ten criteria included factors that the faculty had always considered to be within its competence to decide, such as the "capacity to make informed and faithful articulation of the Christian faith"; but it also included items that the faculty had previously not dealt with directly, such as "commitment to a non-addictive, healthy lifestyle."[7]

Soon after this procedure had been devised, Jones's first term as dean came to a close, and he asked to be relieved of administrative duties so that he could teach full-time. Professor D. Newell Williams was asked to become dean, and he coupled his acceptance with the request that the existing position of assistant to the dean be upgraded to assistant dean, with full responsibility for student-related aspects of the dean's office. Rebecca B. Prichard, a Presbyterian professor of historical theology and former executive on the San Francisco Presbytery, was called to this post, and to her fell the task of overseeing stringent new academic procedures and the assessment for ministry. Working closely with the M.Div. committee and the committee on counsel, Prichard created a system for canvassing faculty to assess all students on ministry-directed degree programs.

Having devoted themselves so completely to the strengthening of Christian Theological Seminary, the faculty and senior staff wondered if they had made progress toward their goals, which President Dickinson had described as serving the world through the church.[8] The approach of their every-ten-year accreditation review in 1998 provided the incentive to assess their work. The faculty sent questionnaires to recent graduates in order to understand as accurately as they could the experiences and evaluations of the people who were putting their seminary studies into practice. They discovered that the perennial problem with CTS degrees—the poor integration of theology and the practice of the ministry—was still with them.[9] This problem, however, showed itself differently with respect to the two major groups of graduates. People who had received the M.Div. degree reported a strong degree of satisfaction with the biblical, historical, and theological studies they had received, but they also indicated that they seemed inadequately prepared to care for a church adequately. Their socialization into a ministerial self-understanding was fragile, so that some of these graduates found themselves unsuccessful and unhappy in their pastoral work.

In contrast, people studying for degrees in pastoral care and counseling reported high evaluations of the way that their studies had equipped them to counsel and to experience themselves as counselors. Where they had trouble was in courses in the theological disciplines. Not only did pastoral care and counseling students feel out of place in courses designed for M.Div.

students, but they failed to see vital connections between the biblical and theological information in these courses and their work as counselors.

In order to think together about their programs of study, the faculty devoted time at its annual working retreat to a book edited by two prominent theological educators: *Shifting Boundaries: Contextual Approaches to the Structure of Theological Education*.[10] In her introduction Barbara Wheeler summed up the four principles that historically had shaped theological programs of study: the division of the curriculum into the fields of Bible, history, theology, and practical ministry; the idea that the theory-to-practice sequence arranges these disciplines with respect to one another; the subdivision of the practical field into functional specialties; and the centrality of historical-critical methods in all aspects of theological study.[11] The article by Craig Dykstra (who had just become senior vice president for religion of the Lilly Endowment) offered a critique of the understandings of *practice* within most seminary faculties, asserting that these ideas emphasized individual practitioners, aiming at getting things done, which meant that historical development was unimportant. Dykstra's critique cut across the entire curriculum, classical and practical fields alike. He proposed a different understanding of practice that was cooperative and called upon embodying the history of the action as well as technical competence. His metaphor was playing baseball, which can be done only by people whose individual actions are incorporated into what the team and spectators are doing together. Action at any moment in a game is conditioned by the knowledge of baseball that is fully embodied among the players. Dykstra asserted that new knowledge is gained through the process of playing so that only players can really learn the game. Following the lead of Marianne Sawicki, he argued that "engagement in the practice of service is a *condition* for the knowledge of a reality absolutely central to faith."[12]

The importance of Dykstra's analysis was that it placed the burden of change upon all parts of the faculty. He was not recommending the radical alteration of existing curricula, but he did assert that this changed understanding needed to permeate all aspects of seminary study. Because he believed that changing curricula would be difficult to accomplish, he hoped that existing programs could be infused with a new spirit of the relationship between the disciplines. Yet Dykstra also yearned for places where radical changes in the curricular structure itself could be developed. In response to that discussion, Calvin L. Porter proposed, only half in jest, that the Bible field should be reshaped so that it would be pointed more toward the life of the church than of the academy. His proposal was that the field be named the field of biblical interpretation. Although the name of the field remained unchanged, one professor—Marti J. Steussy—who had begun her work with the title of assistant professor of Old Testament later became associate professor of Biblical interpretation. The faculty as a whole saw little need to move away from the pattern of curricular design that was familiar to them; but continued to work, both as individuals and as a body, on how they taught their courses.

Midway through the decade, Dean Williams was advised by staff of the Association of Theological Schools that no major changes in curriculum should be made until after the self-study and accreditation review that would be taking place in 1997 and 1998. Furthermore, the dean had promised the Seminary's alumni board that, following the accreditation review, the faculty would begin a "ground up reconsideration of the nature of the church's leadership needs in relation to how CTS might reinvent the M.Div. and that representatives of that board would be invited to work with the faculty on this process."[13] As they finished their self-study for the accreditation review, they concluded that there was "general success and satisfaction" among alumni concerning their work at CTS and therefore reform of the curriculum was "not an urgent matter." They also concluded that people in other seminaries were experiencing similar difficulty in integrating theological and practical studies, which seemed to take the urgency away from the CTS plight. What needed to be done, the faculty concluded, was to "remain in touch with the broader national conversation about how to accomplish practical ministerial education."[14] Their intention, however, was to conduct the "ground up study" that Dean Williams had promised and in the final faculty meeting of the 1997–1998 academic year set dates for the first retreat in which they and representative graduates would begin that work.

At this same time, the professors and staff of the Seminary's Pastoral Counseling Service were preparing for an accreditation review by the American Association of Pastoral Counselors. Required by the AAPC to "think theologically" about their work and program, they wrote an extended exposition of the theology that undergirded their work.[15] While affirming that the leaders of the CTS program sought to "be open to a variety of theological viewpoints," the document stated that "a liberal, social-justice oriented understanding of the Christian gospel is normative." The central assumptions within this world view included the belief that "God's most salient expression of Godself is through loving concern for persons and that all are of value in the sight of God." The central task of therapy is "newness of life." The pastoral counselor "is called to be the embodied expression of God's understanding love and saving grace to those who find themselves adrift on the seas of life. Learning to float in faith when assailed by storms from the world around and sharks from the unconscious below is a life-long task that the pastoral counselor must approach with hope, carrying that hope like a beacon for those whose view of life has grown dim."

The work of psychotherapy, the document continued, consists initially of "confession and ultimately, of conviction, confirmation, and praise." Although couched in the vocabulary of the psychotherapeutic disciplines, the statement insisted that "just as the church provides the structure which houses and lends meaning to the practices of our faith, so the therapeutic hour provides a transitional space where spontaneity and newness of life find expression in the reconstructive work of psychotherapy." In testimonial language, the document declared that "spiritual life is participation in the love of God that created us and will accompany us through all the trials of life, to the grave and beyond. No matter how buried and repressed this voice of hope may become, it is heard by those who come to us for treatment, or they would not come." Theological language was also used in the document's discussion of the philosophy and methodology of supervision at the CTS Pastoral Counseling Center. Supervision was the title of the process by which the faculty and mature staff of the Center guided students in the pastoral care and counseling program who were counseling with clients coming to the Center for help. Some counseling sessions were observed through one-way mirrors, but most of the supervision was based on videotape, audiotape, or written verbatim accounts of counseling sessions. The process also included supervision conferences, reflecting groups, and other procedures by which the staff guided students in their work. The concentrated aspects of supervision were in the practicum that took place all day Monday all through the year except for major holidays.

This faith-based approach to counseling was administered in ways that provided space for people of widely differing theological convictions. In significant numbers, students continued to enroll in the degree programs to prepare for faith-based careers that helped people find meaning and purpose in life. Although some of the graduates expected to serve as ordained leaders within their faith communities, the majority saw counseling as a form of religious service that could be exercised outside of the framework of churches and synagogues.

One part of the Seminary's life that continued to be a place where professors, staff, and students came together as people of faith was in the chapel. Soon after the Seminary moved into Sweeney Chapel, Keith Watkins, who had been appointed the director of Seminary worship, recommended that the celebration of the eucharist be made a major part of the worship schedule. The Friday morning services took place at ten A.M., and most other activities on campus were suspended during that hour so that everyone on campus on Friday mornings would be free to attend. Under the direction of Professor V. Gayle Sarber, the chapel choir, which for many years had been known as the CTS Cantors, increased significantly in membership. With the coming of Garth Baker-Fletcher to the faculty in 1991, a gospel choir was established that offered a contrasting musical character to seminary worship. These groups, along with a bell choir, also provided the opportunity for establishing strong personal relationships among students and staff. Throughout the semester the liturgies would alternate between services of the word, with full sermon, and services of the eucharist, with full celebration of the Lord's supper. The three-year ecumenical lectionary was ordinarily followed for these Friday services, using the readings for the forthcoming Sunday. Each semester the eucharistic liturgies of three or four churches would be used, with professors, students and staff from each tradition taking the lead in preparing and leading the liturgy. The other eucharists were guided by the chapel director, who developed a liturgy that expressed the emerging ecumenical consensus concerning worship at the Lord's table. In the Tuesday morning services in Sweeney Chapel, the ecumenical two-year lectionary for daily prayer was recommended to worship leaders and preachers.

One effort to strengthen the impact of Seminary studies upon students was the developing of a document on experiential learning, prepared by a task force and presented to the faculty in the spring of 1992. The task force had been appointed by Dean Jones and given the assignment to study various forms of experiential learning and prepare recommendations for the faculty. Experiential learning was defined in the dean's instructions as "that process in which a learner is intentionally placed in a situation of experience and practice and in which the learner has the opportunity under supervision to reflect on and learn from that experience and practice." The task force's recommendation was that the faculty redefine their program of study not by revising the current pattern of courses and assigned hours but rather by "contextualizing the curriculum in the experience of the student at three crucial points—the experience of entering seminary, the experience of a significantly different culture, and the experience of leadership in the church." For each of these moments of experience the task force made recommendations that the faculty later enacted into curricular form.

The professors continued their regular duties as teachers and participants in campus life. They were also active as preachers, teachers, conference leaders, and authors. In preparation for the 1997 accreditation review, the faculty compiled a list of the publications during the previous ten years by professors and affiliate professors. Twenty-four persons reported 414 titles of books (written, edited, or translated), articles, reviews, chapters, and journal entries. The caliber of the titles varied widely, from brief comments to major books, but the cumulative impact was impressive.

Responding to Mainline Decline

These efforts to strengthen the Seminary's life were significantly influenced by the continuing decline of mainline protestantism and the rising influence of catholic, charismatic, and pentecostal churches around the world. Although these changes had been taking place for at least three decades, their impact was intensifying during the years of the Liggett-Dickinson era. All of the mainline churches were experiencing a diminished vitality, with Disciples being especially hard hit. In 1925, when the College of Religion began its work at Butler University, the Disciples *Yearbook* listed 706 congregations in Indiana, with a total membership of 160,756.[16] In 1959, as Christian Theological Seminary began its separate life, the *Yearbook* reported Indiana Disciples membership of 139,989 in participating churches and 37,525 in non-participating churches.[17] By 1990, the picture had changed dramatically. In his book *Hoosier Faiths*, L. C. Rudolph summarized the strength in Indiana of the three denominations that he listed under the general heading "the Christians." The conservative branch, called Churches of Christ, reported 39,953 adherents. The Christian Church (Disciples of Christ), which Rudolph described as the "more liberal, ecumenical, and mainline denomination," reported 89,932 adherents. Rudolph referred to "a center group" of Christian Churches and Churches of Christ, which had become the largest segment of the Christians in Indiana, and the third largest denomination in the state, with 160,099 adherents.[18]

This decline of Disciples vitality impacted the Seminary's financial receipts, as President Dickinson reported to the trustees soon after his election. Despite the increasing amount of money received from Disciples sources, the percentage of budget covered went down. From 1982–1983 to 1986–1987, Dickinson told his board, contributions as a category of income decreased from 24.8 percent to 16.9 percent. "One stark conclusion," Dickinson said, "is that the Seminary will have to rely less on Disciples church support unless new church-wide policies are forged."[19] Although the report made no reference to this fact, it was also true that church support would not be coming from other church bodies with large enrollments at CTS. Every previous effort to persuade churches like the United Methodist to include this Seminary in their annual judicatory budgets had failed because they would support only the seminaries directly related to their own ecclesial networks.

The next year Dickinson reported to the trustees that in other schools similar in size to CTS, 23 percent of the budget came from the annual fund and another 17 percent came from the sponsoring denomination. He described, as he would often do in succeeding years, the fact that CTS depended upon its endowment for a larger proportion of its income than other schools. He acknowledged that CTS had been "in a favored position on grants . . . for specific programs and projects, enabling us to engage in numerous experimental and quality enhancing programs."[20] As subsequent developments were to demonstrate, Dickinson was determined to generate more soft-money support for programs by which the Seminary could respond to the crisis of Disciples and mainline protestant church life. With the financial backing of Lilly Endowment, he enlisted members of the faculty to design and sponsor conferences that would explore the challenges facing the churches and help the participants find solutions to these challenges.

Two conferences on the nature of biblical authority, one in the fall of 1989 and the second a year later, were designed to promote dialogue between conservative and liberal protestant traditions. One hundred fifty people representing seven traditions attended the first event and heard the keynote speaker challenge the premise of the conference—its use of the categories of conservative, moderate, and liberal.[21] The second event, intended to foster dialogue between liberal and traditional Disciples, was even less encouraging. It drew only a small number of participants and in his report Charles Blaisdell, conference organizer, concluded: "Any hope of hammering out a consensus at this time may be naïve. The issue for now may be with how much civility we will agree to disagree."[22]

In March 1990 a conference on congregational care and discipline, supported by Lilly Endowment and directed by K. Brynolf Lyon, gathered fifteen scholars and researchers who prepared papers based on congregational studies and dealing with congregational care, discipline, and personal formation. The plan for the conference was that as many as 150 people would attend to hear the papers and share in the discussion. Not only did the organizers want to learn what congregations were doing, but also they wanted to consider implications for theological education.[23] Later that same year, the desire to understand and influence congregational life took a new form when it was announced that CTS and St. Meinrad Seminary would cosponsor still another initiative of Lilly Endowment. The focus of this study would be the way that "seminaries and churches prepare leaders to manage human and financial resources," and the objective was to develop recommendations for seminaries and church leaders so that they could "prepare current and future leaders to be better stewards of the human and financial resources entrusted to their care."[24]

The most comprehensive responses of the Seminary to the crisis of mainline protestantism dealt explicitly with the Disciples of Christ. Again funded by Lilly Endowment, the Seminary sponsored a conference entitled "Christians Only but not the Only Christians: Reappraising the Disciples Tradition in the 21st Century" held in March 1987 under the leadership of Michael K. Kinnamon, acting dean of the Seminary. In his preface to the published papers of the conference, Kinnamon stated that the planning committee had expected between 150 and 200, but was overwhelmed by 550 registrants. The conference was prompted, according to Kinnamon, by the facts that Disciples membership "continues to decrease; our worship frequently seems lethargic; our theological debates are often superficial and divisive." The purpose of the conference was to look to the Disciples tradition for guidance for the future and at the same time become more fully aware of other ways by which the gospel could be expressed. Kinnamon hoped that the conference "by asking the right questions" could serve as "a stimulus for renewal throughout the church."[25]

Eight topics were chosen for consideration—ministry, worship, authority, evangelism, congregational life and discipline, structure, global mission, and church and social transformation—and working papers were prepared for each topic on the historic Disciples perspective, present practice, and future possibilities. The tenor of the conference was stated in Clark M. Williamson's plenary address in which he declared that "one source of our renewal assuredly lies in recapturing the ability to think theologically about our common life." One of the most dramatic statements among the papers, however, held to a different line. Charles H. Bayer, pastor of First Christian Church, St. Joseph, Missouri, and longtime social activist among Disciples, spoke to the future possibilities of global mission. More clearly than any of the other writers, he described the rapid decline of Disciples and other mainline denominations, placing their experience in the context of an even greater diminution of the churches in Great Britain and Europe, "the historic citadels of Christendom." The problem, Bayer continued, was that "what we seem to have misplaced is the evangel, the good news of liberation found in Jesus Christ; the proclamation that the Kingdom of God is at hand."[26] Bayer's assessment of what was happening in seminaries was similar to Williamson's critique of the churches. "Are we creating a generation of marketing experts, soothers of the psyche, captives of a political and social mentality in which the Gospel becomes identified with middle-class values?" He extended his critique to the congregations. "Are our pulpits cluttered with men and women committed to making the church a safe place in which to celebrate the American way of life?"

Bayer's solution to the problem was that North American churches needed increasingly to be the receiving churches, accepting the gifts that could be given by churches in other parts of the world where the dynamic power of the gospel was evident. The four gifts that could be received from the churches of the Third World, said Bayer, were: a revitalized sense of liturgy and celebration; a recovery of Christian spirituality; a new theology of action; and fresh models of congregational life. Bayer claimed that "our task is not to understand the world or provide it a doctrinal system, but to change it, to witness to the breaking out in history of the Kingdom of God which confronts head on the principalities and powers with which we live."

Although the conference was marked by high energy, no plan of action was developed to convert that energy into new life for the Disciples. One result of the conference was that it catapulted Michael K. Kinnamon into national prominence as a leader among Disciples. Already, he was becoming known among Disciples and other churches, too, as a speaker who could galvanize audiences. His addresses combined the best of the faith-and-order stream of ecumenism with major elements of liberationist theology. When he left CTS to became dean of Lexington Theological Seminary, in the summer of 1988, he found his platform and later became a candidate to succeed John O. Humbert as general minister and president of the Christian Church (Disciples of Christ). His candidacy, however, quickly was constricted into a one-issue campaign because of his early advocacy of gay rights in the nation at large and in the life of the Disciples. At the 1991 general assembly in Tulsa, he failed to win the required two-thirds majority by less than a single percentage point.

Another effort to understand the condition of the churches was a case study of the Disciples of Christ funded by the Lilly Endowment and directed by D. Newell Williams. The research topics were chosen and the researchers enlisted following a conference of forty Disciples academic and ecclesial leaders, with brief participation by thirty-two laypersons from Indianapolis congregations.[27] As editor, Williams wrote an introduction and conclusion, affirming sociological interpretations of two divisions that had taken place among Disciples. Around 1900, predominantly urban and industrial Disciples separated from the Churches of Christ that were primarily rural and agrarian. As a result, Disciples became affiliated with the churches that were to be called "mainline," churches that in the early years of the twentieth century were "identified with the religious interests and aspirations of persons associated with the urban and industrial segments of American society and culture that had emerged in the post-Civil War era."[28]

The second division was taking place in the 1920s when the School of Religion was being formed and which Frederick D. Kershner and his colleagues fought. Williams's explanation of this division was more nuanced than for the first division, but could be summarized with two ideas. "In sum, the separation of the Disciples and the Independents, like the liberal-conservative controversy in other denominations, seems to have been the result of different responses to the social challenges associated with the increase of the urban poor that accompanied industrialization and different reactions to the intellectual challenges associated with the application of the developmental hypothesis to history and the study of the Bible."[29] In his summary of the Disciples' decline since 1971, Williams suggested that the portion of the population that Disciples had failed to reach was clear—the current generation of younger adults. What was less clear was the reason why Disciples had lost the ability to reach new generations of Americans; and here Williams, after reviewing the arguments, offered three explanations: "(1) their failure to identify a basis for Christian union that can overcome social and cultural division (the fundamental theological cause of their two major divisions), (2) the difference between the views of their ministers and active laity (the clergy being more liberal on theological, social, and cultural views than the laity), and (3) the failure of their professional leadership to identify a distinctively Christian norm for judging theological statements and moral action."[30]

In his conclusion to the *Case Study* Williams offered his recommendations for the renewal of the Disciples. They needed "to identify a basis for Christian union capable of overcoming social and cultural division that can serve at the same time as a distinctively Christian norm for judging theological statements and moral action."[31] By means of a discussion of the ideas of Alexander Campbell, with brief reference to contemporary Disciples theologians, Williams urged that *the gospel*, which he defined as "God's unconditional love for sinners," rather than the Bible could be that basis for union and norm for faith and action.[31] Williams also offered a series of recommendations for overcoming the theological gap between ministers and church members, mostly aimed at "helping the Disciples to engage in discussion of theological and moral issues over which they divide."[33] What may have been the most important of Williams's conclusions came in the final paragraphs of the book in which he countered the idea that the way to overcome the liberal-conservative gap was to "get rid of the liberal ministers and the Disciples educational institutions that produce them." The most rapidly growing "religious" sector of the American population, he reported, was the "nonaffiliated sector." These people were not likely to respond to a church that opposed liberalism. The church that could win these people must accept diversity but in ways that "are theologically and morally plausible. Beyond this, they must speak a word that adds a quality to human existence not to be found outside of the Christian community. As Alexander Campbell and some contemporary Disciples have understood, this word is nothing other than the gospel of God's gracious love for all made known in the apostolic witness to Jesus Christ."[34]

Although many of the essays in the *Case Study* were marked by a sense of discouragement, one of them reached surprisingly upbeat conclusions. A group of four researchers did a statistical analysis of attrition and retention in Disciples' congregations. They found contextual factors to be less important than they had expected in explaining attrition and retention and proposed that "intrinsic religiosity" might well be the key element. Extrinsic religiosity was illustrated by statements like "Although I am religious, I don't let it affect my daily life" and "I go to church mainly because I enjoy seeing the people I know there." In contrast, intrinsic religiosity was illustrated by statements such as "I have often had a strong sense of God's presence" and "My religion is important to me because it answers many questions about the meaning of life."[35] The writers of this essay concluded in a hopeful way. Churches that could help young adults with children "meet their needs for support in socializing their children in intrinsically religious, prosocial ways" would likely gain and retain members. Their final sentence: "Our results leave us more encouraged about the future of the Christian Church (Disciples of Christ) and, by extension, other mainstream Protestant denominations than others seemed to be."[36]

During these same years several members of the faculty participated in two other efforts to reshape the theology and practice of the Christian Church (Disciples of Christ). In 1983 a consultation began between representatives of the Seminary, the Disciples' Division of Homeland Ministries, and the Christian Board of Publication resulting in an agreement to develop a series of books that would contain services, prayers, and interpretive essays on worship that would be offered to the Christian Church (Disciples of Christ) for study and trial use. These books would be created by a small group of writers working independently and without subsidy, with assistance from Peter Morgan of Homeland Ministries and assurance that the Christian Board would publish them. All of the writers were associated with the Seminary and had previously published in the field of worship.[37]

The first product of their labors, published in 1987, was intended "to connect Disciples worship more firmly with the great tradition of Christian worship stemming from the time of the apostles and from the church of the first centuries after the resurrection of Christ."[38] The book focused upon the celebration of the Lord's supper and sought to be faithful to the Disciples' tradition of extemporaneous prayer at the communion table, offered by the congregation's elders. Yet the book was very different from earlier Disciples' books on worship, including the longtime standard that G. Edwin Osborn had edited and published a generation earlier. A Roman Catholic priest at Catholic University of America, who wrote his thesis for a graduate degree on Disciples' communion prayers, stated that *Thankful Praise* represented the first time that a Disciples book on the Lord's supper entered into dialogue with the other churches.[39] A companion volume focusing on baptism and related aspects of worship was published four years later, with only one of the CTS writers remaining on the editorial team. Like its companion volume, *Baptism and Belonging* sought to broaden the Disciples' understanding and practice of one of the central acts of Christian worship. Although both books were put into use by Disciples across the country, the intention that they be used as the foundation for a comprehensive new worship book for Disciples was set aside by the publishing house that later developed its own book of worship.[40]

The second and more comprehensive effort to shape the future of Disciples ecclesiology was the membership of Seminary-related people on the Commission on Theology of the Disciples Council on Christian Unity.[41] Since its creation in 1978, the commission had focused its work on the church, ministry, and sacraments and had presented a series of closely written reports to the members of the Christian Church (Disciples of Christ). The commission also had published a series of booklets on several of these themes, including two by CTS professors—*Ministry among Disciples* by D. Newell Williams, and *Baptism: Embodiment of the Gospel* by Clark M. Williamson. After two decades of work, the commission published a comprehensive report which sought to answer the "most basic and all-embracing question facing the Christian Church (Disciples of Christ) today: what do Disciples think it means to be church?" An inadequate answer to this question would lead to disruption of everything else the Disciples tried to do, while "a sound and vibrant awareness of what it means to participate in the community God calls forth to be the church of Jesus Christ brings joy, strength, comfort, challenge, guidance, and hope even in times of adversity."[42]

In addition to the sixty-five-page monograph that constituted the main report, the book also included six of the earlier "Word to the Church" reports on ecclesiological themes. The tone of the entire volume was best stated in a few lines in the *Word to the Church on Baptism* (1987). "The task for Disciples today is the critical reappropriation of the fullness of their tradition in the context of the wider ecumenical discussion with a willingness to learn from others and a modest confidence that the Disciples tradition itself, at its best, is a distinctive theological contribution to the larger church."[43] The book as a whole was muted, with no celebration of Disciples history, little critique of the current life of Disciples, and little in the way of testimony to this church's contributions to the church and the world. Its primary thrust, to show how Disciples could shape their current life in order to become more truly "part of the universal Church of Christ,"[44] was significantly different from the way that Disciples like Frederick D. Kershner and Dean E. Walker would have stated it. For Disciples of their generation, the central assumption of their work was that Disciples already exhibited in their ecclesial and sacramental practices the major elements of the one church for which Jesus prayed.

President Richard D. N. Dickinson, Jr., was a constant, although largely silent, participant in these conversations and consultations, many of which he as president had generated. He also continued, on a reduced scale, his longtime participation in the ecumenical work of the National and World Councils of Churches. Following his participation in the Seventh Assembly of the World Council of Churches, in Canberra, Australia, early in 1991, he reported to the Seminary trustees, offering his interpretation of what it meant for CTS to be an ecumenical seminary of the Christian

Church. Three years later a revised and expanded version of these remarks was published in the Disciples' ecumenical journal *Mid-Stream*.[45] To Dickinson, being "an ecumenical seminary of the Christian Church" meant that CTS affirmed the Disciples' conviction that "denominationalism and the fissures which have developed in the Body of Christ" are a scandal. It meant agreement with the intention "to eliminate sectarianism in the name of a whole gospel," and the recognition that all parts of the Body of Christ are necessary if the Body is to be complete. "When CTS describes itself as an ecumenical seminary, it consciously roots itself in the history and ethos of the Disciples of Christ. But its ecumenical vision is informed not simply by a tradition from the past; it is driven also by a hope for the future—the future of the church and the future of society."

In his first version of this statement, Dickinson described six implications for the Seminary growing out of this ecumenical claim: respect for differing denominations and for Judaism; creative interaction of these differing interests; recognition that God's call is to all parts of the world community; commitment to the sustainability of the earth; responsibility for future generations; regionalism as the basis of identity rather than denominationalism.[46] In the later version he added two more, giving them prominence at the beginning of the list. The first was the affirmation that "no one can be truly ecumenical without deep rootage within a community of faith and commitment, because ecumenical commitment flourishes in and through faith, not outside of it." An ecumenist "is deeply conscious of being a member of a specific family and home, but that home is full of windows and doors which invite and permit engagement with the larger global village." The second new implication was that being ecumenical obliged people "to take seriously the institutional manifestations of the ecumenical dream, especially the World Council of Churches and its rich and diverse array of Christian witness."

All of this Dickinson wrote in the context of the Canberra assembly theme, which was titled "Come Holy Spirit, Renew Your Whole Creation." Even at the assembly, this tension between the past and the future had been present, with some representatives relying heavily upon "the history and traditions of the church," while others were following the Spirit in the struggle of the poor for justice and human dignity. In this tension, Dickinson affirmed, "the ecumenical vision is renewed and refreshed."

Already the Seminary was trying to move toward this kind of future. For more than a decade "globalization" had been an important topic of discourse at seminaries across the country. Although imposed by the

Association of Theological Schools, and thought by some to be more "buzzword than concept,"[47] globalization provided an impetus for the administration and faculty to recover a sense of mission that had long been part of the Seminary's self-understanding. Closely linked in the Seminary's activities was a second term—diversity. In its 1997 *Self-Study,* the Seminary used the phrases "cross-cultural," "thinking beyond their own cultural context," and "awareness of diversity" as ways of describing the globalization-diversification aspect of its life.[48] Methods for accomplishing the Seminary's intention were also described, including an "across-the-board emphasis on global awareness" and specific requirements that students have a "cross-cultural experience." Some fulfilled this requirement by taking travel seminars to Latin American, Africa, or the Middle East, while others took courses such as Jewish-Christian dialogue that met in a synagogue. Some white students met the requirement by taking a course in pastoral leadership in black churches, and one of them commented after it was over that as a white, middle-aged woman she found it to be one of the most challenging educational experiences she had ever undertaken. The *1997 Self-Study* acknowledged, however, that the global awareness requirement had not been in place long enough for the faculty to gain "a good sense of its effectiveness."[49]

Other Developments in the Seminary's Work

The Seminary's ability to influence Indianapolis was significantly increased by C. Richard Petticrew, the trustee who had led the Seminary's capital campaign in the latter part of the 1970s. Following up on his pace-setting gift to the campaign, he made additional gifts that created a forum for "dialogue on a wide range of social and ethical concerns." The design for the Petticrew Seminars was that a small group of business, professional, and religious leaders from the larger community would be invited to the campus for a day in which distinguished guests analyzed topics of major importance to the community. President Dickinson was especially interested in these seminars and did most of the work in organizing them, inviting speakers, and soliciting participation by leaders of the Indianapolis community. The first seminar on April 4–5, 1988, set the pace with its title of the conference: "AIDS: Who Should Pay the Costs?" Because Petticrew's gift had been, in part, a tribute to the leadership of the recently-retired president of the Seminary, Thomas J. Liggett was invited to be one of the speakers.[50] In the following years the Petticrew Seminars were planned for one day rather than two, but the tone of the first seminar continued as the seminars during the next years dealt with other topics related to health and medicine, as reflected in the seminar titles: "Health Care After 65: Who Pays?" "Euthanasia: Is It Ever Justified?" and "Abortion." Beginning in 1993, the topics shifted with programs such as "Educating for the Moral Life: The Role of Congregations in Contemporary Society."

The many activities of this decade took place within a framework of President Dickinson's conscience-driven fiscal management of the Seminary. Keenly aware of the high cost of education at the Seminary, and never at peace with these large expenditures, he labored incessantly to develop prudent budgets and to hold all Seminary employees to the fiscal demands of these budgets. Realizing that the Seminary was more dependent upon its endowment than were most other seminaries, he was especially attentive to the issues related to the use of endowments. He fully agreed with the principle that several of the trustees, especially those from Columbus, articulated—that the Seminary should hold its withdrawals from the endowment to no more than 5 percent of its value. Although the budget required and the trustees annually authorized somewhat higher withdrawals, Dickinson and his staff continued to make progress toward their goal of a 5 percent cap. His last budget before retirement called for a 5.2 percent draw.

Dickinson was also aware of the importance of special funding—soft money—to reinforce the program of the Seminary and throughout his administration attracted grants that supported activities beyond the regular budget. The most important source of these special funds was the Lilly Endowment, which consistently centered its grants upon Indiana and Indianapolis and regularly included religion as one of the areas of interest. The endowment's policies made CTS an especially attractive recipient of Lilly money, and through the years, a remarkable list of programs and activities had been energized by this support. The second most important source of funding for special activities was Clementine Miller Tangeman and J. Irwin and Xenia Simons Miller. During these years they used The Christian Foundation as the channel for their ongoing support of programs on campus. Although Dickinson was open to suggestions from faculty and staff, and depended upon staff to help him develop proposals, he took the lead in developing ideas, approaching foundations and other donors, and in overseeing the development of the programs that these funds supported.

Because he devoted such attention to the fiscal administration of the Seminary, Dickinson also realized that the base of support needed further enlargement. Even the successful capital campaign of the middle 1970s had served primarily to stabilize existing program; and the soaring stock market helped the Seminary recover the base that had almost been lost in the early 1970s. New resources were needed to strengthen the endowment, undergird new program, and continue the enhancement of the campus itself. Painstakingly, he developed a new capital campaign, discussing it repeatedly with staff, faculty, and trustees. The trustees consulted with financial advisors and gradually settled upon a $9.5 million campaign that would increase endowments for student scholarships, the library, and faculty support. It would also improve housing for commuting students and provide new facilities for the counseling program by the restoration of the two estate houses on campus.

The centerpiece of the new capital campaign was a new faculty chair in religion and the arts which Dickinson was determined to establish. His conversations with Clementine Miller Tangeman had determined that she was cordial to the idea that the chair be established; she was adamant, however, that the chair not bear the name of any of her family. He consulted with his dean and Disciples historian, D. Newell Williams, and then selected the name of Frederick D. Kershner, the Seminary's first dean, for the new chair. Dickinson listed his reasons to Tangeman, highlighting Kershner's "professional and personal interest in the relation between religion and the arts."[51] Dickinson had long been interested in giving higher priority to religion and the arts. As dean he had appointed a faculty task force to develop a policy document concerning this topic. The task force had described a prominent role for the arts at CTS and subsequently the faculty had given highest priority to creating a professorship for this discipline. Later when President Dickinson, pressed by fiscal constraints, had placed a cap on the size of the faculty, the chair in religion and the arts had been given lower priority. Dickinson, however, was determined that the Seminary move in this direction and his negotiations with Tangeman made it possible for him to override his own cap on faculty size.

Furthermore, Dickinson was confident that he had a candidate for the position—Frank Burch Brown, a Disciples scholar whom he had first brought to campus to discuss the possibilities of his becoming the dean.[52] Brown was a theologian and published author, an organist and composer, who at the time of his second visit to campus as Oreon E. Scott lecturer was described as "something of a Renaissance man—equally at home discussing Mozart's operas, Karl Barth, Appalachian gospel music, and Woody Allen films."[53] These plans all came together on one of the most festive days in

Dickinson's presidency, May 4, 1994. The festivities began at 3:30 P.M. with a tour of the art collection at CTS led by Xenia Simons Miller. Because she and her husband had both developed an extensive knowledge of contemporary art and had given the Seminary most of the art displayed throughout the building, she was the right person to lead this tour. Following a public reception in the common room, Dickinson presided over a program that took place in front of a veiled work of art that was a new gift to the Seminary by Mrs. Miller. Bruce Polizotto, chair of the board of trustees, announced the Frederick Doyle Kershner Chair in Religion and the Arts, and President Dickinson introduced Brown, its first incumbent. Mrs. Miller then presented the new painting, *Praise God,* by Robert Natkin. When she had first seen the artist's work in New York, she had been moved by his use of color. The melon and citrus colors, she said, "made your hearts sing with joy. And we hope that this painting, aptly named *Praise God,* will make your hearts sing with joy."[54]

Following the unveiling of the painting, which was hanging on the wall facing the steps into the common room, the artist gave a gentle statement about his life and work. He compared the process of "editing a painting" with prayer, "that state of communion—that condition—where a person experiences timelessness and that which is beyond us and yet a part of us." Although it is a contradiction, he added, "I must use the words 'Revelation' and 'Mystery' as interchangeable, and just as we capitalize the word 'God,' I must capitalize the word 'Mystery.'"[55]

Despite the exuberance of this day, the work of developing a comprehensive program in religion and the arts proved to be problematic. The faculty statement and the president's hopes were that the Seminary's work in sacred music and the repertory theater could be the foundation to an expanding program that would include the visual arts, dance, and other creative forms of expression. The music program, which had been resuscitated with the calling of V. Gayle Sarber to the faculty, was yet to develop the strength that the faculty hoped for. Even though there were unusually strong musicians and music programs in nearby churches, the Seminary's music activities were largely isolated from them. Efforts to develop strong connections with Jordan College of Music had not been successful. When the chair in church music became vacant again, this part of religion and the arts clearly was in trouble.

The president also found that he faced continuing difficulties with the repertory theater, so much so that comments about this matter appeared year after year in his reports to the trustees. Ever since 1971, when the

Repertory Theatre at CTS had been given its own board and full independence, it had operated as a "wholly un-owned subsidiary" of the Seminary. The relations of the theater to the Seminary often were difficult because of disputes over scheduling the use of Shelton Auditorium. After Alfred R. Edyvean's 1986 retirement from the Seminary faculty, his role with the theater continued, but was increasingly ambiguous and in need of redefinition. The purposes of the theater seemed to be changing and its explicitly religious function was less clear than had formerly been the case. In addition to these matters, the theater even more than the Seminary had to struggle for adequate financial support.

In 1990 these problems had been faced by the Seminary and the theater and seemingly resolved. As part of the theater's twenty-fifth anniversary celebration, and in recognition of Alfred R. Edyvean's contributions to its work, the theater would be renamed the Edyvean Repertory Theatre at CTS. Edyvean would retire from his role as executive director and become founding director, emeritus. The theater's organizational structure would be enlarged. Representatives of the theater and the Seminary affirmed their "desire to recapture the relationship" that the theater and the Seminary had previously enjoyed.[56] During the anniversary year, the Seminary had taken steps that would assist the theater in dealing with its financial needs.

During his final months as president, President Dickinson was again facing challenges from the theater over the use of the auditorium and fiscal practices. When he retired in the summer of 1997, these matters were still in negotiation and relations between the two institutions had deteriorated. During the following weeks, the negotiations continued to be indecisive, reaching impasse over the use of Shelton Auditorium during the inaugural festivities for Edward L. Wheeler, Dickinson's successor, in late October of 1997. Shortly thereafter, the executive committee of the Seminary's board of trustees decided that it would not renew the lease to the Edyvean Repertory Theatre, thus ending the thirty-year relationship between the theater and the Seminary.

Although Dickinson had been successful in creating the chair in religion and the arts and in attracting a distinguished scholar to that post, he had been less effective in generating funds for the program in religion and the arts. He was able to assign a small portion of a Lilly grant for the first year's activities and the new professor began to bring musicians and other performers and artists to the campus. In October 1995, soon after he began his work, Brown announced that the program would be directed toward four goals. The first was to understand "the role of the arts and aesthetics in the Christian tradition and in the life of faith," and thus counteract the "text-oriented" approach to religion. The program would also study the arts within the larger culture and, as its third goal, give special attention to "the sphere of non-Christian religious thought and practice." The fourth goal was "to study artistry—artistic creation and 'performance'—as part of a Christian life and/or vocation."[57]

While the program in religion and the arts was developing, the Seminary was also giving attention to the larger campus. During these same years Butler University was dramatically transforming its campus into a showplace for the city. The Seminary made sure that its grounds were well maintained. A continuing program of tree planting was undertaken, following a design that called for one hundred trees and three hundred evergreen ground covers. The walkway along Haughey and Forty-second streets was extended all of the way to the western drive into the Inter-Church Center. More notable was the redesign and restoration of the O'Neal and Holliday houses—the one to serve more adequately as short term housing for students and the other as the Pastoral Counseling Center and Retreat Center. In appreciation of these efforts, the City of Indianapolis awarded an honorable mention to CTS in the community beautification category for the 1997 "Mayor's Choice" Awards.

As Richard D. N. Dickinson, Jr., prepared for his retirement in the summer of 1997, he could look back over significant achievements during the years of his stewardship of the Seminary. He loved the campus—both its grounds overlooking the White River valley and the buildings themselves—and he lavished that love upon them. He had sustained productive relationships with the entities that traditionally had been the Seminary's strongest financial supporters, and the results permeated every aspect of the institution's life. One result had been the Seminary's participation in the Lilly-supported program to computerize small colleges, small universities, and seminaries in Indiana, so that the Seminary's library was fully on-line. At a deep level of his psyche, Dickinson understood the need to manage the endowment so that its long-term productivity was enhanced; he had the great satisfaction of watching its assets explode during his administration, moving from a value of $26 million when he began his presidency to $75 million as he prepared to leave office. The $9.5 million capital drive had been successful, bringing in more than $10 million in pledges and receipts. His final reports to the trustees were marked by the muted sense of accomplishment that was the most that he could allow himself to express.

He was letting go willingly but reluctantly, recognizing both the strength of the Seminary and the uncertainty concerning the shape that the church and its ministry would take in the years to come. Toward the end he was interviewed in the Seminary's *Link,* and there he commented on why he had chosen to come to CTS when he had had offers from other seminaries. "I liked CTS' ecumenical character, the ethos of the Disciples of Christ, the quality of the faculty whom I met here, and the opportunities CTS seemed to provide for visionary theological education, including commitments to social justice." In his last communication with the trustees, Dickinson reached out to his former colleague and mentor to find the words that described the purpose of the Seminary. "This place is called by God to serve, in T. J. Liggett's felicitous phrase, 'where tomorrow struggles to be born.'" His own closing words were eloquent enough as he assured the trustees of his "sure knowledge" that they would continue "to make CTS the most hospitable environment possible, giving space for that image of God in all humankind which expresses itself indomitably in a spirit ever restless for meaning and wholeness."[58]

12
Memory and Mission

*The Seminary in its
Seventy–fifth Year, 2000*

For seventy-five years the life of Christian Theological Seminary has been shaped by the vision of its founders, Frederick D. Kershner and William G. Irwin. During these years, the faculty has spoken in a series of evolving theological dialects, including the protestant idealism of the Kershner-Walker years, the neoorthodox and chastened liberalism of the Sikes-Robinson-Osborn generation, and the relational theologies that have been spoken on campus in recent decades. Yet, from the origins of the Seminary in Butler University and throughout its years as a freestanding academic institution, its major trustees and professors have been committed to one purpose—to prepare men and women for ministries within the church that will address the needs of all the world. In his inaugural address in 1997, the Seminary's fifth president, Edward L. Wheeler, reaffirmed this purpose, declaring that "the overarching purpose of theological education, in a Christian seminary, is the preparation of men and women, lay and ordained, for excellence in the leadership of the church of Jesus Christ." The Seminary is an extension of the church, "the place where theological discourse, examination, questioning and analysis intentionally take place for the purpose of preparing leaders who will serve God and humanity."[1]

This corporate memory of the Seminary has flourished throughout the years, in part, because of the continuity of leadership. All of the deans and presidents have guided the Seminary during lengthy administrations, marked more by stability and progress than by dissension and decline. They have been joined in their labors by a strong professoriate, with each generation of prominent professors enjoying an extended period of tenure until evolving into another distinctly different generation of teachers. One reason for the cohesiveness of the Seminary's faculty has been its homogeneity. Most professors have been white American males, members of mainline protestant churches, and graduates of prominent universities with advanced degrees in their disciplines. Yet, throughout much of the Seminary's history the faculty has included women, people of color, and people born in places other than the United States.

All these years the Seminary's internal processes have been designed to develop consensus within its faculty concerning academic goals and campus life. Furthermore, the professors have maintained a firm religious relationship to one another and their students through the shared life of the chapel and the personal attention expressed in the classroom and academic processes such as oral exams. Throughout the Seminary's history, it has chosen professors with strong commitments to their own churches and a vocation to prepare lay and ordained ministers; this criterion has created a faculty of people who have worked together constructively despite their differences.

The Seminary's well-being has been maintained by competent and committed trustees whose work has been braced by the example of several generations of the Irwin-Sweeney-Miller family. A tradition of trusteeship has developed through the century and a half of this family's constant participation in the Seminary and the other institutions it also served. Family members have learned how to challenge an institution to higher goals than it would otherwise have chosen, support it in its labors, and stand with it in times of distress. They have discovered ways of being deeply involved without becoming dominant and providing significant financial resources without allowing the institution to become dependent upon the continuation of these contributions. Their example of intelligent, theologically articulate, and organizationally astute leadership has challenged successive generations of trustees to excel in their own service to the Seminary.

The sense of purpose that continues at the center of the Seminary's life has helped it stay focused in its academic form—poised between university departments of religious studies on the one hand and church-related institutes on the other. As a graduate school for a learned profession, the Seminary has lived according to the traditions and requirements of colleges, universities, and schools of theology. Through most of its life, it has valued its connections with its University even though it has always maintained its independence from University control. The Seminary, however, has understood that its mission to prepare leaders for church and world distinguishes it from graduate departments of religious studies in universities. The study of the Bible and related theological disciplines as academic pursuits, the Seminary has steadfastly maintained, is quite different in tone and direction from the study of these same topics in order to use them in religious leadership.

This professional orientation has kept the Seminary focused upon the churches and their needs for leadership. Christian Theological Seminary and Butler University have always been organizationally independent from their sponsoring church and from other ecclesial institutions. One result is that the Seminary has been able to explore ideas that many church people do not understand or accept; another result is that the Seminary has been able to critique the life and thought of the churches. Yet the Seminary has always been dependent upon the churches for trustees and professors, students, and a significant portion of its financial support. In 2000 as in all previous years, the most important validation of the Seminary's work was the readiness of churches to receive its graduates as their ministers and for those ministers to be able to do the work that needed to be done.

One of the challenges facing Christian Theological Seminary as it pointed its life toward a new century was to keep its memory alive. Following the commencement of the year 2000, the only professor from the Norris-Osborn administration still in active service was Clark M. Williamson. As dean, he had to devote significant blocks of time to academic matters such as curricular reform and to the calling of new professors to take the place of the longtime professors who one after another were retiring. Although some of the second tier of professors had been at the Seminary for twenty years and more, their work had always been overshadowed by the people with even longer tenures. As one of the continuing professors noted in a comment upon the retirement a few days earlier of J. Gerald Janzen and Joe R. Jones: "This is going to be a very different place. I hope the next generation of 'senior faculty' can credibly carry forward the best aspects of the tradition that [the retiring] group brought to life so well."[2]

Part of the challenge—perhaps the greatest part—was to decide what should be jettisoned and what should be carried forward. Indeed, during this turn-of-the-millennium moment, the faculty was devoting considerable attention to this very matter by developing a new mission statement and long range plan and once again working at academic reconstruction. The professors started their labors by developing a mission statement, choosing to phrase it in language that was more religious than organizational. They wanted to express the Seminary's connections with the Disciples indirectly rather than explicitly—using language that belonged to the whole church but that would resonate with increased liveliness among members of their sponsoring communion. The new statement, approved by the Seminary's trustees in May 1999, began with a simple declaration: The mission of Christian Theological Seminary is to form disciples of Jesus Christ for church and community leadership to serve God's transforming of the world.

The statement continued by listing the actions that would fulfill this mission:

> *CELEBRATE* the presence of the risen Christ in Word and Table;
>
> *WELCOME* into partnership all who seek God's truth, love, and justice;
>
> *CULTIVATE* the virtues, passions, and practices of Christian leadership;
>
> *REFLECT* critically on the sources of Christian understanding in scripture, the traditions of the ecumenical church, cultures, and experience; and
>
> *ENGAGE* the spiritual and moral issues facing the human community.

Following the development of this mission statement, a committee developed the implications and drafted a long-range plan for the next decade. As might be expected, the section entitled "Vision 2010" affirmed that "a thorough understanding of Christian tradition and thought will permeate the spirituality, creative vision, and practical skills of the seminary's graduates." For years the faculty had been saying something like this as it insisted upon the importance of theological study. Yet, the tone in 2000 was different—less magisterial than it had been for many years. And less self-assured, more collegial—for the statement affirmed that during these years the Seminary "will be an *active partner of congregations and judicatories* in *discovering* appropriate leadership styles for ecumenical churches in their changing contexts" [italics added]. One purpose of this long-range plan was to describe "present strengths we wish to maintain," and here the document stated that the Seminary would "be especially noted for—its strong Master of Divinity and counseling programs and . . . exploring the interfaces between religion and the arts." All of this would be done within a framework that would be faithful both to the Disciples of

Christ and the larger Christian community; and in ways that would consistently work both for diversity and excellence.

The long range-plan also intended to identify "new strengths we wish to develop." Here, the document was less explicit, but certain themes were sounded. In its own life and work it would seek to be shaped by and to exemplify "God's Reign." It would "pursue revitalization of churches through dialogue and partnerships within the Christian Church (Disciples of Christ) and with Midwest congregations and judicatories, including African-American, Asian, and Hispanic churches." Although the statement also affirmed the hope of connections with the church around the world, the regional emphasis would be the focus for the next decade of its life. The emphasis upon the spiritual formation of students was more prominent than it had been in earlier statements.

An important next step was a "sustained conversation" among the professors that was intended to develop a "shared understanding of their vocation as teachers" and would nurture "collegial communion reflection" on their practices as theological educators. The professors would read and discuss seven substantial volumes on educational theory and method, beginning with their annual fall retreat and concluding with a similar venture nine months later, with half a dozen Friday afternoons in between. This refocusing on their primary vocation was funded by a special grant and directed by one of the newer members of the faculty. Through ventures such as these, the Seminary was beginning the process of finding a new sense of identity. The cycle of life that had started with the founding of North Western Christian University had reached its zenith and now was coming to a close. Furthermore, the church and world for which the Seminary had lived had slipped away and new ecclesial and cultural domains were taking their place. Now in the millennial year 2000, the Seminary was seeking to be born again.

In the 1940s, as editor of the Seminary's newly established journal, Dean Frederick D. Kershner annually developed his list of notable events—in the world and in the churches—and commented on them briefly. What list would he have compiled for the year 2000 as the Seminary turned seventy-five—changing prospects for peace in the Middle East, famine and pestilence in Africa, rapprochement between the two Koreas, the surging American economy, Microsoft in the courts, challenges to the death penalty in the United States, global warming, crisis in the National Council of Churches, debates over homosexuality in the churches? And what insight would members of the Seminary faculty bring to society's efforts to solve these problems? In the Seminary's earlier periods religious leaders spoke with considerable confidence for, despite the deep distress caused by world wars and economic depressions, the churches were moving forward, increasingly at the center of the culture. Kershner, Shelton, Osborn, and Liggett, and their colleagues on faculty and in the churches, could be sure that the gospel would penetrate and transform the social structures of their world. They had experienced the seemingly irresistible progress of congregations, denominations, councils, and worldwide ventures both in faith and order and in life and work.

By the year 2000, however, this confidence was greatly diminished. The editors of the *Christian Century,* in a lead editorial on the National Council of Churches, manifested the mood of many leaders of the historic churches. They noted that the thirty-five member churches of the National Council represented scarcely a third of the Christians in the United States, with Roman Catholics, Evangelicals, and Pentecostals not included. Then they asked if there is "any issue today that could possibly bring together the full range of U.S. Christians." They answered their question by stating that only "some loose structure involving minimal organization and commitment" would be possible. The idea of mission to the world, which generated the National and World Councils of Churches, is itself "one of the most divisive issues among Christians." Maybe, the editors concluded, people from these churches could get together "for a joint day of prayer . . . or perhaps even hold a joint meeting simply to share their vision of witness for the next century."[3]

The challenge for Christian Theological Seminary as it moved into a new period was to recreate its witness to the love of God and the renewal of the world and, in keeping with that witness, link itself to the churches in new ways. Around the world, new Christian movements were taking place that were transforming human life; in North America some parts of the Christian community were exploding with growth and impact upon American life. Both in North America and abroad, these dynamic movements were led, for the most part, by people whose call and preparation did not include time in an accredited theological seminary like Christian Theological Seminary. Furthermore, mainline churches and agencies were establishing new versions of short-term theological education, bypassing the very educational institutions that they had always insisted upon as the proper places for pastors and laity to study.

In such a time, what was God calling upon this Seminary to do? Was its longtime purpose still adequate for the future? Should it develop a new mission? How should this new mission be connected to its old memory? How could the Seminary help its churches and graduates reshape their ministries for this new world? Although the long-range plan for the first decade of the new millennium did not answer these questions with strong theological and ethical declarations, one approach was suggested in its emphasis upon integrating the arts into the Seminary's life and work. Since 1966, when the Seminary first entered its campus on West Forty-Second Street, Arnaldo Pomodoro's *Sphere #6* has lived quietly in the entryway near the president's office. This bronze globe is highly polished except in large sections where the smooth exterior seems to have broken away to reveal the irregular membranes and gears that make up the inner workings of the sphere. For more than thirty years people have walked past this work of art, often pausing to reflect upon its message. Children especially have been drawn to it, leaving their handprints as constant witness to their fascination with this silent depiction of our world.

When the sculpture was unveiled, the explanation suggested by a representative of the artist was that the sculpture reveals the "tension between machine-age perfection and man's inner doubts." In the year 2000, as Christian Theological Seminary turned seventy-five, another interpretation could be given—one that was foreshadowed by a photograph of the sphere on the cover of the 1991–1993 Seminary Catalog. Instead of standing aloof and alone as it usually does, the sphere is surrounded by students who are sitting on the floor in front of it, standing to the side, leaning against it, and peering over the top. These men and women, who have befriended the sphere as though it were the rock of ages, include people fresh out of college and others well advanced into their mature years. Some are white, others people of color; some married, some not married. They radiate a sense of confidence and joy that, while it may not always have been present in the classroom, expresses their prevailing mood.

In the year 2000, at this turning point in the life of Christian Theological Seminary, *Sphere #6* represents the tension between memory and mission. By its constant retelling, the storied memory of the Seminary's life serves as *objet d'art*, something burnished and beautiful. Just beneath that polished skin the whole creation groans in labor pains, waiting for its redemption (Romans 8:22 ff.). As the Seminary generates a new sense of mission in that world—a mission to ignite men and women like those in this picture with the passion of the gospel—it escapes from the danger of becoming a museum to past memories. Instead, Christian Theological Seminary—this *College for Applied Christianity*—becomes what Frederick

D. Kershner and all of the others have prayed that it might be, a mighty engine for the renewal of all creation.

Postscript

One of the striking features of the history of Christian Theological Seminary becomes evident only after it has all been told: There never has been a "golden age" in the history of education for ministry in Indianapolis. Every creative period has emerged through intense struggle within the Seminary's church constituency, with its institutional partners, and with its principal donors and supporters. The Seminary has always been poised in uneasy tension between liberal and conservative elements of the churches, faced with the need to define and defend its ecclesial identity. When it has embraced one part of the church and community, the reaction has often been a cooling of affections with another part of its constituency. The faculty's freedom to teach has been honored as important to the Seminary's central identity, but that very freedom has sometimes been the cause of consternation in the churches and community as much as a source of hope and new life. Through all of these struggles, the Seminary has persisted in its mission to be faithful to God, loyal to the church, and useful to the larger human community. It has demonstrated that struggle leads to strength and that suffering leads to servanthood that sustains human community. Christian Theological Seminary has exhibited the truth of the exhortation given by Paul, the church's first theologian—that faithfulness in the work of Christ will never be in vain (1 Corinthians 15:58).

In a period of time when pessimism is widespread in the mainline churches across the land, the story of Christian Theological Seminary is an example that can give hope and direction. The church came into being when the Roman roads and the Latin language were creating a new system for linking the world together. The Disciples of Christ emerged on the American frontier as animal power was giving way to steam, and railroads and telegraph were binding the continent together. When the School of Religion became Christian Theological Seminary, jet engines, interstate highways, and transnational business corporations were shrinking the world into a global village. In each of these periods the Christian faith took shape in institutions that were adapted to the particular needs and opportunities of the time. Now, the electronic revolution, the information highway, the radical consolidation of major commercial empires, and the cultural revolutions among peoples worldwide are shaking every institutional form and cultural value. In such a time, old institutions must be transformed if they are to survive and then flourish as instruments for the peace and well-being of the world.

This is what Christian Theological Seminary has done throughout its history. This is what the Seminary is now seeking to do as it enters into a new quarter century of its life. The example of this school is one that can give courage to all who read it with eyes to see.

Appendix
Faculty of the Seminary
1924–2000

This listing is taken from the catalogs of the College of Religion and the School of Religion, Butler University, and Christian Theological Seminary; it includes all persons who have held positions as members of the regular faculty. During the Seminary's history the definitions of faculty status and rank have changed, and it is difficult to make clear distinctions between the regular faculty and persons who have been affiliated as lecturers or adjunct professors. In early years, for example, Morris M. Feuerlicht was listed in the Butler University catalog as "Professor of Semitics," but his position was closely comparable to what more recently has been classified as affiliate professor. Most people who have carried the title "visiting professor" were employed on a short-term basis and are not included in this listing. A few of these persons, however, functioned as members of the regular faculty. Harold E. Fey, for example, was a full participant in the faculty's work and upon his retirement following four years on the faculty, was elected to an emeritus position and continued to be listed until his death.

The starting and ending years for terms of service have been taken from the catalogs, although the ending date has sometimes been deduced from the disappearance of the name from the faculty listing. A professor's academic discipline has been taken from catalog descriptions. Since teaching areas sometimes changed and the names given to academic disciplines also changed over time, the designations are representative rather than comprehensive. Professors who served over a span of several years usually received advancement in rank, with no change in teaching responsibilities; the rank at the time of the last listing is the one that appears below. Named professorial titles are given for each person who served in these positions. Persons who have held the office of dean and president are all included in this listing and that title appears with other information.

The difficulty in determining the names of professors in the College of Religion, Butler University, is compounded by the fact that in the earlier years the College included undergraduate and graduate instruction, and some people listed on the faculty worked only in the undergraduate division but were active in the College of Religion faculty. Furthermore, during the Athearn presidency of the University a separate College of Religion catalog was not published and the register of the entire University faculty has to be examined to detect the College of Religion faculty. When the College published its own calendar for the fall 1936, it also listed its faculty, which continued six persons from the earlier registers (Frederick D. Kershner, Bruce L. Kershner, T. W. Nakarai, Dean E. Walker, Emory C. Cameron, and Ross J. Griffeth). It also listed two new persons (Arthur Holmes and Ludwig von Gerdtell).

Kershner, Frederick D. Dean; Marshal T. Reeves Professor of Christian Doctrine. 1924–51.

Kershner, Bruce L. Clarence L. Goodwin Professor of New Testament and Church History. 1925–42.

Hoover, Guy I.[1] Professor of Practical Theology. 1925–38.

Ghormley, Hugh W. Associate Professor of Old Testament. 1925–26.

Armstrong, H. Parr. Associate Professor of Practical Theology. 1925–27.

Grafton, Thomas W. Chaplain; Lecturer in Church History and Practical Theology. 1927–30.

MacDonald, Janet Malcolm.[2] Professor of Classical Languages and Archaeology, New Testament Greek. 1927–33.

Reavis, Tolbert F. Professor of Church History. 1927–28.

Moon, Everard Roy. Professor of Missions. 1927–32.

Feuerlicht, Morris M.[3] Professor of Semitics. 1926–51.

Bacon, William F. Instructor in Old Testament and Semitics. 1926–27.

Grafton, Allena. Instructor in Practical Theology. 1927–32.

Garnett, Arthur C. Professor of Apologetics. 1929–32.

Nakarai, Toyozo W. Professor of Old Testament. 1928–65.

Walker, Dean Everest. Professor of Church History. 1928–50.

DeGroot, A. T. Instructor in Old Testament. 1929–32.

Pullin, Morris H. Assistant in Semitic Languages and Literature. 1932–33.

Bachman, Walter Eugene. Professor of Religious Education. 1932–36.

Bailey, Albert E.[4] Professor of Fine Arts. 1932–36.

Cameron, Emory C. Assistant Professor of Practical Theology. 1933–36.

Griffeth, Ross John.[5] Assistant Professor of Comparative Religion and Religious Archaeology. 1933–44.

Homrighausen, Elmer G. Assistant Professor of Church History. 1933–38.

Holmes, Arthur. Professor of Philosophy and Psychology of Religion. 1934–53.

von Gerdtell, Ludwig. Professor of Apologetics. 1935–44.

Moore, William J. Assistant Professor of Semitics. 1937–43.

Canary, Jr., Peyton Henry. Assistant Professor of Religious Education. 1938–43.

Hanlin, Harold Francis. Assistant Professor of New Testament. 1940–46.

Cory, Abram E.[6] Adjunct Professor of Missions. 1941–51.

Calvert, Lucile. Professor of Speech and Dramatics. 1941–45.

Shelton, Orman Leroy. Dean; President; Professor of Christian Ministries. 1944–59.

Burdin, L. Gray. Assistant Professor of Speech. 1945–49.

Smith, S. Marion. Professor of New Testament. 1945–72.

Pellett, David C. Dean; Professor of Old Testament. 1946–76.

Albert, Frank J. Professor of Historical Theology. 1947–65.

Watters, A. C. Professor of Missions. 1948–56.

Gordon, Grover B. Assistant Professor of Speech and Radio. 1949–53.

Osborn, Ronald E. Dean; Professor of Church History. 1950–73.

Rector, Franklin E. Professor of Rural Church. 1950–64.

Norris, Beauford A. Dean; President; Professor of Pastoral Theology. 1950–74.

Robinson, William. Professor of Christian Doctrine. 1951–56.

Miller, James Blair. Professor of Christian Education. 1951–79.

Edyvean, Alfred R. Professor of Communication. 1951–86.

Sikes, Walter W. Professor of Philosophy of Religion and Christian Ethics. 1952–63.

Tobias, Robert. Professor of Ecumenical Theology. 1953–64.

Carley, James R. Professor of Church Music. 1953–73.

Jones, Myrddyn. Librarian. 1953–56.

Smith, Joseph M. Associate Professor of Missions and History of Religions. 1956–64.

Clague, James G. Professor of Systematic Theology. 1956–69.

Stuart, George C. Assistant Professor of Preaching, Pastoral Care, and Urban Church. 1957–60.

Shaw, Henry K. Librarian. 1957–72.

Colston, Lowell G. Professor of Pastoral Care. 1958–83.

Joyce, J. Daniel. Associate Professor New Testament. 1959–62.

Bradshaw, Vinton D. Professor of Parish Ministries; Director of Field Education. 1959–87.

Watkins, Keith. Professor of Worship; Herald B. Monroe Professor of Practical Parish Ministry. 1961–95.

McAllister, Lester G. Professor of Modern Church History. 1961–83.

Porter, Calvin L. Nettie Sweeney and Hugh Th. Miller Professor of New Testament. 1962–99.

Wismar, Donald R.[7] Professor of Psychology and Religion. 1963–85.

Fey, Harold E. Professor of Christian Social Ethics. 1964–68.

Becker, Edwin L. Professor of Sociology of Religion. 1965–81.

Williamson, Clark M. Dean; Professor of Theology; Indiana Professor of Christian Thought. 1966–

Ashanin, Charles B. Professor of Early Church History. 1967–90.

Lord, C. Harvey. Assistant Professor of Church and Community. 1967–70.

Dickinson, Jr., Richard D. N. Dean; President; Professor of Christian Social Ethics. 1968–97.

Janzen, J. Gerald. MacAllister-Petticrew Professor of Old Testament. 1968–2000.

White, Willie. Associate Professor of Theology. 1971–74.

Bates, Robert S. Assistant Professor of Church and Urban Community. 1972–76.

Galbraith, Leslie R. Librarian; Professor of Bibliography. 1972–89.

Liggett, Thomas J. President; Professor of Ecumenics and the Expansion of Christianity. 1974–86.

Towne, Edgar A. Professor of Theology. 1975–93.

Cardwell, Sue Webb. Professor of Psychology and Counseling. 1979–88.

Slater, Nelle G. Professor of Christian Education; Lois and Dale Bright Professor of Christian Ministries. 1980–99.

Roberts, D. Bruce. Associate Professor of Christian Ministries. 1981–

Allen, Ronald J. Nettie Sweeney and Hugh Th. Miller Professor of Preaching and New Testament. 1982–

Burrow, Jr. Rufus. Professor of Church and Society. 1983–

Kinnamon, Michael K. Assistant Professor of Theology. 1983–88.

Lyon, K. Brynolf. Associate Professor of Practical Theology and Pastoral Care. 1983–

Sarber, V. Gayle. Assistant Professor of Church Music. 1983–93.

Williams, D. Newell. Dean; William G. Irwin Professor of Church History. 1984–

Riley, Janet Johnson. Assistant Professor of Parish Ministries; Director of Field Education. 1986–89.

Grant, Brian W. Lois and Dale Bright Professor of Christian Ministries and Pastoral Counseling; Professor of Pastoral Counseling and Marriage and Family Therapy. 1987–

Jones, Joe R. Dean; Professor of Theology. 1988–2000.

Pfafflin, Ursula. Assistant Professor of Pastoral Care and Counseling. 1988–94.

Steussy, Marti J. MacAllister-Petticrew Associate Professor of Biblical Interpretation. 1989–

Pearson, Peet. Assistant Professor of Christian Ministries and SCOFE; Director of Field Education. 1990–97.

Bundy, David D. Librarian; Associate Professor of Church History. 1991–

Baker-Fletcher, Garth. Assistant Professor of Christian Ethics. 1991–93.

Baker-Fletcher, Karen. Assistant Professor of Theology and Culture. 1991–93.

Prichard, Rebecca B. Assistant Dean; Assistant Professor of Historical Theology. 1993–97.

Alvarez, Carmelo E. Dean of Students; Director of Cross-Cultural Studies; Affiliate Professor of Church History and Theology. 1994–

Brown, Frank Burch. Frederick Doyle Kershner Professor of Religion and the Arts. 1994–

Sommerville, Raymond R. Assistant Professor of Church History. 1994–

Helmeke, Karen L. Assistant Professor of Pastoral Care and Counseling. 1995–98

Anderson, E. Byron. Assistant Professor of Worship. 1996–

Kelcourse, Felicity B. Assistant Professor of Pastoral Care and Counseling. 1996–

Johnston, Carol F. Assistant Professor of Theology and Culture. 1996–

Moseley, Dan P. Herald B. Monroe Professor of Practical Parish Ministry. 1997–

Wheeler, Edward L. President; Professor of Church History. 1997–

Smith, W. Michael. Director of Field Education; Assistant Professor of Christian Ministries. 1998–

Yust, Karen-Marie. Assistant Professor of Christian Education. 1999–.

Hearon, Holly. Assistant Professor of New Testament. 1999–

Bailey, Wilma. Assistant Professor of Hebrew and Aramaic Scripture. 2000–

Campbell, Nancy. Assistant Professor of Pastoral Care and Counseling. 2000–

Endnotes

Chapter 1

1. A history of the formation of Indiana's church related colleges is given by Timothy L. Smith in *Uncommon Schools: Christian Colleges and Social Idealism in Midwestern America, 1820–1950* (Indianapolis: Indiana Historical Society, 1978).

2 A good description of Irvington and the role of Butler and its people upon that community is given in Paul Diebold, *Greater Irvington: Architecture, People and Places on the Indianapolis Eastside* (Indianapolis: Irvington Historical Society, 1997).

3 A detailed account of the founding of North Western Christian University, giving full attention to the involvement of the Christian Churches in Indiana and to provisions for ministerial education, is found in Frederick I. Murphy, "North Western Christian University and the Education of the Ministry" (Butler University: unpublished M.A. thesis, 1960).

4. At the time of the college's founding, West Virginia had not yet separated from Virginia.

5. Quoted in *Hoosier Disciples* by Henry K. Shaw (St. Louis: Bethany Press, 1966), 140.

6. The first issue of the *Millennial Harbinger* was dated January 4, 1830. Its purpose was stated to be: "the developement [sic] and introduction of that political and religious order of society called THE MILLENNIUM, which will be the consummation of that ultimate amelioration of society proposed in the Christian Scriptures." It was published monthly for forty-one years, concluding with the December 1870 issue, four years after the death of Alexander Campbell.

7. Lester G. McAllister, *Bethany: The First 150 Years* (Bethany, W.V.: Bethany College Press, 1991), 301, 90–1.

8. McAllister, *Bethany,* 57.

9. D. Newell Williams, *Ministry Among Disciples: Past, Present, and Future* (St. Louis: Christian Board of Publication, 1985), 11–15.

10. J. W. McGarvey, *The Autobiography of J. W. McGarvey, 1829–1911* (Lexington: The College of the Bible, 1960), 14.

11.Albertina Allen Forrest, "The Status of Education Among the Disciples," *New Christian Quarterly* 5 (1896): 408.

12. George M. Waller, "Butler and its People: The History of Butler University 1855–Present" (unpublished manuscript), chapter eleven, 1–2.

13. *Christian Standard* 1916, 1453.

14. Ibid., 1889, 625.

15. Ibid., 1890, 424.

16. Waller, "Butler," 2.

17. Hall was probably referring to Johann Tobias Beck (1804–1878), a copy of whose *Vorlesunger über christliche Glaubenslehre* (1886) is in the Seminary library. It had been owned by Hugh Th. Miller and marginal notations and marks indicate that Miller had read the entire book.

18. *Christian Standard* 1891, 567.

19. Mark S. Massa, *Charles Augustus Briggs and the Crisis of Historical Criticism* (Minneapolis: Fortress Press, 1990).

20. Alexander Campbell, "Principles of Interpretation," in *A Connected View of the Principles and Rules by which the Living Oracles May be Intelligently and Certainly Interpreted* (Bethany: 1835).

21. *Christian-Evangelist* 1894, 324.

22. Ibid., 1896, 50–51.

23. Ibid., 1896, 194.

24. Ibid., 1896, 195.

25. Ibid., 1896, 228.

26. Hugh Carson Garvin, *What the Bible Teaches* (Eldon, Mo: 1908), 5–6.

27. Edward Scribner Ames, *Beyond Theology: The Autobiography of Edward Scribner Ames,* ed. Van Meter Ames (Chicago: University of Chicago Press, 1959), 56.

28. Ibid., 62.

29. The sect to church, with denomination as a variant, was a typology introduced by Ernst Troelsch and developed by later sociologists like J. M. Yinger and Liston Pope. The central idea is that in its early years a religious movement such as the Disciples tends to be separated from the larger society and is exclusivistic in its theology and ethical standards. Gradually the members of the movement make an accommodation with society and their religious movement becomes more moderate. The shift from sect to denomination usually leads to an emphasis upon more education of the clergy and greater consistency with secular standards. For an interpretation of the history of the Christian Churches according to this thesis, see Oliver Read Whitley, *Trumpet Call of Reformation* (St. Louis: Bethany Press, 1959).

30. Edwin L. Becker, *Yale Divinity School and the Disciples of Christ, 1872–1989* (Nashville: Disciples of Christ Historical Society, 1990), 3.

31. *Christian Standard* 1893, 109.

32. An especially lucid account of these choices was offered by J. H. Stockton, financial secretary of Drake University in Des Moines, Iowa (*Christian Standard* 1893, 335).

33. For the history of the Disciples' theological work in Chicago see William Barnett Blakemore, *Quest for Intelligence in Ministry: The Story of the First Seventy Five Years of the Disciples Divinity House* (Chicago: Disciples Divinity House, 1970).

34. From its founding until reorganization in 1943 Butler University had a system of dual governance. Originally organized as a stock company, under a strong board of directors, the University was governed by the president of the board who exercised strong executive power. Academic matters were directed by the president of the faculty whose executive power was significantly limited by the power of the board of directors. During the presidency of M. O. Ross, dual control at Butler ceased to exist.

35. Scot Butler reported Angell's belief that Michigan's school of the English Bible would soon "expand in its work and become a real theological seminary." He continued: "I have long thought other denominations would have done better to plant their seminaries here than in Chicago. Here is an atmosphere of study and scholarship which is inspiring, and the distractions of a great city are lacking." Angell also indicated that the university did serious work in Greek, Hebrew, philosophy, rhetoric, and other subjects that would be useful to students for the ministry (*Christian Standard* 1893, 127).

36. *Christian Standard* 1893, 127.

37. Shaw, *Hoosier Disciples,* 299. Members of the committee, in addition to Sweeney and Jenkins, were John E. Pounds, E. P. Wise, and J. H. McNeill.

38. Ibid., 299.

39. Ibid., 300.

40. Waller, "Butler," 2, 3; Waller cites the minutes of the Butler board for February 2, 1899.

41. Butler board minutes, quoted in Waller, "Butler," 6.

42. Waller, "Butler," 8.

43. Dwight E. Stevenson, *Lexington Theological Seminary 1865–1965: The College of the Bible Century* (St. Louis: The Bethany Press, 1964), 124.

44. *The Declaration and Address* was written by Thomas Campbell on behalf of the Christian Association of Washington, Pennsylvania, and became one of the foundational documents for the Christian Church movement. The one hundredth anniversary of its publication was celebrated at a major convention of the Christian Churches in Pittsburgh.

45. Samuel Guy Inman, "A Gentleman and a Scholar" (Indianapolis: The United Christian Missionary Society, n.d.) n.p.

46. *Survey of Service: Disciples of Christ* (St. Louis: Christian Board of Publication, 1928), 523.

47. Ray D. Stites, "The College of Missions, Indianapolis, Indiana: 1910–1927" (Emmanuel School of Religion: unpublished M.Div. dissertation, 1974), 29.

48. *Survey of Service,* 529.

49. Stites, "College of Missions," 38.

50. Ibid., 45–6.

51. Butler 1911–12, 72.

52. *Butler Alumni Quarterly,* 1914–15, 141.

53. George M. Waller to Keith Watkins, August 8, 1998.

54. Ibid.

55. The battle at the College of the Bible in Lexington was between two generations of faculty who represented two methods in interpretation of the Bible. The younger professors prevailed and this seminary became one of the leaders of the more liberal part of the Disciples movement. The fullest description of the battle is in Dwight E. Stevenson's *Lexington Theological Seminary, 1865–1965.*

56. These debates are discussed at length in the standard histories of the Stone-Campbell movement. See especially Henry E. Webb, *In Search of Christian Unity: A History of the Restoration Movement* (Cincinnati: Standard Publishing, 1990), 249–338; William E. Tucker and Lester G. McAllister, *Journey in Faith: A History of the Christian Church (Disciples of Christ)* (St. Louis: Bethany Press, 1975), 360–410.

57. See Lester G. McAllister, *Z. T. Sweeney: Preacher and Peacemaker* (St. Louis: Christian Board of Publication, 1968), 89–113.

Chapter 2

1. This meeting was the first conference that the Disciples' commission held after it was established under the leadership of Peter Ainslie. It is significant that unity discussions began with the Episcopal Church and that baptism was one of the first topics addressed.

2. *Christian Baptism* (Cincinnati: Standard Publishing Company, 1917), 19. At the time this book was published Kershner was book editor of the publishing company.

3. Ibid., 87, 8. Italics in the original.

4. Perhaps the most mature example of Kershner's method was his book *The Religion of Christ*, published in 1911 by Fleming H. Revell (New York) and republished in 1917 by Standard Publishing Company.

5. The probable reason is that he had married a student.

6. W. E. Jamison to Frederick D. Kershner (FDK), July 16, 1915. MC55.box 11.folder 3.

7. His correspondence with A. C. Smither, managing editor of the *Evangelist*, debated who would retain editorial control over the paper, with Smither insisting that he did. MC55.box 11.folder 5. These files also include correspondence with editors of the *Christian Standard*, the competing journal among Disciples, concerning the topics for Kershner's weekly column in the *Standard*. MC55.box 11.folder 3.

8. *Christian Standard*, December 25, 1915, 398.

9. Ibid., December 11, 1915, 333.

10. FDK to Russell Errett, Nov. 15, 1915. MC55.box11.folder 2.

11. *Christian Standard*, August 25, 1917, 1366.

12. In 1914 when Yale Divinity School changed its name for a brief time to Yale School of Religion, Kershner mentioned the change in his column in the *Christian Standard* (1914, 14) and stated that "Theology in its old sense, is gradually being discarded and the emphasis is being laid where Jesus placed it; that is, upon practical living." He hoped that Yale would continue "to emphasize religion, rather than theology." Quoted by Edwin L. Becker, *Yale Divinity School and the Disciples of Christ, 1872–1989* (Nashville: Disciples of Christ Historical Society, 1990), 9.

13. *Christian Standard*, August 24, 1918, 1423–1425.

14. Thomas Carr Howe (TCH) to FDK, Jan. 31, 1916. MC55.box 11.folder 8.

15. Kershner's knowledge of the development of foundations was expressed in the essay with which he announced the formation of the Christian Foundation: "The Christian Foundation Launched," *Christian Standard*, April 3, 1920, 1–2.

16. FDK to William G. Irwin (WGI), July 12, 1919. MC 55.box 10.College of Applied Christianity.

17. The debate on the mission field was focused on the relation of believer's baptism and church membership. Traditionally Disciples had insisted that only those baptized by immersion when they were old enough to speak on their own behalf could be accepted. On the mission field, especially in China, the practice had developed that people baptized as infants or by sprinkling could be received as members by transfer without being rebaptized. The debates over organization in North America included the relationship between missionary practice overseas and the attitudes of mission executives at home. They also included debates over the legitimacy, from the standpoint of Bible teaching, of having any kind of ecclesiastical organization beyond the local congregation.

18. *Christian Standard*, July 26, 1919.

19. FDK to Harriet Barlow Baker, July 14, 1919. MC55.box 13.folder 1.

20. "In the light of our conversations," Morrison wrote, "I should be deeply grieved, not to say betrayed, if you have actually participated in the present call." MC55.box 13.folder

8. The file contains three versions of Kershner's response to Morrison, implying that Kershner had considerable difficulty in deciding how to explain his actions.

21. MC55.box 13.folder 8.

22. FDK to WGI; March 28, 1919. MC55.box 10.College of Applied Christianity.

23. After taking his degree from Butler and studying abroad, the younger Miller had returned to the campus as professor of modern languages and, following her graduation from Butler, married Nettie Sweeney, daughter of Z. T. and Linnie. Appointed to a position in Irwin's Bank, Miller moved to Columbus where he and his wife joined the family circle in the Irwin home across the street from their church. Miller, eleven years older than Nettie, was only a year younger than William G. Irwin; these two men worked together for the rest of their lives in the business, educational, political, and religious enterprises of their enlarging family.

24. TCH to Miner Lee Bates, July 26, 1917. President's Files 67–3; reported by George M. Waller, "Butler and its People: The History of Butler University 1855–Present" (unpublished manuscript) chapter 12, 4–5.

25. Ibid., chapter 12, 5.

26. "Futile Attempts to Create a College Autocracy," *Christian Century*, November 6, 1919, 7–8.

27. I am using Waller's phrasing, "Butler," chapter 12, 6.

28. Waller, "Butler," chapter 12, 7–8.

29. MC55.box 10.College of Applied Christianity.

30. The entire list, as best I can read it, is as follows. Old Testament: J. H. Marshal, Bennett [no first name given]; New Testament: Vernon Stauffer, W. C. Morro, H. D. Smith; Christian History: M. J. Bradshaw; W. W. Jennings; Homiletics: G. H. Combs, Hugh _____ [not legible]; G. _____ [not legible]; Z. T. Sweeney; Religious Education: W. S. Athearn; _____ [not legible], W. C. Pearce; P. H. Welshimer.

31. *Christian Standard*, December 14, 1918, 254.

32. See his essays in *Christian Standard*, August 25, 1917, 1364 ff.; and October 20, 1917, 60 ff.

33. FDK to W. C. Morro; November 14, 1919. MC55.box 13.folder 8.

34. FDK to T. W. Phillips, Jr., November 4, 1919. MC55.box 13.folder 10.

35. Frederick D. Kershner, "Christian Foundation Launched," *Christian Standard*, April 3, 1920, 1–2.

36. James L. Clark, James W. Nichols, Linwood Crystal, and Ernest E. Owens were from the Danville Church and William G. Irwin, Hugh Th. Miller, George W. Long, William F. Kendall, and William B. Treadway were members of Z. T. Sweeney's church in Columbus. Long was the one Columbus person who did not sign the Articles of Incorporation.

37. This paragraph draws upon the account given by Henry K. Shaw in *Hoosier Disciples*, 328, and undated materials published by the Christian Foundation during the founding years.

38. *Butler Alumni Quarterly* 10 (1921–22), 34–5, 11; (1922–3), 164–6.

39. *Christian Standard*, August 10, 1918, 1376 ff.

40. WGI to FDK February 7, 1920. MC55.box 10.folder 7.

41. FDK to T. W. Phillips, Jr., March 1, 1920. MC55.box 13.folder 10.

42. MC55.box 13.folder 4.

43. WGI to FDK November 13, 1922. MC55.box 10.folder 8.

44. George Waller reports that the efforts to remove Morro were initiated by the committee of five early in 1923, causing distress to faculty president Aley and others on the University faculty. They presented letters of testimonial to the board of directors, affirming that he was one of the best teachers on the faculty, well-liked by his colleagues, a scholar, conservative in religious convictions, in harmony with the belief of the Christian Church. Despite these recommendations, the board of directors decided that he could remain only until the end of the 1923–24 school year but would no longer be department head; or he could leave before then with a full year's pay. Waller assumes that Kershner had wanted Morro out of the way, but the actions that led to his leaving were initiated at a time when Kershner was not intending to take the Butler position ("Butler," chapter 12, 9). Further evidence that Kershner would have kept Morro is the fact that the list that Kershner had drawn up in 1919 had included Morro. Morro's biographer, Dwight E. Stevenson, reported that Morro left the Butler faculty because he was no longer able to deal with the conservative influences that controlled his program: *Lexington Theological Seminary 1865–1965: The College of the Bible Century* (St. Louis: Bethany Press, 1964), 121.

45. Arthur Holmes (AH) to FDK, November 13, 1922. MC55.box 14.folder 21.

46. Examples of this correspondence are FDK to AH, November 17, 1922. MC55.box 14.folder 21; other letters, in the same location, are dated December 5, 1922, April 16 and 18, 1923, May 12, 1923, and February 9, 1924.

47. FDK to AH, December 5, 1922. MC55.box 14.folder 21.

48. FDK to AH, May 12, 1923. MC55.box 14.folder 21.

49. FDK to AH, April 16, 1923. MC55.box 14.folder 21.

50. Holmes seems to have moved into a fulltime position at the University of Pennsylvania. He mentioned in one letter that he had been offered a position as dean of men at "Oregon State AG. University," but he had told the president "a man ought to have ten thousand a year in compensation for the intellectual sacrifices he has to make by going into administrative work, and I have been grinning ever since." AH to FDK, April 18, 1924. MC55.box 14.folder 21.

51 AH to FDK, Feb. 9, 1924. MC55.box 14.folder 21.

52. FDK to AH January 30, 1924. MC55.box 14.folder 21.

53. During this period Irwin was deeply invested in developing the Union Starch and Refining Company. He had recently purchased a major refinery of corn products in St. Louis for $1 million and was becoming a major player in this business. For a full account of these activities, see R. H. Gemmeke, "W. G. Irwin and Hugh Thomas Miller: A Study of Free Enterprise in Indiana" (Indiana University: Unpublished Ph.D. dissertation, 1955), 153ff.

54. FDK to AH, Feb. 9, 1924. MC55.box 14.folder 21.

55. FDK to AH, Mar. 6, 1924. MC55.box 14.folder 21.

56. *Butler Alumni Quarterly* 14 (1925–6), 34–6.

57. *Butler Alumni Quarterly* 16 (1927–8), 153, 156.

58. Throughout this entire process, Irwin said very little in his letters about his conversations in Columbus, although we can imagine that they were frequent and extensive. By the time that these activities were developing, Z. T. Sweeney was suffering from chronic illness that diminished his energies, yet Irwin indicated in a couple of letters that he consulted with Brother Sweeney who could evaluate theological content and strategic plans. When Kershner was preparing an article explaining the idea of their foundation, he had sent

a draft to Irwin who had shared it with Sweeney. It is hoped, said Irwin, that after Brother Sweeney has read it he will "see that there is no question but that organization at the present time is absolutely necessary. For my part, I cannot see how we can safely delay action very much longer. Those who are well grounded in the plea and who have at heart the continuance and growth of it, are gradually passing away and it is from them that we must obtain our help. We can not afford to be without an organization of this kind that will meet their approval." Holmes indicated, however, that Sweeney was active in the conversations, which leads to the conclusion that he and Irwin were close collaborators in the process. Although Sweeney may have been helpful as an occasional participant in the process, Frederick D. Kershner and William G. Irwin were the real founders of the seminary; for a time these two men constituted the new school—Kershner the faculty and staff and Irwin the board of trustees.

Chapter 3

1. Representative of this literature is Leonard Joseph Moore, *Citizen Klansmen: The Ku Klux Klan in Indiana, 1921–1928* (Chapel Hill: University of North Carolina Press, 1991); Kathleen M. Blee, *Women of the Klan: Gender and Racism in the 1920s* (Berkeley: University of California Press, 1991); Shawn Lay (ed.) *The Invisible Empire in the West: Toward a New Historical Appraisal of the Ku Klux Klan of the 1920s.* (Urbana: University of Illinois Press, 1992).

2. Edwin L. Becker, "1923: Year of Peril for Indianapolis Disciples Pastors," *Encounter* 54/4 (Autumn 1993): 369–86.

3. Ibid.

4. George M. Waller reached this conclusion following conversations with people who represented public leaders of Indianapolis during the 1920s. He has also talked with younger historians who have worked with Klan materials and reports that their findings confirm his own inquiries. Telephone conversation with the author, September 2, 1998.

5. *Christian-Evangelist,* December 13, 1923. See discussion and quotation in Moore, *Citizen Klansmen,* 27, 28.

6. *Encyclopedia of Indianapolis,* eds., David J. Bodenhamer and Robert G. Barrows (Bloomington & Indianapolis: Indiana University Press, 1994), 565–66.

7. MC55.XIII.41.

8. *Bulletin (University)* December 1924, 6.

9. Ibid., June 1924, 14.

10. FDK to AH, November 17, 1924. MC55.box 17.folder 68.

11. FDK to AH July 11, 1925. MC55.box 17.folder 68.

12. Frederick D. Kershner's account of Sweeney's death appears in the *Christian-Evangelist,* February 25, 1926, 232.

13. *Bulletin (College of Religion) Supplementary Bulletin,* December 1926–27, 18.

14. Ibid., 1926–27, 15.

15. Arthur Holmes, *The Mind of St. Paul* (New York: Macmillan, 1929).

16. Ibid., 257.

17. *The Indiana Worker,* December 1925.

18. For the stories of churches developing in the community, see Edwin L. Becker, *The Story of Northwood: The First Seventy-Five Years in the Life of Northwood Christian Church*

(Disciples of Christ) (Indianapolis: Northwood Christian Church, 1995), and Hester Anne Hale and Marilyn Harmon, *A Celebration of Faith: The Story of North Church* (Indianapolis: North United Methodist Church, 1994).

19. PRS.I.42; MC151.I.4b.

20. These comparisons are derived from catalogs of the four Disciples' seminaries and from Edwin L. Becker, *Yale Divinity School and the Disciples of Christ, 1872–1989* (Nashville: Disciples of Christ Historical Society, 1990).

21. W. S. Athearn, *Dual Control of an Urban University* (Indianapolis: Privately Published, 1933), 25. In earlier years Athearn had developed a pace-setting program in religious education at Boston University, enrolling as many as 400 students. He had been called from Drake University which had been the first university in the country to offer an accredited course in religious education that could be used to satisfy degree requirements. Athearn had seemed ready to consider moving from Boston to Indianapolis, drawn by the vision of the graduate school for Disciples and interested in helping to make that vision a reality. He was a native Hoosier from a family that had been in Indiana for a century, and as later correspondence revealed, his position at Boston was becoming precarious; he was interested in finding a new place of service.

22. FDK to AH, Sept. 7, 1931. MC55.box 17.folder 69.

23. Athearn, *Dual Control*, 16.

24. Walter Scott Athearn, *An Adventure in Religious Education: The Story of a Decade of experimentation in the Collegiate and Professional Training of Christian Workers* (New York and London: Century Co. 1930).

25. Ibid., 3.

26. Athearn, *Dual Control*, 8.

27. Edwin R. Errett to FDK, Nov. 16, 1932. MC55.Box 31.Folder 49.

28. These discussions were reported frequently in the minutes of the meetings of the College of Religion faculty, handwritten by Ross J. Griffeth who served as secretary during these years.

29. MC151.I.4a.

30. Walter Bachman, Allena Grafton, and Elmer G. Homrighausen.

31. The exemption from tuition is probably explained by a notice in the College's *Bulletin* for June 1931: "Through the beneficence of its friends, the College of Religion has at its disposal scholarships which provide free tuition, not to exceed $200 for a single academic year, for college graduates who are enrolled in the College of Religion. A limited number of scholarships are also available for undergraduate students in the College of Religion," 16.

32. There would henceforth be a Department of Religion within the College of Liberal Arts and Sciences with Professor Bachman and Assistant Professors Grafton, Griffeth, and Homrighausen named as professors. Students could register for either the B.A. or B.S. degree with a major in religion. This major included 30 hours of work, including 12 hours of biblical history and literature, 3 hours of church history, and 6 hours of religious education. Four purposes for courses in this department were stated. They were to help the student: "(1) to gain some measure of ordered knowledge in this field of universal human interest; (2) to develop the attitudes, ideals, and habits, which lead to an enrichment of personal and social life; (3) to acquire a knowledge of the agencies, institutions, and methods necessary to preserve the religious life in his own home and in the community in

which he is to live and to develop disciplined ability for life and conduct as an efficient member of society; (4) to furnish a pre-professional collegiate background for further work in graduate schools of religion, theology, religious education, missions, and social service." *Bulletin (University)* June 1933, 99. This struggle concerning undergraduate studies continued beyond Athearn's presidency. Not until after O. L. Shelton became dean did the connection between the undergraduate and graduate divisions of the College of Religion come to a close. During my earlier years at CTS, Robert Andre and Francis Reisinger were the two professors at the undergraduate level. By now they were completely separated from the School of Religion or CTS faculties. They were, however, Disciples. After these men retired, they were succeeded by Tom Best and Malcolm Clark, both Disciples. Not until Best left the faculty did this Disciples lock come to a close.

33. FDK to William G. Irwin (WGI), March 27, 1933. MC55.box 29.folder 3.
34. WGI to FDK, March 27, 1933. MC55.box 29.folder 3.
35. FDK to Walter Scott Athearn (WSA), February 11, 1933. MCC55.box 29.folder 3.
36. FDK to AH, n.d. MC55.box 17.folder 69.
37. *Bulletin (College of Religion)*, June 1932, 42.
38. The June 1934 Butler *Bulletin* listed Dean Frederick D. Kershner under the department of Christian doctrine; Professor B. L. Kershner, Assistant Professor Homrighausen, and Dr. Todd under Church History; Professor Krone and Assistant Professor Gilley (both of Jordan Conservatory of Music) under fine arts in religion; Assistant Professor Griffeth under history of religions and missions; Professor B. L. Kershner under New Testament; Assistant Professor Cameron, Dr. Hoover, Mr. Gilley, and Dr. Shullenberger under practical theology; Professor Bachman under religious education; and Professor Nakarai and Rabbi Feuerlicht under Semitic languages and literature.
39. "Conference of Bible Teachers in Schools Composing the Membership of the Board of Education" (Indianapolis, February 13, 14, 1928). Quoted in John M. Imbler, "By Degrees: The Development of Theological Education within the Disciples of Christ" (Christian Theological Seminary: Unpublished S.T.M. thesis, 1981), 51.
40. Becker, *Yale Divinity School,* 5.

Chapter 4

1. FDK to AH, July 13, 1934. MC55.box 17.folder 69.
2. A full account of these developments is given by Jeffrey L. Cruikshank and David B. Sicilia in *The Engine That Could: 75 Years of Values-Driven Change at Cummins Engine Company* (Boston: Harvard Business School Press, 1997), 88ff.
3. Interview with Elsie I. Sweeney, March 1, 1967, reported by Lester G. McAllister in *Z. T. Sweeney: Preacher and Peacemaker* (St. Louis: Christian Board of Publication, 1968), 103.
4. FDK to WGI, April 12, 1935. MC55.box 34.folder 85.
5. Ibid.
6. WGI to FDK, April 13, 1935. MC55.box 34.folder 85.
7. FDK to WGI, April 15, 1935. MC55.box 34.folder 85.
8. FDK to WGI, April 24, 1935. MC55.box 34.folder 85.
9. WGI to FDK, April 24, 1935. MC55.box 34.folder 85.
10. Author's conversation with Clementine Miller Tangeman, December 31, 1992.

11. FDK to Edwin R. Errett (ERE), April 25, 1935. MC55.box 31.folder 49.
12. FDK to WGI, May 4, 1935. MC55.box 34.folder 85.
13. WGI to FDK, February 7, 1936. MC55.box 34.folder 85.
14. ERE to FDK, June 12, 1936. MC55.box 31.folder 49.
15. FDK to ERE, June 12, 1936. MC55.box 31.folder 49.
16. ERE to FDK, August 27, 1936. MC55.box 31.folder 49.
17. FDK to ERE, August 23, 1936. MC55.box 31.folder 49.
18. ERE to FDK, December 3, 1936. MC55.box 31.folder 49.
19. FDK to ERE, December 6, 1936. MC55.box 31.folder 49.
20. ERE to FDK, December 8, 1936. MC55.box 31.folder 49.
21. Although I assume that this is Hugh Th. Miller, there is a remote possibility that the reference is to R. H. Miller, Butler trustee.
22. ERE to FDK, June 8, 1937. MC55.box 31.folder 49.
23. The theological statements in these documents related to the Christian Foundation are unusually detailed for Disciples. In contrast, note the simple covenant that had been the basis for forming the congregation in Columbus where several of these people were members. "We whose names are hereunto subscribed believing it to be for the interest of the Redeemers [sic] Kingdom in this place, do agree to organize ourselves into a congregation, to be known by the name of the 'Christian Congregation in Columbus, Ind.,' and, recognizing, as we do but One 'Law-Giver' among God's People, we pledge ourselves to the Lord, and to each other to be governed in all things by the Word and will of God, as revealed to us in the New Testament Scriptures—as Christians we believe we should act honourably with each other, and therefore, as such in defraying the expenses of the Congregation we fully recognize and heartily embrace the Scriptural principle that 'a man should give and cheerfully give, according to what he has.'" Quoted by Margaret Kelly Dismore, "Anatomy of a Congregation: A History of First Christian Church of Columbus, Indiana" (M.A. thesis, Cincinnati Bible Seminary, 1992), 15.
24. Control was exercised in a very close way. Throughout the years Deans Kershner and Shelton regularly submitted two reports of their work at the School of Religion. They were closely typed summaries of enrollment statistics and program highlights for the year, similar in form and content, but slightly different in detail. One report was submitted to the University, to be included in the regular procedures of University administration. The second report went to the Christian Foundation. During the early years following the 1940 contract, all books received by the College library were stamped "Property of The Christian Foundation." Many duplicates, sometimes as many as twenty copies, accumulated because of donations of old libraries. Librarian Enos Dowling consulted Dean Kershner and decided to sell duplications to students for a dollar a book. William G. Irwin heard about it, however, and wrote Dowling a terse letter stating that he had no right to do that and that he should retrieve the books. Dowling had no choice but to recover as many of them as he could.
25. See *Christian-Evangelist,* 1941, 873, 918, 1001, 1009–11, 1125, and 1173–74.
26. *Christian-Evangelist,* 1940, 31. The plaques of Thomas Campbell and Barton Warren Stone are displayed near the Heritage Room in the Seminary Library.
27. Calvin L. Phillips, in Dean E. Walker, *Adventuring for Christian Unity and Other Essays* (Johnson City, Tenn.: Emmanuel School of Religion, 1992), 7.

28. Dean E. Walker, *Adventuring for Christian Unity: A Survey of the History of Churches of Christ (Disciples)* (Cincinnati: Standard Publishing Co., 1935), 14.
29. Ibid., 22.
30. Ibid., 52.
31. *Christian Standard,* January 29, 1916, 590.
32. FDK to H. C. Armstrong; June 23, 1924.
33. Kershner, *Christian-Evangelist*, 1938, 1146ff.
34. The two lists which Kershner quoted use slightly different wording for the same items. The later list, published in 1924, is worded this way: "A catholic name, a catholic confession, a catholic interpretation of baptism and the Lord's Supper, a catholic book, a catholic polity and a catholic brotherhood." Kershner then suggested that "both schedules might have added a catholic spirit and a catholic day of worship." (*Christian-Evangelist* 1938, 1149)
35. Smith's account appeared in *Christian-Evangelist*, 1939, 759–60; Walker's appeared in *Christian Standard*, 1939, 702, 710.
36. *Shane Quarterly*, which continues as *Encounter* (the name was changed in 1956). *Shane* was edited by the faculty of the School of Religion and its dean Frederick D. Kershner. The journal adopted the name of the Irish castle less than a mile from the birthplace of Alexander Campbell, and in an essay explaining this title, Dean E. Walker claimed the central tenets of the Disciples and affirmed their continuing relevance for the world of his time. This Disciples-specific journal, however, had a remarkably broad focus, which Dean Kershner stated in the introduction in which he explained the journal's purpose. Kershner noted in correspondence that most people responded favorably to the title of the journal. Nettie Sweeney Miller was one of the people who did not like it; and she was also critical of the poor proofreading.
37. *Shane Quarterly* 1 (1940): 3.
38. Ibid., 195.
39. Ibid.
40. D. Newell Williams, "Overcoming a Liberal-Conservative Divide: The Commission on Restudy of the Disciples of Christ," in *Christian Faith Seeking Understanding: Essays in Honor of H. Jackson Forstman,* eds. James O Duke and Anthony L. Dunnavant (Macon, Ga: Mercer University Press, 1997), 246–76. I draw extensively upon Williams's work in the next paragraphs.
41. The pertinent correspondence is in MC55.XI.46 and PRS.I.130.
42. Hester Anne Hale and Marilyn Harmon, *A Celebration of Faith: The Story of North Church* (Indianapolis: North United Methodist Church, 1994), 53.
43. This offer, however, did not materialize.
44. MC55.box 4.folder 26.
45. From *The Hancock Democrat,* reprinted in *Shane Quarterly* 3/2–3 (April–July 1942): 216–19.
46. FDK to WGI February 8, 1940. MC55.box 41.folder 25.
47. Hilda E. Koontz, *A History of The National City Christian Church* (Washington, D.C.: National City Christian Church, 1981), 16ff.
48. For a discussion of Sweeney's interest in Hartford Theological Seminary, see D. Newell Williams, "Z. T. Sweeney" (Indianapolis: Christian Theological Seminary, 1987), 11. Although Williams does not report this fact, Sweeney's knowledge of Hartford Seminary

was based on his close friendship with a president of the school, formed during many summers that they vacationed together in Ontario, Canada. Author's conversation with J. Irwin Miller, October 17, 2000.

49. "The Attitude of Disciples to Future Unity Movements," 313.
50. "Butler Cornerstone Address," 395–8.
51. *Christian-Evangelist*, 1941, 601.

Chapter 5

1. The initials stood for Literature of the Restoration Movement; this collection was continued in the library of Christian Theological Seminary in the Heritage Room. The core of the collection had been gathered privately by Enos Dowling, who had sold it to the Christian Foundation for permanent deposit at the School of Religion.

2. Sweeney wrote two research papers concerning baptism and its relation to church membership which she sent to O. L. Shelton after he became dean. Copies can be seen in MC151. series I.folder 13.

3. At this time the School of Religion Committee, which was the managing board of the Seminary, consisted of William G. Irwin, chair, Edwin R. Errett, Hilton U. Brown, Hugh Th. Miller, and Crate Bowen. The deliberations and actions that led to the calling of a new dean appear to have been conducted informally rather than in called meetings of this committee.

4. Nettie Miller (NM) to Orman L. Shelton (OLS), Nov. 26, 1943. MC151. series I.folder 7.

5. This reconstruction is based on conversations that Shelton had with Ronald E. Osborn and Bill L. Barnes. Osborn's account is published in "Portrait of a Churchman: The Ministry of Orman L. Shelton," *Encounter* 20 (1959): 132–67.

6. William G. Irwin (WGI) to OLS, late August 1943. MC151. series I.folder 7.
7. WGI to OLS, Oct. 14, 1943. Ibid.
8. NM to OLS, Nov. 26, 1943. Ibid.
9. Henry E. Webb, *In Search of Christian Unity: A History of the Restoration Movement* (Cincinnati: Standard Publishing Company, 1990), 355,6.
10. OLS to Hugh Th. Miller and NM, February 1, 1944. MC151. series I.folder 7.
11. Death continued to afflict the family with the death of William G. Irwin's sister, Linnie Irwin Sweeney (Mrs. Z. T. Sweeney), on February 3, 1944, at the age of 84. She had survived her husband by nearly two decades.
12. Author's conversation with Ruth Stone Pifer, Sept. 20, 1993. The Millers' visit to Frederick D. Kershner's office took place at 4:00 P.M. on Friday, March 17, 1944. A copy of the memorandum of agreement is in MC151.series I.folder 4a. Letters from Kershner to his family in February and March state that he had no knowledge of what would be taking place until the Millers' visit that March afternoon. MC55.box 56.folder 10.
13. This large number of baptisms in relation to transfers indicates that this church practiced closed membership, requiring all members to be immersed. Many of the 1,019 people would have been adults who had been baptized by sprinkling in infancy.
14. MC65.series I.folder 10.
15. Ibid.
16. This quotation and other information concerning the founding of the European

Evangelistic Society are taken from an account written by Ottie Mearl Stuckenbruck September 1, 1993. In this same letter Stuckenbruck describes the formal beginning of the European Evangelistic Society in a service in Sweeney Chapel presided over by Dean Shelton. MC151.series I.folder 15b.

17. Von Gerdtell was a strange person to add to the faculty. A Christadelphian rather than a Disciple, his theology was very different from that of others on the faculty. People would come out of his classes crying because of his teachings about Jesus, whom von Gerdtell described as a rich young prince with a retinue of 120 servants. Jesus was just a man, but he went to other planets redeeming people. How could he do this? He existed as long as God thought him. God could think Jesus through a closed door and think Jesus to another planet. Despite these ideas in the classroom, von Gerdtell's book on miracles was published by the Disciples publishing house, the Bethany Press, with a strong endorsement by Dean Kershner.

18. Faculty Minute Book, 132–3.

19. MC65.box 1.folder 8a.

20. The Christian Foundation also assumed responsibility to assist the Kershners in completing the purchase of their house.

21. The orientation course for first year students provided discussions of life and work in graduate school and the life of ministry; it also included conferences and discussions based on students' fieldwork with programs in churches to help them in that work. The orientation course for middler students consisted of conferences and discussions based on their fieldwork, and it included a study of church programs and activities in progress in churches. The orientation course for seniors provided study and practice in building programs for the church year; it was to be a clinical workshop, anticipating the actual experiences that ministers go through.

22. This congregation had had a long association with Butler University. It had been formed by a merger of two earlier congregations, one of which had been located at 40th and Capitol Avenue. In the late 1920s, shortly before the merger, the Capitol Avenue church had bought property for a new building at 46th and Capitol (northwest corner), intending to build "at the gateway to the University," which was in the process of moving to the Fairview campus. Several factors, including the Great Depression, forestalled that venture. When the merged congregation later followed through on its intention, the earlier site was no longer in its possession, but rather property at 46th and Illinois streets. The Kenwood building was sold to Second Christian Church; while the new facility for University Park was under construction, the congregation used Sweeney Chapel for Sunday worship. For a brief period of time the congregation's pastor discussed with Shelton and others the possibility of leasing land on the Butler campus for the new facility. Shelton's experience with the university, however, made him wary of the idea.

23. Dean E. Walker, "Presentation of Portrait," *Shane Quarterly* 6 (1945): 168–71.

24. Frederick D. Kershner, "A Personal Word," *Shane Quarterly* 6 (1945): 173 (italics added).

25. October 2, 1944. The correspondence between Shelton and R. H. Miller can be found in MC65.box 1. folder 9.

26. From the chart of the membership of the Christian Foundation it is difficult to determine exactly who were members at this time. Hilton U. Brown, Hugh Th. Miller, his wife Nettie S. Miller, and Girnie L. Reeves were definitely members, and probably Orville

Stevens and Charles M. Setser. Of these persons, Brown and Mr. and Mrs. Miller were also members of the School of Religion committee. It seems likely, however, that the conference prior to the 11:00 o'clock meeting was with Hugh Th. and Nettie Miller alone.

27. Ross's position was especially important because he was the first faculty president to be granted the full powers of the office of president of the university.

28. The dates of this discussion are established by Shelton's letters to R. H. Miller dated April 15 and October 5, 1946. MC65.box 1.folder 9. Also used are indicators in an undated draft of this interpretation of the contract. A copy of the contract between the Christian Foundation and Butler University is in the Shelton papers, copiously marked in red pencil; the same file contains a seven-page, closely spaced carbon copy of a document entitled "Review for the School of Religion Committee of the Contract between The Christian Foundation and Butler University." In the first paragraph the author, who surely was O. L. Shelton, states that more than five years have elapsed since the cooperative arrangement was established. PRS II.folder 21.

29. PRS II.folder 21.

30. Ibid. Shelton's response to this letter was not preserved with the others in this file; in following years he showed little interest in the organization of the course of study. The degree requirements in place when Shelton began as dean continued with little change until the major changes that were made following the establishing of Christian Theological Seminary as a separate institution twelve years after Miller's challenging letter.

31. Orman L. Shelton (dean and Christian ministries); Toyozo W. Nakarai (Semitic languages and literature); Dean E. Walker (church history); Arthur Holmes (psychology and philosophy of religion); Abram E. Cory (adjunct professor of missions and comparative religions); Lucile Calvert (speech); Harold F. Hanlin (New Testament). Three leaders of congregations were listed regularly as lecturers, Rabbi Morris M. Feuerlicht (Semitics); W. A. Shullenberger and T. K. Smith (Christian ministries). A lecturer in church music was listed regularly.

32. Insights into Shelton's intentions in his faculty building can be gleaned from his correspondence, especially the brief, informal communications between himself and R. H. Miller. Shelton's letters summarize matters under consideration by the trustees on the School of Religion committee and by the Christian Foundation. Insights have also been gathered from interviews with professors from that period of time, or with their widows. Limited amounts of information are available from collections of private papers in the Seminary's archives. Shelton's vision can also be seen in the list of people whom he unsuccessfully tried to attract early in his administration: Don McGavran, missionary with the United Christian Missionary Society, who later was to found the Church Growth Movement at Northwest Christian College and Fuller Theological Seminary; Herald B. Monroe, general secretary for the Christian Churches in Ohio; A. Dale Fiers, then pastor in Cleveland, and later president of the United Christian Missionary Society and the first General Minister and President of the Christian Church (Disciples of Christ); R. Frederick West, a Disciple teaching at Wabash College, previously at Texas Christian and later at Atlantic Christian; William Weaver, whom Shelton had known in Texas, as the successor to Holmes (Weaver's subsequent career included many years as assistant dean of the Divinity School of the University of Chicago); and Edwin L. Becker, who refused this appointment but later came following the resignation of Franklin E. Rector.

33. OLS to RHM, June 21, 1949. MC65.box 1.folder 9.

34. RHM to OLS, October 30, 1950. Ibid.

35. McGavran initially asked for a one-year term even though he was ready to leave the mission field in order to develop his ideas about people movements in an American context. Shelton used this one-year request as the basis for withdrawing from the discussion, but his letters leave room to believe that Shelton had developed doubts about McGavran's suitability for the School of Religion.

36. OLS to RHM, January 28, 1948. Shelton mentioned other assets that he believed Watters would bring and then concluded: "If he can make the contribution that Dr. [William] Robinson made in clarifying some of the brotherhood problems objectively, he will be an apostle for good." Shelton had high hopes for how Watters would work. "I would expect him and he fully agreed to participate in interdenominational and brotherhood councils. I would hope to have him sit in on the Disciple-Baptist committee in a session or two since he has been on that in Great Britain."

37. OLS to RHM, June 13, 1948; February 21, 1950.

38. It was understood by students that she was a friend of Clementine Miller and thus, some students concluded, could have been an occasional source of information about campus activities.

39. Although several accounts by students of the time recount these remembrances of Kershner, these paragraphs draw primarily upon Byron C. Lambert's monograph "Frederick Doyle Kershner's 'Intelligent Good Will': A Reminiscence and an Ethical Meditation With Afterward," July 12, 1990.

40. Earl Stuckenbruck, letter to author, September 15, 1993.

41. Author's conversation with Medford Jones, fall 1993.

42. D. Newell Williams, "Overcoming a Liberal-Conservative Divide: The Commission on Restudy of the Disciples of Christ," in *Christian Faith Seeking Understanding: Essays in Honor of H. Jackson Forstman,* eds. James O Duke and Anthony L. Dunnavant (Macon, Ga.: Mercer University Press, 1997), 246–276.

43. Author's conversation with Enos Dowling, October 1, 1993.

44. MC151.series I.folder 13.

45. MC65.box 1.folder 9.

Chapter 6

1. Joining them in the discussion, and writing a summary of the discussion, was G. W. Newlin, who was employed by Miller to manage the family's affairs.

2. None of the issues was dated, and the first two issues did not carry volume and number identifications, but the third issue was identified as Vol. I, No. 3. Although this publication was not named, I am referring to it as *School of Religion Bulletin.*

3. Orman L. Shelton (OLS) to J. Irwin Miller (JIM), July 17, 1952. PRS II,folder 51.

4. Robinson, however, was unable to attend the conference because of illness.

5. *School of Religion Bulletin* II/1. What the article did not describe was the hard work that the Dean had to do in order to bring Nakarai's manuscript to the press: the endless correspondence to find a publisher, getting a publishing subsidy from the Christian Foundation, and then having to deal with the fact that the book did not sell and the whole project went into debt. Nor did these announcements about Nakarai's book reveal the

prickly character of the author's letters to the dean defending his honor and insisting upon his freedom from financial obligations related to this project.

6. *School of Religion Bulletin,* III/2.

7. Ibid.

8. *School of Religion Bulletin,* V/1. Professors, trustees, and students who had some kind of official participation included Robert Tobias, William Robinson, J. Irwin Miller, Orman L. Shelton, Ronald E. Osborn, Harold Cline, Ralph Holcomb, Victor Ramsey, Lucy Hass, and James Merrill. Professor Frank Albert accompanied two of his classes to the assembly. Dean Shelton, an accredited visitor, drove to the assembly in his new, blue Dodge, equipped at doctor's orders with power steering and air conditioning. This was his first major expedition following a heart attack that had kept him away from campus much of the previous academic year.

9. This episode was described by Ronald E. Osborn in a conversation with the author in July 1997.

10. In his lectures at the School of Religion, Robinson frequently mentioned P. T. Forsyth and Karl Barth, noting the similarities in their ideas, and stating that if the world had listened to Forsyth Barth would not have needed to write. Robinson also was interested in Paul Tillich and would sometimes begin a class session by reading a sermon from Tillich's book of sermons, *The Shaking of the Foundations* (New York: C. Scribner's Sons, 1948).

11. Published by Bethany Press in St. Louis in 1948; revised edition in 1955.

12. (London: James Clark & Co., 1922), published one year earlier than Frederick D. Kershner's *Christian Union Overture* (St. Louis: The Bethany Press, 1923).

13. William Robinson, *The Shattered Cross: The Many Churches and the One Church* (Birmingham, England: The Berean Press, 1945), 5.

14. William Robinson, *Essays on Christian Unity* (London: James Clarke and Co., 1922), 31, 45.

15. William Robinson, *The Administration of the Lord's Supper* (Birmingham, England: The Berean Press, 1947).

16. Robert Tobias, "Christian Hope and Ecumenical Responsibility," *Shane Quarterly* 15 (1954): 114.

17. Robert, Tobias, *Ecumenical Studies Series* 1/1 (March 1955): 28.

18. Ronald E. Osborn, *The Spirit of American Christianity* (New York: Harper & Brothers, 1958), 152.

19. Ibid., 165.

20. "Current Issues in Faith and Order," *Shane Quarterly* 14 (1953): 112–15.

21. Osborn, *The Spirit of American Christianity,* 202, 222.

22. Shelton's tabulation of needs (*School of Religion Bulletin* VI,2) was as follows: Ministers needed, 443; Ministers of education needed, 40; Ministers of music, 8; Ministers annually for new churches, 60; Other leaders needed, 50; Annually for future growth, 170. The annual need by 1975 totaled 771.

23. *School of Religion Bulletin* VI/2.

24. Alberta Bible College, 2; Cincinnati Bible Seminary, 4; Johnson Bible College, 29; Kentucky Christian College, 7; Manhattan Bible College, 5; Minnesota Bible College, 8; Northwest Christian College, 22; and Pacific Bible Seminary, 2. The accreditation standard was that not more than 15 percent of the students be from unaccredited schools. The

importance of the undergraduate program of Butler was indicated by the fact that 23 percent of the Seminary's enrollment were Butler graduates.

25. Many students were pastors of churches, living in the communities where they ministered, and were close enough to campus that they could drive to classes each day. A large proportion, however, lived too far away for easy driving. The two-day schedule made it possible for these students living more than an hour's drive from campus to come in early one morning, stay over night, and return to their homes the second evening. While in the city, however, they needed a place to stay, and private homes all around campus opened their doors to these students.

26. *School of Religion Bulletin*, VI/3.

27. The biographical information for Thompson, however, failed to note that he was married to the Shelton's daughter and only child, Orma Lee.

28. Hilton U. Brown, born in 1859, had finally stepped down from the presidency of the board in the University's centennial year 1955. He had been a member of the board since 1885 and its president since 1903.

29. File Memorandum, Nov. 1, 1955. I-S-M papers.

30. As these discussions were taking place, the University was also projecting its needs for the future, with a focus upon the years 1960 through 1965. These projections used 1933 as the starting date for plotting the population of the 18 to 21 age group, the percentage attending college, the enrollments in all Indiana colleges and graduate schools, and the enrollments for Butler University. Total enrollment in the University was projected to grow from 4,480 in 1955 to 8,300 in 1965. Even with an increase in faculty of 85 percent, class size would have to increase. Three new buildings—library, college of music, and administration and college of business administration—would cost $3,500,000, and endowment would need to rise from $4,742,000 in 1956 to $9,000,000 in 1965. With these needs at the University, the challenge of resolving the needs of the School of Religion would be increased.

31. File Memorandum, Dec. 28, 1955. I-S-M papers.

32. The meeting of the joint committee reported in the following paragraphs met at the Columbia Club at 10:00 A.M. on June 25, 1956, with the following people present: Evan B. Walker, Orman L. Shelton, Irwin Mitchell, Jr., Kurt F. Pantzer, Earl Pulse, John R. Rees, M. O. Ross, J. I. Holcomb, and Kathryn Bromley, Secretary. These minutes are in the I-S-M papers. Although J. Irwin Miller was not present at that session, the Christian Foundation was well represented by Pulse, Rees, and Shelton.

33. The Saarinen sketch showed drives and walkways but no other practical reuirements of modern buildings. No parking lots, storage facilities, or utilities were indicated.

34. The Irwin Library is the only building on the Butler University campus to bear a name of the Columbus family of Disciples who more than any other group of persons have endowed the university with multi-generational leadership and financial support.

35. Hilton U. Brown, longtime president of the Butler board of directors and of the Christian Foundation; Theo. O. Fisher, Pastor of Northwood Christian Church, Indianapolis; J. Irwin Miller, Columbus, Indiana; R. H. Miller, longtime member of the School of Religion Committee; Earl B. Pulse, industrialist from Columbus, Indiana; John R. Rees, agriculturalist and Indiana state senator from Columbus, Indiana; and Orman L. Shelton.

36. The charter defined Christian Churches (Disciples of Christ) as those churches

"affiliated with the International Convention of the Christian Churches (Disciples of Christ), Inc., an Indiana corporation."

37. Ronald E. Osborn, "This Name 'Encounter,'" *Encounter* 17 (1956): 77.

38. This study was directed by James Gustafson, Daniel Day Williams, and H. Richard Niebuhr. Its official publications, not yet available when the Faculty Discussion Club began its work, included: H. Richard Niebuhr, *The Ministry in Historical Perspectives* (New York: Harper & Brothers, 1956); Ibid., *The Purpose of the Church and its Ministry: Reflections on the Aims of Theological Education* (New York: Harper & Brothers, 1956).

39. In addition to the School of Religion and Union Theological Seminary, the project was examining Garrett Biblical Institute in Evanston, Protestant Episcopal Seminary in Alexandria, and Louisville Presbyterian Seminary. Although Blizzard and F. E. Rector of the School of Religion faculty were acquainted prior to the beginning of the study, this relationship probably was not the reason for the inclusion of the School of Religion.

40. Samuel W. Blizzard, "The Butler University School of Religion Parish Minister Alumnus and His Training Needs," 1. Blizzard's "Confidential—Not For Publication" report to the School of Religion, dated March 8, 1956, was a fifty-nine-page analysis of the questionnaires received from thirty-six of the forty-two pastors of congregations who had graduated from the School with the B.D. degree in eight classes chosen at three-year intervals beginning in 1930 and concluding in 1952. Although the number was not large, the percentage of respondents was high, and the profiles of their responses compared favorably with those from other seminaries in the study. Dean Shelton took advantage of Blizzard's work by distributing copies of his essays widely and by bringing him to campus as lecturer and workshop leader for students and for Disciples pastors in Indiana. He also arranged for Blizzard to hold a daylong conference in Indianapolis with members of the state boards of the Disciples in the states with which the School of Religion was related.

41. "Special Study of Theological Education," 3.

42. This name was approved by the faculty on June 6, 1957, and it was used when the incorporators were issued a charter for Christian Theological Seminary on September 17, 1958.

43. "Special Study of Theological Education," 20, 21.

44. Ibid., 9.

45. Ibid., 15.

46. Ibid., 8.

47. Ibid., 19, 20.

48. Ibid., 17; the second quotation is from p. 34.

49. During Kershner's last years the faculty had labored over requirements for the B.D. degree. In the 1937 catalog they announced a B.D. program that required ninety semester hours, including twelve hours in Greek or Hebrew, or ninety-six hours if students did not choose the language option. In 1942 they remade the program, reducing requirements from ninety semester hours to seventy-two, and providing four variations. The catalog for the 1953–54 session restored the requirement that the B.D. degree require ninety hours of work. The existing pattern, with its four variants, two examinations, and dissertation, was retained, with slight revisions. The requirement in Christian Ministries was increased from four to sixteen hours, three hours were assigned to practica, and the thesis was awarded three credit hours.

50. "Special Study of Theological Education," 43.

51. This aspect of Shelton's work is described by Ronald E. Osborn in his "Portrait of a Churchman." Especially pertinent to his work as dean was his significant labor on behalf of the seminary and its membership on the Disciples Board of Higher Education.

52. MC65.box 1.folder 9.

53. All three of these organizations were major agencies of the organized life of the Disciples of Christ.

54. MC65.box 1.folder 8.

Chapter 7

1. *Addresses Given at the Inauguration of Beauford A. Norris as President of Christian Theological Seminary.* A description of the occasion itself, with summaries of addresses, was published in *Christian Theological Seminary Bulletin,* Vol. 1, No. 2 (December 1959).

2. *Addresses,* 10.

3. This phrase appeared in J. Irwin Miller's Opening Greetings to delegates and others attending the inauguration of Beauford A. Norris.

4. Joseph M. Smith to KW, January 15, 1998.

5. Fisher had come from Australia to the School of Religion in 1937 to study on a Sweeney scholarship. He had become the student pastor of nearby Northwood Christian Church which at that time had a membership of about 250 with average attendance of less than 100. When he completed his Northwood ministry in 1965, the congregation had 1,900 members. He was the first new person to be brought into the previously closed circle of people who controlled the affairs of the School of Religion.

6. This report of Shelton's counsel was recounted by Fisher in conversation with the author.

7. The congregation began meeting in October 1955 in members' homes on Sunday evenings and then at St. Paul's Episcopal Church. Eero Saarinen, the son of the architect who designed First Christian Church, designed the edifice that the congregation built on Tipton Lane on the north side of Columbus.

8. This report on the election of the president and other academic officers is drawn from private letters of Ronald E. Osborn (REO) to his family dated June 9, June 19, and July 7, 1959. Disciples of Christ Historical Society, PP6.III.16.

9. First Tobias, followed by Clague, Sikes, and Nakarai. REO to Family, June 9, 1959.

10. The business offices and the pastoral care and counseling program used the Griffeth house, later occupied by the Delta Tau Delta fraternity at 940 W. 42nd Street until the property was razed in preparation for constructing the new campus.

11. "Memo to Joint Committee of Butler University and Christian Theological Seminary," April 19, 1959.

12. At this time the administrative council consisted of Acting President Norris, Acting Dean Pellett, Ronald E. Osborn, S. Marion Smith, and Walter Sikes.

13. REO to KW, January 8, 1998.

14. Although the president was required to consult with the faculty, the bylaws of the seminary gave the president the power to advance a nomination with or without faculty support. On at least one occasion in the early years of the Norris-Osborn administration, a candidate was brought to the campus for a visit but because he did not receive a strong affirmation from the faculty the president did not advance his nomination to the board.

15. Tenure had been established by the trustees in their meeting on May 2, 1965. The provisions and procedures had been recommended by the president and dean, and the trustees, with reluctance especially among business people on the board, had approved. Upon the approval, J. Irwin Miller declared that henceforth every tenured professor, worthy of tenure, would do or say at least one thing every year for which they would be dismissed were it not for tenure.

16. E. L. Thompson left the Seminary's staff at the same time, but Jack Sanders continued with the new title of provost.

17. The people called and the year they began were: Keith Watkins, 1961; Lester G. McAllister, spring of 1962; Calvin L. Porter, 1962; Donald R. Wismar, 1963; Harold E. Fey, 1964; Edwin L. Becker, 1965; Clark M. Williamson, 1966; Charles B. Ashanin, 1967; Richard D. N. Dickinson, Jr., and J. Gerald Janzen, 1968.

18. Robert Tobias to KW, March 10, 1998.

19. Especially severe was the reaction of Ross J. Griffeth, president of Northwest Christian College, which for many years had provided close to 10 percent of the Seminary's enrollment. During the later years of Kershner's administration, Griffeth had headed the undergraduate program in religion at Butler and had been a fully functioning member of the faculty of the School of Religion, for some years serving as its secretary. Griffeth had left Butler in 1944 to assume the presidency of this small college in Eugene, Oregon. Although NCC was unaccredited by its regional accrediting association Griffeth had defended its quality by saying that graduates were accepted without question by graduate schools across the country. Now the graduate school to which Griffeth had directed the largest number of NCC candidates for the ministry, would no longer be receptive to his unaccredited graduates. Therefore, he would direct them to schools that would receive them gladly.

20. *CTS Bulletin,* April 1961.

21. The building committee consisted of two trustees, Harry T. Ice and Richard B. Stoner; two administrators, Beauford A. Norris and David C. Pellett; and two professors, James Blair Miller and Robert Tobias.

22. *CTS Bulletin,* April 1961.

23. *CTS Bulletin,* September 1961.

24. A file of correspondence and historical data has been compiled by Austin Greene, vice president of Development, and Professor Emeritus Edwin L. Becker. See MC151.I.10. The estate houses, beginning at Haughey Avenue and proceeding west, were built by Theodore B. Griffith, Caroline Burford Danner, Perry E. and Lucy Holliday O'Neal, and J. F. Holliday.

25. *CTS Bulletin,* May 1962.

26. This figure included the $600,000 that Butler had paid for the School of Religion building.

27. Even in these temporary facilities, the library would have more space in the new building than in the red-brick building on the Butler campus. It was also decided not to install air conditioning because the architect assured the building committee that the air exchange system in the building would make it more comfortable than their existing building. The first summer proved that this forecast was not accurate, for at 8:00 A.M. temperatures in the administrative wing would be 80 degrees of humid Indiana summer, getting worse as the day progressed. The Association of Disciples Musicians held a national workshop in the building with Clementine Miller Tangeman an exceedingly uncomfortable

participant. Before the conference closed she called on President Norris in his office with the promise that she would find a way to underwrite the bill (which was close to $300,000) for the installation of air conditioning.

28. *CTS Bulletin*, March 1964.

29. *CTS Bulletin,* October 31, 1966.

30. The artworks celebrated on this occasion were: Quasar by Victor Vasarely, Mycenae-axe-blue by Ben Nicholson, Sphere # 6 by Arnaldo Pomodoro, the banners of the cross by George Ortman, and the celtic cross by Alistair Bevington.

31. Mead's analysis was published in her book *Culture and Commitment: A Study of the Generation Gap* (Garden City, N.Y.: Natural History Press, 1970). Thomas Luckmann's interpretation of contemporary life was published in *The Invisible Religion: The Problem of Religion in Modern Society* (New York: Macmillan, 1967). Langer's statement was published in *Philosophical Sketches* (New York: Mentor Books, 1964, 141). This paragraph was used by Keith Watkins as the frontispiece to his book *Liturgies in a Time When Cities Burn* (Nashville: Abingdon Press, 1969).

32. Edwin L. Becker, "Christian Theological Seminary in the Late 60s, A Memoir." MC151.I.11a.

33. Room 122 had certain similarities to the space designed by Rudolf Schwarz and described by Frédéric Debuyst in *Modern Architecture and Christian Celebration* (Richmond: John Knox Press, 1968) which as a place of celebration was "probably the most satisfactory ever given us," 60.

34. J. Irwin Miller, "The Church in Russia: Reflections of a Visiting Churchman," *Encounter* 24 (1963): 477–90.

35. *Encounter* 24 (1963): 491–92.

36. *A Church for These Times* (Nashville: Abingdon Press, 1965), 178.

37. Walter Sikes retired at the end of the 1962–63 year during which he turned sixty-seven. Franklin E. Rector left in 1964 to join the staff of the Illinois Council of Churches. In that same year, following a research leave, Robert Tobias left the Disciples to become a Lutheran and accept a position on the faculty of the Lutheran School of Theology in Chicago; and Joseph M. Smith became executive secretary in the department of east Asia of the United Christian Missionary Society. Toyozo W. Nakarai retired at the end of the 1964–65 year during which he turned sixty-seven. In 1965 Frank J. Albert died of a heart attack at age forty-nine. James Clague left the Disciples to become an Episcopalian and in 1969 accepted an appointment to the faculty of the Berkeley Divinity School, New Haven, Connecticut.

38. Vahanian had become a prominent voice in theological and cultural discussion because of his two books, both published by George Braziller in New York: *The Death of God: The Culture of Our Post-Christian Era* (1961), and *Wait Without Idols* (1964).

39. Fey had joined the staff of *Christian Century* in 1940 and had served as editor since 1956.

40. *CTS Bulletin*, December 1963.

41. *CTS Bulletin*, September 1968.

42. *CTS Bulletin*, November 1968.

43. The chaplains with whom Lowell G. Colston developed the Seminary's long term relations were Robert Alexander at Central State Hospital, Kenneth E. Reed at Methodist

Hospital, and John A. Whitesel at Indiana University Medical Center. The first time these colleagues were listed in the Seminary catalog was 1965–66.

44. Johnson was one of the most distinguished teachers and writers in the pastoral care discipline; and his coming added considerable stature to the program of the Seminary.

45. *Master Plan 1967–1977.* MC151.Bound Reports, 11.

46. The first NIMH grant to the Seminary had been announced in 1968, and the first phase of the five-year program had begun in 1969. The first grant for the work-study program was for $66,000, to begin on July 1, 1969.

47. *CTS Bulletin,* October 1969.

48. *CTS Bulletin,* August 1969.

49. *CTS Bulletin,* May 1969.

Chapter 8

1. Robert T. Handy, *History of Union Theological Seminary in New York* (New York: Columbia University Press, 1987), 291–92.

2. Clementine Miller Tangeman to Kingman Brewster, Jr., May 10, 1973. MC151.I.11a.

3. Representing CTS were President Norris and Dean Osborn; trustees Harry T. Ice and A. Dale Fiers; and professors James Blair Miller and Keith Watkins. Among the Lexington representatives were President Welsh and Dean Ralph Wilburn, and Professor Paul A. Crow, Jr.

4. This brief review of the history of St. Maur's Priory and its related institutions comes from its *Bulletin* for 1964–65, 10, 11.

5. This letter dated January 24, 1966, and other documents about the Catholic Seminary of Indianapolis are deposited in FRS.I.1–14.

6. *CTS Bulletin,* November 1966.

7. *Bulletin Catalog Issue 1971–1973,* 5, 7, 12, 13, 23.

8. The third person from the Catholic side of the river to be active in this venture was Mario W. Shaw, a priest and member of the St. Maur Benedictine Community, who was listed as administrator and associate professor of Old Testament.

9. The first seven members of the anticipated twenty-five included Raymond Bosler, pastor of Little Flower Catholic Church; Indianapolis; Joseph Coffin, president of the J. I. Holcomb Company; Gene W. Newberry, dean of the Anderson School of Theology; Sidney Steiman, rabbi of Congregation Beth-El Zedeck, Indianapolis; Matthew Welsh, former Governor of Indiana; and Beauford A. Norris.

10. The creation of the Repertory Theatre and a full history of its first thirty years is published in *Dreaming the Impossible Dream,* by Marian K. Towne (Indianapolis: privately published, 1996). Towne reports (44) that both the theater and the counseling center were encouraged to incorporate as distinct entities. Only the theater did so, however, establishing its corporate status in 1971.

11. This three-volume set carried the general title *The Renewal of Church: The Panel Reports* (St. Louis: Bethany Press, 1963). A major review of these volumes by Walter W. Sikes was published in *Encounter* 25 (1964): 482–93, under the title "A Denomination Looks at Itself."

12. The lectures were published under the title *Toward the Christian Church: Intention, Essence, Constitution* (St. Louis: Christian Board of Publication, 1964).

13. The motion to adjourn the International Convention was made by Elsie Irwin Sweeney of Columbus, Indiana, honoring the contribution of her father Z. T. Sweeney in the creation of the convention in 1917.

14. Ronald E. Osborn, *In Christ's Place: Christian Ministry in Today's World* (St. Louis: Bethany Press, 1967).

15. Lester G. McAllister, Keith Watkins, Calvin L. Porter, Donald R. Wismar, Edwin L. Becker, Clark M. Williamson, Charles B. Ashanin, J. Gerald Janzen, Richard D. N. Dickinson, Jr., Willie White, and Robert S. Bates.

16. Porter's installation address was delivered February 12, 1963: "Principles of New Testament Interpretation," *Encounter* 25 (1964), 41_49. Janzen's was delivered six years later, to the day: "Deep Unto Deep," *Encounter* 31 (1970), 56–65.

17. Lester G. McAllister, "Thomas Campbell: His Significance to the Ecumenical Movement," *Encounter* 24 (1963): 458–76; "Current Literature in Church History," *Encounter* 25 (1964): 381–89.

18. Charles B. Ashanin, "The Church Historian in Dialogue," *Encounter* 29 (1968): 3–13.

19. Clark M. Williamson, "God and the Relativities of History," *Encounter* 28 (1967): 199–218. See also "The Death of God: A Survey," *Encounter* 27 (1966): 283–98; and "Rediscovering Our Grandfathers: Trends in Theology, a Review Article," *Encounter* 28 (1967): 161–67.

20. Edwin L. Becker, "Church Polity and Power," *Encounter* 27 (1966): 323–32.

21. Richard D. N. Dickinson, Jr. "Why International Development? A Christian Perspective," *Encounter* 31 (1970): 164–76.

22. Watkins's essays were: "Liturgy and the Free Church," *Encounter* 23 (1962): 196–203; "Gift to the World: The Relation of Liturgy to Mission," (Ibid., 435–45); and "An Order of Holy Communion for Use Every Sunday," *Encounter* 24 (1963): 303–13. "An Order" was followed by "A Symposium On An Order of Holy Communion for Use Every Sunday," in which seven people from six communions commented on the liturgy, 314–29.

23. Donald R. Wismar, "The Recovery of Preaching: Its Significance for the Theological Seminary," *Encounter* 25 (1964): 324–34.

24. Alfred R. Edyvean and Lowell G. Colston represented professors with longer periods of service and Clark M. Williamson and J. Gerald Janzen represented newer professors.

25. This summary of the faculty's discussion is taken from a report published in *CTS Bulletin*, September 1969.

26. These numbers were the street addresses on W. 42nd Street.

27. Thelma Hodges, longtime cataloguer in the library, was especially skillful in composing the literary spoofs used in these productions.

28. A tribute to Bradshaw's work was published in *Link* (Winter 1997) following his death.

29. One student remembered that there were seven Disciples women who began their work in 1970, but she could remember the names of only four of them. The CTS Directories correct the memory. Five women, four of them Disciples, began their M.Div. programs in the fall of 1969: Joyce Basey, Jacqueline Buck, Deborah Casey, Sherrill Clark, and Claudia Ewing. In the fall of 1970 ten women, eight of them Disciples, enrolled as first

year students for the M.Div. degree: Louise Banks, Christine Hershberger, Carol Krell, Suzanne Martz; Constance Nusbaum, Evelyn Meredith, Margaret Richardson, Judith Slaughter, Ruth Starr, and Linda Weeks.

30. *Christian Theological Seminary Bulletin Catalog Issue, 1971–1973,* 41.
31. *Christian Theological Seminary Bulletin Catalog Issue, 1967–1968,* 49.
32. These four were Joseph Culpepper, William Flewelling, Richard Hamm, and Jan Linn.
33. Edwin L. Becker, "Christian Theological Seminary in the Late 60s, A Memoir." MC151.I,11a.
34. Marian K. Towne, *Dreaming the Impossible Dream* (Indianapolis: privately published, 1996), 47ff.
35. *CTS Bulletin,* April 1970.
36. "Project Understanding (1972–1974): Final Report," August 1974, 146ff. MC98.7.
37. In this regard, people at the seminary were much like the members of First Christian Church in Columbus a generation earlier. They too had moved from a conventional building to a pace-setting example of expansive ecclesiastical architecture. One of their members commented on their experience years later, stating that many people never had felt comfortable in this new home. Yet, it had continued to shape their spirits in a new way.
38. *CTS Bulletin,* February 1974.
39. Clark M. Williamson, "Editorial: Homage to a President," *Encounter* 34 (1973): 271.
40. J. Gerald Janzen, "Art and Gravity," *Encounter* 34 (1973): 361–71.

Chapter 9

1. Liggett studied at Union Seminary during the summer of 1945 and during a one and a half year furlough in 1951–1952.
2. Thomas J. Liggett, *Where Tomorrow Struggles to Be Born: The Americas in Transition* (New York: Friendship Press, 1970), 20–21.
3. The summary of measures to reestablish fiscal stability is summarized from the *Bulletin* , February 1976, 1–3; the three conversations were reported in interviews with Thomas J. Liggett at his home in November 1997.
4. Thomas J. Liggett, "Lilly Endowment Study of the Office of Seminary Presidency Interviews with Thomas J. Liggett, September 14–15, 1992," 32, 33.
5. "Lilly Endowment Study," 83, 84.
6. "Lilly Endowment Study," 31.
7. Memorandum from Thomas J. Liggett to Keith Watkins, August 1998.
8. *The Self-Study Report, Christian Theological Seminary, 1977,* I, 85.
9. Ibid., *1977,* I, 81.
10. *CTS Bulletin,* February 1974.
11. *CTS Bulletin,* November 1974.
12. *Board of Trustees Docket,* May 19, 1976, 44.
13. *Board of Trustees Docket,* May 4, 1977, 52.
14. *The Self-Study Report, Christian Theological Seminary, 1977,* II, 103–08.
15. *CTS Bulletin,* November 1977.
16. *The Self-Study Report, Christian Theological Seminary, 1977,* I, 50.

17. Marian K. Towne, *Dreaming the Impossible Dream* (Indianapolis: privately published, 1996), 79, 82.

18. Bernard E. Meland, quoted in J. Gerald Janzen, "The Old Testament in 'Process' Perspective," in *Magnalia Dei: The Mighty Acts of God,* eds. Frank Moore Cross, et. al. (Garden City, N.Y.: Doubleday & Co., Inc., 1976), 481ff.

19. Ibid., 483.

20. Ibid., 485.

21. See J. Gerald Janzen, "Modes of Power and the Divine Relativity," *Encounter* 36 (1975): 379–406.

22. J. Gerald Janzen, *Job* (Atlanta: John Knox Press, 1985).

23. In another paper published during these same formative years, Janzen used process philosophy to develop an interpretation of religious experience—of the immediate experience of the historical Christ and of the communion of saints. "Modes of Presence and the Communion of Saints," in *Religious Experience and Process Theology,* eds. Harry James Cargas, and Bernard Lee (Paramus, N.Y.: Paulist Press, 1976).

24. In his formal report to the faculty and trustees Williamson mentioned his involvement with Marxist thought but gave no indication of his growing interest in Judaism (See Board Docket for October 17, 1973, 65–66). The detailed report on his encounter with living faiths was published as "Secular Ecumenism: A Different Ballgame," in *Encounter* 34/4 (1973): 343–50. An example of his work on Marxist-Christian dialogue was published as "The Ideal is More Real than the Real (Fichte)," in *Encounter* 35/2 (1974): 132–52.

25. His paper at the conference, with the title "Whitehead as a Counterrevolutionary?" was a response to a paper on "Justice and Class Struggle: A Challenge for Process Thought," by George Pixley, an American theologian teaching in Puerto Rico. Williamson's effort to understand and use Marxist ideas was at the center of a paper, "Notes on a Theology of Work," that he prepared for the Association of Disciples for Theological Education in 1975.

26. Clark M. Williamson, *Has God Rejected His People? Anti-Judaism in the Christian Church* (Nashville: Abingdon, 1982), 7.

27. *CTS Bulletin,* November 1974.

28. *CTS Bulletin,* February 1974.

Chapter 10

1. "Christian Theological Seminary Looks to the Future" (Christian Theological Seminary, 1979), 24. MC151.I.Bound Reports.

2. Ibid., 28.

3. Ibid., 43.

4. *CTS Bulletin,* January 1980.

5. This version of the story summarizes the way Liggett reported it in a conversation with Keith Watkins. A fuller account is given by Liggett in "Lilly Endowment Study," 90, 91.

6. *CTS Bulletin,* June 1984.

7. *CTS Bulletin,* August 1985.

8. *Board of Trustees, Report of the Dean,* October 22, 1980.

9. The series was launched by Keith Watkins, with responses first by Clark M. Williamson and then by Edgar A. Towne.

10. Materials related to the French Lick retreat and curricular developments can be found in MC151.I.11b.

11. "The Chrysalis Program, Summary and Evaluation, July 1985," Evaluation, 23. PRS.V.9.

12. Following Steiman's death, Rabbi Murray Salzman of the Indianapolis Hebrew Congregation, and then his successor Rabbi Jonathan Stein served in that capacity. When Stein left Indianapolis in the early 1990s, Rabbi Dennis Sasso from Congregation Beth-El Zedeck became lecturer and then affiliate professor of Jewish Studies.

13. Mary C. Boys, ed., *Education for Citizenship and Discipleship* (New York: Pilgrim Press, 1989) and Nelle G. Slater, ed., *Tensions between Citizenship and Discipleship: A Case Study* (New York: Pilgrim Press, 1989).

14. In an interview published in the *CTS Bulletin,* Pittenger remembered that in the 1930s only four American theologians had been writing and thinking about theology from a process perspective—Bernard Loomer, Bernard Meland, Daniel Day Williams, and Norman Pittenger. Process theology, Pittenger declared, "is the only system of thought which significantly incorporates a metaphysic of love." Why did he believe in God? Because such a belief is necessary to process thought: "only God gives order and significance." And also because belief in God "is an article of faith and part of my historical context. I believe there is a God because my father told me so." *CTS Bulletin,* November 1981.

15. *Board of Trustees, Report of the Dean,* October 1979.

16. His courses in the sociology of religion had been based on the conviction that "there is no such thing as an isolated individual," and that one must understand communities and institutions in order to understand persons. "I sometimes think that sociology supports the need for the church more than theology does." *CTS Bulletin,* May 1981.

17. Regents of the University of California v. Bakke, U.S. Supreme Court, 1978.

18. *Board of Trustees, Report of the Dean,* October 1982.

19. *Board of Trustees, Report of the Dean,* May 1984.

20. *Board of Trustees, Report of the Dean,* May 1981.

21. *CTS Bulletin,* December 1978.

22. *CTS Bulletin,* May 1980.

23. E. A. Sovik, *Architecture for Worship* (Minneapolis: Augsburg Publishing House, 1973).

24. They were built on Julius Field that had been the football field for Shortridge High School at 34th and Meridian. When Shortridge was closed as a high school, the field had become surplus property and the Seminary bought it for future expansion. A. C. Shortridge, after whom the high school had been named, was a leader in educational activities in Indiana during the nineteenth century. A prominent member of the Christian Churches, Shortridge was for many years a member of the board of directors of Butler University. The suggestion that the apartments be named for Shortridge, thus recovering a significant Disciples' name for the Seminary and connecting CTS with the tradition of Shortridge High School, was dismissed by President Liggett.

25. The tree was blown over in a violent storm in June 1989. Later in the year the Seminary held a special service of joyful remembrance of the tree and what it had meant.

One student later commented on the fact that the Seminary "would hold a memorial service for a tree." At CTS she had learned that "although I am a human being and live life from that perspective, life, itself, is a much richer, fuller enterprise." Brenda Brasher, *Koinoia*, January 31, 1990. Another student wrote a reflection about what that tree may have witnessed during its 300-year life, concluding, "Did I love that old oak tree? No. But hell, it sure had class." Dave Avery, *Koinonia*, September 6, 1989.

26. Carpenter's windows were prominently displayed in Allen Freeman, "Serenely Simple Interior Painted by Light," *Architecture* (June 1988): 86–89. Another publication that described the campus and illustrated its remarkable qualities was *The American Organist* (December 1987), in which a brief statement by Edward Larrabee Barnes summed up his ideas about the chapel as a place of mystery.

27. "Christian Theological Seminary Looks to the Future," 43.

Chapter 11

1. The members were Donald Manwarren, deputy general minister and president of the Christian Church (Disciples of Christ); Marilyn Moffett, active Disciples laywoman who soon would serve as moderator of the general assembly of the Christian Church (Disciples of Christ); and John Bean, pastor of North Christian Church of Columbus, Indiana.

2. *Report of the Trustee Task Force on the Relationship of Christian Theological Seminary and the Christian Church (Disciples of Christ),* July 1, 1986.

3. These revised possibilities included ten presidential scholarships providing full tuition and a $1,000 stipend, in the hope of attracting "the highest caliber students to ministerial study at CTS." Five Martin Luther King, Jr., scholarships were to be awarded to "racial minority U.S. citizens who show promise for ministry." Ten Thomas J. and Virginia M. Liggett scholarships were to provide full tuition for students who were members of the Christian Church (Disciples of Christ) or the United Church of Christ. *CTS Bulletin,* December 1988.

4. Ursala Pfafflin, Marti J. Steussy, Peet Pearson, David D. Bundy, Garth Baker-Fletcher, Karen Baker-Fletcher, Rebecca B. Prichard, Frank Burch Brown, and Raymond R. Sommerville.

5. *Policy Statement on Faculty Recruitment and Development,* approved by the board of trustees May 9, 1990.

6. See Jones's essay "Schematic Reflections on Salvation in Jesus Christ," in *Encounter* 56/1 (Winter, 1985): 18.

7. *Principles and Procedures for Assessing Student Aptitude and Readiness for Ministry.*

8. "Discerning Our Central Purposes," November 15, 1987, n.p.

9. *1997 Self-Study,* 112–25.

10. Barbara G. Wheeler and Edward Farley, eds., *Shifting Boundaries: Contextual Approaches to the Structure of Theological Education* (Louisville: Westminster/John Knox Press, 1991).

11. Ibid., 12–13.

12. Ibid., 46.

13. D. Newell Williams to Keith Watkins, August 31, 1998.

14. *1997 Self-Study,* 1/124.

15. Pastoral Counseling Service, Christian Theological Seminary, "Application for Approval/Renewal," 1997.

16. Indianapolis congregations included Central Christian Church with 2,785 members, Third Christian Church with 1,921 members, and three other congregations with more than 1,000 members each. The Downey Avenue congregation in Irvington reported 922 members. Smaller congregations that were to become the places where seminary professors and their families were to be concentrated were Northwood Christian Church with 330 members and North Park (later to be called University Park) Christian Church with 700 members. Second Christian Church, given a separate listing as a Negro congregation, reported 250 members.

17. Central reported 1,032 members, Third reported 1,649, Downey Avenue reported 1,447 members, Northwood reported 1,590, and University Park 1,039. Second Christian Church reported 764 members. Two newer congregations were East 49th Street Christian Church with 772 members and Speedway Christian Church with 1,950 members.

18. L. C. Rudolph, *Hoosier Faiths: A History of Indiana Churches & Religious Groups* (Bloomington and Indianapolis: Indiana University Press, 1995), 60. In the Disciples 1990 *Yearbook* Central Christian reported 293 members, Downey Avenue 440, Northwood 740, Third 739, and University Park 144. Speedway Christian Church now listed 3,119 members. Second Christian had changed its name to Light of the World Christian Church and reported 2,885 members. East 49th Street Church had relocated to the far northeast corner of the metropolitan area, and under the same pastor who had been its leader since the 1950s was still listed in the Disciples *Yearbook* but had become identified as part of the centrist group. In its most recent report to the *Yearbook* this rapidly growing congregation had listed 3,854 members.

What was happening in Indiana and Indianapolis was also taking place in other parts of the country. Everywhere Disciples were rapidly losing strength. Their decline was part of the widespread restructuring of American religion; all of the mainline protestant churches were losing members, as a growing body of literature reported and analyzed. Disciples, however, were losing even more rapidly than the others, partly because many of their constituents were "going independent." With relatively few exceptions among Disciples, and these primarily African American, the only congregations in the "Christians movement" that showed dramatic growth were among the independent churches. Not only in Indianapolis, but in many other cities—including Louisville, Lexington, Phoenix, and Seattle—churches from this central group were among the largest protestant churches, rivaling the megachurches that had been spawned by the evangelical and revivalist traditions.

19. "President's Report," February 10, 1988.

20. Ibid., February 8, 1989.

21. The quotation is from the report on the conference in *Link,* January 1990. The papers were published in a book edited by Charles R. Blaisdell, *Conservative, Moderate, Liberal: The Biblical Authority Debate* (St. Louis: CBP Press, 1990).

22. *Christian Theological Seminary Link,* January 1991.

23. Ibid., January 1990.

24. Ibid., October 1990.

25. The papers of this conference were first published in *Mid-Stream* 26/3 (July 1987). The references to essays in the series are drawn from that version. Kinnamon's opening remarks are on pages 261–64.

26. Charles H. Bayer, *Mid-Stream* 26/3 (July 1987), 453.

27. D. Newell Williams, ed., *A Case Study of Mainstream Protestantism: The Disciples' Relation to American Culture, 1880–1989* (Grand Rapids: William B. Eerdmans Publishing Company; St. Louis: Chalice Press, 1991). Writers met at a later time to criticize one another's work, and early drafts of the papers were presented to a public conference at the Seminary April 15–18, 1989. Most of the papers and related materials were published in the *Case Study,* a book of nearly 600 pages. Another Lilly-funded case study analyzing the Presbyterian Church was published in five volumes, with the series title *The Presbyterian Presence: The Twentieth-Century Experience,* eds., Milton J. Coalter, John M. Mulder, and Louis B. Weeks (Louisville: Westminster/John Knox).

28. *Case Study,* 5.
29. *Case Study,* 9.
30. *Case Study,* 25.
31. *Case Study,* 562.
32. *Case Study, 565.*
33. *Case Study,* 570.
34. *Case Study,* 574.
35. *Case Study,* 535.
36. *Case Study, 553.*

37. The team consisted of Keith Watkins, chair, Michael K. Kinnamon, Katherine Kinnamon, Ronald J. Allen, and Linda McKeirnan-Allen. Peter Morgan met with the team much of the time.

38. Keith Watkins, ed., *Thankful Praise* (St. Louis: CBP Press, 1987), 8.

39. Gerard Francis Moore, "The Eucharistic Theology of the Prayers for the Communion Service of the Lord's Supper of the Christian Church (Disciples of Christ): 1953–1987" (Catholic University of America, unpublished dissertation for the degree Licentiate of Theology, 1989), 88.

40. When that new book, *Chalice Worship,* was published in 1997, *Thankful Praise* was mentioned in the Introduction and then set aside. Comparing the three Disciples books—*Christian Worship, Thankful Praise,* and *Chalice Worship*—one reviewer concluded that the newest of the books invites Disciples "to step forward without really encouraging us to move." *Thankful Praise,* "with its impetus from Osborn, Robinson, and Campbell, has been side lined by a more palatable, less threatening, updating of the status quo." Douglas B. Dornhecker, "Chalice Worship: How Goes the Reformation?" Western Association for Theological Discussion, February 3–5, 1998, 18.

41. Over the years several people who were at the time related to the Seminary had served on the commission, including professors Ronald E. Osborn and Michael K. Kinnamon and Howard Goodrich, regional minister in Indiana. At the time this book was published the list of members included professors Clark M. Williamson and Joe R. Jones, affiliate professor Paul A. Crow, Jr., and CTS graduate Kenneth Henry. All three consultants were also related to the Seminary—Carmelo Alvarez was visiting professor and Richard L. Hamm and Linda Patrick-Rosebrock were graduates.

42. Paul A. Crow, Jr., and James O. Duke, eds., *The Church for Disciples of Christ: Seeking to be Truly Church Today* (St. Louis: Published for Council on Christian Unity by Christian Board of Publication, 1998), 13.

43. Ibid., 126.
44. Ibid., 25.
45. The report to the trustees was in the "President's Report" for May 1991, and the published version "Christian Theological Seminary Facing the Next Millennium," was published in *Mid-Stream* 33/2 (1994): 205–13.
46. "President's Report," May 8, 1991.
47. Conrad Cherry, *Hurrying Toward Zion: Universities, Divinity Schools, and American Protestantism* (Bloomington and Indianapolis: Indiana University Press, 1995), 66.
48. *Self-Study: Christian Theological Seminary, 1997,* I, 108–9, 114.
49. *1997 Self Study,* I, 114.
50. President Liggett had to cancel his presentation because of illness.
51. Richard D. N. Dickinson, Jr., to Clementine Miller Tangeman, February 18, 1994.
52. Brown was a graduate of the University of Chicago, an authority on theology and the arts, with books on that topic published by Princeton University Press. The most recent of these volumes was still new in the book stores—*Religious Aesthetics: A Theological Study of Making and Meaning* (Princeton: Princeton University Press, 1989).
53. *Christian Theological Seminary Link,* June 1992.
54. Ibid., August 1994.
55. Robert Natkin's remarks were printed in the program leaflet given to participants and summarized in *Christian Theological Seminary Link,* August 1994.
56. Marian K. Towne, *Dreaming the Impossible Dream* (Indianapolis: privately published, 1996), 112ff.
57. Frank Burch Brown, "Religion & the Arts at CTS: Tracing the Contours," photocopied statement dated October 1995.
58. "Report to the Trustees," May 7, 1997.

Chapter 12

1. *Christian Theological Seminary Link*, Winter 1997.
2. Ronald J. Allen to Keith Watkins, June 14, 2000.
3. *Christian Century*, June 7–14, 2000, 637.

Appendix

1. Hoover's position was part-time. His major work was as general secretary of the Indiana Christian Missionary Association, a position that later held the title regional minister.
2. This position was part-time at the College of Religion, with the major part of her work in the College of Liberal Arts.
3. Despite the title, Feuerlicht's position was always part-time, similar to what has in the latter part of this history been called affiliate professor.
4. This position was part time at the College of Religion, with the major part of his work in the College of Liberal Arts.
5. Although Griffeth was listed as a professor in the College of Liberal Arts, and not as a professor at the College of Religion, he functioned with the faculty of the College of

Religion, meeting regularly with that faculty, serving as its secretary, and performing committee assignments.

6. Despite the title, Cory functioned as a full member of the faculty.

7. His appointment was originally in the field of preaching.

Index

Albert, Frank J., 107, 141, 278
Aley, Robert J., 43, 58, 59
All Souls Unitarian Church, 49
Allen, Linda McKiernan. *See* McKiernan-Allen, Linda
Allen, Ronald J., 228, 229, 230, 233, 280
Alvarez, Carmelo E., 281
American Academy of Religion, 210
American Christian Missionary Society, 119
American Schools of Oriental Research, 172
Amerson, Elaine, 243
Ames, Edward Scribner, 12–13, 14, 85
Anderson, E. Byron, 281
Anderson School of Theology, 171
Angell, James B., 15
Armstrong, H. Parr, 51, 54, 277
Ashanin, Charles B., 163, 173, 230, 279
Assembly of the World Council of Churches, 119
Association of Theological Schools, 80, 102, 134, 167, 179, 200, 203–204, 219, 248
Athearn, Walter S., 34, 58–63
   becomes University president, 59
   removed from presidency, 67
Atherton, John W., 43, 50, 59, 62, 67, 76, 77, 79

Bachman, Walter E., 278
Bacon, William F., 57, 277
Bailey
   Albert E., 278
   Wilma, 281
Baker, Dave, 150
Baker-Fletcher
   Garth, 250, 280
   Karen, 280
Barnes
   Bill L., 141, 145, 149, 160, 162, 184, 188, 218
   Edward Larrabee, 148, 171, 176, 198, 200, 234, 235–236, 240
      designs new campus for CTS, 147

Barth, Karl, 173
Bates, Robert S., 183, 185, 230, 279
Bayer, Charles H., 253
Bea, Augustin Cardinal, 168
Beatles, 151
Beaver, R. Pierce, 226
Beck, Johann Tobias, 6
Becker, Edwin L., 163, 170, 173, 183, 190, 223, 230, 279
   retires, 227
Beloat, Larry, 197
Benton
   Allan R., 5, 16
   Gene, 150
Berger, Peter, 208
Berry, E. Wayne, 112
Bethany College, 2, 3, 5, 25, 36, 42
Bible College at Phillips University, 96
Bible College of the Christian Church of Indiana, 16–17
Binford, Thomas W., 185
Blaisdell, Charles, 252
Blake, Eugene Carson, 155
Blizzard, Samuel W., 134
Bowen, Crate, 76, 101
Boyle, George A., 229
Bradshaw, Vinton D., 147, 163, 172, 178, 230, 279
   retires, 227
Briggs, Charles A., 7, 11
Brite Divinity School, 21, 35, 57, 69, 95, 210
Brite, L. C., 35, 43
Brown
   Arthur V., 45
   Frank Burch, 262, 281
   Hilton U., 18, 24, 28, 29, 31, 32, 34, 37, 43, 44–45, 48, 49, 50, 59, 60, 62, 63, 67, 75, 79, 101, 127
      opposition to Ku Klux Klan, 48
Bultmann, Rudolf, 173
Bundy, David D., 280
Burdin, L. Gray, 107, 278
Burner, Willis Judson, 16
Burns and James, 87

313

Burrow, Rufus Jr., 228, 229, 230, 280
Butler Foundation, 37, 45, 77, 144
Butler
  Ovid, 5
  Scot, 5, 14, 17
Butler University, 3, 4, 10, 19, 20, 35
  and creation of seminary, 14–17
  bible college negotiated, 29–32
  est. biblical philology program, 5–7
  graduate College of Religion founded, 44
  loses accreditation, 58

Calhoun, Jay, 193
Calvert, Lucile, 107, 110, 278
Cameron, Emory C., 72, 277, 278
Campbell
  Alexander, 2–3, 5, 7, 78, 80, 85, 103, 256
  Nancy, 281
  Thomas, 80, 81
Campbell Institute, 38
Canary, Peyton Henry Jr., 278
Cardwell, Sue Webb, 210, 226, 228, 229, 230, 280
Carley, James R., 154, 163, 279
Carnegie, Andrew, 18
Carnegie Foundation, 36, 215
Carpenter, James, 235
Casel, Odo, 155
Catholic Seminary Foundation of Indianapolis
  teams with CTS, 168–169
Central Christian Church, 29
Central Indiana Christian Institute, 48
Chailleux, H. L., 84
Christian Board of Publication, 35, 257
Christian Century, 29, 31, 79, 157
Christian Education Resource Center, 224
Christian Foundation, 35, 35–37, 38, 45, 53, 56, 63, 66, 77, 96, 97, 101, 102, 105, 116, 127, 129, 132, 133, 141, 144, 146, 148, 157, 160, 217, 261
  bylaws and commitment with Butler Univ., 77–79
  incorporated, 36
Christian Herald, 19
Christian Ministers Association of Indianapolis, 48

Christian Standard, 25, 26, 29, 34, 38, 71, 74
Christian Theological Seminary
  and civil rights movement, 151–153
  and strong faculty ethos, 230–231
  creates Doctor of Ministry program, 181–182
  creates Master of Divinity program, 179–182
  creates pastoral counseling center, 225
  establishes new contract with Butler Univ., 144
  ground broken for new facility, 149
  growth in the 1970s, 204–208
  incorporated, 133
  initial goals laid out, 135–137
  international scholars program, 223–224
  Jewish-Christian relations program, 224
  mission statement for new millennium, 270–271
  name adapted, 135
  names chapel for Z. T. Sweeney, 236
  new campus dedicated, 150
  repertory theatre
    established, 160
    renamed, 264
    severs ties, 264
  teams with Catholic Seminary Foundation, 168
  upgrades pastoral care & counseling services program, 247–249
  women admitted to M.Div. program, 179
Christian Woman's Board of Missions (CWBM), 15, 19
Christian-Evangelist, 25, 26, 71, 79, 90
Chrysalis program, 223–224, 226, 231
Church Women United, 154
Cincinnati Bible Seminary, 36, 37, 69, 74
Clague, James G., 121, 141, 279
Clark, James L., 30, 35, 66
Cleveland Foundation, 36
Clingan, Donald, 210
Coleman, Christopher Bush, 20
College of Missions, 19–21, 44
College of Religion
  accredited by American Association of Theological, 80

Index

College of Religion (*continued*)
  changes to School of Religion, 88
  competition with other schools, 69
  moves to Northside, 55–56
  opens, 53–54
  opens new facility, 88
College of the Bible in Lexington. *See* Lexington Theological Seminary.
Colston, Lowell G., 141, 159, 160, 163, 172, 176, 183, 191, 210, 230, 240, 279
  retires, 227
Columbia University, 165
Commission on Theology of the Disciples Council on Christian Unity, 257
Compton, John, 162, 191
Consultation on Church Union, 155
Conway, Gerald W., 169
Cooperatives, 95, 119
Cory, Abram E., 85, 108, 111, 278
Culp, Barbara, 140
Culver-Stockton College, 42
Cummins, Clessie, 63, 70
Cummins Engine Company, 171

Daggett, Robert Frost, 49
Darrow, Clarence, 48
Davison, F. E., 47
Dean, James, 151
DeGroot, Alfred T., 57, 277
DeMars, Richard, 234, 236
DePauw University, 1
Derthick, H. J., 35
Dever, William G., 172
Dewey, John, 13
DeWitt, Marsha, 140
Dickinson, Richard D. N. Jr., vii, 163, 173, 185, 198, 201–202, 202, 204, 205, 219, 220–221, 226, 229, 230, 231, 234, 241, 243, 246, 251–252, 258–259, 260–266, 279
  and international scholars program, 223–224
  retires, 265–266
Disciples Divinity House, 57, 95
Division of Homeland Ministries, 257
Dix, Gregory, 155
Dodd, C. H., 120, 155
Dowling, Enos, 114
Downey Avenue Christian Church, 48, 53

Drake University, 14, 25, 38, 39, 57, 69, 166
Drury College, 31
Dykstra, Craig, 247–248

Earlham College, 1
Ecumenical Center of Renewal and Planning, Inc., 169
Edyvean, Alfred R., 117, 141, 159, 163, 172, 183, 230, 240, 264, 278
  retires, 227
Edyvean Repertory Theatre, 209, 264
  separates from CTS, 264
Ellington, Duke, 153
Elliott, Virgil, 99
Encounter, ix, 133, 139, 163, 189
Errett
  Edwin R., 63, 66, 69, 74, 75–76, 77, 85, 86, 89–91, 94, 95, 97, 101, 112
  dies, 100
  Isaac, 78, 87
  John, 26
  Russell, 26
Eureka College, 19
European Evangelistic Society, 102

Fenton, Cassius, 145
  dies, 230
Feuerlicht, Morris M., 48–49, 64, 276, 277
Fey, Golda, 154
Fey, Harold E., 154, 157, 276, 279
Fiers, A. Dale, 138, 150
Fisher, Theo, 143
Ford, Joann, 191
Forrest, Albertina Allen, 4
Foundation for Religious Studies, 169, 171
Franklin College, 5

Galbraith, Leslie R., 230, 279
Garfield, James A., 87
Garnett, Arthur C., 277
Garrison
  J. H., 8, 9, 9–10, 11, 12, 35
  W. E., 16, 17, 80, 87
Garvin, Hugh Carson, 5, 8, 9, 10–12
Gearhart, Herbert, 162
German Evangelical Association, 102
Ghormley, Hugh W., 49, 51, 54, 277

Gilbert, Daniel D., 147
Gordon, Grover B., 278
Gordon Pipers, 190
Gore, F. H., 36
Gorman, Donnette, 140
Grafton
 Allena, 277
 Thomas W., 41, 43, 50, 277
Grant, Brian W., 228, 230, 280
Gray, Larry, 191
Griffeth, Ross J., vii, 68, 72, 100, 277, 278

Hale, Evelyn, 143
Hall
 A. M., 6–7
 Jabez, 16
Halley, Henry H., 52
Hanlin, Harold F., 57, 101, 107, 110, 278
Hardin, George W., 35
Hartford Seminary Foundation, 215
Hartman, Grover, 209
Hastings, Warren, 99
Hearon, Holly, 281
Helmeke, Karen L., 281
Hicks, Luther, 152
Hiram College, 4, 35
Hoggard, J. Clinton, 227
Holcomb, James Irving, 127, 128–129, 130
Holmes, Arthur, 38–39, 40–42, 43–44, 51, 52, 54, 58, 67, 68, 83, 94, 110, 277, 278
Homrighausen, Elmer G., 68, 278
Hoover, Guy I., 51, 277
Hough, Joseph, 185
Howe, Thomas Carr, 27, 29, 30, 31
Humbert, John O., 254
Hurd, Harry Clark, 20

Ice, Harry T., 131, 163
Independents, 95
Indiana Christian Missionary Convention, 119
Indiana Council of Churches, 209
Indiana University, 14
 Law School, 44
Indiana Worker, 55
Indianapolis Hebrew Congregation, 48
Indianapolis Symphony, 190
Institute of Race and Religion, 167

International Convention of the Disciples of Christ, 71
Irwin
 Joseph I., 11, 16, 18, 28, 87
 William G., 18, 24, 28, 30, 31, 32, 35, 37, 38, 39–42, 43, 44, 45, 46, 49, 50, 58–59, 60, 62, 63, 65–67, 70, 72–74, 75, 77, 79, 86, 87–88, 91, 92, 97, 101, 238, 267
  dies, 100
Irwin-Sweeney-Miller Foundation, 133, 148, 162, 165, 198, 199, 243

Jackson, Edward L., 48
Jackson State University, 152
James
 Dick, 131
 William, 13
Janzen, J. Gerald, 163, 172, 189, 210, 211–212, 230, 232, 240, 269, 279
Jenkins, Burris, 16
Jewish Community Relations Council, 212
John Herron Art Institute, 44, 52
Johnson
 Emsley W., 59, 67, 76
 Paul E., 160
Johnston, Carol F., 281
Jones
 E. Stanley, 84
 Joe R., 243, 244, 245, 250, 269, 280
  resigns deanship, 246
 Myrddyn, 279
 Rufus M., 52
Jordan, Arthur, 45
Jordan College of Music, 263
Jordan Hall, 45
Joyce, J. Daniel, 279

Keiser, Marilyn, 234, 238
Kelcourse, Felicity B., 281
Kelly, Robert L., 134
Kennedy, John F., 151
Kennedy School of Missions, 21
Kent State University, 152
Kershner
 Bruce L., 51, 54, 64, 277
 Frederick D., viii, 24–28, 28–31, 32–36, 38–45, 46, 47, 48–49, 49–56, 57, 58–59, 61, 69, 70, 71–76,

Kershner, Frederick D.(*continued*) 77–78, 79, 80, 82–83, 84–85, 86, 87, 88, 90–91, 93, 94, 96, 99, 100, 102–103, 110–111, 134, 255, 258, 262, 267, 271, 272, 273, 277
    and Athearn, 63–67
    and the Ku Klux Klan, 48
    joins Butler faculty, 44
Kim, Heung Ho, 191
King, Martin Luther Jr., 152
Kinnamon, Michael K., 228, 229, 230, 243, 253, 254, 280
Krannert Charitable Trust, 188, 194, 217
Kromer, Helen, 150
Ku Klux Klan
    and Indiana politics, 47
    impact upon churches, 47–48

Langer, Susanne, 151
Laymon, William J., 31
LeSueur, Jim, 191
Lewis, Robert, 125
Lexington Theological Seminary, 57, 69, 80, 95, 166, 210
Liggett, Thomas J., viii, 172, 192–196, 197, 198, 199, 200–203, 213, 214–217, 222, 226, 230, 231, 232, 233–234, 236, 237, 239, 240, 242, 243, 260, 266, 272, 280
    and bookstore enhancement, 225
    becomes president of CTS, 192–193
    inaugurated as president of CTS, 202
Lilly Endowment, 128, 146, 159, 160, 162, 163, 183, 208, 209, 213, 215, 218, 224, 247, 252, 253, 261
Lloyd, Frank P., 162, 185
Locke, John, 13
Loisy, Alfred, 82
Long, R. A., 35
Lord, C. Harvey, 163, 183, 279
Luckmann, Thomas, 151
Lugar, Richard, 164, 182
Lumley, Fred Elmore, 20
Lunsford, D. Wright, 126, 145
Lynn, Robert W., 224
Lyon, K. Brynolf, 228, 229, 230, 252, 280

MacAllister, P. E., 185, 217, 234, 237
MacAllister/Petticrew Chair of Old Testament, 217
MacDonald, Janet Malcolm, 277
Marshall, Frank, 96, 98
Mart, Sharon, 140
Mathias, Theo A., S.J., 226
McAllister, Lester G., 141, 158, 163, 173, 230, 279
    retires, 227
McCash, I. N., 35
McCord, James I., 150
McGarvey, J. W., 3, 8, 18, 25, 103
McGavran, Don, 108
McKiernan-Allen, Linda, 228
McWhirter, David I., 190
Mead, Margaret, 151
Metropolitan Plan Commission of Marion County, 163
Metropolitan School of Music, 44, 52
Mid-Stream, ix, 259
Miguez-Bonino, José, 226
Mill, J. Stuart II, 230
Millennial Harbinger, 2, 3
Miller
    Clementine. *See* Tangeman, Clementine Miller.
    Hugh Th., 30, 31, 32, 45, 65, 67, 77, 86, 96, 97, 101, 102, 105, 109, 112
    J. Irwin, 71, 106–107, 109, 116, 117, 125, 127–129, 130–132, 137, 139, 141, 142, 143–144, 145, 149, 161, 163, 167, 168, 171, 172, 188, 195, 213, 217, 234, 236, 238, 241, 261
        as president of Nat'l. Council of Churches, 154–155
        elected first chair of CTS, 133
    James Blair, 108, 163, 172, 176, 190, 208, 209, 224, 230, 278
        retires, 227
    John Chapman, 5, 30
    Nettie Sweeney, 77, 86, 87, 97, 99, 101, 102, 109, 112, 154, 238
    R. H., 85, 88, 95, 97, 99, 101, 104, 105, 107, 108, 109, 114, 138, 139
    Xenia Simons, 217, 238, 241, 261, 263
Milligan College, 25, 35, 115
Milligan, Robert, 12
Milner, Jean S., 49
Moon, Everard R., 55, 277
Moore, William J., 278
Morgan, Peter, 257
Morrison, C. C., 29, 31, 79, 84

Morro, W. C., 18, 20, 21–22, 28, 29, 33, 34
Moseley, Dan P., 281
Mount, Sister Teresa A., 169, 191

Nakarai, Toyozo W., 55, 64, 86, 94, 107, 110, 117, 118, 153, 277
Napier, B. Davie, 227
National Council of Churches, 154
National Faculty Seminar on Christian Education, 225
National Institute of Mental Health, 162
Nettie Sweeney and Hugh Th. Miller Chair of New Testament, 217
New Oak Society, 243
Newsweek, 79
Niblack, John L., 49
Niebuhr, Reinhold, 156
Nixon, Richard M., 151, 193
Nooe, Roger T., 84
Norris
   Beauford A., 134, 141, 142–147, 149, 152, 157, 160, 161, 163, 163–164, 166, 167, 168, 169, 170–172, 175, 176, 184, 188–189, 193, 202, 218, 278
      appointed first dean of CTS, 133
      inaugurated president of CTS, 142
      retires, 188–189
   Shirley, 164, 218
North Central Association of Schools and Colleges, 74, 86, 128, 203
North Methodist Church, 87
North Western Christian University, 91
   founded, 1–2
Northwest Christian College, vii
Notre Dame, 1
Nouwen, Henri, 209

Oberlin College, 166
Osborn
   G. Edwin, 257
   Ronald E., vii, ix, 108, 118, 119, 121, 122–123, 134, 141, 146, 152, 154, 155, 156, 163, 167, 169–170, 174, 202, 272, 278
      becomes dean of CTS, 144

Osborn, Ronald E. (*continued*)
      founding editor of *Encounter*, 134
      resigns deanship, 170

Pacific School of Religion, 165
Page, Kirby, 52
Pantzer, Kurt, 130
Patterson, Bernardin J., 168
Paul, Charles T., 19, 20, 21–22
Peabody Fund, 36
Peabody, George, 36
Peak, George B., 35, 38
Pearl Harbor, 88
Pearson, Peet, 280
Pellett, David C., 107, 143, 144, 145, 158, 163, 170, 172, 190, 201, 202, 230, 278
Pendleton, W. K., 4
Perkins, J. J. (Mr. & Mrs.), 125
Petticrew, C. Richard, 217, 218, 240, 260
Petticrew Seminars, 260
Pfafflin, Ursula, 280
Phillips
   Benjamin D., 35, 66
   Thomas W. Jr., 35, 38
Phillips University, 35, 57, 69, 77, 95
Philputt, Allan B., 29, 30, 34, 41, 43, 50
Pike, James, 156
Pittenger, Norman, 226
Polizotto, Bruce, 263
Pomodoro, Arnaldo, 241, 273
Pope, Liston, 142
Porter, Calvin L., 141, 163, 172, 210, 230, 247, 279
Presley, Elvis, 151
Prichard
   H. O., 39, 51
   Rebecca B., 246, 281
Project Experteach, 208
Project Understanding, 186
Pullin, Morris H., 277
Putnam, James W., 73, 89

Quillian, Joseph, 160

Raines, Richard C., 131
Ramga, Patrice, 191
Ratti, Gino A., 74
Reavis, Tolbert F., 277

INDEX

Rector, Franklin E., 117, 118, 141, 159, 278
Rees, John R., 101
Reeves, Marshall T., 18, 29, 31, 37, 41, 66, 69
Repertory Theatre at CTS. *See* Edyvean Repertory Theatre.
Restoration movement, 112
Richardson, Robert, 4
Riley, Janet Johnson, 228, 230, 280
Roberts, D. Bruce, 222, 230, 280
Robertson
    A. T., 52
    Alexander M., 132
    Carrie Frances, 132
Robinson, William, 93, 117, 118, 120–121, 278
Rockefeller Foundation, 36
Rockefeller, John D. Jr., 125
Ross, M. O., vii, 100, 101, 102, 104, 105, 127, 127–129, 132, 144
Ruckelshaus, William, 208
Rudolph, L. C., 251
Russell Sage Foundation, 36, 134
Russian Orthodox Church, 154–155
Rutledge, George P., 38, 84

Saarinen
    Eero, 87, 130, 147, 187
    Eliel, 86, 112, 187
St. Maur's Priory, 167–168
St. Meinrad Seminary, 253
Sanders, Jack E., 126
Sarber, V. Gayle, 229, 230, 250, 263, 280
Sawicki, Marianne, 247
Schulte, Paul, 168
SCOFE (Supervised Concurrent Field Education), 245
Scott, Nelson, 191
Scott, Walter, 80
Sealantic Foundation, 160
Second Presbyterian Church, 49
Second Vatican Council, 153, 155
Shane Quarterly, ix, 84, 89, 139
    renamed *Encounter*, 133
Shaw, Henry K., 16, 145, 163, 279
Sheets, Laura, 140
Shelton, Orman L., viii, 85, 93, 97–101, 102–110, 111–112, 114–115, 116–117, 118, 119, 120, 123–128, 131,

Shelton, Orman L. (*continued*) 132, 134, 137–139, 140, 143, 146, 147, 160, 202, 215, 227, 272, 278
    and Dean Walker, 113
    appointed dean of School of Religion, 100
    appointed first president of CTS, 133
    dies, 137
Sheppard, Sally, 140
Short, Dennis, 191
Shullenberger, William, 74, 76
Sikes, Walter W., 117, 118, 121, 141, 144, 156, 278
Slater, Nelle G., 220, 224–225, 230, 231, 280
Sly, Virgil, 108
Smith
    Harlie L., 145
    John, 78
    Joseph M., 121, 156, 279
    Raccoon John, 87
    S. Marion, 107, 110, 118, 134, 163, 176, 180, 278
    T. K., 69, 70, 77, 85, 90
    W. Michael, 281
    Wales E., 84
Solomon, Izler, 149, 190
Sommerville, Raymond R., 281
Sovik, Edward, 233
Sphere #6, 168, 187, 241, 273–274
Spivey, Charles, 153, 162
Standard Publishing Company, 69
Steele, Edward A. III, 225
Steiman, Sydney, 141, 212
Stephenson, D. C., 48
Steussy, Marti J., 248, 280
Stone, Barton W., 78, 80
Stoner, Richard B., 171, 195
Stuart, George C., 279
Supervised Concurrent Field Education (SCOFE), 178
Sweeney Chapel, 236–238
    dedicated, 237–238
    groundbreaking, 237
    Holtkamp organ dedicated, 237
    memorial plate inscription, 236
Sweeney
    Elsie Irwin, 95, 109, 112, 114, 125, 154, 238
    Linnie Irwin, 44, 63, 65, 95, 238

Sweeney (*continued*)
　William E., 36, 85
　Z. T., 8, 11, 12, 16, 17, 18, 22, 24, 28, 29, 30, 31, 32, 33, 36, 41, 42, 43, 45, 50, 53, 71, 76, 89, 90, 92, 95, 96, 236
　　dies, 71

Tangeman
　Clementine Miller, 109, 112, 125, 131, 157–158, 161, 162, 165, 217, 233, 234, 236, 237, 238–239, 240, 261, 262
　Robert S., 165, 238
Teegarden, Kenneth, 193
Texas Christian University, 25, 35, 43, 69, 72
Thompson, Ervin L., 126
Tillich, Paul, 75
Titsworth, John A., 75, 76
Tobias, Robert, 121–122, 141, 144, 154, 156, 279
Towne, Edgar A., 197, 210, 230, 232, 237, 280
Transylvania University, 30, 57, 210
Troelsch, Ernst, 173
Tyrrell, George, 82

Underwood, Charles E., 19, 21
Union Theological Seminary, 7, 134, 165
United Christian Missionary Society, 22, 108
University of California Berkeley, 165
University of Chicago, 12
University of Michigan, 14
University Park Christian Church, 103

Vahanian, Gabriel, 157
Vanderbilt University, 69, 166
von Gerdtell, Ludwig, 72, 102, 277, 278
Vonnegut, Kurt, 151

Wakefield, Dan, 151
Walker
　Dean E., 55, 57, 68, 80–82, 84, 85, 89, 90, 93, 94, 96, 102, 103, 112–113, 114, 119, 120, 258, 277
　　and Orman Shelton, 113
　　leaves School of Religion, 114–115

Walker (*continued*)
　Evan, 131
　Lucius, 226, 231
　W. R., 70
Waller, George M., viii
Watkins, Keith, 140, 153, 156, 163, 190, 230, 233, 234, 235, 279
Watters, A. C., 108, 118, 278
Weinhorst, Richard, 149
Welsh
　Matthew E., 149, 163
　W. A., 166
Welshimer, P. H., 33, 34, 70, 84
Wheeler
　Barbara, 247
　Edward L., 264, 267, 281
Wheelock, John Hall, 173
White, Willie, 153, 163, 230, 279
Whitehead, Alfred North, 173
Wickey, Gould, 102
Wicks, Frank S. C., 49
Wilder, Amos, 150
Willebrands, Johannes, 168
Willett, H. L., 12, 14, 17
William G. Irwin Chair of Church History, 217
William Woods College, 25
Williams, D. Newell, 228, 229, 230, 248, 255–256, 258, 262, 280
　becomes dean, 246
Williamson, Clark M., 157, 163, 173, 189, 210, 211–212, 230, 240, 253, 258, 269, 279
　and Jewish-Christian relations program, 224
　and Judaism, 212
Wismar, Donald R., 163, 174, 210, 227, 228, 230, 279
Women's Christian Temperance Union, 47
World Council of Churches, 154
Wranglers, 49

Yale Divinity School, 95
Yale Institute of Sacred Music, 165
Yocum, Cy, 108
Yust, Karen-Marie, 281

Ziegler, Jesse, 167
Zimmerman, Donald W., 169